NO MAN'S LAND

NO MAN'S LAND

MEN'S CHANGING COMMITMENTS TO FAMILY AND WORK

KATHLEEN GERSON

BasicBooks
A Division of HarperCollins*Publishers*

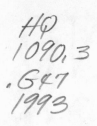

HQ
1090, 3
.G47
1993

Designed by Ellen Levine

93 94 95 96 ◆/RRD 9 8 7 6 5 4 3 2 1

Library of Congress Cataloging-in-Publication Data

Gerson, Kathleen.
    No man's land: men's changing commitments to family and work /
by Kathleen Gerson.
        p. cm.
    Includes bibliographical references and index.
    ISBN 0-465-06316-0
    1. Men—United States—History—20th century. 2. Men—
United States—Social conditions. 3. Sex role—United States. I.
Title.
HQ1090.3.G47 1993
305.32'0973—dc20   92-54520
                                                    CIP

CONTENTS

Part III
The Causes and Consequences of Change

LIST OF TABLES

PREFACE

Suddenly men are a hot topic. For several decades the spotlight has been on the revolution in women's lives, but now we are beginning to recognize that men's lives, too, are undergoing profound change. While it is clear that most men no longer provide the sole or primary economic support to their families, it is less clear what new patterns of commitment they are developing instead.

Today there is no single predominant road to manhood. Men have entered a no man's land, a territory of undefined and shifting allegiances, in which they must negotiate difficult choices between freedom and commitment, privilege and sharing, and dominance and equality. In the face of such upheaval, why do some men hold on to the breadwinner ethic, while others flee the responsibilities of parenthood, and still others involve themselves in family life more than men in earlier generations? What does it mean to be a man in a world where women are almost as likely as men to shoulder the responsibilities of supporting a family?

In the pages that follow, I take a close look at the other side of the gender revolution, at how and why men's lives are changing and why these changes appear more limited and enigmatic than the now obvious revolution in women's employment and family patterns. Unlike the more common approach that focuses on the differences between men and women, this book looks at the differences among men. By analyzing scores of interviews with men from diverse social backgrounds and walks of life, I examine the varied ways in which men are reassessing their commitments to family and work. I focus not just on men's choices but also on how men perceive and construct their options.

By deciphering the different routes men are taking in response to new dilemmas, opportunities, and pressures, I investigate how social circumstances shape men's lives as well as how men are taking an active part in either promoting or resisting change. My analysis provides a key to understanding the more general processes by which men develop, or fail to develop, commitments to family, parenthood, and work. My intention is that this will help us respond more meaningfully both as a society and as individual men and women to what remains an unfinished revolution.

To make sense of men's lives, I began with C. Wright Mills's recommendation: "Problems of biography, of history, and of their intersections within social structures. . . . are the coordinate points of the proper study of man. . . . The problems of our time—which now include the problem of man's very nature—cannot be stated adequately without . . . develop[ing] a psychology of man that is sociologically grounded and historically relevant."[1] If Mills's use of *man* as a generic term for all humans seems outdated, his method remains fitting. The history of the last two decades provides strong evidence that men's and women's natures are not innate or unchanging; they are shaped by social institutions and practices. Studying how individual biographies intersect with structures in flux provides a powerful tool for making sense of these social processes.

The men best positioned to clarify the causes and consequences of change are those who came of age during the recent period of rapid change in family life, work organization, and the relations between the sexes. Such men are now facing critical choices about marriage, work, and parenting. Most of the men in the study were in their thirties, but their ages ranged from late twenties to mid-forties (only 4 percent were under thirty, while 16 percent were over forty).

I wanted in particular to discover how and why men made choices about family and work.[2] Practical exigencies limited me to the New York metropolitan area, where I chose from two sample sources that provided a rich range of backgrounds and living situations. An alumni list of men who had attended a local university offered a pool of men who were likely to be employed in professional and white-collar occupations. A labor council list of employees in a variety of blue-collar and service-sector jobs offered a pool of working-class men who were less likely to have gone on to higher education. The lists were sorted according to residence, and names were then selected randomly from a range of central-city, outer-city, and suburban locations.[3] This process yielded 138 interviews.

In terms of education and class, the sample targets a group into which most American men fall.[4] Although I could not include a representative number of African-American, Hispanic, or Asian men, of homosexual men, or of those who number among the very poor and the chronically unemployed, I have placed my findings as much as possible in the larger national context by relating them to demographic trends gleaned from the census and other surveys. Percentage breakdowns among the interviewed men describe the contours of this sample, however, not the size of certain groups in the general population.

The interviews took place at a location of each man's choosing, usually his home. They were conducted by me or by one of my two research assistants and typically lasted about three hours each, although many extended well beyond four hours.[5] We used an open-ended but highly structured approach to elicit the men's life histories from early childhood to the present, and we concentrated especially on events, experiences, and choices in the family and at work.[6] We probed for transition points in men's lives and encouraged them to use these points as triggers for memory.[7] Memory may sometimes be undependable, but how people perceive, recount, or interpret past events is surely as important as the events themselves. It shows how they make sense of their experiences and use them to cope with the present and make decisions about the future.[8] The quoted material is taken from verbatim transcripts. Occasionally a quote was condensed or a grammatical error or confusing phrase was slightly changed to clarify it. All of the men's names have been changed to protect their privacy.

The in-depth life-history interview offers some unique advantages over a large-scale survey with precoded, closed-ended answer categories. It captures a picture of men's lives as they develop over time, thus providing a way to chart the processes that link causes and effects. It allows an analysis of subjective experience and the reinterpretation of experience in response to specific events. And it is well suited to discovering little-known or poorly understood social arrangements and practices.

Through a comparative analysis of the interviews, I developed a typology of men's varied commitments to family and work, especially to parenthood. This typology is based on two dimensions of commitment: economic contributions to a family and participation in domestic work, especially child rearing. If a man ranked relatively high on the first dimension and relatively low on the second, I called it a *breadwinning* orientation; if he ranked relatively low on both, I called it an *autonomous* orientation; and if he ranked relatively high on the second, irrespective of his standing on the first, I called it an *involved* orientation.

These categories are, to use Weber's language, ideal types. They make it possible to distinguish among different patterns of commitment and to discover the forces that are pushing and pulling men toward different destinations. Of course, some men's lives more closely resemble these ideals than do others, and deciding which type best captures the contours of a life was difficult in a few cases. These categories nevertheless reflect general trends in contemporary America and thus provide a framework for analyzing how and why men's commitments are changing.

I have chosen my terms carefully, but I am aware that they do not all have a shared meaning in our culture—particularly the word *family*. Amid the confusion and uneasiness wrought by widespread change in our most intimate attachments, it has become virtually impossible to discuss family life, or even to define what a family is, in a language everyone would consider neutral. My focus on relationships that are linked by legal, blood, or residential ties is not meant to imply that other relationships could not constitute a family.

The fact that we are beginning to ask questions about the meaning of manhood and the legitimacy of male privilege suggests that a major social upheaval is under way. Men's role in, and resistance to, the gender revolution profoundly affects not only their lives but the social, economic, and political fates of women and children. By linking men's experiences to their wider social and institutional context, I offer an explanation of this poorly understood aspect of change.

ACKNOWLEDGMENTS

In the late 1970s, I began research on how women make choices about work, career, and motherhood. At the time, many believed that the apparent revolution in women's work and family patterns was a fragile and fleeting development. My interviews with women from a variety of class backgrounds convinced me that a genuine social revolution was under way. These interviews revealed something else that contradicted the received wisdom of the day. Many of the women with whom I spoke did not describe the men in their lives in the ways that social theory and common belief have come to portray them. Rather, these women spoke of men who were nurturant, not especially ambitious, and more interested than they in having children. This unanticipated finding about how women perceived men sparked my interest in studying men more directly. To start at the beginning, then, I would like to thank those women who so generously shared their lives with me and who helped me to realize that there is as much to learn about men's lives as about women's.

Needless to say, it has required the help of many to convert that initial insight into this book. I have been blessed with so much support and accumulated so many debts along the way that it is hard to know where to begin, when to stop, or what to say. Although I know that my words are destined to fall short, I would like to express my gratitude to the colleagues, friends, and confidants who made it possible for me to bring this project to fruition. Without their intellectual, emotional, and practical assistance, I simply could not have done it.

A number of organizations provided essential financial support. A Presidential Fellowship from New York University gave me a semester's leave to conduct interviews, and a grant from NYU's Research Challenge Fund provided support for collecting and transcribing interviews. These grants were administered through the Center for Social Science Research, where Barbara Heyns, Richard Peterson, and Patricia Hartmann provided much-appreciated administrative and intellectual aid. At a later stage in the research, support from the dean's reserve fund and the sociology department's research apprenticeship program provided additional aid for data analysis. I am grateful to Dean C. Duncan Rice and my department colleagues for this assistance. My thanks go also to the people and organizations who helped me find my sample. Their names must remain anonymous to protect the confidentiality of my sample sources, but my gratitude can be openly expressed.

My research assistants, Vera Whisman and Nancy Wohl, were gifted and dedicated, the best interviewers for whom anyone could hope. I learned almost as much from their interviews as I did from my own. Angela Danzi, Vania Penha-Lopes, and Felinda Motino were expert coders and data analysts. Elinor Bernal once again proved to be an incomparable transcriber, providing good-humored insight along with verbatim transcriptions of the interviews. And Carrie Aaron came through in the crunch, searching out bibliographic details on short notice.

As the writing stage began, I was fortunate to spend a year in academic paradise as a visiting scholar at the Russell Sage Foundation. Surrounded by a uniquely inspiring and stimulating group of colleagues and provided with an exceptionally dedicated support staff, the latest in computer technology, and delicious food, I enjoyed that rarest of commodities in academic life: time to think, analyze, and write amid a community of committed researchers. My deep appreciation goes to Eric Wanner and Peter de Janosi for creating this environment and giving me the opportunity to be part of it. Equally heartfelt thanks go to the other visiting scholars, all of whom have become lifelong friends as well as true colleagues: Lee (Chip) Clarke, Faye Lomax Cook, Tom Cook, Cynthia Epstein, Kai Erikson, Patricia Gurin, Bill Kornblum, Ted Marmor, Robert Merton, Jon Rieder, Charles Tilly, Steve Vallas, and Viviana Zelizer.

My thanks also go to the many colleagues at New York University and elsewhere who read, listened to, or in other ways critiqued my ideas. Even though I was not always wise enough to take their advice, I thank them for helping me to do better. I cannot begin to name them all here, but those to whom I am especially appreciative include Bob Alford, Steve Brint, Arlene Daniels, Jo Dixon, Debra Friedman, Naomi Gerstel, Harvey Goldman, David Gordon, Dinni Gordon, Andrew Hacker, Sydney Halpern, Michael Hechter, Rosanna Hertz, Robert Max Jackson, Jerry Jacobs, James Jasper, Sandy Jencks, Carole Joffe, Michael Kimmel, Rebecca Klatch, Magali Sarfatti-Larson, Edward Lehman, Jane Mansbridge, Caroline Persell, Bernice Pescosolido, Richard Peterson, Joseph Pleck, Barbara Risman, Patricia Roos, Susan Shapiro, Carmen Sirianni, Theda Skocpol, Vicki Smith, Judith Stacey, Peter Stein, Ronnie Steinberg, Beth Stevens, Lise Vogel, Harrison White, Norma Wikler, Alan Wolfe, and Eviatar Zerubavel.

The people at Basic Books are every bit as talented, helpful, and inspiring as their reputation suggests. It has been an honor to work with a group of gifted and dedicated editors. Judith Greissman and Susan Arellano supported me with enthusiasm, creativity, and intelligence. Martin Kessler is a masterful editor whose unerring eye helped me shape the book in a new way. Linda Carbone, my development editor, rescued me from my worst stylistic habits, helping me to see the point and get to it. Whatever grace and good sense can be found in these pages is in large measure due to Martin's keen insight and Linda's deft editorial touch. They have made this book much better than it otherwise would have been, and I am very grateful. Many thanks also go to Kermit Hummel for coming up with a title, to Jo Ann Miller and Alec Moore, and to Akiko Takano, for grace under pressure.

Special friends and relatives sustained me and kept me sane through this long project. My parents, Rose and George Blum, and my sisters, Linda Gerson and Betty Gerson, provided continuous encouragement and strength. Sydney Halpern and Robert Jackson nourished me intellectually and emotionally, remaining treasured friends and supporters during the worst as well as the best of times. Jane, Michael, and Daniel Wolchonok provided warmth, friendship, sustenance (both psychological and culinary), and happy times away from my computer. Cynthia Reynolds, the third parent in my postmodern family, was always there with the nurturance, love, and good cheer needed to keep my spirits up and get my work done. Immeasurable thanks go to all of these people for making my life not only full, but fun.

It is impossible to find the right words to thank my husband, John Mollenkopf, and my daughter, Emily. They make my life and my work worthwhile. John is my best friend, my most trusted intellectual confidant, and my editor of first resort. He, too, put a lot of hard work into making this a better book—helping me to develop my ideas, providing the support I needed, and taking time out from his own busy schedule to read and edit every page. His generosity and strength kept reminding me just how off the mark our prevailing notions about men can be. Emily has known very few years when I was not working on this project. She not only put up with it but remained a constant source of sustenance, inspiration, and joy. I hope this book helps in some small way to make our society a better place for her and her generation.

Finally, I wish to thank the men who shared their lives with me. Their openness and kindness gave this project life and made it seem worth doing. May the future bring them opportunities for growth and viable ways to meet the challenges of social change.

I dedicate this book to John, in gratitude, and to Emily, in the hope that she will inherit and help to build a more just and equal world.

PART I

MEN'S QUIET REVOLUTION

1

INTRODUCTION

No Man's Land: An area of anomalous, ambiguous, or indefinite character.
An unowned, unclaimed, or uninhabited area.
An unoccupied area between two opposing armies.

—Webster's Dictionary

A husband relaxes in front of a television, beer in hand, while his children play unattended and his weary wife labors in the kitchen after a long day at the office. A muscle-toned, well-dressed bachelor parks his shiny new sports car and enters an apartment filled with luxurious furniture and the most advanced stereo equipment. A young father nestles his infant in a baby carrier while attending to his toddler on a playground.

These popular images offer conflicting views of men's lives in the closing decades of the twentieth century. They also stand in stark contrast to the dominant assumptions about manhood that prevailed only thirty or forty years ago. In 1950, breadwinning husbands (and their female counterparts, homemaking wives) accounted for nearly two-thirds of all American households. Most young men could expect to marry, have children, and provide the sole or main economic support to their wives and children.[1] They could also expect to leave child rearing and housework to their nonemployed or intermittently employed wives. Those men whose wives did work typically viewed those earnings as secondary and the work commitment as tenuous.

To be sure, the primary breadwinner pattern never accounted for all men, even during the height of domestic resurgence in the 1950s. In 1955, for example, almost 22 percent of all households contained an employed wife, and almost 9 percent were headed by single mothers. By 1960 the breadwinner-homemaker arrangement barely accounted for a majority of households, having dropped to less than 52 percent. Even though over 23 percent included an employed wife, 11 percent were single-parent families, and almost 15 percent were single adults, these other family forms were still considered not only deviant but dysfunctional by most analysts.[2] Those men who did not or could not conform to the ideal of the good provider were typically judged to be failures. The reigning ideology defined mature manhood almost exclusively in terms of achieving economic success and providing for wives and children.[3]

Since this period, women's lives have undergone a revolution, one that once seemed fragile but is now incontestable. In 1990, about 74 percent of women between the ages of twenty-five and fifty-four were in the labor force—up from 43 percent in 1962; 77 percent of them worked full-time (at least thirty-five hours a week); and about 80 percent of unemployed women were looking for full-time jobs. [4]

Changes in the kind of women who work have been equally dramatic. In 1990, over 58 percent of married women and 67 percent of mothers were employed or looking for work. Among mothers with school-age children, 75 percent were in the labor force, and among those with a preschooler, over 58 percent were either employed or looking for a job, up from 12 percent in 1950. Indeed, over half the mothers of children under the age of one were in the paid labor force. Among employed mothers with preschool children, close to 70 percent held full-time jobs.[5]

Women of all ages and family statuses have streamed into the workplace, rearranging the balance of their ties to employment and child rearing. They have also mounted a conspicuous challenge to men's longstanding privileges both at home and in the workplace. As we approach the twenty-first century, women's strong attachment to paid work shows no sign of abating. We may debate the political and social significance of these changes, but there is no doubt that fundamental changes have occurred.

Successful revolutions, by their nature, can never remain confined to one social group. Revolutionary change reorganizes the basic foundations of a society, changing the rules and dynamics of social relationships among dominant as well as subordinate groups. Just as changes in race relations involve whites as well as people of color and changes in class relations involve the economically privileged as well as the economically disadvantaged, a gender revolution must include men as well as women. Alongside the revolution in women's lives, there is another, less familiar story to tell.[6]

The Uncertain Contours of Change

Are men changing, or are they remaining steadfastly traditional despite the shift in women's lives? If some men are changing, then how? Are they becoming more egalitarian in response to women's insistent demands, or are they rejecting their historical responsibilities in a continual search for unbridled freedom? Experts and lay observers have characterized change—or the lack of change—in men's lives in all of these ways.

The decline of the male as primary breadwinner is the most apparent aspect of change. Men who provide the sole or major economic support for their families have not disappeared, but as a group they no longer predominate and are unlikely to do so in the foreseeable future. By 1990, the percentage of American households consisting of a married couple dependent on a sole male breadwinner had dwindled to less than 14 percent, down from almost 60 percent in 1950. Even taking into account the 16 percent of households where the wife did not work full-time year-round and the 3.1 percent of households headed by a single father, it appears that only about a third of American households now depend solely or primarily on a male earner.[7] (See appendix, table 1, for a graphic representation of these changes.)

As the proportion of men who are sole or primary breadwinners has declined, so has their cultural support. A once-uncontested belief in the superiority of the "good provider" has given way to new debates about men's proper place in society. It is no longer clear what goals a man should pursue, much less how he should pursue them. Indeed, it is no longer clear what it means to be a man. As women have become almost as likely as men to shoulder the responsibilities of supporting a family, it has become harder for men to defend and justify advantages based solely on being born male. The demise of a cultural consensus on the meaning of manhood has left men in a no man's land, searching for new meanings and definitions of maturity. It is no wonder that books about men and masculinity are frequenting the best-seller lists, men's studies has become a growing field, and television talk shows that once dealt almost exclusively with women's concerns now discuss men's frustrations in tones that imply a current or impending crisis.[8]

One important aspect of the gender revolution is the slow and limited degree of change in men's domestic participation. Men's family involvement has not kept pace with women's increasing commitment to paid employment. This "housework gap" has left most women with more work and less leisure than their male counterparts. According to some estimates, married women average two to three fewer hours of leisure per day than do married men.[9] And when the time spent performing paid

work, housework, and child care is added together, men work an average of eighty-eight fewer hours a year than do women.[10] From this van-
tage point, the movement toward gender equality, which once appeared
to be an attainable if distant goal, has become stalled at the domestic
doorway.

While most married men continue to resist responsibility for domestic
work, other men are making different kinds of choices. One has been
termed a male "flight from commitment," which is as significant as the
more explicit feminist revolt of the last two decades.[11] Men in this group
have chosen autonomy, either by moving away from marriage and parenthood altogether or by not maintaining involvement with children they
have brought into the world. The rise of divorce and singlehood as acceptable alternatives to marriage has allowed a growing group of men as
well as women to choose freedom and autonomy over economic and social ties to parenthood and family life. Several factors have contributed
to this trend.

First, more men and women are postponing marriage, remaining permanently single, or getting divorced. Divorce rates doubled between
1950 and 1985, and even though they have declined slightly since then,
they appear to be leveling off at a high rate. By 1991, the average age of
first marriage among men had risen to 26.3 years; one in four Americans
over eighteen had never married, up from one in six in 1970. More significant, over 17 percent of men between the ages of thirty-five and thirty-
nine had never married, up from less than 8 percent in 1980.[12]

Many of these unmarried men are likely to remain so: once he reaches
forty, a never-married man has only about a 12 percent chance of marrying; by forty-five, his chances fall to 5 percent. According to recent estimates, 10 percent of the adult population of men and women may never
marry, up from 5 percent in earlier decades.[13] When the growing proportion of never-married men is added to the ranks of divorced men, the result is a large proportion of men who are single. In 1990, over 17 percent
of American men were single adults who lived either alone or with an
unrelated adult, up from about 8 percent in 1970. Among men between
the ages of forty and forty-four, that figure remains high. In 1991, close to
16 percent of white men and close to 24 percent of black men in this age
range did not live with a spouse, a parent, or a child.[14]

As divorce, postponed marriage, and permanent singlehood have become more common, so has the tendency for men to postpone becoming
a father, to eschew fatherhood altogether, or to lose contact with their
children. Although studies of men's childbearing patterns are rare, it appears that men, like women, are more likely to postpone parenthood or
to remain childless than were their counterparts three to four decades
ago. In 1986, 28 percent of women between the ages of twenty-five and

twenty-nine did not have a child in their household, up from 18 percent in 1960. Among white women in their late twenties in 1986, more than 40 percent were childless.[15] Indeed, among all women born in the 1950s, 17 percent appear to be remaining childless, up from 9 percent of women born in the 1930s.[16] These trends surely apply to men as well.

An even more dramatic rise has occurred in the percentage of children who do not live with their fathers. Between 1970 and 1991, the proportion of children living with two parents declined from 85 percent to 72 percent, while the proportion living with one parent—usually the mother—rose from 12 percent to 26 percent.[17] In 1991, 19 percent of all white families and 58 percent of all black families with children were headed by a single mother. Most white children who part ways with their fathers are the product of divorce and separation, even though the percentage of white mothers who never married rose from 3 percent in 1970 to 19 percent in 1991. Among African-Americans, out-of-wedlock childbearing has become the primary cause of a father's absence: 54 percent of one-parent black families in 1991 were headed by women who had never married, up from 15 percent in 1970.[18]

Whether through divorce or their parents' decision not to marry, the ranks of children who are growing up without sustained financial or emotional support from their fathers are swelling. A 1987 survey found that only 30.1 percent of divorced women received the full amount of court-awarded child support (which may or may not have been adequate). Forty-one percent were awarded no support; 14.8 percent received less than the full amount; and 14.2 percent received nothing despite a court decree.[19] For never-married mothers, who find it difficult to establish paternity or make any claims on the men who fathered their children, the situation is even worse. Fewer than one-third of these children can be legally tied to their fathers, and fewer than 15 percent of unwed mothers collect any child support.[20]

The economic vulnerability of children and their mothers is a serious new development.[21] In a world where women's earnings average 72 percent of men's, women and children who do not live with a man are at distinct financial disadvantage compared to married couples or single men. In 1989, the median income of families headed by a woman was only $16,440 a year, compared with $38,550 for married couples and $27,850 for single men.[22]

Men's estrangement from family life has fueled a rise in female and child poverty. In 1989, over 32 percent of families headed by a woman were struggling below the poverty level. Non-Hispanic white female-headed households had a poverty rate of 25.4 percent, while the rate for black female-headed households was 46.5 percent. In contrast, only 5.6 percent of married-couple families and 10.3 percent of all American fam-

ilies lived in poverty. Sadly, the poverty rate for children reached close
to 20 percent that year, higher than that for any other age group.[23]

It is clear that some men are remaining aloof from domestic work despite their increasing reliance on women's earnings, while others are relinquishing parental ties altogether. These developments have troubling
implications for the well-being of American women and children. They
do not, however, tell the whole story. Alongside these trends, another
kind of change has occurred: the rise of the nurturing father.

Although the gender gap in domestic work persists, men's domestic
participation has increased, even if slowly and to a limited degree.
Whether the glass looks half empty or half full depends on the point of
comparison. When men and women are compared, men's participation is
clearly lower. When men's current behavior is compared with their behavior of several decades ago, however, a rise in participation becomes
apparent. From 1969 to 1987, the average time men spent at household
work rose by 159 hours per year for men with two children, by 162 hours
for men with one child, and by 173 hours for men with no children.[24] Men
increased their share of housework from 15 percent in 1965 to 33 percent in 1985. They continued to spend most of this time on traditionally
male tasks (such as outdoor chores, repairs, gardening, and paying bills),
but they spent more time on traditionally female tasks (such as cooking,
meal cleanup, housecleaning, and laundry) as well—from 8 percent in
1965, to 11 percent in 1975, to 20 percent in 1985. As a result, women
spent 7.5 fewer hours a week doing housework in 1985 than in 1965,
while men spent 5.2 hours more.[25]

More pronounced changes have taken place in men's involvement in
child rearing. In a recent study, married women reported that their husbands' share of housework remained low but that their participation in
child care was much higher, averaging just over 40 percent of the total.[26]
Taken together, these figures show that although inequality persists, the
domestic labor gap is shrinking.

More important, these averages mask important differences among
men. While some continue to avoid all domestic involvement, others are
more involved in domestic work than the averages convey. This is especially true of child care. Among married couples with an employed wife,
12 percent of the women reported in 1988 that the father provided the
primary care for their children when the mother was at work. Among
those with a child under five, 17.9 percent reported relying on the father
as the primary caretaker. An additional 5.4 percent reported relying on
the father as a secondary provider of care.[27] Social psychologist Joseph
Pleck thus concludes that "taken together, it appears that married men
on average perform one-third of the housework, and one of five fathers

with an employed wife is the primary child care arrangement for his preschool child."[28]

The situation for divorced and single fathers is also more complicated than the averages convey. Although the overwhelming majority of children in single-parent families live with their mothers, the percentage of fathers who retain some form of custody, including residential custody, has risen.[29] In 1990, 3.1 percent of American households were headed by a single father, up from 1.8 percent in 1950. Men now head 12.5 percent of all single-parent households. Among children whose fathers did not retain any residential custody, 40 percent reported in one study that they had seen their fathers within the last thirty days, including 28 percent of those whose parents had been divorced for ten years or more.[30] These figures in no way mitigate the crisis that has developed because the majority of divorced fathers neither see nor support their children in a systematic way; they do, however, point out that not all divorced and single fathers have abandoned their children.

Paradoxically, a pattern of involved fatherhood has emerged alongside this retreat from family commitment. A growing group of fathers, most of whom are married to work-committed women, are changing diapers, pushing strollers, cuddling their children, and generally sharing in the pleasures and burdens of child rearing.[31] Although equal sharing with mothers remains rare among these involved fathers, they are nevertheless demonstrating a capacity, a willingness, and an enthusiasm for parenting not seen in their fathers' and grandfathers' generations.

Each of these trends represents a piece of the puzzle of how men's lives are changing. Viewed as a whole, change in men's lives has been ambiguous and multifaceted. It is not a simple matter of things getting worse, getting better, or staying the same—all three are happening at once.[32] A once-predominant pattern has given way to increasing, and perhaps unprecedented, variety.

Studying Change in Men's Lives

The current generation of adult men has come of age in a period of rapid change and growing confusion. Their responses to new freedoms and new constraints have challenged some long-standing beliefs about the nature and experience of manhood. Examining their lives thus provides a rare opportunity to chart the process of change and to uncover the reasons for men's behavior. The life histories of a sampling of this strategic group will reveal how and why men who came of age at the same time developed differing commitments to women, work, and children.

I conducted in-depth interviews with 138 men from diverse social backgrounds. Although not a statistically representative sample of all American men, they were carefully selected to illumine the diverse paths men are taking. The men were chosen at random from two sources: alumni lists of a private university located in the New York metropolitan area (including some who never graduated) and lists of workers maintained by a labor council also located in the New York metropolitan area and representing a wide range of blue-collar and service occupations (including workers who were not union members). The men lived in a variety of locations, including the central city (31 percent), the outer city (10 percent), and the suburbs (59 percent). Since more than three-quarters of the U.S. population now resides in a "megalopolis" that mixes cities, suburbs, and sprawl, the residential locations of these men are in keeping with where most Americans live.[33]

Although they claimed diverse racial, ethnic, and social backgrounds, the men in the group were predominantly non-Hispanic white. Sixty-three percent reported predominantly Northern European ancestry; 19 percent reported Eastern European ancestry; 13 percent reported Southern European ancestry; and 6 percent reported African, Hispanic, or Middle Eastern ancestry.[34] I found no relationship between the ethnic background of these men and their choices about family and work.

These men were between the ages of twenty-eight and forty-five at the time they were interviewed. The average age was thirty-six, and only 4 percent were below the age of thirty. As young and middle-aged adults, they were in the family- and career-building stages of their lives—old enough to be making consequential life decisions about work, marriage, and parenthood, yet young enough to be directly affected by the gender revolution of the last several decades. Their lives offer a lens through which we can view the dynamics of change.

Approximately half (53 percent) held college degrees and were employed in white-collar, managerial, and professional occupations. The remainder lacked college degrees (and usually any significant college experience) and were employed in a variety of blue-collar and low-level white-collar occupations. This diversity in occupation and class position makes it possible to analyze how work experiences and occupational opportunities shape men's family and work commitments. It also allows us to explore the similarities and differences between middle-class and working-class men. We will see, for example, that the image of the "macho" working-class man, who opposes any move toward gender equality, is as misleading as the image of the "liberated" and "sensitive" middle-class man. The variation within both class groups is far greater than the differences between them.

The men also varied in their family situations and choices. Sixty percent were married at the time of interview; 11 percent were divorced, separated, or widowed; and 29 percent had never married, including five men who were gay or bisexual. Among those who were married, 45 percent had wives who were employed full-time; 26 percent had wives who were employed part-time; and 29 percent had wives who were full-time homemakers. Over half (53 percent) had at least one child. These men had traveled a variety of routes in adulthood and displayed diverse orientations toward work and parenting. Within both class groups, there were men who viewed themselves as primary breadwinners, men who wished not to have children, men who had become estranged from their children after divorce, and men who had become or hoped to become involved in caring for their children (including some divorced men who had retained some form of custody).

Approximately 36 percent of the men who were interviewed came to define their family and work commitments in terms of primary breadwinning (a percentage that is similar to the one-third of American men who now provide sole or primary support to their families). Of these men, 92 percent had married (or were engaged), and 74 percent had become fathers and were working to support their families. (All those who were not yet fathers planned on having children soon.) Among those who were married and had children, 49 percent were supporting nonemployed wives as well as their children, 35 percent had wives who were employed part-time, and 16 percent had wives employed full-time. Whether or not their wives held paid jobs, however, all of these men saw themselves as the *primary* earner, the one upon whom the family depended. In turn, they resisted involvement in caretaking and domestic work.

Another 30 percent had eschewed parenthood or significant parental involvement. These men had either opted not to have children (86 percent of the group) or had become estranged from their children in the wake of divorce (14 percent of the group, or about half of the divorced fathers interviewed). They were not committed to parenting either economically or emotionally.

Finally, about 33 percent had moved toward more rather than less family involvement. They developed an outlook on parenthood that included caretaking as well as economic support. Most of these men (63 percent) had already become fathers and were involved in caring for their children, while the others were looking forward to having a child in the near future. Most were also involved with a work-committed woman with whom they shared economic responsibilities, although 17 percent had a part-time-employed wife and 4 percent were supporting a nonemployed wife. An additional 9 percent were divorced and not currently in a committed relationship, and 15 percent had yet to marry and were not currently involved with one special person.

While only a minority of those with an "involved" outlook (about 39 percent, or 13 percent of the total sample) had become or planned to become equal or primary caretakers, all were, or wished to become, significantly more involved in parenting than men who developed "breadwinning" or "autonomous" outlooks. These nurturing fathers point toward the progressive potential of current change.

Controversies in Explaining Men's Lives

There are inherent perils in any analysis of men. Since they are members of an advantaged group that still enjoys disproportionate power and privilege, it is necessary (if difficult) to strike a balance between sympathetic understanding of the problems men face and appropriate awareness of their uses and misuses of power. As a woman who considers herself both a humanist and a feminist, I am aware of the complexities of my attempting to make sense of men's experiences and outlooks. We cannot completely set aside our personal experiences, even in pursuit of understanding the experiences of others. But we are not prisoners of them, either. The power of social science analysis is that it allows us to find answers that stand on their own, apart from the predilections of those who seek them. While values have surely influenced the questions I posed, they should not have determined the answers I found.

Although we have grown accustomed to using gender as a category for analyzing women, we are less comfortable when the subject is men. Yet it is unquestionably true that men's outlooks reflect their experiences as *men* rather than as prototypical humans.[35] This means we need to examine how social opportunities and constraints shape men's lives no less than women's. To do this, I have chosen an approach that differs from most other studies of men. I focus on variations among men rather than on differences between men and women. I analyze men's dilemmas and constraints as well as their privileges and advantages. I explore how men perceive, construct, and justify their choices, even when those choices appear self-serving or implausible. And I search for signs of positive change as well as signs that change is limited or harmful.

EXPLORING DIVERSITY AMONG MEN

It has once again become fashionable to argue that men are essentially alike and fundamentally different from women.[36] Women, so this account goes, are nurturant and caring; men share a need for achievement at work and for domination at home—they are driven toward control but lack a well-developed capacity for sustained nurturance or deep emotional attachment. These visions of gender, which assume homogeneity among men, reinforce the belief that a "masculine personality" is inherent and male dominance inevitable.[37]

I have chosen, instead, to examine the forms and causes of a variety of patterns among men. Ordinary men's experiences are more richly diverse than any homogeneous conception of men can capture, and exploring differences among them helps us move beyond stereotypical notions of the "typical" man. Equally important, it allows us to discover how different social arrangements promote diversity in men's experiences, outlooks, and relationships.

Explaining variety among men has practical as well as theoretical uses. Only by understanding why some men support equality and others do not can we locate the obstacles to progressive social change. By taking a close look at a small but theoretically significant group of men who are attracted to more egalitarian family forms (often for reasons that are not simply altruistic), we can locate the social arrangements that would allow and encourage more men to become supportive partners and nurturing parents. Understanding men's varied and sometimes unexpected family and work choices will help us discover the conditions that foster more equal and loving relationships.

ANALYZING MEN'S PRIVILEGES, DILEMMAS, AND CONSTRAINTS

In addition to presuming uniformity among men, discussions of men's lives tend to focus either on their power, privilege, and ability to control *or* on their problems and constraints. Yet it is misleading to depict men as either free agents or victims. Men assemble, protect, and justify the prerogatives of being born male, but they must also cope with dilemmas, constraints, and uncertainties.

Men as a group may possess disproportionate power and privilege, but many individual men do not *feel* powerful.[38] To some extent, this perception is akin to the proverbial fish who does not notice the water in which it swims. Most members of dominant groups take their privileges for granted—until they are taken away. Nevertheless, even dominant groups are not entirely free. Just as subordinate groups often find ways to create power and opportunity, so powerful groups rarely control completely.[39] Privilege can impose its own constraints, and even very privileged men face some constraints (or perceive that they do). Just as we need to understand that women, though disadvantaged, are not mere passive victims but also active molders of their lives, so we also need to investigate the ways in which men, while an advantaged group, are also constrained by social conditions.[40]

Also, the benefits of being born male do not fall equally on all men. Men vary in their opportunities and constraints, their privileges and burdens. Men's lives are changing in paradoxical ways. The increasing difficulty of earning a "family wage" may lead some men to reject family life and others to share economic obligations more equally with women. The entry of women into the workplace has made it easier for men to move away from economic obligation, but it has also made it harder for men to avoid domestic sharing. As their once secure advantages erode, men can try to hold on to domestic power and privilege or they can take advantage of the opportunity to escape breadwinning burdens. In rejecting the sole-provider ethic, they can reject the obligations of family life or agree to share them more equally. Even those who continue to act as primary breadwinners are not immune from these dilemmas. The rise of new patterns among other men challenges the male breadwinner's historical privileges and poses new uncertainties for us all.[41]

Investigating men's dilemmas as well as their privileges has more than purely theoretical uses. Men need reasons beyond pure altruism to concede power. To discover the conditions under which some men become willing to support greater equality between the sexes and others decide to resist equality at all costs, we need a more complex view of men's interests than one that stresses only male advantage. We need to understand how and why men feel constrained as well as free, burdened as well as privileged, controlled as well as in control. How those conditions vary across individuals and change over time is part of the story of how men's lives are changing.

Some men may be uncomfortable admitting that their choices have costs, that dominance and equality both exact a price. Some women may protest that since most men have far more power than most women, it is beside the point to look at the constraints or costs of being a man. Yet men are coping with the burdens as well as the privileges of traditional definitions of manhood, and it is possible to acknowledge their power and still take account of their constraints.

LISTENING TO MEN'S ACCOUNTS

My analysis focuses on men's personal accounts, even though there is good reason to approach them with a skeptical eye. There is often a gap between what we say and what we do. Since circumstance and perception force all of us to distort reality in systematic ways, the challenge is not to distinguish between "accurate" and "false" accounts but to discover how different groups make sense of the world in different ways. Some men may claim to be more egalitarian than they are, for example, while others may act in ways that are more egalitarian than they claim to be.[42] Some men may exaggerate their domestic involvement the better to fit the image of a sensitive, caring man, while others may underestimate their domestic contributions to protect an image of "macho" strength and control.

While it is important to distinguish between reliable accounts and those that merely state what someone believes others want to hear, this challenge should not prevent us from listening to men. There is no reason to assume that men are any more or less truthful than women, even when their accounts diverge. To understand the changing meaning of gender, we need to make sense of men's perceptions. By focusing on differences among men, my aim is to place men's accounts in a social, historical, and comparative context.

EXAMINING (POSITIVE) CHANGE

There is no doubt that some men's resistance to equality in the family and other men's turning away from the family altogether are two major components of recent change. Yet change has a third aspect as well: the movement of some men toward greater equality with women and more involvement in the home. Moreover, most men are perceiving their domestic responsibilities in new terms: contemporary men are much more likely to feel they *should* participate even when they don't. Whether change appears progressive or retrogressive, significant or inconsequential, depends on what is being singled out for attention.

For practical and theoretical reasons, I focus on the liberating as well as the retrogressive aspects of change. Examining both aspects not only presents a fuller and more accurate picture but allows us to discover the forces that promote or inhibit more fundamental transformations. A narrow focus on how things are getting worse fosters the view that women have lost, not gained, from their fight for equal rights.[43] Acknowledging the positive elements of change along with the negative ones puts us in a better position to direct inevitable change in more progressive directions.

Gender Stereotypes and Ideals

In exploring the diverse ways that men are responding to new pressures and opportunities, I have tried to avoid juxtaposing "good women" against "bad men" or even "good men" against "bad men." My aim is to explain how social arrangements shape men's choices and world views, not to pass judgment on individual men or women. Virtue is not distributed by gender, and no one choice is right for everyone.

Yet explanations of how men behave cannot be entirely divorced from considerations of how they *should* behave. Are egalitarian men merely compliant, or are they enthusiastic partners in the creation of a more humane world? Are single and divorced men irresponsible deserters of women and children, or are they bewildered survivors of an escalating sex war? Are traditional breadwinners holding on to unearned patriarchal privileges amid a changing social order, or are they struggling to remain responsible in an ever more uncertain economic environment? All of these judgments swirl around the intensifying debate over the meaning of manhood and the nature of change in men's lives. All too often, the man who expresses nurturance and sensitivity is judged to be weak and unmasculine, just as the woman who appears strong or ambitious is often declared selfish and unfeminine.

My own starting point is that posing the debate in these terms is misleading and dangerous. Men and women share a range of human capacities that belie the gender stereotypes we have inherited. It is inaccurate to view men and women as inhabiting opposite ends of a single psychological continuum in which caring women are contrasted with strong men. It is even worse to condemn those who appear to deviate from these ideal types. Strength and caring are not mutually exclusive categories, but essential human capacities we all need. Armed with a better understanding of why change is occurring but still remains limited, we will be in a better position to build social institutions that foster generosity *and* strength in everyone. If we fail to understand the causes of change, however, we are unlikely to discover how to build a more humane, just, and tolerant future for all.

2

THE CHANGING CONTOURS OF AMERICAN MANHOOD

Received models of fatherhood are not writ in the stars or in our genes. Our ancestors knew a very different pattern than our own, and our descendants may have another that is no less different. Fatherhood, history reminds us, is a cultural invention.
        —John Demos, "The Changing Faces of Fatherhood"

To make sense of men's lives, we first need to lay some myths to rest. Consider the belief that breadwinning is a traditional or natural pattern with a long legacy. In fact, men's behavior and our wider cultural ideals about manhood have not consistently conformed to this model throughout American history.[1] To the contrary, the idea that men should provide sole or primary economic support for their households in lieu of participating in domestic work did not develop until the emergence of industrial capitalism and only gradually came to describe the behavior of most men. However much some may mourn its decline, the good-provider ethic has not been a continuous historical pattern. It was the product of social forces that converged in one fleeting era, and its reign as a predominant form of behavior and a prevailing cultural ethic has been relatively short-lived.

Masculinity in American History

Before the rise of industrial capitalism, economic survival required that all able-bodied family members contribute to the common family enterprise of economic survival. Even youngsters were not treated as children—that is, economic dependents—for very long. In all but the most affluent households, all family members contributed what they could, as soon as they could, to secure the family's survival amid the natural and social uncertainties of rural, farm, and small-town life.[2]

Although husbands and wives shared the economic burdens and domestic hardships of preindustrial life, their relationships faced a shaky future. High rates of premature death and desertion made unpredictable and untimely marital breakup common. Life expectancies for both sexes were shorter than they are today. Deaths among mothers with young children, often from complications with pregnancy and childbirth, left many men to rear their offspring alone or to find surrogate parents to look after their children. Male death and desertion left widows and abandoned wives in a similar plight. Despite the low incidence of legal divorce, short life spans meant that young married couples could not safely assume that they would share a long life together. As many analysts have pointed out, divorce has merely replaced death as a modern form of marital disruption.[3]

Contemporary American men have inherited an ambiguous legacy. The "lone man against the world" image extolled in popular myth has its roots in the early period of preindustrial expansion, when men could, and often did, leave home and family to seek their fortunes alone. Yet the preindustrial period also offers a vision of men and women jointly shouldering the risks and responsibilities of work and family. Both visions have persisted in American mythology, but each lost a large share of real-life adherents as industrial capitalism developed throughout the nineteenth and twentieth centuries.[4] The rise of the wage-earning worker produced a new definition of manhood and, indeed, a new kind of man.

The birth of the industrial system did not immediately produce the primary breadwinning model that today is mislabeled "traditional." Women were heavily represented among early industrial workers—for example, in the emerging textile industries. As the traditional weavers of cloth in the home before the advent of factories, many women initially followed the shift from production in the home to production in a communal workplace. As the economic organization of production shifted from personal use and barter exchange to earning a wage, it was not preordained that men would become the primary earners while women became economically dependent on men. Rather, the breadwinning male—as a pattern of behavior and as an ideal—was constructed through protracted conflict. The sequence and causes of this transformation remain a matter of debate, but the process of change was clearly marked by political struggle.

As the physical and economic separation of home and work grew, wage workers began to organize in an effort to gain some control over the terms and conditions of their work. According to the economist Heidi Hartmann, male workers struck a fateful bargain with owners and employers, who agreed to exclude women and children from important sectors of the emerging occupational structure in order to improve male workers' bargaining power with employers as well as their leverage over women. Of course, women also faced convincing reasons to pursue domesticity instead of wage work, since working conditions were generally poor and it was not easy to meet the needs of children while in the public workplace. Whatever the causes, protective labor legislation and other policies of occupational sex segregation eventually took hold. The belief eventually emerged that a "family wage" or "living wage" should pay men enough to support their wives and children.[5]

None of these developments encompassed all families, of course. Real wages often fell short of the family-wage standard.[6] And women have always worked: working-class, minority, and poor women have usually had no choice but to find low-wage work in the least desirable sectors of the economy. Single women, whether never married, divorced, or widowed, have always had to support themselves and their children. It follows that even when breadwinning became the predominant form, it was never as widespread as commonly assumed—especially outside the white middle class.[7] Nevertheless, as the nineteenth century drew to a close, most men and women occupied separate economic, social, and spatial spheres.

The rise of the primary-breadwinning husband, based on the ideal of a family wage and the "protection" of women and children, provided some obvious benefits. It afforded middle-class women and children relief from the sometimes dangerous and often squalid conditions of early industrial workplaces. It freed children from the burdens of wage earning, allowing them an extended childhood devoted to learning and play under the watchful eyes of mothers, teachers, and other female caretakers. As the sociologist Viviana Zelizer points out, children became economically "useless," but socially "priceless."[8]

Despite these real benefits, the barring of women from highly paid, secure jobs reinforced and exaggerated inequality between men and women and between adults and children. The "modern family" became synonymous with a sharp differentiation between the sexes, a glorification of the mother-child bond, and an expectation that men should provide economically for their wives and children.

The consolidation of the modern family, with its reliance on a male family wage, transformed the justification for male control over women and children. Patriarchal dominance could no longer be easily asserted as a male birthright; men now had to earn it through economic success in the marketplace. Male power and privilege became tied to good jobs that paid enough to support the family in a certain degree of comfort. In exchange for assuming economic responsibilities, men "earned" the right—and gained the economic power—to head the household and to control the family purse strings.

Many men, of course, were never able or willing to conform to these new standards of manhood. Working-class jobs often paid too little, and poor men were hard-pressed to find any work at all. Periodic recessions and depressions swelled the ranks of the unemployed, but even during good economic times many men fell short of these new definitions of success. A significant proportion of working-class women, and even children, have always supplemented their husbands' limited incomes or lived without the help of any male support.[9] Similarly, men, especially those with poor labor market prospects, have always been able to use desertion or divorce to escape the economic burdens of breadwinning. These alternatives did not disappear, but they became harder to choose and defend as the breadwinner-homemaker model became the dominant cultural ideal, if not the only behavior in reality.

A range of ideas emerged to justify and reinforce male breadwinning and female homemaking. A "cult of domesticity" arose in the mid-nineteenth century, which held that a woman's proper place is in the home, providing for her family's emotional needs and moral education.[10] The advent of psychoanalysis at the end of that century transformed the case for male breadwinning and female domesticity into scientific language, suggesting that these arrangements were not just morally superior but biologically necessary. These ideas were first and most enthusiastically accepted among the middle class, where more families could afford to heed their prescriptions, but they eventually spread throughout the common culture. An ideology of manhood as "good providing" could not force men to conform, but it did judge those who would not or could not to be inadequate husbands, failed fathers, and immature adults.

Yet even as male primary breadwinning came to predominate, the social foundations that made it possible showed signs of eroding. By the turn of the century, white-collar and service jobs were expanding and women were beginning to fill them. Although their numbers were small at first, the growth of white-collar and service jobs in the early twentieth century foreshadowed the postindustrial revolution that was to take place after World War II. Men were among the first clerical workers, but a ready supply of educated women began to replace them (at lower wages) in the early decades of the twentieth century.[11]

In this early period, the growth of the female labor force did not appear to threaten the preeminence of the male breadwinner. After all, the vast majority of women workers were young, single, childless, and only temporarily employed. Marriage and pregnancy sent most employed women home to care for newly acquired husbands and children. The economic prosperity that followed the Great Depression and World War II, coupled with veterans' benefits and preferential treatment for male workers, gave male breadwinning a new boost and temporarily suppressed the long-term erosion of the good-provider pattern. However insignificant the emergence of large numbers of employed women may have appeared at the outset, it was a portent of more widespread changes to come.

When changes did become apparent, they made a revolutionary transformation in women's lives.[12] Streaming into the labor force in ever-increasing numbers, women have developed a commitment to the workplace that has come to resemble the career pattern once reserved for men. A burgeoning proportion has also postponed or rejected marriage, reduced their reproductive rates to an unprecedented low, and fashioned a variety of alternatives to full-time mothering. By the mid-1970s, over half of all American women of working age were in the labor force, and the birthrate had dropped below the replacement rate of 2.2 children per woman for the first time in American history.

Since then, women's movement into the work force has continued unabated, topping 58 percent for all working-age women in 1990 and accounting for two out of every three mothers with preschool children. Since the precipitous rise in women's employment rate is fueled by the entry of younger rather than older cohorts of women, the percentage of mothers with young children who are employed has risen faster than the percentage of all women who are employed. Most employed women have entered female-dominated occupations, but a notable proportion has broken the barriers to entry into male-dominated fields such as law (up from 4 percent in 1972 to 21 percent in 1990), medicine (up from 10 percent to 19 percent), computer programming (up from 20 percent to 36 percent), and even bus driving (up from 34 percent to almost 52 percent).[13] Other women have not been so fortunate, however, as rising marital instability and the decline of male support have left them economically vulnerable in an economy that continues to allot most of the best-rewarded jobs to men.[14]

Men have also undergone a revolution in family and work commitments, albeit a quieter one. Since 1970, men's earnings have stagnated, eroding their ability to earn a "family wage." From 1979 to 1988, the median hourly wage for men fell 5 percent, and the bottom 75 percent of the male work force experienced wage reductions.[15] For white men serving as a family's only breadwinner, median inflation-adjusted income fell 22 percent between 1976 and 1984.[16] Families have been able to maintain a comparable standard of living only because women have joined the work force and experienced slightly rising wages.[17] Men's relative economic contributions to family survival have thus declined over the last several decades, while pressure for them to share in the work of the home has mounted.

Although the economic prospects of most men have contracted, their options about whether to share their earnings with women and children have expanded. The rise in divorce, nonmarital sexual partnerships, and out-of-wedlock childbearing has given men an escape hatch from the demands of primary breadwinning.[18] Many men may now find it difficult to support a family alone, but they have a choice about what to do instead: they can rely on an employed partner to share the pressures of economic survival, or they can simply remain single and thereby keep their earnings to themselves.

Few Americans now live on farms or in small towns, where preindustrial men, women, and children joined in a common physical and economic struggle to survive. Men no longer depart the household to seek their fortune on an expanding frontier. Outside the inner city, premature and unexpected death is less likely to take young men from wives, lovers, and dependent children. Social conditions have changed irrevocably, but the historical ambiguity and diversity of male commitments have reemerged in a new form.[19]

Now, as in an earlier era, "good providers" vie with "autonomous men" and "involved husbands and fathers" for ideological and social support. But no clear successor has taken the place of the once-ascendant but now embattled ethos of male breadwinning. Contemporary men— whether primary breadwinners, husbands and fathers in dual-earner marriages, or confirmed bachelors—face new choices and circumstances. Models from the past, however unambiguous or attractive, provide little help in navigating these uncertain waters.

Alternative Paths in Men's Development

Just as it is incorrect to assume that men's breadwinning is a pattern that has prevailed throughout American history, it is also erroneous to assume that contemporary men are a homogeneous group. Despite the common belief that a shared set of experiences binds all or most men together, modern men inherit an ambiguous cultural legacy and face a variety of social circumstances. Pushed and pulled in diverse ways, they are moving in different directions. Some continue to choose breadwinning, but others are forging alternative paths. To make sense of this diversity, we need to distill the complexity of men's lives into some general patterns. In particular, men differ in two important ways: whether or not they developed a breadwinning outlook in childhood, and whether or not they have sustained or changed their outlooks over time.

Among men who expected to become breadwinners, some have maintained this outlook into and throughout adulthood, following a stable path toward good providing. But others experienced unexpected change, either moving away from family commitments or moving toward parental caretaking.

Men who did not develop a breadwinning outlook in childhood have followed a similar range of paths. Some of these men have sustained an autonomous outlook. Others have undergone some kind of change, either becoming breadwinners despite an earlier reluctance or unexpectedly turning toward involvement in child rearing.

These six paths do not exhaust all of the complicated patterns emerging among contemporary men, but they illustrate some of the most important contours of change. Taking a close look at how individuals are traversing these alternative routes provides a way to decipher how and why men are changing. Consider, then, the paths taken by the following middle-class and working-class men.

Jim and Brian come from very different economic backgrounds, but they share a life trajectory toward breadwinning:

Jim grew up in a comfortable home located in a well-to-do suburb outside a major Eastern city. His parents moved there shortly after his birth, attracted by the spacious lawns and high-quality public schools that seemed ideal for their children. Each day, his father commuted to work in the city, leaving Jim and his sisters in the care of their mother.

His parents stressed education, and his father's income as an advertising executive ensured Jim's access to a good college. From his earliest memories, Jim aimed for and expected to achieve professional status. In his eyes, a professional job would provide the income to support a wife and children in the same degree of comfort he enjoyed as a child. It would also bestow him with the mark of success.

In college, Jim partied more than he studied, and his grades suffered accordingly. Though a pre-med student, he had little chance of being accepted into an accredited U.S. medical school. But being a doctor seemed the most appealing way to achieve the material and social rewards he desired, so Jim gained entry to a less selective medical school abroad. Four years later, he returned to the United States with a medical degree and an appointment as an intern at a small suburban hospital.

*In his late twenties, with the demanding—and impoverished—
years of medical training behind him, Jim met and married Theresa,
a nurse five years his junior. She shared his vision of creating a home
and family in which he earned the bread and she baked it. Jim was finally able to cash in on his "investment" in a lucrative, if demanding,
private practice, and he and his wife are expecting their first child.
She has quit her nursing job to devote all her time to child rearing, and
he puts in long hours as a doctor to support his growing family in
style.*

Although less privileged and further along in his work and family "careers," Brian has followed a path parallel to Jim's:

*Brian grew up in a modest attached house in a crowded Irish neigh-
borhood on the outskirts of a large city. His father was a plumber who
loyally stayed with the same company, despite low pay and poor working conditions. His mother, a devout Catholic, never held a paid job or,
to his recollection, expressed any desire to do so. She seemed content to
look after her six children.*

*Brian spent his boyhood playing in the crowded streets of his neigh-
borhood. He never enjoyed school and, like his father, preferred to work
with his hands rather than his head. When his father was able to get
him a plumbing apprenticeship, he jumped at the opportunity to quit
school at seventeen and learn a "useful trade." His parents, who
stressed hard work and making a good living, were happy with this
decision.*

*After completing his training, Brian went to work as a plumber for
his father's boss. He also married his neighborhood girlfriend, Donna,
shortly after they discovered she was pregnant. He can't say he "really
loved" her, but it was the "right thing to do." Besides, she shared his
background and outlook on life, and the timing seemed right. Shunning birth control, they had two daughters within the first three years
of marriage and planned for an even larger family.*

*As his family grew, Brian chafed under the insecure working condi-
tions of private contracting. When the opportunity arose, he took the
appropriate civil service exams and moved to a more secure job with
the city. He has been there ever since. Now that he has four children to
feed, he cannot afford to leave. The security, pension benefits, and
other protections of a civil service job offset his irritation with tedious
working conditions and bureaucratic procedures.*

*Today, Brian, Donna, and their four children share a small but
comfortable house in a working-class suburb. Donna "rules the roost"
and complains that he is never home. He rejoins that he has to work
overtime and take extra jobs "off the books" to meet the heavy expenses*

of a large family. He also admits he prefers hanging out with the guys to "taking orders" from Donna at home. She has no desire to work, and in any case he would not "allow" it until the youngest child begins school. They both agree that "a mother belongs at home."

Jim and Brian found the social and economic support to maintain their early outlooks on work, family, and breadwinning. Indeed, both attributed their later success to following the model their parents had set for them. And why not? They had little reason to question the logic and value of their upbringing, since the promises of their childhood were relatively easy to fulfill. Through hard work, they reason, they have been able to obtain the rewards of being a man: supportive wives to care for their homes, healthy children to carry on their names, sufficient income to meet their material aspirations, and the respect of family and friends for having accomplished so much at home and at work.

Other men, however, have not found the process of becoming a breadwinner as straightforward or attractive as they had anticipated. Beginning with similar backgrounds and aspirations, Walter, Alan, Robert, and Larry moved away from primary breadwinning over time, although not in the same direction:

Walter's background, like Jim's, was solidly middle class. His father was a modestly successful accountant, who supported his family and was "moderately" involved in raising his young son and daughter. His mother was home daily, never feeling the need or desire to work outside the home. Walter "always assumed" he would marry and have children some day. He knew he would be a professional, too.

He was good in math and science and attracted to the financial rewards promised by a medical career. But he was not attracted to the pressures and long training doctors must endure. He thus chose dentistry, a well-paying but less demanding medical occupation.

In college, Walter had his first serious relationship with a woman and married her three years later. His wife worked as a film editor but quit when their son was born. By then, Walter was making ample money in his private practice, and she had hit a dead end in her career. They moved to the suburbs, and he commuted to work in the city each day.

But Walter gradually tired of his life at work and at home. His private practice was lucrative but uninspiring and excruciatingly predictable. He longed for more time to himself, but the financial demands of a nonemployed wife and child made that impossible.

Walter also became estranged from his family. Commuting kept him away from home much of the time, and his resentment of their dependence on him made tensions high when he was there. These tensions created a subtle but palpable barrier between him and his young son.

By the time it came, Walter's divorce merely ratified his emotional distance from his family. It also allowed him to move to the city, where the emotional distance took physical form. He now lives close to his office, but has cut back on his working hours to enjoy the leisure activities that city living affords. He pays only modest alimony, since his ex-wife now works, and his child support payments are less than the expenses he bore when married. He tries to see his son every weekend, but his new girlfriend is taking an increasing amount of his time. Mostly, he says, he likes being alone.

Alan also avoided parental commitments even though he initially held a breadwinning orientation:

Alan was raised by his grandparents. His parents were divorced before he was five, and his memories of his father are dim. He lived with his mother and maternal grandparents, who were like parents to him. His grandfather took his father's place as family breadwinner and patriarch. His grandmother "spoiled" him, and he remembers her as "terrific."

Alan's expectations for the future were vague, but he was confident he could "take care of whatever came up." He always "figured" he'd get married and get a job. He gravitated toward retail sales, where his relaxed, unaffected charm made finding jobs easy.

Alan went to work right after high school selling hard goods in a department store . He was an effective salesman and able to make "good money" on commission. With money in his pockets, he married young, had a child, and became a breadwinning father when he was barely into his twenties.

After a few years, an economic recession hit, sales fell drastically, and Alan found himself out of work. He was not especially concerned; he knew he could find another job and was happy to enjoy his leisure until the unemployment checks ran out. His wife, however, was horrified at Alan's sudden change of fortune. When she asked for a divorce, Alan learned that she was involved with another man.

Within weeks of his wife's revelation, divorce proceedings were under way. In court, she asked for and gained full custody of their daughter, citing Alan's poor work record and lack of involvement with their child. She also claimed Alan assaulted her, although Alan denies this vehemently.

When the divorce was final, Alan's wife moved across the country with her new boyfriend, taking his young daughter far away. Alan considered contesting his ex-wife's move, but he believed the judge would not support him and would have little power to enforce compli-

ance even if he did. After several attempts to contact his daughter, all of which his ex-wife opposed, Alan ceased trying to be a father. He has not seen or heard from his daughter for over a decade.

Since his divorce, Alan has held a variety of jobs and remarried twice. He rarely stays at one job for long, choosing instead to alternate between periods of work and periods of play. He has no desire to have any more children. He prefers the freedom of childlessness to the risk of loss that fatherhood would entail.

Walter and Alan turned away from an initial adherence to the good-provider ethic toward an ethic that stresses personal freedom and autonomy.

Like them, Robert and Larry expected to become primary breadwinners but ultimately rejected this pattern. Instead of distancing themselves from domestic life, however, these two men embraced parental involvement, developing ties to their children that extend far beyond providing for economic needs alone:

Robert grew up in the privileged surroundings of an affluent suburb. His father, a doctor, provided a stern, imposing, and demanding figure for his two sons. His mother also had a strong personality, but fewer outlets for its expression. She worked part-time, but poured most of her considerable energy into her family. Both parents stressed discipline and achievement. Robert was not close to his father, but he did respect his father's accomplishments. Like his father, he expected to become a successful doctor and good provider for his own wife and children.

In college, Robert realized that science was not his strength and that becoming a doctor was not his, but his father's, aspiration. He switched to a humanities major over both parents' objections and went on to graduate school in art education. He liked working with people, especially children, and eventually became a high school teacher.

In his early twenties, he married a fellow teacher. They had two children, a boy and a girl. Since he and his wife earned limited incomes but enjoyed flexible schedules as teachers, they both continued to work and shared fairly equally in the child-care duties not absorbed by day-care centers and baby-sitters. Robert found himself to be a devoted and nurturing father, far different than his own father had been. Indeed, he took to parenthood with greater enthusiasm than did his wife.

Shortly after the birth of their second child, the marriage began to deteriorate. Robert's wife became dissatisfied with teaching and began to feel "confined" by marriage and motherhood. As she struck out on a new career in advertising, they "grew apart." Divorce seemed a wel-

come relief to both, but Robert was determined not to lose his children.
They agreed on a joint custody arrangement, in which the children
split their time equally between the two parents. This arrangement
gave her the freedom she desired and him the parental involvement he
needed. The divorce reinforced rather than undermined the shared
caretaking that had already developed between them.

Robert now lives with his new wife, Rhonda, an editor with a pub-
lishing company, in an apartment a few blocks away from his former
wife. His children, now nearing their teens, have rooms in each
dwelling and move back and forth easily between their two homes.
They spend every other week with Robert, who proudly displays their
art on the apartment's walls. He has remained a devoted teacher and
has recently begun to write innovative educational texts. He is eager to
have another child with Rhonda.

Larry's economic origins were more modest, but he held equally traditional expectations:

Larry's father was a boat captain, and from his earliest memory that
is what Larry wanted to become. As the oldest son, he was often looked
to as the man around the house during his father's frequent absences
at sea. Larry's mother, a strong woman who stressed the values of hard
work and honesty, doted on him. His father died when Larry was in
his teens, but his father's pension kept the family out of poverty .

Larry joined the seafarers' apprentice program shortly after high
school graduation. It takes years to become a licensed captain and
many are never accepted into the ranks of this elite group, but Larry
was confident that his father's connections, combined with his own
skills, would secure a place for him among the captains' ranks.

For seven years he worked as a crew member on tugboats that pulled
barges out to sea. The work was tedious, but he was learning to be a
captain and never doubted that his promotion would come at the end
of the probationary period. During this period, he married and had
two children. His wife, Rita, continued to work as a flight attendant.
In addition to recognizing the need for two incomes, she was commit-
ted to working and aimed, as she still does, for a promotion to man-
agement. They have been able to coordinate two erratic work schedules
so that one parent has always been home to care for their toddlers or
get them to the baby-sitter.

Several years ago, Larry's lifelong dream was shattered. The board
refused to promote him to captain's rank. If he remains at sea, he will
have to do so as a member of the crew. Rita, he says, has kept him
"afloat" economically and spiritually during this rough time. As he
has struggled to adjust to his thwarted ambitions and to search for

new, if less stimulating, work in the everyday world of the "land-locked," his family, and especially his children, has become the emotional center of his world.

Unlike their own distant fathers, Robert and Larry actively participate in rearing and providing emotional sustenance to their young children. Although unexpected, parenting has become one of their most fulfilling life experiences. They not only share but *enjoy* sharing the economic and nurturing responsibilities of parenthood. It is difficult to distinguish their contributions to the family from those of their wives. The trajectories of these involved fathers provide a sharp contrast to those of Jim and Brian, who remained stable breadwinners, and of Walter and Alan, who avoided parental involvement, even though all three groups grew up with similar aspirations.

Those early aspirations are quite different than those of the following six men, who grew up hoping to find freedom and to avoid the demands of becoming a good provider. Gus and Tony never veered from the path they initially hoped to pursue:

Gus grew up in a small Southern town. His mother was a full-time homemaker, and his father a lawyer who worked out of a small office attached to their home. Unlike most fathers of his era, Gus's father was close at hand and even joined the family for lunch whenever the children were home. Both parents were well educated and stressed professional careers and marriage for their three children. Gus, however, was a gifted artist and wanted to find an occupation that drew on his artistic skills. He also felt bored and confined by small-town family life, attracted instead to the glamour and excitement that a big city promised.

Despite his parents' wishes, Gus moved to New York City after high school graduation to pursue his interest in art and design. In place of the comfort and security of small-town life, New York offered insecurity and economic hardship, but also the freedom from "middle-class" values and the opportunity to explore alternative lifestyles. He enrolled in a design school, subsisted on part-time jobs, and moved in with a woman he met at school.

After finishing the design program with honors, he took a job as designer-planner for a social service agency. Living with a woman, however, confirmed Gus's aversion to family life. He found sharing an apartment, much less his life, too confining. As her demands for commitment escalated, he concluded that he preferred living alone, where he could be free to devote his time to work.

As middle age approaches, Gus has few regrets. He has become increasingly self-confident in his work and has grown restive with the

*limits of working in a bureaucracy. He plans to start his own business
soon. Although a risky move, Gus can afford to take it, for he has
avoided the economic and social entanglements of marriage and fatherhood. Children appeal to him in the abstract, but the concrete circumstances necessary to become a father do not. His own material
needs are few, and time rather than money is his most valued resource. He breathes a sigh of relief that he has managed to avoid the
"trap" of family life and is grateful to his sister for giving his parents
the grandchild they so desired. He feels little nostalgia for the small-
town world he long ago left behind.*

Like Gus, Tony never wished to become a father or a breadwinner,
and his aspirations did not undergo significant change:

*Tony was not completely averse to having a child of his own; it just
never seemed like a realistic goal. Orphaned as a young boy, he was
sent to live with his older sisters, dividing his time between the two so
that he would be less of a burden to each. As soon as he was old enough
to earn money, he worked at any odd job he could find. The lack of financial resources made college out of the question. He did not like
school anyway. When his uncle offered him the chance to be a mechanic in his gas station, he quit school in the tenth grade and began
to support himself.*

*Within a few years his uncle hit hard times and let Tony go. Tony
was good with his hands and always able to find work, but no job
lasted more than a year, and none seemed to provide much promise for
the future. He moved aimlessly from one job to another until he finally
joined the army. His army stint was short and comparatively pain-
less, since he was sent to Europe instead of Southeast Asia. Once dis-
charged, he returned to his sister's home and the modest but bearable
life he had left behind.*

*Not long after his return, Tony met Vickie, a teenager who lived
down the street. Over her father's strong objections, they began to date
steadily and were soon making plans to marry. She seemed to have the
self-confidence and ambition that Tony lacked. She began working and
saving money for the house they would buy someday. Tony went along,
handing over most of his pay to her. She stayed in school, graduated,
and trained to become a nurse. She also pushed Tony to apply for a job
with the city, where he was hired as a provisional worker.*

*As soon as Vickie reached the age of consent, they married and set-
tled into a bungalow financed primarily by her savings. Since that
time, they have discussed having children, but she states flatly that she
is too ambitious to take the time out to raise a child and that, with
high blood pressure, a pregnancy would threaten her health. As a pro-*

visional worker, Tony does not earn enough money to support a family alone in the style his wife wishes. He hopes to find job security some-day, but holds little hope that the work will pay well. He nevertheless has no desire to be a househusband. He hates housework and leaves most of it to Vickie, who demands a high standard of cleanliness. His marriage gives him more of a family than he ever expected, and he feels no need to press for a child over his wife's objections. Her judg-ment has proved correct so far, and he is willing, indeed happy, to abide by her preferences.

Despite the cultural and social injunctions that encourage men to trade personal freedom for family responsibilities, specific social cir-cumstances converged to reinforce Gus's and Tony's early aversion to the breadwinning ethic. They differ from Paul and Steve, who both moved from an early rejection of breadwinning toward conformity to the good-provider pattern:

Paul was a child of the sixties. Raised in a solidly middle-class family, he concluded in adolescence that he wanted no part of the establish-ment to which his parents belonged. At the height of the youth rebel-lion, he moved to Vermont with Nancy, his college girlfriend, where they opened a store together. They were happy as equal partners in their food store, and although some extramarital affairs brought strains to the marriage, their commitment to each other survived. Fol-lowing one especially rough period, when his wife got seriously in-volved with another lover, they decided to forgo all extramarital li-aisons and cement their bond to each other by having a child. They shared in the care of their young daughter, just as they shared in the running of the store.

Paul was very happy living the life of a country hippie, but "making ends meet" got difficult. Expecting a second child and facing the eco-nomic burdens that parenthood brings, he and Nancy decided to move back to "civilization" in search of jobs with steady paychecks.

With the proceeds from selling their country store as a down pay-ment, they bought a house in the suburbs and went looking for jobs in the "real world." Hindered by her lack of work experience, Nancy was disappointed to find nothing better than a low-paying job as a clerk-typist. Paul was more fortunate, landing a job on the bottom rung of a social service agency. His managerial skills, concern for the needy, and sheer energy were appreciated and rewarded. Paul found himself moving up the ladder of success despite himself. He missed the time work took away from being with his family, and especially his two young children, but the rewards of success were seductive.

Within a few years, Paul was making enough money to enable

Nancy to quit her job. She had never planned to become a housewife, but her job was leading her nowhere. Paul urged her to stay home, for he was working sixty hours a week and felt someone needed to be with the kids.

Now an agency director, Paul feels remorse when Nancy and the kids complain of his long days and nights at work. He admits he has discovered work ambitions he once scorned, but he loves his job and the lifestyle it affords him. Much to his own surprise, he has become a breadwinner and a member of the establishment.

Steve also became a breadwinner without ever intending to do so:

From as far back as he can remember, Steve recalls that he was wild. His parents tried to keep him off the streets, but as soon as he was big enough to stand up to his father, he was out of the house and hanging out with the guys. He sought in his friends the warmth and cama-raderie he never had from his unaffectionate father, a military man with a cold, stern demeanor. His friends offered more than support, however. By the time he graduated from high school, he was well schooled in sex and drugs. He made no plans for the future.

Following a brief period of immersion in the hippie counterculture, he was drafted and sent to Vietnam. There he acquired several tattoos and a serious heroin addiction. By the time he returned home, his life had less direction than ever. He drifted from job to job; whatever income he could muster was quickly depleted to support his drug habit, and he sought work that enabled him to stay high as often as possible. His strongest memory of that period is being fired from a mail-carrier job for driving a truck while stoned.

Eventually he moved in with Elaine, who seemed to care about him in ways he had never known before. With a steady job of her own, she urged him to break his drug habit and aim for something better in life. He joined a methadone program and gave up the "hard stuff." When Elaine got pregnant, they married.

Faced with the new and overwhelming responsibilities of father-hood, Steve panicked and reverted to drugs as the most convenient escape. Elaine supported him and their child singlehandedly. He found that arrangement even harder to take and moved out of the house they had purchased with the help of his in-laws.

On his own for the first time in years, Steve realized how accustomed he had become to domesticity and how little pleasure he now derived from his freedom. On the advice of a friend, he applied for a job working with computers. He tested well, for he had always had an aptitude for math. In his new job as a computer programmer, he discov-

ered talents he never thought he had and a love of work he had never known. Recognizing his talent, his boss offered him a promotion.

Elaine agreed to let him move back in with her and their young daughter if he would stay straight. She had tired of the double burden of full-time work and sole responsibility for child rearing. Steve was now earning enough to support the whole family, and she was ready to have another child.

Off drugs for two years, Steve is now a full-time breadwinner. Elaine works part-time to provide some extra income, but she spends most of her time caring for their two young children. Steve gets up every morning looking forward to a job he enjoys. He expects to be promoted to management soon and ultimately plans to run the whole department. In his view, the support of his boss and his wife saved his life.

Paul's and Steve's stories show how strong the social pull toward breadwinning can remain for some. In contrast, the life histories of Frank and Todd demonstrate how the pull toward the good-provider model is waning for others:

Frank grew up in a Midwestern household, where a stress on education and achievement groomed him for the fast track of occupational accomplishment. Although his parents also stressed "family values," Frank sensed that making money and climbing the corporate ladder were more important ingredients of success than marriage and family. From as early as he can remember, Frank recalls that work ambitions crowded out any strong desire to have children.

Proving himself to be an able student and a dedicated worker, Frank launched a promising career as a corporate economist after completing graduate school. He fell easily into the habit of working eighty-hour weeks, usually arriving home only to eat a quick meal and fall into bed. His hard work and quick intelligence were rewarded with frequent promotions and hefty raises. In the early years, amid work demands and rewards, he hardly noticed that a personal life was missing.

By his late twenties, however, Frank had begun to sense an emptiness in the skewed balance of his life. He was growing weary of long days at the office and short nights alone. He started to drop in bars after work and even gambled on a few blind dates. Within a few years, Frank met Sharon, a woman he could envision sharing his life with. She, too, was a busy professional who shared his enthusiasm for hard work. She moved in with him. They settled into the busy life of two childless professionals and married after a few years.

Several years into the marriage, Sharon began to raise the subject of children. Her pleas to start a family increased in frequency, but Frank hardly noticed. He was too pressured at work and did not need another responsibility. He had never taken her suggestions seriously, for he knew she was as committed to working as he.

One morning, Sharon announced she was leaving. She explained that he was too distant, inaccessible, and tied to his work; she wanted a more balanced life, with a child and with more sharing and intimacy. Frank had heard these complaints before and so was skeptical of her sincerity, but when he arrived home that night she was gone. He was devastated. The prospect of losing Sharon made him realize how much he needed and loved her, how important their life together had become to him.

After a few days of disorientation and despair, Frank came to a fateful conclusion: for the first time since adolescence, he realized some things mattered more to him than money, success, and power. He resigned from his high-pressured job and set about to find less demanding employment. His occupational future looked less promising, but he looked forward to having more time to pursue other pleasures.

It took months to convince Sharon that she meant more to Frank than his job did, but after six months of separation she agreed to reunite. They bought a home in a nearby suburb.

Frank and Sharon now have a four-year-old daughter. As an assistant vice president in a major corporation, Frank is an achiever by most people's standards. He nevertheless feels downwardly mobile compared to the goals he once set for himself and the path he once traveled. He will never be president of any corporation; nor does he wish to be. Instead, he leaves the office by 5:30 each day so that he can relieve the baby-sitter. As he awaits Sharon's return from work, he bathes his daughter and prepares her for bed. He marvels at how much joy he has found as a father and how little regret he feels for choosing a slower track.

Like Frank, Todd moved from avoiding family life to becoming closely involved in rearing his young daughter and deeply committed to supporting his wife's professional career:

Todd's memories of his mother are vague, for she died of leukemia before he started school. His father was a hard-working insurance salesman who could barely support his two young sons, even working nights to bring in extra cash. He had neither the time nor the desire to be their mother as well as their father, and soon married his deceased wife's sister to provide a mother for his boys. Not without bitterness, Todd remembers his father as an emotionally remote man in a marriage devoid of passion, tied to a secure but ultimately unfulfilling job. His father stressed these conservative values to his sons, warning them that if they did not work hard at school and go to college, they would end up as ditchdiggers or on the breadline.

Todd viewed his father's life as sadly truncated and did not wish to pursue the same safe but constrained existence. Instead, he wanted to be a singer or an actor. Freedom, excitement, and self-fulfillment, not security, were his life goals. After a few frustrating semesters at a local community college, Todd left home with a small suitcase and a guitar. He moved to Florida to eke out a living singing in coffeehouses while he developed his musical and acting skills.

But freedom proved an elusive goal for Todd. The Vietnam War was growing abroad, and the draft board was breathing down his neck. With no student or health deferments to shield him, Todd decided to enlist before he was drafted. Like countless other working-class boys of his generation, he decided that defending his country was the right thing to do.

Todd came back from the war irrevocably changed. The experience had been painful enough, but the discrimination he encountered on his return added insult to injury. He could not land a decent job as, time after time, the image of the unstable Vietnam vet foreclosed employment possibilities. He moved from one temporary job to another, pursuing his dream of a music and acting career in his spare time. He also married, but divorced within several years as financial and other difficulties took their toll on the relationship. When he did, he left a son in his ex-wife's care.

One night, Todd met and was immediately attracted to a self-confident, assertive, and graceful woman named Sally. As a professional dancer, she knew what she wanted and where she was going. They moved in together, and he found a satisfaction that he had never known when he was "free."

Then Todd had another good experience. Through a special program for displaced Vietnam veterans, he was offered, and accepted, a job as a water and sewer repairer—work he would have rejected a decade earlier as boring and restrictive, beneath his abilities. Much to his surprise, he enjoyed the physical work and the split-shift hours. For the first time in his adult life, he had a steady income and a secure job. With Sally's career as a professional dancer and teacher blossoming, they felt ready to get married and have a child.

Todd is now delighted to take care of his infant daughter during the day while Sally takes and teaches her dance classes. In the evening, he digs ditches and repairs pipes, chuckling to himself that he has ended up just as his father warned he would. But he has never been so happy and already looks forward to having another child. He still dreams of an acting career, but his priorities have *changed: a strong, supportive relationship with his wife and close in-volvement in raising his daughter now come before all else. He feels a deep sadness that his own distant (and now deceased) father missed the joy he is now experiencing taking care of his child. He also regrets that he could not care for the child of his first marriage as he now does for his daughter.*

These life histories suggest some of the most prevalent patterns of commitment that have emerged as men's choices have diversified over the last several decades. They show not only that men can develop a variety of expectations and desires in childhood but also that these outlooks may be sustained or changed as men encounter unexpected circumstances later in life.

Regardless of class background, young boys confront a contradictory and ambiguous array of definitions about what it means to be a man. They may accept the good-provider ethic, or they may develop a more skeptical view of breadwinning. For those who aspire to breadwinning, marriage, fatherhood, and a good job offer the promise of domestic power and public prestige. For those who do not, breadwinning commitments are more likely to appear risky and dangerous. On the one hand, failure to become a "good enough" provider or a "successful enough" worker means failing more fundamentally as a man. On the other, successful breadwinning can trap one in boring work or stifling domestic obligations. From this perspective, the search for personal autonomy offers a more promising route to manhood than does lifelong commitment to marriage, parenthood, and work success.

Both of these outlooks are deeply rooted in the American cultural tradition to which children are exposed.[20] Yet adopting either as a child is no guarantee of achieving it as an adult. Rather, men may sustain, modify, or reject their early outlooks as they grow up and face the unexpected contingencies of adult life. As men have encountered new options and constraints, they have built their lives in a variety of ways. Many have developed outlooks that bear little resemblance either to earlier cultural definitions of manhood or to the aspirations they held as children.[21]

Either by sustaining or unexpectedly developing a breadwinning outlook, some men have reaffirmed the good-provider ethic. Either by maintaining an early outlook or by moving away from parenthood in adulthood, other men have stressed a more autonomous vision of manhood. Still others who expected to become breadwinners or to remain autonomous have become caretakers and nurturers instead. Each of these patterns contains much diversity, and the variations among men can be as much a matter of degree as a matter of fundamental difference. Yet comparisons between those who underwent significant change from their early outlooks and those who did not make all paths instructive.

These paths provide a framework for moving beyond a uniform vision of men to examine a range of choices and outlooks. By identifying the crucial events and experiences that propelled men down these different paths, we can uncover the causes, shape, and consequences of change in men's lives.

PART II

PATHS OF CHANGE

3

THE CHILD AND THE MAN

Psychologists, in expecting to find a relation between what parents do and a particular outcome in the child, have generally failed to appreciate that the child is always interpreting the actions of parents. . . . Rarely will there be a fixed consequence of any single event—no matter how traumatic—or special set of family conditions.

—Kagan, *The Nature of the Child*

Men who have reached adulthood in recent decades have confronted confusing circumstances. The stagnation of wages has undermined their capacity to support a family alone. Women's entry into the workplace has challenged their preeminence as breadwinners and workers. The sexual revolution has eroded the double standard, and the revolution in cohabitation and divorce has loosened the bonds of marriage. These trends have undermined the foundations of men's modern privileges, but they have also given men opportunities to pursue new paths, claim new freedoms, and develop new identities.

Born into the post–World War II period of economic growth and a resurgent breadwinner-homemaker household, these men had few clues that they would ultimately encounter a revolution in family patterns and gender relations. Even before these changes became apparent, however, many of these men had experienced ambiguities, contradictions, and doubts about what the future would and should hold. Such childhood concerns set the stage for the unforeseen twists and turns that occurred later in their lives. Childhood experiences provide only limited clues for explaining men's adult commitments and choices, but they provide a point of departure for men's life trajectories.

To construct a picture of these starting points, we must rely on men's own retrospective accounts. Whether they represent a form of selective remembering or a way of interpreting the past, these accounts show how men actively use and make sense of early experiences rather than simply being molded by them. Indeed, the experiences these men recount cast doubt on a number of widely held beliefs about the determining influence of childhood experiences on later life choices and outlooks.

Sons and Fathers

Among the men we will meet in the following pages, only a minority became a sole or primary breadwinner. But this was not the case for their fathers, almost three-fourths of whom had been the primary or sole family breadwinners—although fathers with blue-collar and lower white-collar jobs were more likely to have shared breadwinning with a wife who worked full-time (see appendix, table 2). Taken together, these fathers showed a strong attachment to the workplace and not much participation in child rearing. Only 4 percent of the men recalled significant periods when their fathers were out of work. Of the remaining 96 percent, across classes and occupations, none reported fathers who averaged fewer than forty hours at work per week and many reported longer work weeks (ranging from a low of 13 percent among fathers with lower white-collar jobs to a high of 81 percent among the self-employed).

Most sons concluded that their fathers were "generally satisfied" with their jobs, and many felt that their fathers were "very satisfied" (ranging from a low of 25 percent for fathers in lower white-collar jobs to a high of 63 percent in professional occupations). Overall, only 34 percent reported that their fathers spent some time with them every day, but 50 percent of those whose fathers held lower white-collar jobs did. While there are some exceptions worth noting, most fathers embodied the prevailing masculine norm of distant parenting and good providing.

While fathers' level of job satisfaction may bear some relation to sons' outlooks as children, this relationship weakened with the passage of time (see appendix, table 3). In adulthood, sons' orientations toward breadwinning are only loosely and ambiguously connected to perceptions of how much satisfaction fathers derived from a job or career. Among those whose fathers appeared moderately satisfied or dissatisfied, there was little change over time in the percentage who rejected breadwinning. Among those who perceived their fathers were very satisfied, however, 59 percent held a breadwinning orientation in childhood, but only 30 percent sustained that outlook through adulthood. As time passed, those men whose fathers were very satisfied came to resemble those whose fathers were not.

Fathers' degree of participation in child rearing had a similarly weak and ambiguous relationship to sons' adult orientations (see appendix, table 4). Of sons who perceived their fathers to be involved in child rearing on a daily basis, fewer than 40 percent ultimately developed an orientation of parental involvement. A similar percentage of sons who perceived their fathers to be uninvolved or only sporadically involved also developed an involved outlook. Why do fathers' employment and parental patterns bear so little relation to the ultimate choices and outlooks of their sons?

FATHERS AS WORKERS AND BREADWINNERS

One reason a father's choices about work and breadwinning are not straightforwardly reflected in his son's choices is that there is often a discrepancy between what a father does and what feelings he conveys about doing it. Equally important, a son may judge his father's choices in very different terms than did his father. Whether a son concludes that breadwinning is mostly a privilege or mostly a burden depends on many factors beyond a father's choices, hopes, or dreams.

Most of the respondents had fathers who worked steadily when they were growing up, and 45 percent concluded that their fathers were satisfied with their work—that is, that they found their work sufficiently fulfilling that they would not have chosen a different occupation. Another 33 percent concluded that their fathers were moderately satisfied, but found little fulfillment in their work. An additional 14 percent concluded that their fathers would have preferred a different line of work or not to have worked at all.[1] Many sons thus perceived a gap between a father's stress on hard work and his feelings about working. This discrepancy, which for some appeared to resemble hypocrisy, planted early seeds of doubt in some sons. Edward, an unmarried physician, recalled how his father's obvious distaste for his job undermined the admonition to work hard and achieve success:

> It's quite clear my father hated his job. Certainly his goal was that we have careers that we be happy with, that we could even get a certain amount of control and get more out it. But at the same time, even though instilling that attitude, there was the image that work is not a positive thing.

Fathers could extol the value of work, but their specific choices might serve as a cautionary tale. Sam, an architect, explained how his father's refusal to leave a job he disliked did not convey the message that sacrifice is admirable:

> My father would never complain. He only told me one thing: "Be happy with what you do and if you're not happy, change." Because he wasn't happy, but he always did the same job. He was stuck, didn't try to do anything else.

Discrepancies between what fathers did and how they felt about it sent children mixed messages about the value of work commitment and economic security, but their feelings spoke louder than their actions or words. When a father appeared more frustrated than fulfilled, he conveyed the message to avoid the same fate, to take chances, and to think twice about sacrificing personal happiness at the altar of financial security. Edward explained:

> My father obviously didn't find his job satisfying. He was very much a martyr, whose whole focus was supporting and sacrificing for his family. I don't see that ability to martyr myself. I look at the grief and anxiety my father had by being the sole provider, and I would like to change that definition of being a man. So if being a man is being the rock and support of your family, that doesn't look very good to me.

The example of an unhappily employed father could make other patterns—even those reserved for women—more attractive. Edward found his mother's domesticity more appealing than his father's job. He longed for the option not to work, an option his father never had:

> I'm my mother's child. She went most of her life without working and seemed happy, content, and able to do worthwhile things. If I didn't have to work, I would be able to do that, too. I don't feel I need to be working in order to be self-satisfied.

Yet as we have seen, most fathers did *not* convey strong dissatisfaction with work or provide an ambiguous message about the value of breadwinning. Clearly, sons can react in a variety of ways to the images and messages their fathers provide. Over time, as sons age and establish greater personal independence, the meaning of their fathers' choices is also increasingly open to reassessment and change. And even when sons perceive little or no dissatisfaction on the part of their fathers, they may still choose a different path.

Ian, a freelance writer, avoided long-term commitments to secure jobs even though his father found success in a twenty-year career as director of a public service organization. Ironically, his father's fulfillment so raised Ian's standards of what makes an acceptable job that he ultimately found them nearly impossible to achieve:

My father was always doing something that he liked. He liked the idea of work, the idea that a person's worth was built on work. He never hated what he did. So I never was exposed to a situation where, "God I hate my job, I hate my boss." That may have influenced me to make me unwilling to accept a situation like that.

A father's commitment to the work ethic in the face of frustration and disappointment can inspire a corresponding response in a son, but it can also provide an example of what to reject or avoid. Although his father was a "downtrodden" lawyer who stressed the importance of "compromise," Paul, the director of a social service agency, interpreted his father's work commitment as timidity, cowardice, and uninspired conformity:

My father was very phobic about change. He would say, "Life is a compromise." He had an obsession about fitting into the crowd. I was very idealistic, rebellious, and we had a million clashes. I lived through a real hippie, dropout period. Once I quit a teaching job because I didn't like it, and my father said, "You're not supposed to like work. That's certainly not a legitimate reason for quitting."

Sons, moreover, do not look exclusively to their fathers when forming goals and aspirations. Other models and messages may provide a more attractive alternative, even when a father seems content with his choices. Despite his father's satisfaction as a breadwinner, Ian found the hippie culture of his youth far more appealing:

I had all these rebellious, Abbie Hoffman–type idols when I was growing up. I read all those books about how there was another way of living. Up until a certain point I had no idea you could do it any other way, and then it hit me that there's plenty of other ways to do it. That kind of reading and listening to people influenced me more than my father or close friends.

Whatever its sources, a divergence between the outlooks of fathers and sons is likely to produce a painful struggle. The outcome of this struggle is indeterminate even in the short run. Chuck, a thirty-five-year-old systems analyst, learned at an early age that he did not share his father's skills or his definition of manhood:

My dad worked in a factory. He wanted me to be interested in sports and be the All-American boy based on sort of a John Wayne model. But I realized very early that I wasn't particularly adept at sports. I used to read a lot, write, draw, go to museums. I was interested in things like cooking and art that were not what a young boy should be doing. It took me a very long time to know that he was really proud of me, because he had a different framework about being a man or being successful.

Even a boy who identifies closely with his father as a child does not necessarily maintain that identification as he matures. Over time, as a son faces the tasks of becoming an independent adult, he may see more clearly the costs as well as the benefits of his father's choices. He may discover fundamental differences between himself and his childhood models. And he has the advantage of being able to assess the long-run consequences of the choices his father made.

This process of distancing and evaluating may take place regardless of what the father chose or how he felt about it. Vern, a thirty-five-year-old park maintenance worker planning to remain childless, learned—amid some pain and regret—to distance himself from a father he came to believe had sacrificed too much for the sake of earning a living. He felt some guilt about not following in his father's footsteps, but it did not prevent him from pursuing a less constrained life:

I'm not a pusher like my father. I have my forty-hour week with my time off. I'm not an ambitious person, which is sad to a point and not a nice thing to admit. My father was ambitious, but I feel that twenty-five years of his life were spent just working. He did nothing else.

Neil, a graduate student hoping to become a professor, came to see his father's reluctance to aim high at work as a warning to avoid "playing it too safe." He wished for the success his father had not pursued:

The older I got and the more success I had, the more I started to think, "Why didn't your dad do as well?" Lots of kids grow up with hero worship of their dads, and that clearly was not my case. I keep trying to understand why somebody as bright and funny as my dad is working in some little job instead of managing some corporation. And there's an anger the older I get. He had potential, but that potential wasn't realized. If he were a little bit more ambitious, a little bit more driven. . . .

Anger, guilt, resentment, and sadness can accompany the process of separating from a father. These emotions are most likely to emerge when the son does not emulate his father but uses him as a foil to push against.

Those who rejected their fathers' breadwinning model endeavored to account for the differences between their fathers and themselves. Aware of differences in generational opportunities, they felt fortunate to have escaped the constraints to which their fathers appeared to succumb. Most rejected the preoccupation with security that seemed to prevail among this older generation, which grew to manhood during the Great Depression and World War II. They defined themselves in opposition to this ethic of security, glad to be able to take more risks. William, a thirty-five-year-old accountant, drew a clear line between his father's search for stability and his own willingness to take chances. He accepted his father's disapproval as part of the price of freedom:

> He puts a lot of stock in stability, in sticking with it. He was from the generation that you stay with one company and you're loyal. . . . So it was difficult for him that I have changed jobs several times, changed careers, done a number of things. It's difficult for him to understand.

Others blamed their fathers for failing to rise above the social constraints of their era. As they strove for independence and meaning in and outside work, they came to judge their fathers harshly for refusing to be masters of their fate, for not living up to the masculine ideal of being in control. Yet they also held a grudging respect for them. Neil concluded that he was fortunate to have avoided a trap his father had not been able or willing to transcend:

> My father survived a job that he hated for thirty years. I couldn't do it. I think a lot of his choices were self-imposed. He could have been one of those few guys who found another job he would have been happy at, but he didn't do it. I'm from a different generation, who assumed that we were gonna be able to get a great job no matter what we do. I just feel I'll be a success no matter what I do. But my dad's generation didn't feel that way; they were just happy to get a damn job.

Whether they attributed the causes to social or psychological differences, men who veered away from their fathers' breadwinning models developed an identity and self-image different from—indeed, in opposition to—their fathers. The process of distancing took these sons in many disparate directions. For some, it meant becoming more ambitious and successful, with some attendant ambivalence. Michael, a psychotherapist and custodial father of two, felt some guilt and "fear of success"[2] for exceeding his father's accomplishments, but he succeeded in any case:

> My father felt threatened by my ambition and was always quick to tell me that no matter how good I got, he would always be better. He would become very angry and envious of my success, especially at school. So I'm very proud of my accomplishments, but I experience it as a problem at the same time.

Others came to accept themselves as less ambitious, less capable, or less talented. Ray, a childless financial officer in a small company, ex-

plained the discrepancy between his achievements and his father's this
way, even though his father had built financial success in an expanding
postwar economy while Ray's working years were intertwined with a
more stagnant economy:

> I'll never reach the level of my father. These people are just financial
> whizzes, and they're better, and you can't help it. You can't be any bet-
> ter than you are. I'll be happy if I have a nice job and enjoy it. That's
> fine.

Whether or not they "blamed" themselves, those who did not climb as
high as their fathers came to see themselves as less work-oriented, less
dedicated to job success, and less committed to upholding the good-
provider ethic at all costs. They pondered this difference with ambivalence, concluding that, although they had rejected a highly touted definition of masculine identity, they had also escaped its negative consequences. Carl, an ex-printer currently working for a utilities company,
marveled *and* shuddered at his father's single-minded devotion to his
job, a devotion he could not and did not wish to muster:

> My father loved his job, and I certainly don't. He's old-fashioned, a
> throwback. He had the same job for forty-nine years, but me and him
> are opposites. He was very dedicated, and I was always talking about
> last night's game or having a cigarette in the bathroom.

When sons turned away from a model of manhood based on work
dedication and self-sacrifice, it held implications for how they judged
their fathers' family commitments as well. When work responsibilities
seemed like a trap, family responsibilities could assume a similar appearance. Arthur, a sanitation worker who was single and childless at thirty-
six, concluded that his father's "sacrifices" were anchored in breadwinning obligations that might be best to avoid:

> I could see what my father went through, and I realized I'd have to
> make a lot of sacrifices to be married. I'm selfish. You're willing to
> give up your freedom when you date somebody, but with a family
> comes responsibilities, and you begin to resent it.

A father's work pattern thus does not account for a son's relationship
to work and family life. Fathers present ambiguous, contradictory models to which sons respond in a variety of ways. Over time, they gain new
perspectives on their fathers' lives. Their long-run reactions grow out of
a series of personal experiences and lessons that make fathers' teach-
ings increasingly less determinate.

FATHERS AND PARENTAL INVOLVEMENT

If most fathers were strongly committed to working, they showed a correspondingly low participation in child rearing. Hank, a paramedic who hoped to become an involved father, forgave his father's distance because he knew his need to earn a living precluded the kind of participation Hank would have liked. His father, a security guard and elevator operator, was locked out of fatherly involvement because he was locked into caring for his family through economic support:

I can't remember playing sports. It wasn't a father-son relationship that you see in the movies. He couldn't. He worked double time. You never knew when he was coming home. His work ethic was that you did what you had to do to put a roof over your head and feed the children. He was trapped, too.

Despite this pattern among the fathers, a notable proportion of sons report a closer involvement, or the desire for a closer involvement, with their own children. Yet even in the unusual cases where their fathers were reported to be highly involved, the sons did not necessarily follow this model (as table 3 in the appendix shows). Why is there so tenuous a relationship between a father's pattern of participation and his son's later orientation?

The processes that led some men away from their fathers' work model also set the stage for different approaches to parenthood. Ernie, a physical therapist who became closely involved in rearing his daughter, recalled his father's absence with bitterness and disappointment. This memory spurred him to reject his father's choices and develop a different definition of fathering:

There was no support, no one I could talk to, no male role model at all. I got the sense that he thought he was the provider, but I wasn't looking for a roof and clothing; I was looking for a father. I think he felt he was serving his role well, but there's more to it than just that.

When asked what he would have liked his father to be like, Ernie explained it this way:

A lot of the opposite. More like how I try myself to be—expressing a lot more what you feel, more honesty, spending lots of time, participating in the growing-up stages. My father's negative influence has turned positive for me. He taught me how *not* to be a father.

Some of the men recalled that one of their first memories involved yearning for a more involved father. Their disappointment provoked an early determination to give their children what they had not received. Dean, a driver for the park service, realized early in life that his father didn't have time to spend time with him. He vowed "to go out of my way to try to change that."

Aware of the futility of wishing for more, most turned to their mothers for nurturance and support. Some, like William, the accountant who ultimately became an involved father, even identified more closely with their mothers than their fathers:

> I'm probably more like my mother than my father, more emotional than rational in some respects. I don't think that he was a bad parent. I just think he had limits in terms of his ability to deal with people. It was difficult for him to show his emotions and that reflected in his relationships with everyone. I would have liked him to be more involved but, given where he was coming from, maybe I'm just as well off that he wasn't.

Since most fathers did not participate in caretaking, those who did stood out. But involved fathers could send a message as ambiguous as the one sent by distant fathers. And a father's involvement, like a lack of involvement, can be judged in diverse ways. A son might be thrilled to spend time with his father, but he might also notice the sacrifices and trade-offs. Gus, a planner, observed his father's dedication to child rearing and concluded that involved parenting was too time-consuming:

> I would say my father was overly involved. If he didn't like the outcome of a situation, it was Mother's fault, but otherwise *he* brought us up. He was always home by a certain hour. The first thing was the family. So I feel that you can't just have children and show up at your own convenience.

Most fathers, of course, were not "overly involved." And most sons did not pay much attention to or feel much concern about their fathers' absence. As time passed, however, many sons changed their outlook. They concluded that having a distant father—and being a distant father—could have a range of unappealing consequences. When they faced their own choices, they reconsidered the meaning of their fathers' lack of participation.

Some discovered that their fathers paid an unanticipated long-run cost for their lack of involvement. Neil, the aspiring academic, observed his father's descent into unhappiness after decades in a dissatisfying job. He decided that his father had little to show for a life so detached from caretaking and so focused on unrewarding work:

I think he's unhappy looking at his life. He can't have a good self-image of himself without a good career. And since he can't fall back on his relationships with his kids, it makes him a very unhappy person at sixty.

Even when a father did not appear to pay a heavy price for being uninvolved, some sons concluded that the price others paid was too steep. Events in their own lives made them aware, often for the first time, of opportunities lost and pain endured. Some came to resent the costs that their fathers' absence had imposed on their mothers. Carlos, a social worker, learned a painful lesson from his divorced, philandering father:

Reflecting back, I don't want to do to my children what my father did to me or to my mother. . . . She was left alone to raise a child by herself, and she had to make a lot of sacrifices.

Others concluded that having a distant father had cost them heavily, even if no one else appeared to suffer. And they wished for the fathering they had missed. In the process of grieving for what would never be, they looked to parenthood as a way of redeeming the past. Michael, the psychotherapist whose father resented his success, wanted to have children, at least in part, so that he could be the kind of father he never had. In speaking of why he wanted to become a father, he said:

Maybe part of it was to make things different than when I was a kid, to be a different kind of father than I experienced, to work through some of the unresolved conflicts and feelings that I had with my own father. I would be more available, more nurturing, more giving, more of the things I wished for from him. I was, in a way, trying to give to myself by giving to my kids.

Some discovered only after having a child that parenthood could provide an arena for reworking unresolved conflicts. They took the opportunity to break out of a cycle of neglect that extended back longer than they could remember. These men discovered in themselves a desire and capacity for nurturance that they had hardly glimpsed in their fathers. Ernie, the physical therapist, found the experience redemptive:

It's kind of filled a void and brings me back to all the things I missed. It gives me a chance to give it back to someone else. I wanted to do the things that didn't happen to me. It's like a mission. So it feels good that I help my daughter and spend time with her and share things and express the love that was missing.

Those who became more nurturing than their own fathers tried to account for the discrepancy between the parenting they received and the parenting they were giving or planning to give. Some blamed social constraints and were grateful for a different set of opportunities. Neil realized that his father faced obstacles he did not:

I missed him, but I don't hold it against him. Things have changed so much since he was a father. I spend so much more time with my daughter, but my job is completely different from his job—it has allowed that.

Others focused on personal, not social, differences. They concluded that, for unknowable reasons, they simply did not share their fathers' desires, goals, or limitations. Parenthood provided the most important occasion for these men to recognize the differences between the kind of father they had and the kind of father they wished to be. It allowed them to develop a once-suppressed awareness of what they had missed. Tom, an editor, learned after the birth of his son just how much he hoped to diverge from his father's example:

In my relationship to my own child, I became quite aware how different a father I wanted to be from the way my father had been. And I think that was the biggest revelation in really understanding what I felt I had missed.

And this revelation affected his relationship with his son:

I am aware that I'm a very different kind of a father than my father was with me. I didn't consciously say, "What my father did was bad, so I'm gonna do this because it's better." My relationship with my child has been very instinctive. It's just been interesting that it has been so different. Because this is basically just what I wanted and felt was the right thing to do.

Some nurturing men were convinced that they were reacting directly against the negative example set by their fathers, striving to be different. William said:

I didn't want my relationship with my son to be as unemotional as mine was with my father. I don't think it ever would have been the same because my father and I are such different people. But there are times when Peter wants my attention, and I stop and think, "I don't want to be my father." So my parenting is somewhat a reaction to my father.

Warren, a thirty-seven-year-old engineer and father of one, said he didn't like the way his stepfather brought up children:

He was very cold and not touching, so I never really looked at him as someone to look up to. He was either yelling at me or trying to straighten me out. So I hope my daughter has very different memories—taking her camping, fishing, teaching her to ride the bike—because I don't even have the memories that other kids have.

By consciously reacting against their own experiences, these men had to learn to be creative and self-reliant, to trust their desires more than the content of their past experiences.

A son might choose to become more involved than his father, as we have just seen, but he might also reject his father's model by choosing not to have children at all. Afraid that he might repeat his father's mistakes or recreate the disappointment he experienced as a child, a man, as Chuck explained, might "try to spare somebody the type of childhood and life I had."

Of course, a son might also react by choosing his father as a model and emulating him in later life, as most childhood socialization theories predict. In these cases, distant fathers produce sons who also become distant fathers, perpetuating the cycle across generations. Over a third admired their breadwinning but distant fathers and resolved to follow their example. Some envied their fathers and looked back longingly on the "good old days" when fathers were not expected to participate in the daily routine of child care. Marvin, a lawyer with three children under the age of five, admitted that his father did very little: "In high school, he was available for Ping Pong, and that was about it." But, he went on:

> I understood why he didn't take much interest in his kids. I don't think he had much patience with children, and I understand now the time such work takes. I think he had it lucky . . . because he had fewer responsibilities with the kids. People shouldn't have to do what they don't want to do.

The lesson of these reactions is not that distant fathers produce nurturing any more than non-nurturing sons. The dynamics between fathers and sons are more complicated and less determined than can be captured by theories that focus on processes that reproduce psychological capacities and proclivities across generations. Fathers provide an example, a set of experiences, and one side of a relationship to which sons are exposed. Sons can respond, however, in a variety of ways. Their responses can also change as they age and face adult conflicts over parenting and other life choices. Sons can and will appropriate the "meaning" of their fathers' lives and their own relationships with them in ways that take time to emerge. Neither the father's behavior nor the more general childhood context determines the son's early reactions, interpretations, desires, or capacities. More important, neither foretells how a son will make sense of these experiences as he grows up, faces a range of new options, and struggles to make his own choices.

Sons and Mothers

The family and work patterns among mothers of the men who were interviewed reflect the social trends of post–World War II America, when women's domesticity encompassed large segments of the working and middle classes. Forty-four percent of these men reported that their mothers were never employed outside the home during the time they lived with their parents. Twenty-six percent reported that their mothers were employed, but only part-time or intermittently, and 24 percent reported that their mothers began full-time work only after they (and their younger siblings) had entered school. Only 10 percent (8 percent of the middle-class and 14 percent of the working-class men) reported that their mothers worked full-time before they started school.

Most sons believed that their mothers were generally satisfied (see appendix, table 5). Among middle-class men, 72 percent of those whose mothers were never employed reported that their mothers seemed to prefer it that way. Similarly, among those whose mothers worked full-time before their sons began school, 83 percent reported that their mothers appeared satisfied. The pattern is similar for the mothers of working-class men. Among this group, 54 percent reported that their mothers seemed satisfied with full-time domesticity, while 89 percent of those whose mothers joined the labor force full-time before their sons began school reported that their mothers appeared to prefer working.

So even though the postwar period did not offer a wide range of choices to women, most mothers in both class groups conveyed the message that they preferred to do what they were doing. Of course, we do not know how these mothers actually felt, only what their sons believed they felt. However a son's perception of his mother's feelings is exactly what is most likely to affect his own outlook.

Despite the fact that the mothers of most of these men had depended on breadwinning husbands and put their families first, only a minority of men reproduced (or wished to reproduce) this pattern in their own relationships with women. We have already seen that about half of the men developed a breadwinning orientation in childhood, but only about a third held such an outlook as adults. Is there a relationship between a mother's employment pattern and her son's outlook? Childhood socialization theories suggest that this should be the case, but the effects of mothers' choices on their sons appear to be as uncertain as the influences of fathers.

A boy's early outlook is linked to his mother's situation, but his adult orientation is not (see appendix, table 6).[3] Most men whose mothers were strongly committed to work rejected a breadwinning outlook, but so did most men whose mothers were homemakers or intermittent workers. A mother's situation, like a father's, does not determine how a son will interpret, react, and use this model in either the short or the long run. Whether or not their mothers were employed, sons responded in diverse ways—including disapproval and ambivalence as well as support—to their mothers' choices.

HOMEMAKING MOTHERS

About 40 percent of those whose mothers never worked and 26 percent of those whose mothers worked part-time or intermittently ultimately became (or aimed to become) breadwinners. For these men, the link between their mothers' domesticity and their own adult preferences appeared obvious. Marshall, single at twenty-nine, hoped to recreate the pattern that had seemed to work so well in his childhood:

Probably my mother has had the greatest influence—how she totally devoted her life to the children and how much we benefited from it. We had happy childhoods and have fairly happy dispositions now, which I think is a direct result of her spending so much time with us. So I saw this as the right way to do things, and something I would want to do also.

Others realized, even as children, that their mothers had paid a price for such family devotion. Max, a supervisor of park workers who married a policewoman, recalled his homemaking mother:

She was a typical mother of the fifties. . . . She was always there. I was happy that she was home, but I think she felt a little left out. It didn't fulfill her, but she never complained.

Even when a mother appeared to prefer domesticity, a son could conclude that she paid a heavy price for investing all her energies in the transitory job of being a wife and mother. Wesley, a paramedic who welcomed his own wife's return to work after the birth of their two daughters, concluded that his mother's serious problems later in life could have been avoided if she had had more to her life than child rearing:

She never worked for money; she did a lot of work in the house rearing seven kids, which is not easy. She didn't want her independence, but I think she would have been a lot better off, because unfortunately my mother has had a lot of problems. She's under psychiatric care; she's really snapped. I think she feels all the kids are gone, and now there's nothing.

Similarly, Sidney, a businessman with a young daughter, dramatically shifted his view once the long-run costs of his mother's domesticity became clear:

My mother . . . certainly was able to take a great deal of pride in my father's career, but I became aware in college and immediately after my father died that she was quite at loose ends. That's when I started to think that if she had more of an independent life, she would have something more to get a toehold on. Just knowing what she could have done and should have been able to do and simply didn't because of the mores of the time—that experience confirmed me in being a strong feminist.

Men with domestic mothers could see the drawbacks for their fathers as well. Roy, a divorced paramedic and father of one, eventually resented his mother's willingness to remain economically dependent in the face of his father's financial struggles:

In later years, I felt that she should have worked. He was the only one bringing the income in, and it was really a big hardship. You could see the pressure was put on my father because he had to work those extra jobs. I felt that she didn't help out, but I never asked her, "How come you didn't help Dad out? You could see he was hurtin'."

The sons of domestic mothers could also conclude that even if mothers and fathers had not paid a price for a mother's domesticity, the children had. While most sons appreciated their mothers' continuous presence, some felt stifled by it, as Grant, a thirty-four-year-old plumber, makes clear:

I think she preferred staying home, but I wished she had worked. She was there *all* the time. She was there too much of the time. There was no privacy. Home was her headquarters, and she watched everything we did. I wanted more freedom.

A son's discomfort with his mother's domesticity does not assure that he will avoid choosing a similar kind of woman as a wife, but it does temper the effect of using his mother as a model. It can trigger the search for an alternative pattern, and may make a son more open to alternatives if they arise. Dennis, a data processor and father of two, resented his mother's obsessive attention. He ultimately decided that it was better not to "overprotect" his children but to provide his daughter with a different vision of womanhood:

> I see a kind of confidence in my older daughter in terms of what she thinks about doing that would not be possible in a household where a woman was performing a more, quote, traditional role.

When social change makes it easier for a man to avoid marrying a domestic woman (either by finding a partner who is committed to work or by deciding not to marry), it also becomes easier for him to acknowledge any doubts he might harbor about his mother's choices. In the brave new world where men and women are more likely to share breadwinning, a mother's domesticity can seem more than disadvantageous; it can seem morally wrong. Patrick, a lifeguard married to a nurse, breathed a sigh of relief that social changes had allowed him to escape the burden of an economically dependent wife:

> My mother's world, when a woman could just stay home and depend on a man, is gone. Good riddance! My mother just let everybody else take care of her. She's into a free ride. My wife and I have a better handle on things. I don't want to lock her out of anything. I want her to be able to take care of herself. Everybody ought to pull their own weight.

EMPLOYED MOTHERS

A range of reactions also emerged among men who grew up in homes where their mothers worked full-time. About 36 percent did choose work-committed partners as adults, but another 23 percent chose not to marry (or have children), and the remaining 40 percent eventually became primary breadwinners with domestically oriented wives. Among those whose mothers worked full-time before their sons started school, 29 percent developed a breadwinning orientation in childhood and 21 percent held that outlook in adulthood. Among those whose mothers worked full-time after their sons began school, 42 percent were oriented toward breadwinning as children and 48 percent as adults.

Most men with work-committed mothers found it hard to ignore the discrepancy between their parents' arrangement and the more prevalent pattern of the period. A social milieu that stressed the advantages of women's domesticity made it easy for sons to feel that having an employed mother was not something to be proud of. Threats to his father's standing in the community, for example, bothered Harvey, a betting clerk:

My father resented my mother going to work. There were fights. He was frustrated, and his pride was gone. I knew my father was trying. He did what he could, but it was tough. Now it's acceptable because everything costs. He was in the wrong era.

In an era when occupational opportunities were reserved for men, others worried about the obstacles their mothers faced and the sacrifices they had to make. Carlos, whose parents were divorced, recalled how his mother's truncated options took a toll on both of them:

My mother worked all her life, doing factory work. Deep down I think she probably would have preferred not having to work, but she's the type of person that does what has to be done, and so I never heard her complain. . . . If she had achieved a higher-status job, she might have been able to give me more or simply made it easier for both of us.

Sons' most common objection to their mothers' employment, however, was based on their sense of not receiving as much attention as the children with homemaking mothers appeared to receive. If a homemaker could provoke a reaction against overprotectiveness, an employed mother could elicit resentment for not being constantly available—especially when she appeared to be working by choice rather than necessity, as was the case for Dick, a twenty-nine-year-old, single director of a small company:

She always worked as a secretary. She despised cooking and cleaning. The work got her out of the house, and she preferred that. . . . But it bothered me, because I would see all my friends' mothers at home.

But there were also advantages to having an employed mother: the economic benefits, for example, as well as the pride children could take in their mothers' accomplishments. Neil, the aspiring academic, not only felt such pride but chose it as his personal model when his father's career fizzled out:

When I was about fourteen, she got a job as a secretary, and she's worked her way up. She said that she had to go to work for us to go to college, so there was kind of a trade-off. I thought it was great because she would get excited about it. My mom's a very bright, ambitious person. . . . I'm real proud of her. A lot of my ambition came from my mother.

The freedom from parental intrusion could also be appealing, especially if the son did not enjoy a smooth or close relationship with his mother. In these instances, a mother's employment offered him freedom from the conflict that would ensue if she stayed home, as Peter, an art installer, pointed out:

> I liked having both of them out of the house. It was a very mixed feeling because I really craved to have a good family life and get along with them. On the other hand, the situation was unbearable, and it was better when they were both gone.

The mix of advantages and disadvantages offered by an employed mother usually produced ambivalent reactions. To make sense of their mothers' choices amid a different cultural norm, most sons tried to discount the personal costs and focus on the benefits. They also tended to separate the consequences for themselves from others' reactions. Edward, the physician, was not bothered by his mother's return to the workplace, even though he knew his father was unhappy. He rejected his father's definition of women's appropriate behavior and searched for other models instead:

> When my mother first went back to work, it was a major blow to my father. He'd always been the provider, and so it was very hard for him. But I wasn't bothered by it. It wasn't like any particular role model had gone and crashed. Maybe that's because most of my teachers were married women. It didn't seem anything abnormal or unusual.

They could also distinguish their concerns for their mother's welfare from their own needs for support. Carlos wished his mother had been able to find a better job, but nevertheless admired her achievements and appreciated her efforts on his behalf:

> I never had any resentment, because her work didn't interfere with the nurturing. I never had any doubts that I was loved. I didn't feel abandoned. I knew that she was working for my benefit, and she made sure that I was cared for. I know there's been a lot of studies lately about latchkey children, but it wasn't a negative experience for me. It taught me a lot of strengths in terms of being responsible and knowing what it means to work.

Short-run ambivalence could also dissipate over time. Charles, a lawyer, had some misgivings when his mother went to work, but he finally concluded that there were no significant long-run drawbacks. "Maybe occasionally I wanted her at home," he told me, "but it certainly didn't have any lasting impact. I just can't imagine it being otherwise."

The long-term consequences of having a work-committed mother, like the long-term consequences of having a domestic one, were varied and unforeseeable. In most cases, it provided a positive image of women's employment. In some cases, it also encouraged an orientation of domestic sharing. Juan, a financial analyst, used his experiences growing up with an employed mother as a model for his own cooperative relationship:

> I took it for granted that my wife would work because my mother was always working. I've realized that it's not fun to come home and cook and clean. And since my mother was working, we had to help, and I learned to cook when I was nine.

Carlos rejected a submissive image of women when his own family experiences led him to appreciate his mother's strength and reject the "macho" ethic that permeated his cultural milieu:

> The image that I was getting from the media and society didn't coincide with what I saw the women in my family doing. I saw them as being equal to any male, and that there shouldn't be that dominance-submissive type of relationship. I would not have wanted my mother or my aunts to be treated in that manner. I wouldn't want to be treated that way, and I shouldn't treat someone else that way. So even though my father was a more traditional Hispanic, it didn't fit with my own home.

Morrie had a very different reaction, as he watched his mother work too hard for too little reward and concluded that it was better not to marry than to falter as a breadwinner:

> My mother worked and worked and worked her whole life, and that left a deep impression. That's part of me being extremely cautious about getting married and having children—because if I'm going to, I really want to do it the right way.

A final group of men wound up choosing a domestic partner despite their pride in having an employed mother. Phillip, a thirty-two-year-old developer, married a woman who embraced domesticity and full-time motherhood even though he had always been "kind of a women's libber because of my mom, because she was so strong a working mother." Such a choice meant moving against the tide of change. More commonly, those who focused on the advantages of having an employed mother found that social circumstances in adulthood reinforced this early preference.

It is clear from the range of reactions among these men that whether or not a mother becomes committed to working outside the home, her employment pattern per se does not account for her son's orientation. As a boy, he may take pride in his mother's choices, feel confused and ambivalent about them, or resent them fiercely. Over time, experiences with women may undermine or reinforce these early responses. For most, later life experiences will reflect the larger forces of social change.

The Uncertain Influence of Childhood Experiences

Childhood socialization processes provide popular explanations for men's parenting and work choices. Theories that focus on these processes argue that little boys form a "masculine personality," marked by an orientation toward achievement, a preference for domination, an aversion to intimacy, and a constricted capacity for nurturance. These proclivities develop in the crucible of the family and produce adult men who eschew family caretaking in favor of workplace commitment and domination over women and children.

Various theories emphasize different aspects of the socialization process. Psychodynamic theories, such as Nancy Chodorow's analysis of the "reproduction of mothering," argue that unconscious interactions between mothers and their children produce boys with "rigid ego boundaries" who repress their relational capacities and ultimately become "not mothers." Role-learning theories, in contrast, stress how male children identify with and ultimately adopt the behavior of their fathers and other significant male role models. Psychoanalytic and social learning theories postulate different causal processes, but they both argue that childhood is the crucial arena in which adult orientations are produced. While they isolate different mechanisms of transmission, they predict a common result: men who share a package of psychological traits that leads them to prefer *and* to choose work accomplishment over family involvement and individual achievement over interpersonal attachment.[4]

These theories, though appealing, present an incomplete picture of how men's childhood experiences influence their later orientations and choices. They fail to take account of the wide variety of capacities and orientations that men develop; they underestimate the degree of contradiction in the socialization context of little boys; they do not adequately distinguish between the context and the child's reaction to it; and they overlook or discount the possibility of change in adulthood.

Children respond to the varied and ambiguous contexts of childhood in varied and changing ways.[5] Among the men whose life paths we will trace, some recreated the patterns of their childhood environment but most did not. Over time, these men had experiences that led them to reassess the meaning of their parents' lives and their own early outlooks. Childhood experiences neither prepared them for the obstacles and challenges of adulthood in a rapidly changing world nor determined how they would react. The childhood context simply provided them with a point of departure.

Those who did not expect to become breadwinners—51 percent of the men—provide the clearest evidence that processes of childhood socialization are incomplete and uncertain. Their early rejection of traditional models of manhood is best examined against the backdrop of expectations held by those who, as children, did adopt the breadwinning ethos.

The Breadwinning Ethos

Those men who, as children, adopted a breadwinning outlook saw in it an ineffable but alluring image of the good life. In this dream, material affluence formed the foundation on which other goals were built. Robert, the teacher with joint custody of his two children, "always kind of blandly assumed that, no problem, I'll be rich." And Reid, a businessman with one child who hoped to re-create the suburban affluence that had surrounded him as a child, did not expect to find that economic times had made the American dream elusive: "I never dreamed I'd be stuck in a one-bedroom apartment with a wife and a child."

Of course, the breadwinner outlook means aiming for sustained and successful participation in the labor force. Even to someone like Carlos, whose parents were divorced and whose father never contributed to his support, the need to earn a good livelihood came first: "The emphasis in my family was get a good education, get a good job, and you have enough finances to meet your needs."

Those who expected to become breadwinners assumed that they would work and, more significantly, that success at work would make it easy to accomplish any other goal. Henry, a construction foreman and primary breadwinner, explained that he "always worked, even as a kid, and figured everything else would take care of itself."

For men from the middle class, success meant more than securing a steady job. It meant finding a professional career that would furnish ample social, personal, and financial rewards. Julian relinquished hopes of becoming a teacher because it could not offer sufficient compensation to support his anticipated family responsibilities. He became a lawyer instead:

> In college, I admired a lot of historians, but unanimously they dissuaded me from pursuing an academic career. When you think in terms of a good career—a career that will allow you to fulfill that role of breadwinner—everything sort of gravitated toward this one.

Hard work and a successful, well-remunerated career formed the foundation on which these men could pile other goals, such as getting married, having children, and supporting a family in comfort. Marriage, by most accounts, could simply be assumed. As Robin, a stockbroker contemplating divorce, put it, it was "the natural state." In Reid's description: "I thought, 'Fine, sure, I'll get married someday. It will happen when it does, just like crossing the street.'"

Marriage was seen as a crucial step on the road to maturity, which for these men meant stability. Ernie, the physical therapist, hoped marriage would give him the security his parents had failed to provide: "I looked at marriage as a way to stabilize me, because I always felt I was scattered. I was floating all the time."

Like Ernie, some men longed for a happy family not because they enjoyed one as children, but because they did not:

> I fantasized about having children and a "Leave It to Beaver" family. I didn't have it, and I wanted it almost to pay back myself, to make sure my children got what I didn't have. I realized how much it was missing in me.

Others viewed marriage as something that "just happens to you." Ian, the single writer, used to see it as his inevitable, if not altogether inviting, fate, especially after a married cousin told him, "Enjoy this, because it will be your last taste of freedom." For Ian, as for most, marriage was "the normal way to live." It would simply find you sooner or later, and once it did, you were permanently and irrevocably in its grasp. Michael, now divorced, recalled: "I had a feeling that I would get married and . . . stay married. Absolutely, I would be the breadwinner, and the woman would take care of the other things."

For those who aspired to breadwinning, then, the wish to get married involved a set of assumptions about themselves as men and about the women they would choose as mates. Like Dennis, they defined women in opposition to themselves: "I never envisioned getting into a relationship with a woman who was working full-time. I think it was just the stereotype."

Those aspiring breadwinners either did not notice the flow of women into the labor force or did not let it change their expectations. They often belittled the importance of women's employment and continued to assume that they, not their wives, would become their household's economic head. Julian's point of view was that, "even if you marry a professional woman, she's got to take some time off and start a family."

These men also assumed they would become fathers, seeing parenthood as the inevitable outcome of a smooth process of building a career and finding a mate. Like the idealized image of living happily ever after often attributed to women, such men envisioned a contented future in which children would be their reward for success at work. Since they expected their wives to care for the children, parenthood provided a way to confirm a masculine identity, but it did not appear to be a time-consuming job. Carlos initially saw children as a way of demonstrating his manliness, but later changed his view:

> I went through a phase where I was caught up in the idea of creating someone in my image. As I got older, I said, "That is not a reason to have children." I got concerned that I would not like someone seeing me as an extension of themselves and imposing their values on me to complete the dreams they didn't complete for themselves.

Aspiring breadwinners also sensed, a bit uneasily, that the responsibilities of a job, a wife, and children could exact a substantial toll. Edward, although he always expected to become a husband and father, so far hasn't:

> I remember when I was a little boy, my folks used to call me Peter Pan, because I knew what an adult had to do and I didn't understand why everyone was in such a hurry to get there. I looked at the responsibilities and the hassles and the troubles, and I just didn't see what the up side of it was. . . . But I always figured, yes, I'd eventually be married and have a family.

Aware of the dangers, these men nevertheless focused on the rewards and minimized the potential difficulties of becoming a breadwinner. Contemplating the unanticipated problems adult life had wrought, Gus, the planner who ultimately decided to remain childless, compared his childhood dreams to his adult realities:

> I always had grand fantasies of how things should be, and it was difficult because nothing could ever meet them. . . . I thought I would have a family, and I had no idea life would be so difficult. We were very sheltered. I never thought it would be hard to make money or find an apartment.

Although working-class men faced more constricted employment options, the aspiring breadwinners in this group also expected a relatively easy road. Grant, the plumber with three children, explained:

> I was married at nineteen, so I learned real early that you have to get a job. I looked toward something physical, definitely not white-collar . . . but I never thought breadwinning would be a problem. . . . It really came as a shock when I lost my job and was out of work for a year.

Regardless of their class origins, these men took it for granted that they could not only survive but prevail. They believed that the world was theirs for the taking, that all they needed was the confidence and the energy to pursue their goals. Jeremy, a forty-year-old manager, for example, claimed that "because of my upbringing, I never worried about the future. I always assumed I am one of those people who will land on their feet no matter what the circumstances." Alan, a property assessor with no college degree, concurred: "My attitude was, 'If you have confidence in yourself, no matter what comes up, I can take care of it.'"

Men who embraced the breadwinning ethos saw it as a commitment to a set of interconnected responsibilities and privileges involving work, money, marriage, and parenthood. Most recognized that it could and probably would entail difficulties, but all expected the attendant privileges to offset the potential problems. More important, whether they viewed the road to manhood as smooth or strewn with obstacles, they could envision no other path.

Alternatives to Breadwinning

Slightly more than half of the men did see other paths, ranging from a vague attraction to adventure and lifelong freedom to a strong distrust of the work ethic or family life. Fourteen percent of this group (8 percent of the total sample) planned to share economic responsibilities with a woman; 46 percent (24 percent of the total sample) hoped to remain childless and often single as well; 32 percent (17 percent of the total sample) did not form any future plans about family and work; and, sadly, 9 percent (4 percent of the total sample) succumbed to an especially acute form of pessimism: they did not expect to live to adulthood. These outlooks are united more by what they oppose than by what they affirm. Highly skeptical about the desirability of breadwinning, these men were unclear about what to put in its place.

EXPECTING TO SHARE ECONOMIC BURDENS

Those who expected to share economic responsibilities with a spouse believed that a working wife would make a more fulfilling and fulfilled companion than would a homemaker. Even at an early age, these men were not attracted to women who wanted or expected to be supported by a man. Neil, the single graduate student, recalled how his earliest visions of the ideal mate involved a woman as dedicated to work as he expected to be: "I just could not see myself being attracted to somebody who was not gonna have their own career, and have the same kind of in-

terest and passion about what they want to do as I had about my career."
Joseph, a blue-collar worker who married his childhood sweetheart, had
much the same thought: "I never expected my wife to sit around and
bake pies. She's very intelligent, and she's got a mind of her own."

In addition to finding employed women more attractive, these men
hoped their prospective spouses would lessen their own economic burdens. They looked forward to marrying and having a family, but they did
not equate family commitment with becoming the sole, or even primary,
support of their households. They wanted the freedom to seek personal
fulfillment and not just economic security at work. This would help them
avoid the greatest danger of male breadwinning: being trapped in a stifling marriage and saddled with the need to earn a big paycheck. Unlike
the vast majority of their peers, this small group developed an egalitarian
outlook, at least in terms of employment. They did not, however, consider the implications that sharing economic responsibilities would hold
for their participation in child rearing. Eager to avoid the burdens of
breadwinning, even these men did not anticipate taking on new burdens
in the home.

EXPECTING TO REMAIN AUTONOMOUS

By far the most popular alternative to breadwinning was to evade the
dangers of domesticity rather than to minimize them. For some, early experiences made marriage look more like a trap than a reward. Hank, the
paramedic, recalled that marriage was the furthest thing from his mind
and claimed never to have seen a happy marriage. Others watched people they loved go through painful divorces. Gil, although his parents
seemed happily married, focused instead on the unhappy ones:

> My older sister was divorced several times, so that broke the mold for
> the family. She had two children, and it was difficult for the children
> to go through. Maybe I was selfish. I was more interested in my fulfill-
> ment. Why get married?

Some found plenty of evidence that marriage was either an extremely
fragile state or a kind of perpetual purgatory—risky in either case. Doug,
a sanitation worker who eventually married and had two children, originally saw much to lose and little to gain by marrying:

> When I was a teenager, everybody was like, "Get married? What for?
> Leave all this?" We thought we were pretty cool. And as I got older, in
> the marines and after, I knew I would never get married. I was having
> a great time, and no way I was going to get married. . . . I didn't think
> it was such a good deal.

If some hoped to avoid marriage, others doubted they would be able to achieve it. These men felt insecure, vulnerable, and unattractive. Norm, an attorney and father of two, worried that he would never be considered sexually desirable or even adequate, so he "never took marriage for granted." Lloyd, a worker at a sewage plant, wanted to find a partner, but assumed that his homely appearance put marriage and family out of reach:[6]

> I'm one of the ugly guys. . . . When you look like Arnold Stang, you don't get many dates. . . . You stand all alone, with a bunch of guys who are also all alone. I wanted a woman to share my thoughts with, but it was very lonely.

Sexuality was an especially acute concern for those who began to question their sexual orientation. Len, a dentist, had no emotional room to develop goals that required a female partner after he began to wonder about his sexual identity:

> When I was about nine, I started to think I might be gay, and that was a conflict, trying to figure out where marriage and family would come in. . . . I was trying to deal more with sexuality than family—whether I could have a relationship with a woman. That's about as far as I got.

Even those who were not plagued by sexual matters feared that they would be unable to find the right woman for an exclusive, long-term commitment. Ernie, the physical therapist, longed to have children, but doubted he would ever find a partner to make that possible:

> Having children and getting married—I did separate the two. I always wanted children, but not necessarily a wife. I wouldn't have been surprised if I never would have gotten married. I didn't know if I would ever meet the right person, and it used to worry me. How would I get children without the wife? The woman can have children without being married, but the man can't. I really felt that it was unfair that I didn't have options that women did.

But negative experiences with children left some men wondering whether they wanted to have a family of their own. After taking care of his younger siblings in adolescence, Harry, a social worker, began to ask himself whether having children was worth the trouble:

> When I was very young, I thought I would get married and have a family, because everyone was married and had children. But in my teens, I carried a lot of responsibility with my brothers, and I really felt that I had done my time. So after college, I determined I was not going to

get married. I was not going to have a family. I was really going to try
to put some things together for myself.

Children could appear to threaten high work ambitions as well as personal freedom. Like many women, some men felt they had to choose between having a child and having a successful career. Frank, a bank officer, feared that children would rob him of opportunities:

> Very soon after I got out of school, I started seeing the person who's
> currently my wife. And she quizzed me on my attitudes about child
> raising. And I told her that I had absolutely no use for children, that I
> was enthusiastic about getting down to work, and I wanted to do
> something constructive, and I didn't want any children.

In contrast, most men viewed children as a threat to their freedom *not*
to succeed at work. Fearing that becoming responsible for economic dependents would rob them of the option to pursue unpredictable careers
or less demanding jobs, these men rebelled against a whole package of
domestic and work commitments that embodied the established definitions of masculine success. So Rick, a junior high school teacher (and
now the father of two daughters), kept "postponing with no end in sight";
Tom, the editor (and divorced father), "didn't see my life following any
kind of pattern—in fact, I was probably doing whatever I could to prevent it falling into the pattern"; and Steve, an ex-addict (and now a computer programmer), embraced the 1960s counterculture and dropped out
of college: "Being a breadwinner? No, thank you. Out the door."

If for some, remaining autonomous meant not having to find a challenging job, for others it meant the freedom not to take a tedious, ordinary one. Drawn to an alluring cultural symbol—the lone, often rebellious man who strikes out on his own against the system and against the
odds—they hoped to seek their fortunes and lodge their identities in
work that promised freedom, adventure, or risk. These men were attracted to occupations that hold a glamorous, almost mythological cultural aura. Some involved physical danger and violence. After fighting in
Vietnam, for example, Doug

> ran around like a wild man. First I was contemplating being a merce-
> nary, then some jobs on the oil pipeline in Arabia. They all included
> the possibility of violence. That's what I was trained for. Those were
> the only jobs I contemplated.

When Norm thought about the future, it was flights of fancy—sports
figures, astronauts. Similarly, Felix, a hospital administrator, said that:
"When you're a kid, you have dreams of being a professional athlete, entertainment, something like that. You don't think of being a doctor or a
lawyer, tedious stuff."

These potentially unstable and even dangerous careers were linked to a wish for freedom from having to support a family. Ron, a surveyor and father of two, preferred physical risk to the risk of domestic boredom:

I wanted to just have fun. I wanted to be a smoke jumper for the forest service, those sickos who jump out of planes and get into the fire lines. Then I was going to join the merchant marines, but I got my draft notice, so I joined the navy.... Marriage was for those other guys. I'd stay single, have my fun, and continue on until the day I die.

Aspirations for glamorous jobs also tended to conflict with the stress parents placed on security and stability. Todd eventually became a utilities repairman, but originally pursued an acting career despite his father's admonitions:

I would look out the window and wonder what the rest of the world was like. I didn't want the dull, safe life of my father. I never gave much thought to family and responsibilities growing up.

In rejecting the breadwinning ethic, some hoped other types of commitments could take the place of family life. Stuart expected to find his family among a community of men, having decided at an early age to become a Franciscan brother: "The Church was teaching that this was a worthy sacrifice, but I didn't understand, really, what it meant.... I had a very romantic concept of the monastery and this community life."

More common was a vague hope of remaining free and independent indefinitely—like Scott, a paramedic who sought safety in solitude after serving in Vietnam:

Vietnam makes you want to be away from everybody. When things are starting to fall apart all around you and the world is hanging by someone else's decision, you want to hide. I saw a lot of guys breaking down, so I decided to play little mind games. I could sit in a crowd of people and just tune myself off completely from them. So the loneliness, it was kind of preferable. I thought I'd never get married.

REFUSING TO THINK ABOUT THE FUTURE

Another group did not consciously oppose marriage, parenthood, or steady work. They simply did not formulate any well-defined goals or expectations. As Theodore, who ironically became a planner, put it, "I always had a reluctance to think about the future. I was never a person who said, 'I want to be this when I grow up.'"

Such passivity stemmed from two opposite and apparently contradictory assumptions about the future. One was that men enjoyed the luxury of not having to plan. Men who made this assumption believed that everything would work out fine with or without forethought. This unexamined optimism was most pronounced among those whose middle-class affluence guaranteed them a good start in life. When Paul, the social service administrator and a father of two, was asked whether he had any expectations about what he'd be doing at this age, he replied:

> Goodness, no. I was very bad at that. I am fortunate that things ended up as well as they have for me. I was not good at planning, foresight, determination, or any of those traits. I started off very bad scholastically. . . . My career planning was nix, horrible.

The second, more pessimistic orientation was espoused mostly by working-class men, who were more likely to feel that constricted opportunities would take any future "choices" away from them. Dean, the driver for the parks department, graduated from high school while the Vietnam War raged:

> One brother was in the marines; the other in the army. I figured my destiny was controlled, so I wasn't really thinking ahead. If I was drafted, I was drafted. Otherwise, if you learned how to do roofing or how to fix a car or something like that, it seemed you could always get by.

Those from the working class who held no aspirations were more likely to assume that even their best efforts would not be good enough to ensure future success. With limited economic resources and meager parental and social support, these men saw little reason to make plans that could not and would not be achieved. As George, a supervisor for the park service, saw it, "Everything you plan just seems to fall through anyway, so why bother?"

Since supporting a family depended on finding a good job, declining to formulate occupational goals made it harder to plan for marriage and parenthood. Zachary, a divorced business manager, focused on short-term pleasures rather than long-term commitments:

> I had no desire to be a father, to raise children, be the breadwinner. I had no interest in college; I had no interest in a special career. I was a know-it-all wise guy who wouldn't take lessons from anybody. . . . I just wanted to have a good time. It was hang out and don't think about next week, much less graduating from high school.

Whether the future looked bright or dim, those who gave little or no thought to it assumed that forces outside their control would determine their fate. In contrast to the common assumption that men are reared to plan for the future and to feel and act as if they are in control, these men developed a passive, nonchalant outlook.

EXPECTING AN EARLY DEATH

None exemplify this fatalistic approach more vividly than those who expected to die young. This small but notable group expected to succumb to the dangers of growing up long before the chance to face adult challenges arrived. For these men, all from the working class, future planning seemed irrational since they did not expect to have a future. Gary, a separated custodian with sole custody of his young daughter, told me: "I thought I'd be dead by now. I got involved with gang fights. I did drugs. I sniffed glue. I sniffed carbon. It's a wonder I have a brain left."

The chilling truth is that exposure to gangs, drugs, and street violence made these expectations seem reasonable to some working-class boys. For others, the Vietnam War posed even greater dangers. Those who could not afford college were vulnerable to the draft. Lacking the necessary credentials to obtain a good job, they were also more likely to see the armed forces as a palatable alternative to the civilian labor market.[7] Patrick had served in Vietnam and seen close friends die:

> I never thought I'd make it to this age. I was into motorcycles, parachuting. I went into the army at twenty-one, and I really didn't think I was going to come home. I never thought about the future.

Steve fell into drug addiction and lost all interest in planning for the future:

> I didn't really think of getting married and having kids as something real. I never figured I'd get past thirty, so I didn't worry about it. . . . I became a heroin addict, so this distracted me from certain things.

These men were painfully aware of the dangers that could and probably would arise on the road to adulthood. While other boys looked forward to reaping the social benefits of manhood, they expected instead to pay a high price for having been born male.

Diversity and Change

Despite the modern emphasis on breadwinning as a man's proper adult status, boys and young men form their aspirations in an ambiguous cultural and social context that stresses both breadwinning and its discontents. The contradictory quality of these cultural values allows and encourages men to form diverse, vague, and conflicting expectations in childhood. Whatever goals and hopes a child forms, moreover, there is no guarantee of their being reached. They may become firmer as later experiences confirm early expectations, or they may change as adult experiences undermine their foundation.

Becoming an adult involves a process of relinquishing past attachments and dependencies while assuming new responsibilities and commitments. In modern societies, the process can be steady or abrupt, but even under ideal circumstances it is demanding.[8] When the structures that constrain and regulate adult development contain contradictory and rapidly changing guidelines, it becomes more difficult to navigate the process of growing up and to predict the outcome. Among the whole group of men, change in adulthood was as prevalent as diversity in childhood. Regardless of the point of departure, the majority changed their orientation over time.[9]

Only 38 percent of those who developed a breadwinning orientation in childhood sustained it as adults (see appendix, table 7). Thirty-two percent preferred to affirm personal freedom and independence instead. The remaining 29 percent became, or hoped to become, involved in caring for their children. These men developed greater parental involvement than they could have imagined as children.

A similar pattern of change can be seen among those who developed nonbreadwinning expectations in childhood, which in most cases meant remaining autonomous. In adulthood, 29 percent still hoped not to forge parental ties. But slightly more than a third became oriented toward breadwinning despite their earlier aversion to it. More surprising, 37 percent of this group became, or expected to become, involved fathers.

This pattern of diversity and change applies to both professional and working-class groups. While more college-educated men expected as children to become primary breadwinners (55 percent compared with 43 percent for the working-class group), this disparity declined over time. Indeed, the percentage of working-class men who held a breadwinning outlook in adulthood exceeds that of men with college degrees. Only a few percentage points separate the middle-class and working-class men who moved toward involved fatherhood. The variation that exists within each class is more noteworthy than the small differences between them. A diverse and complex set of parental and family patterns emerged among men across the class spectrum, as experiences of personal change were a dominant motif among the more and less educated alike.

Whatever the direction of change, the process of changing provoked a wide range of reactions. Most who became breadwinners felt fortunate, but some longed for the freedom they had relinquished. For Peter, the art installer who had spent a large portion of his adolescence in reform school, the stability he ultimately achieved seemed a reasonable outcome to his earlier, wilder experiences. It also seemed a far better fate than the alternative:

I tend to look on things philosophically—even negative experiences really are learning experiences. It's not a cliché. While I was an adolescent, everybody else my age was walking the line, and they all wound up on drugs. By that time, I had been arrested, played hooky, been thrown out of school, all kinds of troubles. I didn't have a good family life, but I was the one who turned out in some ways as a very strong person. It's not by accident, but that's the way it was.

Paul, the ex-hippie who became a successful social service administrator, did not feel so fortunate:

That concept of a breadwinner was sort of alien to me. At one time, I was proud of the fact I don't think about these things. It's disgusting that society does this to you. I'm doing it, but there's a part I'm still against, a lifestyle that I still don't believe in.

A similar sense of disillusionment, lost possibilities, and even guilt haunted many of those who moved away from breadwinning. Genuinely happy childhoods and misplaced faith in idealized cultural mythologies left some ill prepared for the harsher realities of family and work life. This is what Max, a thirty-two-year-old gardener and divorced father, had to say:

My childhood was very Ozzie and Harriet . . . the American dream. I wanted to be like my father—have a good job, a happy home, a family with a wife and kids. And maybe I still do, in a way. But it just didn't turn out that way. You wake up one day and realize life is not a television show. Life is very hard and very ugly, and it's what you make it.

These men found that adulthood did not offer the "happily ever after" endings they had once expected to find. Neither did it offer the older avenues for establishing meaningful bonds in the world. As men have lost the abiding power to enforce paternal authority, the bonds between fathers and children have become more complex and more discretionary. Michael, a custodial father, welcomed a richer parental relationship than one based solely on patriarchal power, but he also grieved for the lost world of his childhood, which seemed so much simpler:

I grew up in the early fifties, and there was a belief in institutions—in authority figures—that isn't there today. Parents had a certain authority that was unchallenged. Now, if you can't get what you need from your kids because they love you, you're really kind of lost. It has to be voluntary. Because falling back on authority and the belief in authorities is sort of like believing in Santa Claus. And giving that up was, for me, a very painful realization . . . like letting go of my own childhood.

Even liberating change is rarely purchased without some cost. Yet some embraced the newly emerging possibilities and opportunities more tightly than they lamented the loss of old privileges. Larry, the limousine driver with a young daughter, preferred the present confusion and future uncertainty to his father's more predictable, but also more confined existence:

> My father had ground rules. He knew that dinner was going to be ready, and he was going to watch TV. He wouldn't change a diaper. But I have no ground rules. With a woman's role being much more expanded, this is like uncharted territory. That's why some men have a lot of problems . . . but I think it's much better for men. The macho holdout types are really missing the boat. I look at my daughter, and I see the future, and it feels right.

Whether the process of change is judged beneficial or harmful, welcome or odious, the perception of change is distinct from its actual causes. Just as we have seen that childhood experiences do not preordain the trajectory of adult development, so some who underwent change were also aware that childhood provided only limited preparation for negotiating the bends and forks in the road ahead. Max explained:

> At the age of twenty-one, I figured I knew everything; at the age of thirty-two, I find out how little I really do know. You can only learn that from living it. Listening doesn't help. Sometimes you've got to live your own life and make your own mistakes.

If childhood predispositions do not foretell men's later life choices, then how and why does change occur? Why are some protected from change, while others are cajoled, seduced, or forced to undergo it? To answer these questions, we need to make sense of the social forces and personal experiences that led most men to undergo a change in outlook and life direction. Although the same forces that led some to change also allowed others to sustain an early outlook, it is easier to find the factors that produce change in the lives of some than to see how the same factors produce stability in the lives of others. Those who changed are also less likely to take their choices for granted or to see them as predetermined. When men are sheltered from the experiences that produce change in others' lives, their life choices are more likely to appear natural or ordained—the outcome of values, personality attributes, or even biological predispositions acquired in childhood or before birth. Paths of change, in contrast, make it clearer that encounters with social institutions can either support or undermine early experiences as life proceeds. The causes and processes of choice are thus easier to discover when change takes place. The lives of those who changed provide more information about the social and institutional forces that affect everyone.

We will examine the life trajectories and personal dilemmas of three groups of men: those who initially did not expect to be breadwinners, but who moved toward that choice; those who initially expected to become breadwinners, but who eventually chose to remain autonomous; and those who initially hoped either to become breadwinners or to remain autonomous, but who then became (or wished to become) involved fathers. By comparing these different paths and strategies, we will be able to discover why men are developing such diverse commitments to family and work and how they are negotiating the currents of change.

4

TURNING TOWARD BREADWINNING

What I thought was important six years ago I don't find important now. I was hanging out with my friends, chasing women, and getting drunk. What's important now is my job, my kids, and my wife.

—Eric, a thirty-four-year-old property manager

Even in an age when stagnant earnings and employed mothers are eroding the popularity of male breadwinning, many men choose to base their identity, their sense of themselves as men, on being a good provider. This outlook reflects the real responsibilities some men continue to shoulder. After all, about a third of American households are still supported by either a sole male earner or a married couple in which the wife is employed either part-time or intermittently. And, in a telling practice, many men whose wives are employed outside the home argue that they themselves are the primary and least dispensable earners in the household.

Before married women became such a large part of the labor force, men's good-provider responsibilities helped to justify their claim to the best jobs and highest paychecks. Even today, when both partners in most marriages are earners, men continue to enjoy an economic edge at the workplace that is used to claim advantages inside and outside the home.[1] This sense of being *responsible* for the family's economic well-being—whether or not a wife is employed—means that a man may not feel his status as a breadwinner has changed regardless of the changes in women's lives. When a man believes his job is to furnish the ingredients required to make the bread, he will expect someone else to bake and serve it.

Holding on to a breadwinner identity offers obvious benefits, but it also poses dangers and drawbacks. If personal worthiness is measured by the size of a paycheck, then those who cannot or do not earn an "adequate" income (according to very subjective criteria) face failure as earners and as men. Success at breadwinning also exacts a price, for good-provider responsibilities may tie one to an unfulfilling job or marriage. Given this mix of demands and privileges, it is not surprising that many men approach breadwinning with ambivalence. As children, more than half of the men who were interviewed hoped to avoid becoming breadwinners. Yet 34 percent of those men ultimately did (or planned to) marry, have children, and become the sole or main support of their households.

What made so many of these early resisters eventually turn toward breadwinning? Why did they trade independence and freedom for the privileges and obligations of supporting a household? As work, marital, and parenting decisions interacted over time, unanticipated experiences produced unintended consequences for these men.[2] Here I examine the causes and consequences of this process of change, especially for men's involvement (or, more accurately, lack of involvement) in the non-economic aspects of family life. Understanding why some men become breadwinners despite an initial resistance offers important clues about the social forces that continue to reproduce traditional patterns.

Finding Employment Stability

The key to becoming a breadwinner is finding job stability. Without a predictable, steady income, a man lacks the means to support a household. Yet three out of four formerly reluctant breadwinners reached adulthood with a deep distrust of the work ethic. They had little desire to conform to the demands of stable employment and formulated virtually no future plans concerning work. Skeptical of the benefits of working for a wage and doubtful of their abilities to secure or maintain rewarding work, they viewed employment as a necessary evil that could be minimized. They were attracted to the promise of freedom that could be achieved only by shunning high work commitment.

This early outlook was prevalent among the working-class men, who had good reason to doubt their chances in the labor market. From the perspective of limited opportunities, it was easy to romanticize a life of adventure, free from the demands and tedium of a steady job. To such men, aimlessness was a virtue, not a vice. Kevin, a paramedic, hoped for nothing more than a life exploring the countryside like a character out of the 1950s television show "Route 66," which he no doubt watched as a child:

I had absolutely no idea what I was going to be doing with my future. I wanted to go see the country. I got a job with a guy who let me drive on the road. I drove the Eastern half of the United States. There were scattered periods of unemployment.

An equal proportion of those who grew up in more privileged surroundings also rejected the work ethic of stable employment—even though their fathers had been successful and their education positioned them to reap the financial rewards of a professional career. In place of the working-class image of the lone adventurer, these men romanticized a hippie lifestyle, free from the constraints of blind obeisance to the middle-class norm of material success. Paul, who ultimately became a successful social service administrator, recalled:

Even during the hippie years, there was never a time for more than a week or two when I wasn't working, but I had *no* career movement. Nor did I want one. I was consciously opposed to it. I didn't want to be part of the establishment; I didn't want an established job or that kind of thing. I was very "anti." I had real long hair and wore an earring.

True to such an outlook, reluctant breadwinners started out with erratic, unstable work histories. In early adulthood, most moved from job to job, rarely stopping at any one for long or looking for work that offered a future as well as an immediate payoff. As Peter, the reform school graduate who eventually became a successful art framer, explained it:

Most of my life, I remember being in a state of anger and rebellion. I was very unhappy with the results, never understanding why I'd continually get into trouble. My rebelliousness and anti-authority posture—it doesn't make for the corporate type. I floundered for many years. I had difficulty getting involved in something and staying at it. I tended to get involved for a while and then break away from it.

For some of these men, events and encounters that made job instability less palatable or even less possible pushed them out of old ways of life. Expanding work opportunities pulled others toward stronger work ties. Either alone or in combination, these pushes and pulls provided an opportunity for change and promoted a new outlook on work.

The pushes could take the form of seemingly fortuitous or catastrophic events that became significant because idealized visions of freedom began to crumble under the weight of real experience. As the dream began to fade under the bright light of economic realities, unanticipated events led these men to change their outlook on paid work. Paul recalled how a fire at his country store foreclosed an old way of life and prompted him to rethink what he wanted from life:

> People grow in and out of things, and I obviously grew out of my hippie years. The store burned down. There was nothing happening for me vocationally, and cabin fever set in. That was a real crossroads in my life. . . . I had this opportunity at about thirty years old to say, "What do you want to do?" I came back and got this job in a nursing home as a social worker. I knew I had a career, something I enjoyed immensely. I still had long hair, but I wore a jacket and tie. . . . Now I'm executive director.

For Kevin, unfortunate events also became an opportunity. Theft plus the untimely death of a good friend led him to forsake his one-day-at-a-time lifestyle:

> My tractor-trailer was stolen, and the same summer a neighbor passed away. I started to think, "Gee, I've been very selfish. I've only been trying to gratify myself, and maybe there's a higher purpose." I got a call for a job as a health-care professional. It was fate. That was a turning point in my life, definitely.

Less visible but more socially structured pushes exerted an even more powerful influence on these men. The experience of unemployment, in particular, tarnished the sheen of freedom and led some, like Steve, the Vietnam veteran and recovering heroin addict, to question their earlier rejection of the work ethic:

> I was on methadone and welfare for a couple of years, and that was real degrading. I didn't need much, and it seemed like easy money. But it's no way for a human being to live. After a while it just didn't feel right anymore. I didn't like not working . . . just lying around, wandering around. I went and got a job.

Even highly educated men with advanced degrees were not immune from the sobering effects of being out of work. Sidney, a businessman, held money, career movement, and security in low regard when he graduated from college. A long period of not working and fruitless job searches led him to relinquish his original idealism and focus on more practical concerns:

> It was a tough time in my life. Here I was—single, no dependents. Money wasn't particularly a problem. And yet this was a dehumanizing, painful experience. Unemployment is a terrible thing, something I

found horrifying. I'm not particularly accustomed to failure. I decided to refocus and say, "Look, you've got to be a little bit more specific about what you're doing." And I applied to business school.

Experiences that produce disenchantment with job instability or not working have little impact, however, if real opportunities for rewarding work do not arise. For most reluctant breadwinners, the pull of unexpected opportunities was essential to establishing stable employment commitments. These reluctant workers all found satisfying, well-rewarded jobs. Although these opportunities seemed fortuitous, they occurred in a context that affords white men a greater chance than other groups of being "lucky."

In some cases, a social network of both close and distant connections opened a door into a new realm of opportunity.[3] David, a city planner, learned how strong "weak ties" could be when he was fired for union organizing and sought work after a protracted period of unemployment:

> I wasn't doing anything, just collecting unemployment insurance. And then I got bored, so I decided I better go to work. I saw an ad and was interviewed here for a job, and the guy who interviewed me recognized my name from my organizing days.

Network ties can be especially important for working-class men, who lack the educational credentials to compete for the best jobs on their own and who thus need a geographically proximate web of kin and friends to help open doors. Doug, a Vietnam veteran, explained how his sister saved him from self-destruction on his return to civilian life by finding him a steady job with the promise of a future:

> I used to hawk on the street, selling plants and hustling stuff. It wasn't easy coming back here. I was like a bomb ready to go off. Then my sister helped get me a job as an ambulance driver. I really liked it; it was exciting.

Steve drove cabs and delivered mail until a friend pushed him to apply for a computer programming job. He got the job and loved the work: "I couldn't believe that they'd pay me for sitting round and designing systems and playing with computers." For the first time, he found pleasure in paid work and was rewarded with promotions for doing well.

Others moved toward stable work via a path that seemed so serendipitous and unpredictable that it simply appeared to be good luck. Phillip moved haphazardly from job to job until a knock at a nightclub door led to a career in entertainment and hotel management:

> Right after I graduated, I did a lot of jobs—taxi driver, busboy, waiter. I read about a nightclub that was opening, and that's what I wanted to

do—theatrical things, my dreamy ideas. I knocked on the back door in the rain, almost leaving, and some kid come out and walked me through the security guard. They hired me to be the janitor two days before the place opened. . . . I was the assistant manager and then the manager. Now we're building a hotel, and I'm the project manager. . . . If I had turned around and walked away, if I hadn't stood there and waited for a few minutes for somebody to come out, I don't know what I'd be doing today.

Since luck and accident seemed the overriding determinants of personal fortune, the arrival of a job opportunity appeared to be part of a disorderly process. For Jeff, who found a challenging job working at a zoo, there was no conscious search for meaningful work:

I drifted right into my job, fell into it. I actually found the work to be pretty interesting. I'm surprised. I have a lot of stimulation, enough problems to make life interesting. I found my level. I like to be somebody's good second man. That's my slot in life, even though I was probably a fourth man.

Of course, such good fortune did not result from a random process. These men entered labor markets that tend to favor men. In such a context, where even passivity may eventually succeed, a bit of persistence is likely to pay off. But since most men take their competitive advantage for granted, luck seems to pervade the process of locating rewarding employment. Fred, a real estate developer, floundered for months, enduring the agony of over a hundred rejections until "luck" intervened:

I called this one company and was scared to death, because the person they said to talk to was the president. The guy turns me down. Then out of the blue I asked him how you get started in the business. I don't know where those words ever came from, but it got him talking. He was ready to hang up the phone, and he says, "I always promised the person who taught me that I would teach somebody else. Why don't you come in tomorrow? We'll see what we can do." I went in the next morning, and they offered me a job.

One wonders how this company president would have reacted to a woman's voice or an ethnic accent at the other end of the telephone. Chances are high that he would have been far less likely to take the same risk and open the same door. Luck, like other social goods, is not distributed equally.

For most reluctant workers, finding a good job meant finding a job with an advancement ladder. Internal promotions thus provided a third, and critically important, route to expanded job opportunity. Those who experienced upward mobility did not necessarily actively seek it. As initially reluctant workers, they typically began their jobs with a casual attitude toward paid work. Instead of looking for rapid movement up the organizational ladder, they sought the fringe benefits offered by a job and resisted attachment to the work itself. David, a political organizer who later became a city planner, initially viewed his job as a place to fight the system as a union organizer rather than a place to achieve his personal fortune. Yet he "liked the work environment and didn't have to wear a tie." As a well-educated and skilled worker, however, he found himself being promoted despite his casual attitude. He eventually rose to the highest ranks of his division:

> It was a slow progression. I started here as a junior programmer. I took tests and got promoted and at some point they had to promote me in order to promote somebody else—otherwise I wouldn't have gotten promoted. I found that very funny. I didn't really care. I didn't care about the money that much either. But my job was secure.

Reluctant workers from working-class backgrounds also experienced unanticipated upward movement, often after choosing an occupation with little forethought. A problem student in high school, Sam was transferred to a technical school, where he earned a certificate to be an architectural draftsman. Once channeled into a practical and challenging occupation, he rose high up the ranks. To him, the process felt almost effortless, a gift from heaven:

> In high school, I was a juvenile delinquent. I had to pick something, and I couldn't draw freehand, so I went into architecture. It worked out terrific. I went straight up. In nineteen years I went from junior draftsman to assistant director. It's crazy. It was strictly God.

Organizational promotions, like network connections and lucky encounters, were not as arbitrary as they seemed. All of these routes to job stability were supported by a structure that continues to provide men, especially white men, with a wide range of avenues to success at work. In this context, the odds are good that a substantial proportion of men, even among those who begin adult life highly skeptical of steady work and their chances of finding it, will eventually "stumble" upon or "drift" into employment opportunities.

High Job Demands and Rewards

Whatever the route to stable employment, it increased both the rewards and the demands of working. For these reluctant breadwinners, new commitments at work had a ripple effect, producing a host of changes in their personal lives as well. For the first time as adults, they enjoyed a measure of economic security and a sense of being protected from social calamity. Ken, a court reporter for fifteen years, finally found stability after a succession of dead-end jobs:

> I always was lazy. I'd get interested in something and then get bored with it. I didn't stay in a job longer than a year or so. But it's not good to go from job to job. You don't gain benefits; you lose things. I've had problems in this job, but I'm staying with it. I've come a long way. I started very low on the ladder, and I've come up quite a bit. The security has been the benefits, the money, just knowing I have a job until I retire.

After years of living from day to day, planning for the future became possible and attractive. Job stability encouraged a new interest in the future, an orientation that makes little sense when a steady income cannot be assumed. When Greg, who had been a cabdriver, became a court aide, he began to look forward to promotions. He also began to see himself as the main support of his family:

> When I first started working, I didn't worry about security. Driving a cab, there was really no future; I'm not going to wind up with a pension fund. As a court officer, there's a lot more doors that will open. I can move up. I feel more secure than I have with any other job. Now, unless I was making enough of an income to support my wife, I wouldn't be happy at all.

Stable employment bestowed unanticipated benefits, especially when it involved a promotion. Moving up the occupational ladder provided growing power, prestige, and control. George, a park supervisor, explained how four promotions had given him authority and saved him from the malevolent whims of other employees. As he put it, "I'm so high now, nobody can screw me."

Such rewards proved seductive. They enticed these men to invest more in the workplace and develop a new outlook on work. Similar to an ex-homemaker discovering the pleasures of being recognized in a more public arena, Paul, the onetime hippie, enjoyed the accoutrements of success as an administrator:

> I like getting out of the house and going someplace completely different where I am Paul, job person, instead of Paul, family person. I enjoy the prestige and going to fancy meetings and people saying, "There is the executive director." I don't want to build it up, but within my own little world, it's nice to have a carpet in the office, to make decisions, to have a certain power, a certain responsibility.

Along with economic security and social prestige, job stability fostered a new self-image based on work accomplishments. Men who had once resisted defining themselves in terms of labor market success began to shift their identity. Steve, the recovered drug user who became a computer analyst, changed his outlook as he moved up the hierarchy and found surprising satisfaction in his job. Although he once viewed work as a place where he had to suppress his true nature for the sake of a paycheck, he now began to see it as an arena for achieving personal "authenticity":

> I didn't want to be working just for money. I never liked wearing suits. Now work is a big part of how I define myself. If someone says, "Who are you?" I might say I'm a Buddhist, but more likely I'd say I'm a computer programmer. . . . The way my ethics are now, you have to work to support yourself . . . but I have the best of both worlds because I get to be really authentic and go to work because I like what I do.

A new and enlarged set of demands tends to accompany stable employment. Work begins to absorb a larger proportion of time and energy, even as it offers more rewards. For these reluctant workers, work inevitably soaked up time previously reserved for their private lives. David, the political organizer who became a planner, began to take work home at night and on weekends as he became more enthusiastic about his job:

> There was a complete change in my interest towards my career, a complete turnaround. I started putting a lot of hours in, started working a lot of overtime, taking work home with me, working on weekends.

Rod, an upwardly mobile lawyer, complained that his unexpected success depended on sacrificing even the most basic aspects of his private life: "I don't have much time at all to myself. In fact, I feel very nervous taking a week off for a honeymoon."

Most reluctant workers, however, welcomed the rising time demands of their newfound success. They found pleasures in work that had once been found only in more private pursuits. For Phillip, the aspiring film director who "lucked" into nightclub and hotel management, job demands also provided a primary source of "fun." He suspected, somewhat nervously, that his wife paid a higher price for his increased work demands than he did:

> This is a hell of a lot of fun. I'm making an awful lot of money, and I'm learning a lot as I go along. I work very long hours—seven days a week, ten to fourteen hours a day—and my wife might never see me.

But every day is a challenge, and I am having a good time working very hard.

We can see how rising work commitment had paradoxical effects on family life: secure employment tended to increase these men's subjective commitment to family life while decreasing their actual participation in it. First, stability at work tended to encourage stability in other areas as well. Since employment rested at the base of a hierarchy of goals, reluctant workers could not consider making other long-term commitments until they could count on having and keeping a job. Their outlook on marriage and especially parenthood changed as they achieved a measure of financial security. Fred, the real estate investor whose persistence on the telephone opened the door to success, began to look forward to fatherhood only after a successful career seemed assured:

> Your goals start changing. Right now, it's money and career. And then, when you get that, other things start playing a role. I've achieved, luckily, some level of that. I'm doing very well financially. I want to be completely financially secure when I have a child.

But as these reluctant breadwinners shifted their allegiance away from private pursuits and into the workplace, involvement in work and family took the form of a zero-sum game.[4] The sheer amount of time spent on the job kept them away from home and drained them of energy when they *were* there. As George, the park supervisor, explained:

> The amount of hours I work, I can't come home and be the soap-opera type of husband who's going to cook and clean. I'm not going to work seventy-five hours a week, come home, and cater to my wife. I'm just not physically able to do more, and I wouldn't.

The shift involved a change of emotional focus as much as a decline in actual time spent at home. According to David:

> It's not the time, really. It's mostly the focus, because basically I've been focused on what I can do at work, so when I get home I'm tired, and I have less focus on the children.

Rising economic resources enabled reluctant breadwinners to become *primary* breadwinners. Their fears about the burdens of good providing subsided as they realized they could support a household. They gained the means and the motivation to support a domestic wife, whose first responsibility would be to care for the family whether or not she worked outside the home. Sidney, the early idealist who turned to business school when he could not find a job, was ultimately able to support a wife and children. When their first child arrived, he considered his wife's earnings from her public relations job optional. Her income is "not important at this point," he said. "We have a very comfortable income. I don't want her to go to work just to make money."

Along with the vast majority of men in America, all of these men could count on higher earnings than their wives could hope to command. Since women on average earn only seventy-two cents for every dollar earned by a man, superior earnings give most men the leverage to evade domestic work even when their wives are employed. (The men for whom this is not the case will be discussed in chapters 6 and 8.) Doug, the Vietnam vet who became a sanitation worker, admitted that his wife took care of the housework and children, even though they both worked full-time, "because women don't get paid, and I was making most of the money."

With the economic resources to define their wives' income as surplus, once reluctant breadwinners began to push their wives toward domesticity. They also took pride in their newfound status as good providers, arguing that they offered their partners security and material comforts in exchange for domestic service. They converted their economic contributions into power at home. George felt he earned the position of "head of the household" by providing his wife with consumer luxuries:

> There has to be a leader. And the responsibility of the leader is to be fair, not just to boss people, but to make a decision, right or wrong. I provide the money, so it's a success. There has to be system, and that's ours. . . . My wife loves her lifestyle; she's got it made. She drives a new car, has great clothes, her friends, no responsibilities. What the hell does she need a job for? She's got her freedom. What more could you want?

In a larger sphere, job stability affected the general outlook of initially reluctant workers. As they moved from a precarious to a more secure lifestyle, some even concluded that stable work had saved them from a disastrous fate—spiritually and actually. Ron, a surveyor who had once dreamed of fighting forest fires, saw personal destruction at the end of the path he had decided not to take:

> The more I think about what I wanted to do, I'd probably be either stabbed, shot, or thrown into the gutter. Being a smoke jumper is great when you have a fire, but what do you do afterwards? Sit around and do nothing. The navy taught me that when you sit around and do nothing, you start drinking. If I had done that, I think I wouldn't be here.

Reluctant workers entered the labor force with a deep skepticism about the value of earning a living. But unexpected opportunities yielded unexpected economic, social, and psychological rewards, nurtured a growing commitment to the workplace, and prompted a change in outlook on family life as well.

Unexpected Commitment in Marriage

Most reluctant breadwinners—almost 90 percent—held an early aversion to marriage. Marriage, like paid work, appeared to be a trap that threatened to steal their autonomy and ensnare them in a web of unwanted economic, social, and emotional responsibilities. As Jesse, a construction worker, explained:

> I really didn't want to get married because I didn't want to have to answer to anybody, be home for dinner. I didn't want the responsibility of a wife and having to make sure the landlord got his rent, the electric company got their money. As an independent, I could care less if they turned off my lights.

And Sam, the upwardly mobile architect, recalled how:

> I was on my own and enjoyed it. I never had a doubt about handling myself. I'm a great cook. The only thing I don't like to do is dust, but I could handle everything. It was great just to have my freedom.

Yet these skeptics eventually said "I do." Even more, they became committed husbands who sustained their marriages over a long period of time. How did this come about?

Some confirmed bachelors simply tired of the single life. Ron turned to marriage after years of self-indulgence began to wear thin and the dangers of living life on the edge became more apparent:

> I took care of all my fantasies, dreams, ambitions in the navy. I did all the things I heard about. After the drinking and trying to keep up with everybody else, I said, "What am I doing? I'm trying to kill myself. I could get hurt." It turned me off after a while. After you've drunk a whole bottle of vodka, it kind of sets you on a new course. I got everything out of my system. Marriage was the next logical step.

These initially reluctant husbands began to miss the intimacy and sense of being rooted in the world that freedom could not offer. Fred, the real estate broker, grew tired of the short-term relationships he used to enjoy:

> The single life—it just doesn't appeal to me anymore. It's nice to go out with different people, but it gets a little old. It lacks that special commitment that you get from one person.

Others did not consciously tire of being single. Instead, despite earlier skepticism, they found fulfillment in one relationship. For Eric, a property manager, unexpected contentment with one woman undermined earlier doubts about the possibility or desirability of being in a committed relationship:

I was still dead set against marriage. I perceived marriage basically as a loss of freedom, financial responsibilities, personal commitment that I was not geared up to. But when we got together, it was really unbelievable. I don't know how to explain it, but I felt so comfortable with this woman—so relaxed and so good. Getting married seemed like the most natural thing to do.

Having also discovered the benefits of involvement with one woman, Kevin, the truck driver who became a paramedic, said:

Up until I met Joanne, I thought I was never going to get married. But she made me happy, made me warm. It wasn't a sexual thing. It was a caring thing. She would get up at two in the morning when I came home from work. I was very important to her. I decided this was the kind of thing I wanted. I'm lucky to have her. She takes very good care of me. My life wouldn't be worth shit without her.

Others gravitated toward marriage more passively. Marriage never became the preferred choice, but it came to be seen as a social requisite they would not be able to resist. Sam, the architect who loved his freedom, felt inexorably pushed toward marriage:

Going through this whirlwind and getting married, I thought, "What am I doing?" But I'm the kind of guy who just wants to get the day over with and wake up tomorrow. Everything is getting through to the next day. That's all I am.

Far from feeling powerful and dominant, many reluctant husbands felt defenseless. After a four-year courtship, Lee, an ambulance driver and medical technician, agreed to marry despite considerable doubts; it "just happened." When asked why, he explained:

Are you familiar with the term, "Shit or get off the pot"? All of her friends had been getting married. We went to all of their weddings. She kept hounding me. She was like a shadow I couldn't get rid of. I finally said, "I guess this is the way to go." I liked her. It wasn't like I couldn't stand being with her.

Despite the passivity and lack of conscious planning with which some stumbled into marriage, the result did not always confirm their worst expectations. In these cases, the domestic trap of marriage became a caring nest. Jeff, the zookeeper, harbored deep doubts about his ability to form a lasting, powerful emotional attachment to anyone, but his indifference gradually turned to love. As the years passed, he discovered and developed a capacity for intimacy he once thought would elude him forever:

> Looking back on it, I shouldn't have gotten married for the reasons I had at that time. I'm glad I did now. I should have felt like this, like the way I do now. I was lucky. I mellowed. I just met somebody I loved and wanted to be with. It turned out okay.

Others were not so fortunate. They remained entangled in what seemed to them a tight, uncomfortable net of domesticity from which they felt unable or unwilling to escape. Doug, the sanitation worker and Vietnam vet, explained how his wife's persistence coupled with his own desire for children led him to enter and remain in a marriage marked more by convenience than a strong emotional bond:

> We're certainly not a match made in heaven. We've lasted for thirteen years, but there's still a long time ahead. Who knows what's going to happen? She's a good girl, a good mother, and she loves her children. She loves me, too—God only knows why. So I could have done a lot worse.

What kept reluctant husbands like Doug in their marriages when so many others are choosing to divorce? About 17 percent of reluctant breadwinners did indeed consider divorce, and several went through a period of marital separation. But changes in their outlook on long-term commitment led almost all of them either to reunite with their original partners or to search for a more fulfilling permanent relationship. (Only two of the twenty-four reluctant breadwinners had been divorced.)

Some found that years of marriage transformed their earlier preference for solitude into a distaste for being alone. When Jerry, an attorney, separated from his first wife, he discovered how much he needed and wanted a partner in life. Although he still viewed himself as a "loner," he explained eloquently: "I want to take a left turn when everybody's going right, but I want someone to take that left turn with me."

In some cases, these initially reluctant husbands had to struggle to win back wives who demanded that they change or leave. Faced with an ultimatum to stop drinking or face a divorce, Joseph, who had held jobs as varied as longshoreman and child-care worker before becoming a highway repairer, chose family commitment and stability over the freedom to be a lonely alcoholic. When his wife decided that they should separate,

I hated it. It was terrible. I'm not the kind of person who can be alone. I don't like it at all. There wasn't any other woman. . . . My family is the most important thing I have. So there's nothing more I want than to stay sober. Janet said, "Three strikes and you're out."

Other reluctant husbands were enmeshed in a web of personal ties and obligations that kept them in unsatisfying marriages despite a desire to leave. Responsibilities to other dependents won out over personal preferences. Although Jesse, the construction worker, yearned to escape the confines of what felt to him like a suffocating marriage, he nevertheless stayed with his wife and needy in-laws:

I got the seven-year itch after four years. There were things I wanted to do, and I couldn't appease everybody. My wife isn't very independent, and there was another person who was willing to give me the freedoms I was looking for, a more independent person. I had asked for a divorce. I was totally at the bridge. We had started a legal separation.

I talked to a few counselors, a priest, my eighth-grade nun, my mom and dad. They were supportive of the marriage, but I don't think they really understood how I felt. I couldn't in good conscience leave and let people more or less fend for themselves. At that particular time, my brother-in-law was dying. He and my sister-in-law were living with us. I was the sole supporter. I swallowed it hook, line, and sinker. I think if I were to have my life to live over, I would go in the other direction.

If close-knit networks of kin obligations kept some reluctant husbands in unsteady marriages, then the arrival of children created another cementing force. Unexpected pregnancies led some to marry and others to remain married. Indeed, married couples with children get divorced less often than childless couples. Kevin, the paramedic, felt ill prepared to assume the economic responsibilities of marriage and parenthood:

I had to buy two wedding dresses. She had outgrown one by the time we got married. When she told me she was pregnant, I tried to convince her into not having the baby. I even took her to a place called a family planning center, where they gave such a graphic description it was bizarre. She ran out crying. I said, "Okay, that's it, have the baby." I'm not unhappy. I'm in love with both my daughters.

For Doug, commitment to his marriage didn't develop until his first child was born. Every time his attachment to his wife wavered, his attachment to his daughter strengthened enough to keep the marriage together:

I really didn't want to be married. I think we stayed married because I worked days and she worked nights. We stayed away from each other. Then three years after, my daughter came along, and I was in awe for a while. That was my little girl. She was around three, and I didn't want to be married, but I said, "Wow, this is a really big deal, having her around. I guess I'll be married for a while."

Forging stable bonds, whether happily or unhappily, had a similar set of consequences for all of these reluctant husbands. First, marital commitment strengthened their ties to paid work. Marriage produced a concern for the future in men who had previously taken pride in their casual attitude toward work and their ability to live from day to day. Even when their wives worked, reluctant breadwinners felt responsible for the long-term economic support of their spouses and the children who followed. This concern for future economic obligations led them to seek employment that promised a career as well as a current paycheck. Jesse lamented the bargain he felt forced to strike. In his early construction jobs,

I was as happy as you could be. My time was my own. I didn't have to answer to anybody because if you showed up, you got paid, and if you didn't show up, you didn't get paid. My boss was like that.

Once married, he felt obliged to give up autonomy for security. As he put it, "Security is a definite must because of my responsibilities."

Work and economic security became more important because marriage meant an inevitable turn toward parenthood as well. Herbert, an engineer and father of two, asserted that even a begrudging agreement to marry also meant an implicit agreement to have children: "If you weren't going to have children, what's the point of getting married?"

In some cases, wives made the demand for children explicit. When faced with a choice between remaining single and becoming a parent, reluctant breadwinners were surprised to find their commitment to a valued relationship overrode their fears of having a child. Jeff, the zookeeper, finally agreed when he discovered just how important his marriage had become to his own well-being:

I thought I had accepted the fact that I would be single, and I even had plans of going out west, working as a ranger. I'd be single again, play around, stuff like that. When it really came down to it, I couldn't deal with that. We said to each other, "How can two people split up and love each other?" A Hollywood scene. Well, I caved in. Now it doesn't seem that terrifying to be a father. It's not *that* bad.

He added that becoming committed ultimately meant relinquishing his "free choice":

> If I had my own free choice, I wouldn't have a kid. But she left me no choice. Last time, I had free choice—I forced her to have an abortion. I had a feeling deep down she hated me, or that part of me that forced her to have the abortion. Just agreeing to have a kid dissolved the hatred. Didn't repress it, dissolved it.

Reluctant breadwinners stayed in their marriages despite previous doubts and current sacrifices. They traded personal freedom for the largely unanticipated benefits of a committed relationship. Marriage, like steady employment, created stability in lives that had been marked by rootlessness. It constrained the range of freedom, but it also provided a reason to go to work, to create a family, and to plan for the future. From one perspective, it transformed romantic social rebels into mainstream conformists. To most who underwent the transition, however, it gave meaning and form to aimlessness. For a few, like Steve, it seemed to save their lives:

> I was getting more and more into drugs. She wanted me to stop taking drugs, and she left. I felt abandoned for a year. Then after I spent Christmas in a drunk tank, I went for help out of desperation. I got straight and got a job. We got back together, found a big apartment, and became a family. We even decided to have another kid.

The Pull of Parenthood

Almost three-fourths of the reluctant breadwinners began adulthood with an aversion to the prospect of having children (the rest were neutral on the topic). Parenthood represented the primary responsibility they hoped to avoid, implying as it does so many other economic and emotional commitments. They equated fatherhood with all the bread-winning burdens they saw in the lives of their own fathers and other male figures of their childhood.

Yet, just as they found secure employment and developed committed marital bonds, these men moved from hoping to avoid parenthood to feeling willing and, in some cases, enthusiastic about becoming a father. They established (or planned to establish) lasting emotional and economic ties to their children. Peter explained:

> At one point, I would not have been able to say I wanted a child. I was very much afraid to end up like my father. But that wouldn't be the

case now. I really do love children now. I find that I get along very well with them, and I'm not afraid to deal with them. I want to have children as soon as possible.

The change did not involve an eagerness for taking care of children, however. The bonds they developed, or started to plan, involved having and supporting children, not participating extensively in rearing them. What caused this change in outlook, why was it limited to procreation and economic support, and what were its consequences? Either alone or in combination, a variety of experiences made childlessness less attractive and fatherhood more so.

First, reluctant fathers lost many of the supports that made remaining childless attractive. Over time, the alternative outlets for their energies began to shrink and grow less satisfying. As their friends married and built domestic households, they lost earlier networks of male support and faced a growing incentive to turn from more public to more private pursuits. David, who became a committed bureaucrat despite his start as a union organizer, made a willing but unenthusiastic transition to parenthood when his friends and political cronies began to withdraw from political life to raise families:

> Our political activity was slowing down. And other people in this group were having kids. So when everybody decided to have kids, we did too. The group dissolved, and things turned into nuclear families. We all did it at the same time. . . . It was something that we were just going to do. It wasn't strong feelings.

Others decided it was time for a change when they tired of the freedom they had worked so hard to achieve. Fatherhood, like marriage, offered a new challenge and a new identity. Phillip discovered that the steady pursuits of work and play could get tiresome after a time:

> I'm getting bored having so much fun all by myself. I make a lot of money. I've traveled a lot. I work very hard and play very hard, and I've been playing very hard for the last five years. I want another challenge. I'm just bored with the two of us having such a good time.

More often, however, reluctant fathers did not turn toward parenthood of their own accord. Rather, they became involved in relationships with women who pushed strenuously and, in these cases, effectively for having children. For men who were ambivalent rather than totally opposed to fatherhood, strategic nudging generally overcame their halfhearted reluctance. Lee, the ambulance driver expecting his first child, gave up his resistance in the face of his wife's determined efforts:

In the long range, I guess I've always felt that's what I wanted, but I had to be convinced, and she helped with that. I'm still scared silly about having children, but she's been having the neighbor's kids come over, and the attitude is changing. She's exposed me a little more to the idea.

More resistant men faced more determined efforts to overcome their opposition. Even those in the habit of dominating their wives found that trying to exert control could sometimes backfire. For Jeff, the zookeeper, marriage had unintended consequences. After agreeing to two abortions at his request, his wife stopped deferring to his wishes. He had been used to being "sort of domineering" in the early years of their marriage, but then things changed:

> As my wife has gotten older, she wanted to have a kid. There was this mounting pressure as she was approaching thirty. Where in the past, I would shrug it off, I couldn't anymore. Finally, it reached the point where I knew she was going to leave. I knew I didn't want her to leave. I just said okay . . . to keep the marriage together.

For these men, a growing and unexpected commitment to their wives overcame an opposition to parenthood. They adjusted to a situation they found somewhat frightening, but not completely under their control. In the face of an unplanned pregnancy, Sam, the architect and draftsman, transformed his initial anger into a passive, controlled acceptance of his fate:

> I was very annoyed when I found out she was pregnant. I wasn't making good money, and I wanted to make sure I had enough so when the child came there's not any grief. I guess I was really a bastard for a while. I was upset with myself because I wanted more out of myself before the child came. But the whole thing changed somewhere in the sixth or seventh month. I kind of resigned myself to it. I said, "Hey, I'm going to have a kid. This is happening."

As initially reluctant fathers accepted the prospect of having a child, they endeavored to overcome their fears and to focus instead on the dangers of childlessness. With his wife's delivery date approaching, Lee, the medical technician, began to view fatherhood as the lesser of two evils. To offset his concerns, he took solace in his deliverance from a worse fate:

> I have no great love for children. They're still scary to some extent. This seems much riskier than getting married. But I look at myself when I'm forty-five, and I say, "What would it be if I didn't do it now?" That idea seems scarier than going through with this. I'm praying it all

works out. Everybody says the attitude changes when the child comes. They don't regret it. I guess I'm not totally fearful.

Whether they greeted the change enthusiastically or begrudgingly, becoming a parent had similar consequences for all. Some were anticipated; others were not. Some were beneficial and provided unexpected pleasures; others produced the very drawbacks that reluctant breadwinners had once hoped to avoid.

Becoming a father usually provided unanticipated pleasure and fulfillment. Kevin, the paramedic, fearfully awaited the birth of his first child, but then found that it was like falling in love unexpectedly:

In the hospital, my wife came down with a fever and couldn't nurse the baby. They sent me to the nursery, sat me in a rocking chair, and said, "Here's a bottle. Feed the baby." A radio was playing soft music. I held her in my arms and danced with her. That was it. She had me. It was one of the happiest moments of my life. These have been probably the best years that anybody could be granted on this earth. I have been so happy watching her grow.

When Steve, the recovering drug addict, became a father, he discovered a wellspring of emotional and personal resources he had not known existed:

I thought she was going to be pregnant forever. I just didn't think what it would be like when the baby was born. Then each time a baby arrived, I panicked over the responsibility. I became unglued emotionally and went back to drugs to escape.

But it turned out that I could love them even more than I expected. If I let myself think about the fact that they almost weren't born, I could feel real sad. I don't know what would have happened, but it doesn't seem that my life would be as full.

As for the unanticipated responsibilities and burdens parenthood entails, Doug, the sanitation worker and father of two, said he felt "proud as a peacock" when the baby came, but

the fright came later when I realized the awesome responsibility and the hard job you're taking on. If I knew, I don't think I would have been able to conceive a child. I really don't think I would have been able to concentrate.

For reluctant fathers, the "awesome responsibility" of fatherhood meant providing financial support for a rising number of dependents. Even more than marriage, becoming a father compelled commitment to work. This change was generally not unforeseen, since it was one of consequences that reluctant fathers feared most. Peter, the childless art framer who tired of an autonomous but lonely lifestyle, presumed a child would force him to work harder and to take work much more seriously:

> I'll have to hold my nose to the grindstone much more. I've been shunning commitment to many things in the past, especially to work, and I would have to make much greater strides in what I'm doing than I am now.

Whether or not changes in job commitment were anticipated, they entailed costs as well as benefits. The need for financial security took precedence over other wishes and posed a potential dilemma. If the work they preferred failed to offer sufficient income or protection against economic uncertainty, then reluctant breadwinners were forced to choose between intrinsically fulfilling work and secure, well-paid jobs. Men in poorly paid human-service jobs were especially likely to face this trade-off. Joseph, who had been a dock worker and restaurant manager, had found genuine gratification working in a day-care center: "Working with a child is a lot more important than fixing the transmission of a car. I enjoyed it more than anything." Yet the need to support his own two children pushed him back into the high-pressured world of restaurant management:

> I went back into hotels and restaurants where I could make money. I felt it was necessary even though I enjoyed the child care more. But along with the gratification there has to be security. I have my family to worry about.

The need for a secure income led other reluctant fathers to forgo the search for more satisfying work. They forfeited earlier dreams in order to stay in uninspiring jobs they could not afford to leave. Like many frustrated workers, Herbert, the engineer and father of two, dreamed of starting his own business.[5] As the family breadwinner, he concluded that economic risk taking, especially in the form of self-employment, was a luxury he could no longer afford:

> There was no way I could ever go into business for myself because what if you become a total failure? How are you going to support the wife and children? I probably could have left, but psychologically I couldn't. I never wanted children, but when I had them, I did accept them.

Children promoted work ambition as well as a concern for security. Once the freedom not to work—or at least not to move from job to job— was lost, getting promoted became more important. The need to think about and plan for the future gave what was once "just a job" the significance of a "career." For some, this newfound ambition came to seem natural and inevitable, as in the case of Eric, a former truck driver who stumbled into property management:

> My wife was pregnant, and I needed benefits, and the first job that came along got me. . . . Now, I'm making the most of it. I'm getting a promotion now. I definitely have intentions of climbing the ladder.

As economic pressures mounted, other reluctant fathers grudgingly gave in to the need to move ahead. They conceded to the new requirements they faced, but they also tried to limit parenthood's impact. Jeff, who had agreed to have a child in the face of his wife's threats to leave, raised his minimum standard for job success but hoped to resist the pressure to aim for unbounded heights. He feared the costs of work success and kept a ceiling on his goals even as he raised the floor:

> Hopefully, it doesn't cause me to be too ambitious. I'm going to try to be sort of strong about it. Having kids might push me more to move up the ladder, where it's not really good for me. I've got to keep my integrity. There's a certain point I can't fall below, but I don't have to make sixty thousand a year to be happy.

For better or worse, becoming a parent had a stabilizing effect on men's commitment to work. It had similar effects on their family ties, their personal goals, and their lives in general. In cases where the emotional bond between spouses had been weak, the arrival of children dampened the desire to leave if not necessarily the sense of emotional distance. Doug credited his two children with keeping him married and even drawing him closer to his wife:

> I'm not really the family man she would like, but I love her a lot— more now than I ever did. The children pulled us together. I don't know if there would be enough of a bond to hold us without them. It might be over; we'd go our own ways.

Stable work and family ties produced psychological changes. Parenthood encouraged a turn away from illusions of remaining forever young and free.[6] The social demands of fatherhood led Sam, the architect, to trade a childlike self-image for a more adult one:

> It pushed me more, the responsibility of having a child. I'm like a normal middle-class type person now. Getting that responsibility, having a kid that I got to take care of—that was a big push. It said to me, "You're an adult," because up until that time I was a child.

The men who had resisted stable commitments at work and in the home greeted these changes with mixed reactions. While a few grieved for the freedom they had lost, most preferred to emphasize the unexpected rewards of parenthood. Like Doug, they viewed the outcomes they had once feared in a more positive light: "Without children, my life would be a lot emptier. Now, I don't think I'll ever be a bum. Just knowing that they need me, having that responsibility, gives me strength."

Indeed, those who had traveled a particularly rocky road to parenthood, such as Vietnam vets and reformed addicts, came to see their children as saviors. Joseph believed that fatherhood had saved him from his own worst impulses:

> I think probably if the children weren't on the scene, I wouldn't be sitting here talking to you. God only knows where I'd be. It's not the most pleasant thought. I guess basically I realize that Janet would get along fine without me, she wouldn't wither away, but at this stage in their life, they need a father. So it's been a stabilizing effect.

George, the park supervisor and father of two, concurred:

> Maybe I wouldn't be here today if I didn't have children. I could have gotten on a plane, flew somewhere, crashed. I was pretty wild, and the family more or less slowed me down, calmed me down.

It is important to distinguish between the occurrence of change and how people perceive it. Since these men became fathers despite an initial resistance, they had a strong incentive to justify their choices. Most agreed with Steve that parenthood gave them a needed direction in life, a base on which to build, a reason for becoming what at some deeply submerged level they had wanted to be:

> I always wanted to be responsible and good and honest and all those things I rejected because I threw some stuff out with everything else. Taken in the whole context of drugs and losing touch with the ground, what's important now is trying to give my children the best. I feel responsible for that. I've been compensated . . . I might have offed myself if I didn't have something else to turn to.

Even while these men began to conform to the prescriptions of breadwinning, however, they retained a social and psychological distance from family life. They adopted a limited definition of fatherhood. To them, it meant extending their social and genetic heritage more than molding their offspring through active participation. Ken, the court reporter, saw his daughter as the carrier of his family name and thus his only link to the future—even though he knew she might change her name if she married: "you leave nothing else in this world but children. That would have been the end of the line for my name." To Peter, "it would be like becoming extinct if I had no children. I could see myself becoming very bitter, very lonely later on in life."

The demands of work provided an important rationale for maintaining a distance from caretaking, especially from the "dirtiest" tasks of child care. Herbert, the engineer, had two children despite considerable hesitation. He decided that being a father meant earning a living, not caring for a child: "I never changed a diaper. I felt that wasn't what I was supposed to do."

Because reluctant breadwinners were nudged into parenthood, they retained the leverage to avoid extensive involvement. They struck a bargain with their wives: in exchange for consenting to have a child, they would be excused from the more demanding aspects of child rearing. Jeff agreed to have a child only after extracting a promise that he would not be expected to care for it:

> Consuelo wants to have the kid. I had to be bribed, so she has agreed to take on more than her share, to do the care, the nurturing part. She said, "I want to have the kid; I'll take care of it." So I'll just work and be the playful father. It sounds too good to be true. I don't know what's going to happen but she gives me a lot of freedom.

Without supportive partners, reluctant breadwinners could not negotiate or maintain the boundaries they drew between supporting children and caring for them. How did these men find, become involved with, and secure the support of women willing and able to relieve them of the bulk of child-rearing responsibilities?

Choosing a Domestically Oriented Partner

Many reluctant breadwinners moved from a relatively egalitarian outlook on relationships with women to one that recognized a sharp division between work and family tasks.[7] One route involved an unexpected attraction to a woman who preferred domesticity to a career. Whether or not these women were employed outside the home, they put family responsibilities first. They did not define commitments to paid work as a primary goal or as a career. Philip, the nightclub and hotel manager, broke his own rule "not to go out with anyone who works for me" and started dating an employee who checked coats. He felt an "emotional spark" that had been missing in earlier relationships with more career-oriented women:

> I had preconceived ideas of what I wanted from a wife, a woman. I used to be a real women's activist. I thought I wanted someone who

was an equal in every way, especially on a work level. It took me a long time to realize what I really wanted from a wife was not an equal. And Lisa was it. There's nothing special about her professionally. She's just a wonderful girl. She cooks great. She's very smart, but she doesn't have any ambitions to do professional stuff. She just makes me feel good.

Despite his concern that his friends would not approve of his choice, he discovered he wanted different things from an intimate relationship than they seemed to be seeking:

At first I was embarrassed to tell people we were going out. I thought people would think she was substandard—not up to par with who they thought I should go out with. A lot of that thinking came from being around these guys—a lot of what they do is who they're seen with. But that was never really me. It took me a year or two to realize that, and when I came out of the closet with Lisa, it wasn't hard at all. Everybody was thrilled.

Another route toward choosing a domestic spouse involved a more forthright rejection of equality. In these cases, dissatisfying experiences with career-committed women led reluctant breadwinners to seek less ambitious partners. They complained—as women are often said to do— that a focus on career makes a partner less available emotionally and practically for a close relationship. Peter, the art installer, now separated and involved with a less ambitious woman, did not support his first wife's dedication to her career:

My wife was a workaholic. She devoted herself entirely to her work. She was working at home almost every night. They gave her every opportunity for promotion because no company could survive without a person like her. Eventually we literally began to drift apart. Part of it was my anger; part of it was her remoteness.

As his feelings about parenthood began to change, her disinterest in having children became a liability instead of an asset:

She didn't want children and neither did I. But I changed my mind over the last five years. Now I feel far more confident. She just didn't want it.

These men worried about being superseded by an accomplished woman, preferring instead to occupy a more central position in the relationship. Jerry, an attorney whose mother worked outside the home until he left for college, originally thought he wanted a career-committed partner. But he began to feel overshadowed by his wife's success in business, and soon the marriage ended: "In my mind, I was competing with her, and I didn't like that. That put a tremendous strain on our marriage."

His initial interest in an egalitarian relationship turned to skepticism. As successful women became less attractive to him, he began to search for a different kind of partner:

> I learned what I didn't want. I wanted a girl who is a little bit softer, more feminine, not wanting to compete with me. I don't mind her working, but I want her priorities to be me more than her career. . . . I'm selfish.

Peter chose someone who was willing to meet his desires to have a child: "she is willing to have a child to please me. That's very important to me."

Some reluctant breadwinners had married work-committed women who were unexpectedly pushed toward domesticity. In these cases, circumstances transformed a relatively equal relationship into a "traditional" one. For Paul, the upwardly mobile social service administrator, a shared family business in a country setting had produced an unusual equality in the early years of his marriage:

> That lifestyle was perfect, because we took turns going into the store. I would stay home one day, and Judy the next. It was the most egalitarian child raising for those three years that I've ever seen or heard about. . . . But right now it's pretty traditional. She's doing the child caring, and I'm doing the breadwinning.

Despite their preference for sharing work and caretaking, a return to the city foreshadowed the demise of equal sharing:

> When we came back from Vermont, Nancy didn't have a degree nor the skills. She had never had a job, never gone for an interview. Someone had to bring in money, and I was much closer to jumping on the career ladder than she was. So I think it was necessity that she said, "You run with the ball. I've got a kid, and I'm pregnant with twins."

Blocked opportunities at work also changed these wives' outlook on relationships and family life.[8] Sidney, the ex-lawyer who became a businessman, remained "ardently feminist," but accepted his wife's change of attitude when poor treatment at work convinced her to stay home with their young daughter: "It was not the nicest agency. It was a relief for her to get out of there." For Jesse, the unhappily married construction worker, his wife's firing ended hopes of her building a career and sapped her desire to work outside the home:

She was a manager in a responsible position, a very devoted employee. She'd get there at the crack of dawn. It hurt her a great deal
when they fired her. Finally, I told her, "To hell with them. It's not
even worth it."

The chance for more equal sharing also diminished when accidents
and unexpected health problems reinforced a wife's already growing discontent. A disabling accident on the job allowed Eric's wife to escape
from a work situation that had grown increasingly untenable:

One of the patients threw a wheelchair at her, and she hurt her back.
It was very painful for her, but I think it was actually a blessing in disguise. She was getting pretty fed up. Compared to that job, almost
anything is more fun.

Occasionally, wives were forced to relinquish cherished careers.
These husbands became primary breadwinners in spite of their wives'
and their own preferences. When a serious injury ended his wife's career
as a paramedic and co-worker, Kevin became the sole earner:

I think secretly she hates not working, because she had a career she
wanted to pursue. She was involved in the same thing I was; she was
an emergency medical technician. Her back was injured on four separate occasions, and they said she couldn't go back in the streets again.
She gets teary-eyed because she can't go back. I know she'd like to do
something, but she's very limited. The only thing she really knows is
patient care, and that's totally out of the question now.

All of these routes led toward unexpected commitment to a domestic
spouse, which had similar consequences. First, if children were not already present, wives began to push for having them. When they grew
frustrated by paid work or found their ambitions thwarted, children offered a new challenge in life. Reluctant breadwinners faced growing
pressures to become fathers. Lee, the emergency medical worker expecting his first child, watched his wife's ambivalence about having a
child dissolve:

When we got married, neither one of us had a great interest. That
changed. Maybe she got bored. Maybe this was a challenge. So she
sort of changed her feelings from "No, we're not going to have children" to "Yes, we are." She persisted, and I started thinking.

A wife's domestic orientation became as important as her wish to
have children. Both partners shared the incentive to create a division between breadwinning and caretaking, even when a more fluid and egalitarian arrangement had prevailed in the past. Phillip had once loved to

cook, but found himself expelled from the kitchen when his girlfriend moved in:

> I used to be the greatest cook. But when Lisa moved in, I lost control of the kitchen. I joke about it a lot, but the kitchen is her place and I'm there only on permission. If I put things away wrong, I get yelled at.

He also anticipated, with mixed feelings of relief and regret, that the same rules would apply when children arrived: "I can visualize myself trying to get involved and getting thrown out."

Their wives' domesticity pushed some men out of the kitchen and the nursery. It tied all of them more tightly to the workplace, as work became the primary means by which their suitability as husbands and fathers could be assessed. This put a special pressure on men who could not find well-paid work. Kevin, the paramedic, acknowledged wistfully that "no matter what happens in this world, I have to provide for my family. She likes nice things, and unfortunately I haven't been able to get her nice things."

Whether or not these reluctant breadwinners welcomed their economic obligations, they developed justifications for assuming them. Most cited their children's well-being. Doug, the sanitation worker, explained:

> I wanted her to work in the beginning. I said, "Hey, I'm out there hustling, working all the time. Why don't you help?" I thought she could work because I know other people that do it. But I worked it out in my head that it's a benefit to the kids that she's there all the time.

By choosing a domestic partner, sometimes unwittingly, these men enjoyed freedom from domestic work. But they also relinquished financial assistance and some domestic control. Kevin, the paramedic whose wife became disabled, adjusted to losing a vote in how to run their home: "This is *her* house. I may live here, but this is her house."

In return for these concessions, primary breadwinners reaped substantial benefits. The time, energy, and freedom afforded by having someone else take care of domestic matters gave them significant advantages. They gained the traditional rights and privileges of manhood: status and power as heads of their households and relief from the unpleasant parts of child care and housework. Lee planned to rely on his paycheck to "buy" his way out of the dirty work when the baby arrived:

> One of us, obviously, will have to have a full-time job, and since she's not in a position to get one, and I still have one, and she's the one who overwhelmingly desires this child anyway, it's assumed that's the way things are going to continue. She hasn't made any major objections,

and I'm hoping it falls into place. There are things I hope I won't be doing. I don't look forward to waking up at four A.M., having her throw me out of bed saying, "It's your turn." Changing diapers is not my great ambition in life, nor is sitting there for twenty minutes holding a bottle. I'm hoping I can just get the pleasure aspect and not too much of the dirty work.

Reluctant breadwinners saw this division of labor as fair and even optimal, given men's advantages in the labor market. By assuming the duties of good provider, they also viewed their economic contributions as a gift to their wives, who were thereby saved from the dual burden that many employed wives assume. George, the park supervisor and father of two, concluded that equal sharing in the home was not acceptable under any circumstances:

> My wife cooks, shops, cleans. I provide the money. To me, to run a home and raise children is a full-time job. If you do more, that's where you lose your children and you lose control, because you can't skate and ski at the same time. I'll work my full day, but she *must* be here for those kids so they can get good guidance.

Traditional arrangements came to seem natural or inevitable, no matter how reluctant these men had once been. For David, the city planner, his wife's blocked mobility at work combined with his own expanding opportunities to send the two along divergent paths. Despite differences in their options, he nevertheless took the view that his wife "naturally gravitated towards taking more responsibility."

But the decision to separate breadwinning and child rearing is not simply the outcome of natural inclinations, abilities, or even preferences. Gender differences in workplace opportunities led some men to become breadwinners even when they felt better suited than their wives to domestic activities. For Paul, the welfare administrator, the disjunction between abilities and responsibilities was clear and sometimes painful:

> I think I could be more of a homebody than Nancy. I have a more natural inclination to kids. I enjoy spending time with the kids, especially now because I spend less. I look forward to coming home and cuddling with them, touching them, being near to them, finding out how their day was. Nancy basically does not view herself as a mother; it doesn't come easy to her. From the time our first child came home, she realized she really wasn't cut out for motherhood. Nancy is more to the point where they're driving her nuts. She has made the ultimate sacrifice in doing it, but it's taken a toll on her.

Conclusion

What caused such significant change among these men? Since they are united precisely by their initial aversion (or, at least, indifference) to "traditional" definitions of masculine success, personal preferences cannot explain the movement toward breadwinning. Indeed, some retained their distaste for the good-provider ethic even after they became primary breadwinners. Paul, the social service administrator, believed that "one shouldn't work all that much; one should have some free time; one should be able to sit around," but found himself "setting goals for myself that are conflicting."

Some reluctant breadwinners held on to earlier preferences even as their behavior changed, while others changed their beliefs to better fit their new circumstances. In neither case, however, did the beliefs or preferences cause the change. Rather, changes in opportunities and options preceded and prompted the ensuing changes in behavior and desire.[9]

Compared to men whose initial aversion to breadwinning did *not* change in adulthood, those who did ultimately become breadwinners were disproportionately exposed to social forces that allowed, encouraged, and in some cases compelled this choice (see appendix, table 8). Only 45 percent of those who kept an autonomous outlook found job stability and opportunity, while 75 percent of reluctant breadwinners were able to do so. Unexpected opportunity pulled these men into the workplace, where they found unanticipated rewards in stable jobs. They became committed workers in spite of themselves. Work success, in turn, made breadwinning possible and lessened the risk of making family commitments. Their apprehension about becoming husbands and fathers abated as they grew more secure at work. The high demands of their jobs, on the other hand, lessened their ability and willingness to share in domestic chores.

Experiences with women and children (that stably autonomous men were less likely to undergo) also pulled these men toward breadwinning. A full 88 percent of reluctant breadwinners established stable marriages, even though most had doubted their desire or ability to do so at the outset. In contrast, only 25 percent of stably autonomous men had either stayed married or found a partner they felt committed to in a permanent way. The remaining 75 percent had either remained single or divorced (among this group were three who identified themselves as homosexual). Among those who were stably married, 67 percent of the reluctant breadwinners had chosen partners who either were not employed or were employed part-time. In contrast, all of the partners of men with an autonomous outlook were strongly committed to full-time work.[10]

Finally, 71 percent of the reluctant breadwinners developed an unexpected commitment to children and parenthood, while none of the stably autonomous men had become fathers or planned to do so. The desire to sustain these attachments, along with their unanticipated pleasures, pushed reluctant breadwinners toward stable jobs and marriages. Unlike their counterparts who successfully avoided breadwinning, reluctant breadwinners became enmeshed in personal commitments and attachments that lessened the appeal of freedom from the family and made it more difficult to avoid breadwinning.

Comparisons with stably autonomous men underscore the social forces that pushed and pulled reluctant breadwinners down the road toward marriage, parenthood, and steady work. Unexpected stability at work and in marriage led these men to become good providers despite their early doubts and fears. Because all reluctant breadwinners underwent a process of unexpected change, they greeted their destiny with surprise, puzzlement, and sometimes amazement. As they moved from a decidedly antiestablishment outlook to enjoyment of the fruits of establishment success, many felt grateful as well. Steve, the ex-addict who found himself working steadily and supporting a family, exclaimed:

> I always lived out of boxes and never had any place I could call home. Now I have a family; I have a home instead of drugs. It's like that song where you wake up and say, "Is this my house? Is this my car? Where am I?"

As the advantages of breadwinning became increasingly apparent, most redefined their earlier freedom in terms of selfishness, emptiness, or loneliness. They came to view family commitments, and especially economic responsibilities, as redemptive. Like many studies comparing single and married men,[11] these men concluded that marriage had salutary effects on their health and well-being, while singlehood posed dangers they had escaped.

Since reluctant breadwinners could not easily attribute their achievements to their own desires or efforts, they were prone to construct one of two explanations. Some acknowledged that economic and social advantages had eased their way toward breadwinning, admitting that they had benefited from forces beyond their control. Paul thus concluded:

> I think it worked out this way a lot because of sex roles in society and our abilities to be a breadwinner. In theory, I don't believe in that, but it's not anything to debate. I'm the one who has the potential to make money and is making it.

Most, however, thought that luck had propelled them toward their current situation. Phillip, the nightclub manager and developer, credited the vagaries of time and space for his success:

> I've been very lucky, being in the right place in the right time. I can't imagine what I'd be doing if I hadn't gotten in the door and on this runaway train with these guys nine years ago. I've been very lucky that way. . . . What can you chalk it up to—other than luck?

Unexpected change thus came to be seen as good fortune and much less often as the result of the advantages men enjoy. Luck provided a rationale for opportunities that were not actively sought and sometimes felt undeserved.[12]

Men's comparative advantages nevertheless buttressed the "luck" of reluctant breadwinners. They gave even those men who adopted passive strategies the means to succeed.[13] A passive stance toward life may not lead to the top, but it often suffices to reach the middle. What's more, the process of passively riding the current can look and feel active. Because reluctant breadwinners were drifting with the tide, their passivity did not undermine the stereotype of masculine aggressiveness and action.[14] However, some, like George, did recognize that "most of the good things that happened in my life happened without too much effort on my part. There was no real plan or goals or anything like that. It was like I knocked on a door, and it opened."

Since luck, by definition, is fickle and beyond one's control, those who attributed their accomplishments to luck were uneasily aware that their attainments were fragile and had not been preordained. Other outcomes were not only possible but at one time likely. Some reluctant breadwinners thus took note thankfully of the short distance between them and their earlier compatriots, those autonomous men whose lives had not changed course. Irv, a supervisor of gardeners, felt grateful for his escape from a life not anchored by job or family ties: "A lot of my friends, who were like me, are in jail or still hanging out on street corners. They didn't change. I could have been one of them. I'm glad I settled down."

They were also aware of the social changes that have sent other men veering away from breadwinning. In this period of uncertainty and change, they defined success as having avoided the dangers they felt others had encountered. As George put it, "When I look around and see the by-products of this society—the homeless, the broken marriages, the depression, the problems of today—I say I must have done pretty good."

Even as these reluctant breadwinners moved toward a traditional package of family and work commitments, other men encountered different options and moved in different directions. Some moved toward greater personal autonomy, while others moved toward greater family involvement. The experiences that pushed and pulled initially reluctant men toward primary breadwinning contrast clearly with the experiences that sent other men down these different paths.

5

TURNING TOWARD AUTONOMY

Nobody has a hold on me. I do as I wish, and if tomorrow I don't want to, I don't have to. It's very important that I never feel trapped, locked in. It leads me away from feeling angry, mad, hostile, all those sort of things.
—Jeremy, a forty-year-old computer consultant

While reluctant breadwinners were making commitments to wives, children, and steady jobs, another group of men were turning away from the burdens and joys of family commitment. These men are part of a recent development that has been termed a "male revolt." It actually involves two trends. Growing numbers of men are choosing to remain single and childless. And, in a more disturbing development, as the rates of divorce and single motherhood have risen, growing numbers of divorced and never-married fathers are relinquishing economic and emotional responsibility for their children.[1] Ironically, the men who are now contributing to these trends grew up during the post–World War II period, when widening affluence, sexual conservatism, and stable family structures offered few socially acceptable alternatives to breadwinning.

In this chapter, I examine the process by which some of those who initially expected to become breadwinners ultimately turned away from parental commitments. Among men with breadwinning aspirations in childhood, 32 percent avoided or rejected parental commitments as adults. With the exception of one married man who chose to remain childless, these men either never married or underwent an unexpected marital breakup, including those who became estranged from children after divorce. Most were heterosexual, but two discovered a preference for homosexual or bisexual relationships in early adulthood. Twenty-seven percent were currently married or living with a sexual partner, but most were living alone. Whether or not they were currently in an exclusive relationship, all chose to avoid the risks and dangers (as well as the rewards) of fatherhood.

What social forces allowed and encouraged these men to postpone or reject parental commitments? Why did they choose autonomy instead of attachment? What distinguishes them from their good-provider counterparts? Unanticipated instability in the labor market and unhappy experiences in their personal relationships with women and children led them to conclude that the benefits of fatherhood were not worth the costs. In eschewing parenthood, they endeavored to retain male privilege while sidestepping its historical burdens. Their journey was part of a growing trend, but they were only dimly aware of being part of a larger social shift.

Instability in Employment

Of those who moved from an orientation toward breadwinning to autonomy, most entered the labor force expecting to build steady, secure, predictable careers. Over time, however, their experiences at work and in the labor market led them to reject this search. Instead, they began to emphasize freedom, personal fulfillment, and independence over the promise of security and economic reward. This in turn lessened their desire and ability to make family commitments.

All of these men found some type of steady employment in early adulthood, but most concluded that it was not worth the price it exacted from their lives. Disillusioning work experiences led them to reject the regimentation of a nine-to-five job. Ian, single at thirty-five, gave up steady work as a bookstore manager to become a freelance writer:

> When I got out of college, I worked in a number of different bookstores and for a book distribution company. I hated having to be someplace at nine o'clock in the morning and having to stay there and not having control of my time. I decided that I just couldn't work a regular nine-to-five job for a long period of time. It's intolerable to me.

Ian's discomfort with workplace control is emblematic of these autonomous men. They chafe under the regimentation of a daily schedule and under the authority of bosses they cannot respect. Chuck, a thirty-five-year-old systems analyst, left a budding career in hospital administration after working for a series of "authoritarian" bosses:

> I stayed for twelve and a half years. Initially I liked it, but I became really soured. Management brought in some *real* losers. The man they brought in as director was the same type of authoritarian, rampaging

father figure that I will not work for. I will not work for a person like that again. I will not do it.

The experience of working in tightly organized, bureaucratic settings left them determined to avoid similar situations in the future. Frustration with hierarchical control and arbitrary rules led Jeremy, a forty-year-old computer consultant, to renounce work in public institutions forever:

> The entrenched bureaucracy—I didn't like the way it functioned. To get any sort of decision, it was six weeks' worth of memos and meetings. It seemed to me to be a stifling atmosphere. People simply lost their spark, fire, drive. . . . I realized I could earn a great deal more money in private industry. But money was not the only criteria; it was just very frustrating.

If middle-class professionals found it difficult to work under overbearing bosses, the blue-collar workers who became autonomous tended to find an even lower position intolerable. Herman, a separated father of two, went from job to job seeking to escape hierarchical rule. He even abandoned a decade of training and experience as an air-conditioning reparier because he resented the constant interference of supervisors:

> I felt the boss questioned me, and then I couldn't work for him, because I knew my job. If you give me the job and let me do it, fine, but if you're going to question me and say, "No, it's got to be done this way," I can't take it. Because I felt I could always get another job if I wanted it.

Some autonomous men chose jobs and careers that appeared to offer a relatively independent work style only to discover that they were regulated in more subtle ways. Although Edward expected considerable autonomy as a physician, he discovered that the tyranny of his beeper and the sheer demands of his job were as stifling as having a boss:

> Other people say, "Oh, a beeper, very impressive," but it's not. Wherever you are, they beep and you have to answer. I remember when I was up all night, and I'd wanted to go to the bathroom for several hours. And no sooner had I sat down, than my beeper beeped, and I thought I was going to cry. All I could think of were those poor hamsters, where they turn on the light and give them shock and there's nothing you can do to stop it. If this beeps, I throw up. That's my gut reaction. I hate it.

After years of disillusionment, he began to reassess his commitment to medicine and to develop dreams of finding a less demanding (if less prestigious) job:

Where once upon a time I never would have considered it, now I'm very much on the edge. I really don't like surgery. It's very stressful. Do I want to do something I don't like for the rest of my life? Basically, this career has not turned out the way I dreamed it was going to be.

Those who lacked college degrees and professional training were also disenchanted by jobs that appeared to offer independence but were actually subject to indirect supervision. After working as a salesman, Alan, a forty-three-year-old divorced father, found the atmosphere of high-commission sales too competitive and left to escape the pressure:

I'd take odd jobs, work my twenty weeks, and then go back on unemployment. I was having a ball. When I got my unemployment check, I felt guilty because I had a suntan. If you're not doing something you like, work is a lot of grief.

Bart, a former bus driver, grew tired of arbitrary bosses, complaining passengers, and even uniforms. He decided to quit suddenly after almost a decade on the job:

I drove a city bus for nine years, until it started getting too picky. The management complained about everything. The people abuse you every day. It's your fault it's raining. If they waited twenty minutes for a bus, they yelled at you.

Frustration on the job provided a powerful push for both middle-class and working-class men, but escape was not the only motivation for those who left organized careers. Most of those who summoned the will to quit the rat race also encountered unexpected opportunities to pursue more attractive, if less secure, employment. A fortuitous chance to change direction prompted Andrew to leave a promising career in film production to pursue a riskier path as an interior designer:

I was doing very well, but I got to hate it. I couldn't stand the people, so I stopped doing well. This other thing just sort of evolved. Somebody had asked me to help him with his apartment, and somebody else asked me, and I had a business. So I don't really feel I chose to do it. I felt like it came from the outside, like winds shifted or something. The opportunity came, so I did it. It wasn't a conscious decision.

Others found new paths when old ones became blocked. Just as Chuck was growing weary of his administrative duties in a public hospital, he was unexpectedly moved into a new job that not only sparked his enthusiasm but allayed his fears about choosing a new line of work:

It took a lot for me to leave the hospital. I was afraid of the private sector. Fortunately something happened which was really a blessing in disguise. I was being phased out of one job and managed to get into the computer area. I always thought to get into computer programming, you needed a degree in computer science. But I had the opportunity to do it, and this is the field for me. It's hard to get your first break, but once you get in it, it's wide open.

The departure from stifling jobs was not always a voluntary choice, since resignations occasionally preceded or coincided with being laid off or fired. When this happened, autonomous men struggled to interpret it positively. Amid intimations that his job was in jeopardy, Hugh, a thirty-nine-year-old lower-level manager at a large private university, resigned:

I held my university job for fourteen years, but I recently resigned. I was stuck in a rut. Also, I'm trying to break into public relations and I have a lead on a pretty good job, and if I get that job, I will have made a major improvement in my career plans. So leaving would be one of the best things that ever happened to me.

Relinquishing stable jobs required taking a risk. Moonlighting helped one security-minded worker to change his outlook on his regular job. Josh, a single thirty-three-year-old, found working for a real estate agency much more exciting than his safer job as a sanitation inspector. It inspired him to start his own travel agency:

When I first took the job at the real estate agency, I tasted the freedom to make my own decisions. I had the taste of something different and saw the monotonous nine-to-five operation at the city job, where you can close your eyes and just fill the forms out. I was kind of scared to make the change. Am I going to make it? I have to go out and order the phones, order the sign. But I liked dealing with people and putting it together. I had a great time ... I got a little chancier.

A glimpse at the gratification possible in a less secure setting not only made it easier for these men to take a risk; it also lowered the value they placed on immediate economic reward. Although Andrew had no prior experience in interior decorating, he decided to forfeit the assurance of a decent income to build a business of his own. "It was no money for almost two years," he told me. "People thought it was strange, but it wasn't a hard decision."

These job and career shifts did not necessarily involve a decrease in the importance of success at work. Rather, they raised the value of autonomy relative to economic security. Above all, these men sought jobs that emphasized discretion over supervision. Like a growing number of American workers, they found that working without a boss offered an attractive alternative. Indeed, the 1980s witnessed a rise in the proportion of Americans who chose to become self-employed.[2]

Autonomy could also be found in part-time, short-term, erratic work patterns. For Ian, the freelance writer, temporary work and self-employment provided an escape from the pressures of highly structured jobs:

> All my jobs are part-time. I have no full-time job in the classic sense of the word. Right now I'm working from nine to five—but I can see the end of it. I know it's only a couple of weeks, and it will bring me a little extra money between writing jobs.

Employment in small businesses and newly emerging organizations provided another sanctuary from the control typical of large corporate and public bureaucracies. Jeremy, the computer consultant who rejected public organizations, found more opportunity in the move to a small, less established private company:

> In a larger, more structured company, can you imagine them making somebody who didn't know the computer from the front door manager of computer operations? It would never happen. That was what appealed to me. This company was in those growth stages, and you could literally define the role you want to play.

Others sought refuge in less demanding jobs that provided substantial buffers to bureaucratic control. Herman, the former air-conditioner repairman, found a public-sector job with minimal supervision and pressure to perform:

> I inspect apartments. If the landlord doesn't make repairs, the tenant complains, and they give me a case. It's nice because I'm my own boss, really. I make my own schedule. I'm out in the field. If I want to stop and have coffee four times a day, nobody's there to say I'm not supposed to. There's no pressure at all. Like today, I did one case the whole day.

As financial prospects became less predictable, these men came to value the intrinsic pleasures of work more than its financial payoff. Ian concluded that money was less important than avoiding boredom:

> It hurts on the financial end. I'm always struggling for money, but I don't really mind. I see a lot of people constantly complaining and bored all the time, and I'm never bored. . . . The things I do with writing and music, most probably if I wasn't doing that for money, I would be doing it anyway.

Indeed, some, like Herman, even chose to forgo promotions and higher pay in order to protect whatever measure of freedom they had found at work:

I could have taken a higher-paying job, but it means I would have been inside all day, and I said, "I'll take a lower-paying job and be out in the field." I'd like to make more money, but that's secondary. I love my job. When I did air-conditioning, it was a hassle to get up every day and go to work; now it's not a hassle to go to work.

These men could seek satisfaction in the intrinsic aspects of paid work or, alternatively, by maximizing their freedom from it. For Andrew, the interior designer who set up his own business, work became a source of nourishment rather than a way to accumulate wealth. When asked what the most important things in a job are, he said: "More important than money is growth and just to feel that you're nourished by your work, that your mind is connecting with it."

Others who turned toward autonomy chose to expand their freedom *from* work rather than their freedom at work. Working-class men faced fewer opportunities for intrinsically fulfilling work and were thus more likely to reduce their emotional investment in the workplace. Herman explained:

This job is like a paid vacation. That's the way I look at it. You put in your seven and a half hours a day, but you don't kill yourself. Nobody says nothing if I sit and read the paper for an hour.

After leaving a demanding job in retail sales to spend over a decade "bumming around," Alan, the real estate appraiser, stumbled into a thirty-five-hour-a-week job that demanded very little. He was thrilled to find a job that is "like semiretirement."

Whether autonomous men sought fulfillment in paid work or endeavored to minimize their exposure to work demands, they all began to place a high value on the pursuit of pleasure and leisure. Even more, they strove to dissolve the distinction between labor and leisure.[3] Ian explained:

There are people who separate their lives into two sections and call one "work," and the useful, creative things are called "leisure." But I can't do that. I felt like a zombie when I was working in bookstores. It wore me out, the routine of work. Even though I'm doing more now, it's not as tiring as the regular grind. If I had to, I probably could do it maybe for a year, but longer than that I don't think I could do it.

Avoiding preoccupation with work's economic payoff gave these men a sense of having escaped the traps that ensnared breadwinning men.

While other men performed alienated labor for the sake of an income, they were able, according to Ian, to pursue a "less fragmented" life:

> The work I do has probably made me see myself as less divided than other people are. . . . It's not a job; it's not someplace I go to work and then I go someplace else to do something else.

Refusing to pursue the dream of economic security, these men had to justify the risks they chose to take instead. After nine years as a bus driver, Bart left his job just one year short of qualifying for a pension. In doing so, he rejected the importance of economic security and advancement:

> I just said, "The hell with it." And I was married. But I figured I'd get another job the next day. They're out there; you just have to go look for them. Anyway, I was fed up and didn't care.

Uncertainty about job security and concern for personal independence unavoidably spilled over into intimate relationships. These men became wary of any personal attachments that might lead to breadwinning obligations. Some simply refrained from involvement with any one partner. Andrew, the interior designer, chose to focus on work and planned for a future of solitary travel and adventure:

> One of my fantasies would be to go to Italy and study architecture and don't work and find a funny little place and just live. That would be what I'd like to do. Nothing includes family.

Others redefined the kind of relationship they wanted. They eschewed partners who were looking for a time-consuming or long-lasting commitment. Chuck, who became openly gay, broke off a relationship with a lover who disliked his commitment to his work:

> I was putting a lot of time in on the job, and I was made to feel guilty about that, that somehow I should be spending more time with him. I was ridiculed for taking work home with me. It drove home to me that my next lover will have to understand more where I'm coming from. . . . The types of people I find interesting are people who are at least as busy as I am.

He also realized that he needed more solitude:

> In terms of free time, there are times that sharing is very important to me, but there's a period that I need to be alone, where it's quiet, staring-at-the-wall time.

This growing desire to seek autonomy and avoid economic burdens extended to having children. Edward, the disillusioned surgeon, came to fear that fatherhood would tie him more securely to the work from which he was struggling to escape:

> Unfortunately, I see the biggest drawback to having kids is that I don't know that I want to be giving up certain things in order to have them. I take the biblical approach that man was not meant to work. It was really only as a result of Original Sin that as punishment we were supposed to work. I view it that if I get to the point where I don't have to work, I've obviously reached a higher level.

Paradoxically, his profession also provided a reason for not having children:

> I may become the, quote, selfless physician where I'm not going to raise a family in order to devote myself to my career. I think that's one of the nice things about medicine, that it's socially acceptable to be not married, not have a family, and that's nice having a cover, as it were, an excuse.

Some, however, were already husbands and fathers when they changed their outlook. The unexpected shift prompted these men to pull away from their existing obligations. For Bart, the desire to quit his job superseded his sense of economic duty to his wife and two young children. Asked about what he was risking in giving up his pension, he replied:

> It didn't even occur to me. I just didn't care. I had to get away. If you're not happy with what you're doing, get the hell out. That's the way I looked at it. I'm not going to go to a job I don't like for anyone.

Indeed, the decision to leave a stifling job could also trigger divorce in an already shaky marriage. It did for Roy, a paramedic and forty-two-year-old father of one, who quit looking for secure work after years of "going nowhere" in a series of dead-end jobs:

> I got a divorce because I wouldn't try to find steady employment. I wanted to get anything that was easier for myself rather than do a certain type of job that's more beneficial for a family than for anything else.

Whether they were single and childless or had already married and fathered children, autonomous men who rejected or were unable to establish a stable work life were also inclined to reject the economic obligations of primary breadwinning. Unlike men who moved toward greater family involvement, however, they were not able or willing to establish a long-term relationship with a partner who could share the economic and social responsibilities of family life.

Instability in Intimate Relationships

Disappointment and disillusionment in intimate relationships provided another incentive to turn toward autonomy. Among those who expected to become breadwinning fathers but did not, only 27 percent were currently involved with a steady partner. More important, over 90 percent had undergone some type of significant trauma in their relationships with women. Slightly more than half had never married, even though all had expected to do so at an earlier stage in their lives. Eliot, a forty-three-year-old confirmed bachelor who is a therapist, once longed for the stability and support of marriage:

> Especially in my twenties, I saw marriage as something that would settle me down. It would give me some structure; it would help me grow into something I wanted to be, whatever that was. . . . When I look at it now, I see it as a fantasy, reclaiming the lost family. What I wanted to do was have a family to have the situation that was originally lost returned to me.

Among those who did marry, only one remained married to his first partner. The rest either divorced, separated, or became widowers. These men established a variety of living arrangements in the wake of a marital breakup. Although two eventually remarried, the others either had a series of live-in partnerships or chose to live alone. All were unprepared for the changes they experienced, changes that often involved pain, loss, and a strong sense of personal betrayal. Jeremy, the computer consultant, never recovered fully from the breakup of his marriage to his "life-long love": "We were childhood sweethearts, and I was absolutely sure I would be with that person."

Two men in this group ultimately decided that they preferred either homosexual or bisexual liaisons, even though they too had once hoped to marry and have children. Whether they perceived this change to be the discovery of once-submerged desires or the emergence of new ones, the result was the same. Like their heterosexual counterparts, their orientation changed in response to intimate experiences. Ian, who ultimately "chose" to engage in a series of relationships with both women and men, had once assumed there was little choice but to get married: "I thought by the end of college I'd be married and settled down. I didn't have an idea that there was any other alternative."

ROUTES AWAY FROM COMMITMENT

The turn away from seeking a committed partnership took a variety of forms. In particular, the process differed depending on whether a man avoided marriage completely or underwent an unexpected and usually bitter marital breakup. In either case, the result was disillusionment with marriage and rejection of breadwinning.

Those who never married, despite nearing middle age, were led away from breadwinning via one of two routes. Many bachelors seriously considered marrying during their early adult years, but all the close relationships they formed ended in disappointment and frustration. Some were discomfited to find that most of the women they met expected to have an equal voice in the relationship. Mark, an environmental-protection consultant, who "almost got married a couple of times," rejected one possible mate because she envisioned having an equal say in important marital decisions:

> I was talking about moving to Texas, and she said, "And then what am I going to do with *my* job? I don't want to go to Texas." And I had always assumed that you go where I go. So I saw trouble with that.

Confirmed bachelors did not always play the role of the rejecter, even if most preferred to interpret their choices in such a light. Many of them fared poorly in the sexual marketplace. They concluded that they lacked some quality, or set of qualities, that would attract the kind of women they wanted, that they could not attain such late-twentieth-century ideals of manhood as physical attractiveness, "manly" behavior, and the ability to earn an ample income.[4]

Worries about physical attractiveness made it difficult for some to find any sexual partners. They subverted the confidence and will needed to pursue even casual dating. Adam, a thirty-seven-year-old computer operator, used his obesity to withdraw from social life into the overprotective confines of his mother's home. Asked about his relationships with women, he said:

> I've had none. Up until last year, one girl approached me, but that didn't work out. . . . I was always heavy, so that's one of the reasons I stopped going out, and my mother preferred having me home, so being heavy and maybe not having enough self-confidence, it was easier to stay home.

A pleasing physical appearance, however, is certainly no guarantee of success in relationships. Hugh, the thirty-nine-year-old financial manager who had floundered in a series of jobs, was also unable to build a lasting bond. He blamed his interpersonal difficulties on his ineptitude at mastering superficial ideals of masculinity:

> Several years ago, I was seeing a woman, and she met a ski instructor who swept her off her feet. She said that "he makes me feel like a

woman," implying that I didn't make her feel like a woman. I'm not a macho-type person. This ski instructor was that kind of guy. He went fishing, he knew how to work with leather, he knew about sports, and all this stuff, none of which I knew about or cared about. . . . When I was younger, girls had the same complaint about me.

For others, the link between sexual attractiveness and economic success was more obvious. Andrew feared that his refusal to pursue a secure, high-paying career had prompted the end of his most recent relationship:

It just got too difficult. It sort of drifted off. I just think I didn't live up to her expectations. I think she was looking for someone with more money.

Since many bachelors had rejected working toward a career, their choices often collided with women moving in the opposite direction. Not only did they feel spurned for their lack of ambition but they also felt uncomfortable being compared to women who took their own careers more seriously. Edward felt rejected by his "be-all and end-all girlfriend," but he also felt that, like ambitious men, she was excessively focused on work over love. He preferred to interpret her rejection in less personal terms—as an inability to commit to anyone:

I loved her more than she loved me. I had truly thought about marriage, but it was also clear from the beginning that there were major problems *towards* the marriage. Her point of focus was going to be her career, and she wanted freedom where she didn't have to adapt or adjust to someone else. The major issue was her ability to be in a relationship at all. I think she's got a real fundamental inability to commit to a relationship.

These experiences help to explain why unmarried men fare poorly on indexes of health and well-being. Not only do they lack the support of a nurturing partner, but they have also lost out in a competitive "sexual marketplace."[5] Whether they felt rejected or played the part of the rejecter, the result was the same: a growing fear and wariness of exposure to loss. A series of disappointments made Edward reluctant to pursue future possibilities:

I wonder if part of my reaction is, "Here you got close, and you really tried for something, and you don't get it. How much are you going to withdraw and be protective?" With each of those other three women, it was quite clear to me that if at any point, they said, "Well, do you want to get married?" the answer clearly would have been yes. It certainly raises questions in my mind about what they want out of marriage, since it's so clear how I felt.

Others, determined to view unhappy experiences in a positive way, concluded that they had narrowly escaped being caught. After recovering from the breakup of his one serious relationship, Andrew said he felt relieved:

> After being apart for a long time, I liked her less. When you're not with someone, you get distance and you think, "I'm glad I'm still not under their influence, not being dominated; I'm glad they're not in my life anymore," and that's the way I feel. It just took me a long time to know how I feel.

Among never-married men who rejected breadwinning, some felt stifled in relationships and actively fled long-term commitments; others felt rejected and incapable of acting to overcome their fate.[6] Most agreed with Ian that an equal, mutual attraction between two people is an elusive, perhaps unattainable goal:

> All the serious relationships I can think of have been more serious on one side than the other. Usually, it's been on my side, but not always. It's been difficult. My most stable relationship, I think, is with my computer.

Over time, these experiences promoted an ambivalence about the viability of long-term commitments. Eliot, the therapist, felt confused and helpless by the continuing dissonance between what he wanted from women and what they offered him:

> When I was in my early twenties, I was looking for somebody, but nobody was available. It's understandable. I was a mess, so no woman in her right mind would want to be involved with me. I was grossly immature, unintelligent, just this entity. . . . But later on, as I developed, I got so invested in what I was doing, I don't think I was very available. They were looking, and I wasn't interested. And now, in my forties, I don't know where I am. I don't want to be a confirmed bachelor the rest of my life, but I'm scared shitless of moving in with somebody.

There are good reasons to conclude that many of these bachelors will remain so. According to recent research, never-married men over the age of forty are not likely ever to marry,[7] and the average age of these autonomous men was thirty-six. Moreover, never-married men are not the only ones who turned away from breadwinning in the wake of painful heterosexual experiences. Bitter marital breakups also pushed once-married men away from marriage, breadwinning, and parental involvement. Of course, the men who experienced some form of marital disruption (legal separation, a wife's death, or divorce) did not respond in uniform ways. While a small number (10 percent) hoped to remarry and become breadwinners, most either hoped to avoid parenthood (48 percent) or, paradoxically, to become involved fathers (43 percent).

More important, the men who had children before getting a divorce (exactly two-thirds of the divorced group) moved in two contrasting directions. Well over half (57 percent) minimized responsibility for their offspring in the aftermath of divorce, while 43 percent maintained or strengthened their parental bonds.[8] Thus the experience of marital disruption can have ambiguous and contradictory implications. (Fifteen percent of the sample had undergone some form of marital breakup, but only 5 percent involved marriages where the men had become estranged from offspring. The negative consequences of divorce are probably more widespread in the general population.) Since divorce is more likely to estrange fathers and children than to bring them closer, we need to untangle which aspects of the process of divorce allow and encourage men to recede from their children's lives.[9]

As did their counterparts who never married, divorced men who moved toward autonomy had once expected to spend their lives as breadwinners. As their marriages deteriorated in ways that they could not or would not overcome, their outlook changed. For some, the estrangement was mutual. Roy, the paramedic, married young in order to have "somebody to take care of me." As marital conflict escalated, however, independence became more attractive than being cared for:

> Probably at the beginning, we needed somebody there; but it was rocky from the beginning. We'd fight about everything. I'd want my way, and I just didn't want to share certain things. I'd go off in a corner by myself. We just sat down one day and said, "Hey, we can't keep on going like this. Either one of us is going to take out a gun and shoot each other." Both of us realized that we had no marriage.

These divorced men encountered many of the same disappointments and frustrations that greeted their never-married peers. They, too, felt constrained by women they came to see as "domineering." Often they anticipated a compliant and indulgent spouse, but discovered that their mates wanted, and sometimes demanded, equality instead. In these cases, frustrated husbands felt betrayed by unforeseen changes in their wives' lives. Alan, the real estate appraiser, expected his second wife to be more acquiescent than his first. When she decided she wanted a career, however, she no longer met his expectations of what a wife should be. He divorced for a second time, blaming the breakup on "bad influences":

I knew this girl from West Germany. We got married with no planning. We got along fine for about four years. Then she went to college—I call it getting "Americanized"—and she got into too much of a "what's-in-it-for-me?" type attitude. She got into such a career-type orientation that it was like the spectrum went 180 degrees the other way. I couldn't cope with that.

Some men became abusive in the face of such challenges, triggering an emergent independence in once-acquiescent wives. As Herman's violent behavior escalated, his wife became increasingly assertive:

I brought her out of her shell, and then she stabbed me in the back. I made her stand up, and she started arguing with me all the time.

Occasionally I hit her. She'd be arguing with me, and I'd say, "If you don't calm down, I'm going to hit you. Leave me alone for ten, minutes," and she'd keep badgering me. So she'd end up getting hit. . . . Towards the end, she'd start on me, and I just walked to the front door. I'd go out and walk away. I didn't even argue with her anymore. One day, she went shopping. She took the little girl—my little boy wouldn't go with her—and she never came back.

For others, breaking up was neither mutual nor eagerly greeted. These men felt abandoned by wives they cherished but could not understand, a process that left them feeling angry and betrayed.[10] After ten years of marriage and the birth of three children, Toby, a sanitation supervisor, discovered that his frustrated, unhappy wife had decided to leave him for another man who she said gave her more attention:

I didn't spend enough time with her. I didn't realize the time you've got to put in with her. I was just doing my own thing. She cheated on me and told me about it. I said, "All right, I understand. Because I'm away from the house, I understand how that happened." Then she hated me because of that.

Men who felt rejected also felt incapable of affecting a course of events set in motion by someone else. Much like the stereotype of the woman who molds herself in hopeless pursuit of an unattainable man, these men undertook urgent but futile efforts to retain lost loves. Toby concluded that no matter what he did, he could no longer meet his wife's changed standards:

I tried everything. I wore hairpieces. I changed the way I dressed, who I hung out with. . . . I was messed up for a long time. I saw a counselor for a long, long time.

The loss of a cherished mate was more poignant when there was no convenient target on which to place the blame. For Jeremy, the computer consultant, his "once-in-a-lifetime" partner's psychological problems halted the dream of living happily ever after:

> My feeling is that in this life, there's a number of people, not many, who are "your ideal mate." I was lucky enough to find this person, one of the first people I ever got involved with. We were each other's best friends, lovers, whatever. . . . Then she had a mental breakdown.

This loss left him with a diminished sense of his power to control his life and the lives of others:

> I always thought that I had a great deal of personal power in terms of being able to interact with people, influence them, particularly with this individual. We were so involved with each other that I thought my love, my attention, my personal energy could overcome anything. I was shocked to find that wasn't true.

Sudden death, though rare among young adults, produced an even more painful and unexpected end to one relationship. When Marty, a thirty-eight-year-old paramedic, lost his wife to a sudden stroke, it left a void he could not fill. Because her death was not perceived as a willful rejection, his lost love was easier to idealize and harder to replace:

> About a month or two before she died, Melanie said, "You don't know how much you love me." I just didn't know what it was all about. Now I do. It's a learning process. The day I die, if I was to have a vision, it would be opening the door of that apartment and seeing her standing there in her red robe and just being able to hold her. I don't ask anything out of life anymore because it's all insignificant. Some people only get blessed once in their life. If this is my only blessing, I would not trade it.

Similar experiences sent once-married men and confirmed bachelors toward more solitary goals. Like their never-married peers, some divorced and widowed men left intimate partners, while others felt spurned by them. Some were relieved to escape untenable relationships, while others experienced deep pain in the loss of a cherished bond. All nevertheless underwent unexpected change that made breadwinning less possible and less desirable. They found it difficult to recover from their loss, from their sense of having been betrayed or abandoned, and from the experience of lost possibilities. As Roy discovered, the pain of a bitter breakup may never completely dissolve—even when it ends an equally bitter marriage:

> During the early years of our marriage, there was a lot of hurt between us. If we had stayed together, the hurt would still be there, but I still feel hurt. It never heals.

CONSEQUENCES OF INSTABILITY IN RELATIONSHIPS

In some cases, rejection and loss sparked resolute reassessments of who these men wished to be. Their broken alliances tested their notions of selflessness and giving. They emerged more determined to retain a large measure of independence and self-sufficiency in any future bond, never again to "lose themselves" in a relationship. The breakup of his seven-year homosexual "marriage" left Chuck with a more autonomous but less trusting sense of self:

> I was really devastated. I looked like I was hit by a truck. I really bent over like a pretzel trying to accommodate to his way. I learned that the overriding thing was I placed far too great ego investment in the relationship, and I started recognizing the incompleteness of my own personality—that you can't have two sort of half people trying to come together and be one person. I realized that whoever the next one was going to be, whenever and if ever, was absolutely going to have to have more my interests, my orientation, stuff like that.

Painful breakups did more than alter self-images. They also increased men's skepticism about commitment. Those who felt betrayed and abandoned, especially by philandering spouses, concluded that most partners, and not simply theirs, were untrustworthy. They vowed to protect themselves by maintaining a safer distance in future relationships. Still in love with his ex-wife and recovering from a rift with a subsequent live-in lover, Toby became reluctant to trust again: "To me, girls were totally deceiving because my ex-wife was deceiving."

Discounting the ways in which their own actions provoked rejection, men who felt betrayed focused on what they saw as the unattainable standards women imposed. Alan, the property assessor whose wife took a lover and then divorced him, felt placed in a double bind: he was expected to work hard to earn a living, but also to be an attentive and involved husband:

> What went wrong was I was away too much working. That's why she had a boyfriend. Sometimes I hear from a lot of women that they want their husband to get a second job, and if he does, they complain that he's not giving enough attention at home. Physically, you can only do so much.

But if "traditional" women wanted too much attention and care, then "modern" women wanted too much independence. Mark, the environmental-protection adviser who had never married, explained how a relationship with a career-oriented woman left him with lingering suspicions about all contemporary women:

She had been divorced once, and that bothered me. How can you trust somebody who's already been divorced? She must have been totally with this other guy, too. And along with these suspicions, she wanted to do her own thing. That bothered me and reinforced some of the things I had already suspected: that women are irrational, you never know what to expect, and expect the unexpected.

Autonomous men longed for the imagined "good old days" when women were presumably more supportive, but they had little desire to take on the economic and emotional obligations that accompany the choice of a domestic partner. They came to view domestic women as needing too much support and attention and work-committed women as demanding too much say in their lives. Since both groups posed formidable, if different, demands and dangers, they turned away from commitment altogether.

As they lost faith in modern relationships, these men also lost faith in the possibility of forging permanent bonds. Some resolved to live in self-sufficient solitude. This outlook marked a departure from an earlier desire for nurturance and care. Having married for companionship and attention at twenty-one, Roy, now forty-two, sees things differently:

I didn't think about getting married; it just happened all of a sudden. I was living by myself at the time and just got tired of coming home to an empty place. You need somebody to take care of you. I just wanted to cling to somebody.

When asked why he hadn't seen anybody steadily since the divorce, he replied:

Maybe afraid. I just don't want to get involved. I don't like being changed. Even though you're on your own, you get into a steady way of doing things, and when somebody wants to change it, you're very mad.

Few avoided all relationships, but most endeavored to limit their significance and scope—either by defining sexual involvements as ephemeral or by declaring oneself ill suited for more lasting ones. Andrew, the interior designer, sought temporary relationships:

My major relationship was a negative experience. Other than that, everything has been very short-lived. So I don't go around looking for relationships because I feel it's a very difficult thing for me.

But they were not all aware of the transformation. Some, like Marty, the grieving widower, were painfully cognizant of the change:

Normally you have the wild side, then you get married and settle down. With me, it's the reverse. If sex was in the Olympics, I'd carry the American flag. But I never want to get married again. I don't want to put another person through what I went through. I never want them to experience the pain I experienced. Even now, it hurts, and it hurts bad.

Others felt they were merely acknowledging dormant but long-standing desires their marriages had forced them to suppress. Toby set about to recapture his lost youth:

> We were happy for ten years, but we just didn't get a chance to grow up. When we got divorced, I started living through the years I missed. Both of us have gone back in time. That's why none of my friends are over thirty.

In either case, autonomous men became disillusioned with love, romance, and commitment. And if women came to be seen as untrustworthy, then marriage came to be seen as a dangerous entanglement. Only 22 percent of the divorced (or widowed) men in this group had remarried (compared with 50 percent of the divorced men who became involved fathers). Among never-married men who became autonomous, only 33 percent expressed any plans to marry. They concluded that marriage, like commitment, was not viable in a world that had changed in ways they could not control.

Rancorous divorces promoted a particularly skeptical outlook on marriage. At thirty-six, Bart had been living happily with an older, fully employed woman for several years. Despite his contentment, he resisted legalizing the bond, fearing marriage would change the relationship and undermine his sense of freedom:

> She wants to get married, and I don't think I'm ready. We might as well be; we've been together long enough. It's just that word scares me because I had an unpleasant experience. . . . Not that I have any intentions of leaving her, but I'd feel tied down with that little piece of paper.

It is not surprising that bitter, rancorous divorces promoted fear of marriage. Yet never-married autonomous men also developed a skeptical view of marriage. Josh, who gave up a secure job to set up his own travel agency, had never experienced a long-term relationship, but he nevertheless began to view marriage as essentially fragile and insecure. The separation of two apparently happily married couples in his family subverted his faith that marriage offered a safe haven. He decided, "Why bother?" The best way to avoid divorce, these men concluded, was to avoid marriage. Edward explained:

> Sometimes I think some of my reticence towards just getting married has been that so many people get divorced. I'm not so proud as to say

statistics don't affect me. I don't want to get divorced, and almost rather than getting divorced, I'd rather not get married.

Instability in relationships affected men's outlook on employment as well. Moving away from interpersonal commitment created the opportunity either to avoid employment or to work harder than ever. Either way, jobs became worthwhile primarily for their own sake, not as a means to support a family.

Since working-class men without college degrees were less likely to have secured highly rewarding jobs, they were more likely to use their receding concerns about family obligations to avoid steady employment. In contrast to the achievement-oriented man so often portrayed in popular culture and psychological theory, about 80 percent of this group loosened their ties to work as their breadwinning outlook ebbed. The chance to refrain from unsatisfactory work became an important benefit of moving away from family obligations. Alan, the property assessor, thus greeted his newfound independence with a sense of relief:

> With my divorce, I felt a tremendous pressure relieved. I said, "Jesus, here I am working. I'm in my mid-thirties. It felt like only yesterday I was twenty-one." I was missing so much—like nature, going fishing, walking along the beach. So I took a couple of years off. I felt great because I was having a ball.

College-educated men, who enjoyed better opportunities, tended to respond differently. Among this largely professional group, 64 percent developed stronger ties to work as they moved away from family commitments. Not only did they have more time to devote to work, but work also became a more important source of reward and identity, a compensation for lost or undeveloped family ties. When his long-term "marriage" to another man ended, Chuck filled the ensuing space with work:

> I think as a single person, work has taken on a very large amount of importance, a large part of my life. It's a time-structuring device, and a lot of meaning comes out of it. I feel more worthwhile when I'm doing something like that.

These apparently opposite reactions have in common the wish to pursue fulfillment through individual pleasures rather than shared responsibilities.

Finally, men who moved toward autonomy became less inclined to parent. Men who were childless decided that they no longer desired or expected to become a father. Even for those who had assumed they would one day have children, the unexpected loss of an important attachment postponed those plans. Single and childless at forty, Jeremy recalled how his ex-wife's mental collapse derailed his unspoken plans for parenthood:

> In my previous marriage, I'm sure that children would have happened, but life threw me a curve ball. Right at the point where my life was starting to come together—I was financially able, and I was in a job that allowed me to think about those sort of things, and we both finished our degrees—at that turning point and shortly thereafter was when she started having problems. Otherwise, I'm sure we would have had children. But life didn't turn out that way.

The loss of a "perfect" and seemingly irreplaceable partner also foreclosed fatherhood for Marty, the widowed paramedic:

> The highest honor I can pay any woman, which I only paid Valerie, was, "I'd want you to be the mother of *my* children." To me, that's very important. I want *you* and only you to be the mother of *my* children.

Of course, women can, and increasingly do, bear children without being in a committed relationship. Single motherhood is on the rise among whites and blacks alike. White women are more likely to become single parents as the result of divorce, whereas African-American women are more likely not to marry. In any case, the proportion of households headed by a single mother has risen precipitously over the last two decades. Single mothers now head about a quarter of all families with children. Single fathers, in contrast, head slightly under 4 percent of these families.[11]

Obviously, it is harder for men to become parents alone. Fatherhood and commitment to a woman are closely linked. Men who could not forge a heterosexual relationship thus found parenthood out of reach. When Mark could not find an intimate partner, he realized:

> I never really got to the point of having children. I always assumed that you had to get married, and then kids automatically followed. That would be one and the same to me—getting married and having children. But I never established a long-lasting relationship.

Single parenthood seemed virtually impossible to never-married men. Edward lamented:

> I've thought about the concept of, "Well, you can still have your own child," but I said no, that would be a little bizarre because I don't think it's the ideal way to raise a child. I think single parenting is very hard. For me, at least, that hasn't been a viable option.

As the hope of establishing a suitable bond eroded, childless men lost enthusiasm for having children either in the short or the long run. For those who had become fathers before experiencing a breakup, the consequences were much more serious. Just as contentious divorces produced apprehension about sexual commitment, they also weakened and sometimes severed some fathers' attachments to their children. Herman, the separated housing inspector with two young children, complained:

> I see them two nights a week, but I don't take an active part. It's tough, but I really have no say whatsoever as far as the children are concerned. My wife and I do not speak except in court, and if I fought her, she'd take it out on the kids. So I don't bother. I don't like it, but ... there's nothing I can do.

Ex-wives, eager to put as much distance as possible between themselves and a painful past, also discouraged some fathers' involvement. Alan welcomed his divorce, but blamed his ex-wife for "turning his son and stepdaughter against" him in the aftermath of their separation. His meager attempts to stay in contact after they moved across the country were not reciprocated. The perception of being rebuffed, regardless of its accuracy, gave him the rationale to cease all contact:

> When the breakup first started, my son was very close and my step-daughter was close. But my wife started being manipulative, saying, "You're not related to him. He doesn't want you." She was very narrow-minded.

After the divorce, he felt:

> relieved, if it wasn't for the kids. The part that was most difficult was having her manipulate the kids against me. I'm glad the divorce happened, but the kids went through hell. And I haven't seen them in seven or eight years.

Most autonomous fathers felt that the process of divorce was beyond their control. They blamed unfair judges, a biased court system, and angry wives for the minimal contact they maintained with their children. They perceived a double standard that required them to continue to support their children, but limited their access to them. They responded by withholding their love and concern as well as their paychecks. According to Bart:

> I had nothing to say about it. The judge did all the talking; I did all the listening. They're always unfair in family court. You're wrong; she's right; and I'm going to tell you what you're going to do. They don't

want to hear your side of the story at all. I was allowed to see the kids on Sunday from ten to five, and that's it.

These perceptions fueled the belief that they—not their ex-wives or children—were the victims of forces beyond their control, not the perpetrators of irresponsible acts. Yet mounting evidence contradicts this perception. Recent research shows that courts tend to favor men's economic interests over women's and children's, and that rates of nonpayment for child support are high, with almost 70 percent of divorced mothers either receiving less than the full amount awarded by the court or being awarded no support at all.[12] These perceptions do, nevertheless, suggest an important link between divorce and men's parental involvement. Whether accurate or not, the perception of being expected to remain a good provider even while being denied access to children furnished a powerful rationale for withholding money and affection.[13]

Whatever the causes, these fathers willingly abdicated responsibility for their children. As breadwinners, they had not been involved in the daily chores of child rearing. With the loss of their wives, who had always been their children's primary caretakers, they had to choose between significantly more involvement or significantly less. They chose the latter. After his wife's departure, Herman began to refer to his daughter by using an impersonal article instead of her name:

> She went to her mother's, and that was it. She took the daughter. My son stayed with me for a week, but I didn't think it was right to separate the kids, and I didn't feel I could take care of them.

However victimized they felt, these men lacked the desire, and the confidence, to learn how to become involved parents. They did not wish to take on responsibilities they had successfully skirted in the past. Parental involvement would threaten the freedom they had taken for granted, even as married fathers. Bart neither sought nor wished custody of his two children:

> After the divorce, getting thrown out and everything, I felt like, to hell with it all. They were still my kids—I knew I had to support them— but as far as taking them home, making sure they did their homework—I wasn't ready for that.

The wish to minimize contact with an ex-spouse exacerbated the desire to avoid the responsibilities of fatherhood. An especially contentious divorce helped to curtail an already tenuous connection between fathers and their children. Bart refused to pay child support, ostensibly because it provided a benefit to his ex-wife as well:

I didn't think she was giving them the money that was coming for them. She'd be out, hiring baby-sitters, and I felt that was where the money was going rather than buying them clothes, feeding them, and stuff. She was using it for her own advantage, to go out and party. So I felt like, "No, I'm going to take care of it myself." I would tell her, "I'm not going to give you no more money. When I see the kids, I'll buy them clothes or whatever they need, and that's it." She didn't go for that. Neither did the court. I told them, "You just garnish me so I don't have to see it."

And the court did just that. Bart also avoided the few caretaking duties expected of him, using his ex-wife's perceived irresponsibility as a justification:

> I wanted to see them for a weekend, but she wouldn't go for that unless she was going away. Then it's, "Oh, do you want to watch the kids for the weekend?" So I'd say no. She could care less. So why should I? She's a thorn in my side; she's going to stick it to me as long as she can.

A contentious divorce also made autonomous men reluctant to have more children even under ostensibly better circumstances. Despite two subsequent marriages, Alan refused to have another child because the consequences appeared unpredictable and dangerous:

> It's such a hardship on any man right now, because if something goes wrong—and statistics say one out of every two marriages end in divorce—he's stuck with child support for eighteen years. It's tough. I'm living proof that the courts do not do anything. They favor whoever is more ruthless. You might be paying for the support and still not see your kids. I wouldn't want to put another kid through it.

Whether never-married or divorced, childless or with children, these men changed their outlook on family and work in response to disappointing and often painful experiences in intimate relationships. Apprehension about repeating the pain encouraged them either to turn away from commitment altogether or to view relationships as ephemeral.

Although social theory and popular belief continue to stress men's limited ability to develop deep, intimate bonds of caring, many of these men did not experience relationships in this way.[14] Like the stereotype of a woman who sacrifices herself for another, these men felt lost in relationships over which they had little control. The self-protective distancing that emerged did not represent an unchanging personality trait peculiar to men. Rather, it was an understandable, if not laudable, defensive reaction to painful experiences.

Like many women, many men who moved toward autonomy experienced conflicts between the desire for commitment and interdependence and the wish to avoid further pain or loss. While these men may appear to have responded to such developmental conflicts in peculiarly "masculine" ways, the turn away from commitment was not a consistent, unchanging aspect of their personalities. Although they ultimately came to fit this image, their choices developed in the wake of socially organized experiences that are making intimate relationships harder to sustain for some men. (The next chapter shows how different experiences pulled other men toward more lasting interpersonal commitments.)

Dissatisfying Experiences with Children

Dissatisfying experiences with children also pushed men away from family attachments. This process affected childless men as well as fathers, albeit in different ways. In both cases, encounters with the reality of parenting, whether it involved their own or other people's children, could trigger a change.

Slightly more than two-thirds of those who became autonomous after once aspiring to be a breadwinner were childless, so their sense of the burdens and joys of parenthood was secondhand. In some cases, their friends provided a negative example. As their peers became parents, these men began to wonder whether they really wished to follow a similar path. Viewed from a safe distance, fatherhood appeared more a risk than a fulfillment.

In an earlier era, when fathers could more easily escape the chores of child rearing, these men might have embraced limited parenthood. But their friends' circumstances lent weight to their growing concern that this was no longer possible: their wives could and would demand significant involvement from them. Andrew, the interior designer, began to turn away from parenthood as he watched his friends get married, have children, and become increasingly immersed in the daily tasks of rearing children. Although he had always wanted a child, in recent years he had come to the conclusion that "it's very different now. The men all participate a great deal, and the women expect it of them, and it's just not for me."

Exposure to the changed reality of parenthood also provoked doubt about the pleasures of raising children. Getting to know his nieces and nephews made Adam realize that he did not like children as much as he once imagined:

> I'd go to my sister's and see my nephews. They're not my kids, so basically I'd just watch them and go, "Yuck. I'd wring your goddamned

neck if you were my kid." But I can just say, "See you guys. I'm going home." I realized I can't stand kids.

Chuck, single and gay at thirty-five, projected his view of life onto potential offspring and used this vision to reinforce a choice that was largely out of reach anyway:

I didn't ask to be born, and I'm not particularly thrilled that it happened. I think it's a tough world to live in. I personally find I'm struggling to do it; why am I going to bring somebody into the world to struggle?

Most of those who moved away from parenthood also became reluctant to shoulder other obligations, as though having a child would mean losing the luxury of remaining young. This ambivalence grew as the years passed, even though the option to become a parent did not disappear. Edward, the physician, adopted a short-run strategy of avoidance, while keeping his long-run options open:

I guess a few years back, as some of my friends had kids, I realized I wasn't that sure I wanted them. Now my feeling is I don't necessarily want to have them. Part of me does, but . . . they have a major impact on your life and a major lifestyle change, and I think you have to really be ready to have them and understand what's entailed. I'm not.

A third of those who discovered they weren't ready for parenthood had already become parents. These divorced fathers had minimized or severed their connections to their offspring. Divorce alone surely does not explain their flagging interest in the welfare of their children, since about half of the divorced fathers in this study became very involved in their children's lives. The estranged fathers, unlike their involved counterparts, met disappointment in fatherhood even before their marriages broke apart.[15]

Most did not have children under propitious circumstances. Lax birth control often meant having fatherhood thrust upon them. Only after the birth of his three sons did Toby conclude that he had not been ready for such enormous responsibility:

It never crossed my mind to deliberately make her pregnant. It was no decision of mine. I was busy; I didn't even consider that stuff. But she got pregnant, so we just dealt with it. We were so into going to bed with one another that when she came out of the hospital, she was pregnant in a month. My two oldest guys were only ten months apart.

When fatherhood was not planned, it heightened men's sense of being trapped. Bart, the ex-bus driver who later became a dump-truck driver, not only felt forced into a loveless marriage by his girlfriend's unplanned pregnancy. He also concluded that she was using the children to restrict his behavior. He transferred his sense of anger and regret from his wife to their two children:

> She used them more than anything as a crutch just to keep me down. "You have a kid here; you have two kids." Like I don't know that? She was always throwing it up to my face about the kids this, the kids that. . . . If I had been with a better person, it would have been better. It should have never happened, but it did.

Disappointment following the birth of children was expressed in a variety of ways. In a switch on the more common desire of men to have a son, Toby wished for a daughter:

> I was very disappointed when I had all three children, because I wanted a girl all three times. I had three boys. I didn't like that. I knew they'd be exactly like me. And the oldest one is. He's such a carbon copy of me that sometimes I want to smack him because I know the things that I did wrong and he's followed my footsteps completely.

Whether or not they planned or welcomed their children's births, all of these men chafed under the demands of parenthood. They found parenting more a sacrifice than a joy, even though their wives assumed the lion's share of the child rearing. Walter, a divorced dentist, decided never again to place a child's needs so far above his own:

> When we had him, it was like we totally denied ourselves everything for the baby, and nothing really needs to be that way. If I had more children, which I don't plan to do, I'd still want to be able to maintain my life as it is now as much as I could, not just forgetting all the things that are important to me for the sake of the baby.

Pressures to provide economically for their children could overwhelm the more gratifying aspects of parenting for these men. Preoccupied with keeping food on the table, Alan, the property assessor, was not able to spend time with his son and stepdaughter before the marriage ended:

> When you're out six, seven days a week, it's tough. Back then, I was so pressured working that I never spent the time with them. I was happy, but again, I didn't appreciate it like I could have. But now it's out of the question.

Dissatisfying experiences with children held important consequences for both childless men and divorced fathers, but the consequences were surely gravest for the children who lost their fathers to divorce. These autonomous fathers became reluctant to invest time, energy, or money in rearing their children and expressed their emotional avoidance through physical avoidance. Bart's contact with his children had almost ceased by the time they reached puberty:

> I used to see them every Sunday, but they were only babies. One was four; one was a year. I'd be at my sister's for dinner, stuff like that. Now I haven't seen them—actually been with them—in about six months. Maybe a couple of hours here, an hour there, but nothing where they stayed for the day or anything.

Financial support also declined as these fathers lost their concern for being a good provider. With the decline of emotional involvement, they strove to substitute sporadic economic contributions for the fixed financial obligations of breadwinning. Though securely employed, Toby clung tightly to control of his own earnings, dispensing it to his children if and when he chose:

> I got away cheap. I didn't pay much alimony or support, but we were friends. When she gets in a money game, she calls and asks me for money. Sometimes I give it; sometimes I don't.

As the distance grew, the children developed defensive postures toward their wayward fathers, including reactions of hostility and indifference. Alan found that his son and stepdaughter spurned his infrequent, halfhearted overtures:

> They turned hostile, sent the money back, tearing it up. So I figured, "If that's the way they want it to be. . . ." I could have forced the issue, but who was going to suffer? I figured, "They'll come back," but it never materialized.

Estranged fathers adjusted to these lost parenting possibilities. Roy accepted his loss with regret:

> As far as participation with my daughter, I did very little. Once in a while, she would say something to me about, "My mother did this, my mother did that." You could see she knew I wasn't there. Now I suffer because I should have participated more. I can look back and think, "You missed all this—your child, your precious years."

More commonly, they resigned themselves, deciding that their estrangement was inevitable and preferable to the alternatives. Alan responded philosophically:

> Now that I'm here, I'll make the best of it. That's the way life is. You can feel bad, but then it's not the end of the world. You have to remember that things go on.

Only one of these autonomous fathers ceased all contact with his children, however. Most developed an attenuated relationship in which they simply felt less responsible. While remaining in restricted contact, Herman, the housing inspector, acknowledged that he was enjoying his release from parental responsibility:

> I would like to be more involved in their lives, but also sometimes I would *not* like to be involved. I'm really happy that they come here, but I don't have to be worried. If I want to go out Friday night, I can go out. I really don't have the responsibilities that I should.

Divorce allowed autonomous fathers to develop a more discretionary form of parenting. Having never enjoyed or participated much in the daily labor of child rearing, they began to emphasize the fun aspects of parenting. Toby replaced the self-image of father with that of sidekick to his sons:

> They were kids—five, six years old—when I was divorced. I never did fatherly things with them. I'd get involved with them only when it's fun for me. We'd go out on dune buggies and motorcycles. I let my oldest son hang out in bars with my friends.

Most divorced fathers who became estranged from their offspring did not plan to have more children (86 percent). They either did not remarry or married women who did not expect them to have children. The growing desire to turn away from parenthood also made it easier to get out of deteriorating marriages. Herman admitted:

> After the kids were born, things really started to go downhill. The last three years, I realized it wasn't going to work, and I was just waiting for the time. It was a hostile atmosphere. We were fighting continuously, and it wasn't healthy for the kids.

The movement away from fatherhood offered increased freedom from dissatisfying work as well. The breakup of Herman's marriage allowed him to choose a less demanding job:

> I stayed with the air-conditioning work because I had kids. I was more tied when I had the kids. Now, because of the separation, I wouldn't see changing jobs as being a problem. Financially, it's still tough, but I really don't take an active part in supporting the kids anyway.

And Harry, a social service worker, realized that having no children allowed him to focus on doing work he found enjoyable regardless of how well it paid:

I've been able to sort of play with my career and really just have a lot
of fun without having that responsibility. If I had a child, I probably
would have had to make other choices because the field I'm in doesn't
pay a terrific amount of money, and with children, you have expenses
and college and stuff like that. Children require a lot more future planning than I have to do with my current situation.

Conclusion

Like those who moved toward primary breadwinning, those who moved
away from family attachments were tested in unanticipated ways. A
comparison with the stable breadwinners highlights the forces that propelled those who abandoned breadwinning in a different direction. The
latter were more likely to encounter both unexpected roadblocks to becoming breadwinners and unexpected opportunities to escape its obligations (see appendix, table 9).

Whereas all the stable breadwinners remained satisfied with a stable
job, occupation, or employer over the course of their careers, 59 percent
of autonomous men felt stifled and frustrated in secure, but uninspiring
jobs. These men changed jobs, occupations, and professions in search of
either freedom from work or freedom at work. They are part of a growing trend among American men, who are not only seeking self-employment in greater numbers but also switching careers more frequently.[16]

A similar history of instability in intimate relationships distinguishes
autonomous men from stable breadwinners. Among those who married,
all the stable breadwinners remained married to their original partners,
but only one of those who moved away from parenthood remained in his
first marriage. Ninety percent of the ever-married men in the autonomous group underwent some form of unexpected breakup.

These stark differences in intimate experiences also hold among the
never-married. Among those few who continued to plan for breadwinning although they hadn't yet married, all reported satisfying past experiences and optimism that the right woman would soon appear. In contrast, 92 percent of the never-married men who became autonomous encountered unexpected difficulty and disappointment in their relationships with women—most of these men had never enjoyed a satisfying,
long-term heterosexual relationship. They came to feel destined to remain single.

Finally, the two groups responded differently to encounters with children, fatherhood, and domesticity. Whether or not they had become fathers, none of those who maintained a breadwinning orientation had had

disillusioning experiences with children. But 40 percent of autonomous men who were childless and 86 percent of autonomous fathers found their encounters with children to be more disappointing than fulfilling.

Men who moved away from parenthood were thus considerably more likely to experience instability in employment, loss and rejection in intimate relationships, and disenchantment with their own or other people's children. They responded by turning away from family life, seeking personal happiness in more solitary and independent pursuits. They greeted this change with varying mixtures of disappointment and relief. But the movement away from breadwinning was not a simple result of personal preferences. Indeed, some felt a persistent gap between their desires and their choices. Josh, the travel agent, remained torn between what he had escaped and what he was missing:

> My preference is to be married and have a family. But just look around and see how happy my friends are. The chances of happiness are about fifty-fifty, I guess.

The move away from family life encouraged the belief that a worse alternative had been avoided, but it did not necessarily produce a conviction that the best alternative had been found. This left most still searching. Toby mused:

> I know what the worse is like, but I don't know if I'm happy. I don't know what I want to make me happy. I keep trying to find out those things, but it all comes down to me getting bored. When I get bored, I go on to something else, and I get bored with everything.

The focus on personal freedom also promoted the perception that passive drifting rather than active choice accounted for life's outcomes. Adopting a fatalistic outlook made it easier for these men to adjust to the consequences of their actions. Bart did not know whether to hold himself or fate responsible for his estranged relations with his son and daughter:

> It could have been a lot different, but I guess I didn't give it a chance. I thought, "I'm going to do what I've got to do for myself. When I'm happy, I'll make them happy." It just wasn't meant to be, that's all.

Those who eschewed family commitments fit the models of masculinity that stress a wariness of intimate attachments, a concern for self-fulfillment over caretaking, and a strong sense of a separate self. It is thus tempting to attribute both these men's move away from personal commitments and their wish to protect patriarchal interests against the putative rights of women and children to enduring, unalterable psychological proclivities.[17]

Yet we should not overlook the real, if often unexamined, constraints these men faced. While their growing pursuit of autonomy may appear to reflect an unchanging emotional stance, they developed such orientations in response to unexpected losses and foreclosed possibilities. In any case, their experiences do not fit the model of aggressive, achievement-oriented, forward-looking men. Their own accounts reveal a sense of feeling acted upon by uncontrollable social forces. These subjective accounts, of course, reflect only partial, one-sided truths. They nevertheless make clear that visions of masculinity that stress men's active pursuit of calculated ends provide an incomplete and misleading picture.

The men who turned away from parenthood chose one alternative to primary breadwinning. The lives of those who chose greater rather than less family involvement provide a more compelling challenge to the prevailing view that men as a group resist forming close emotional attachments or that they share a common resolve to protect male advantages at any cost.

6

TURNING TOWARD FAMILY INVOLVEMENT

For the first years of our daughter's life, I was always home, always play-ing games, giving her a bath and, during infancy, getting up in the mid-dle of the night and giving her a bottle. We were always very close. She's called me "Mommy" and called her mother "Daddy."
                                              —Warren, a thirty-seven-year-old assistant engineer

Some have contributed to the major changes in the lives of American men by becoming more involved in family life than previous genera-tions of men have been. These men have acknowledged a deep emo-tional attachment to their children and, even more significant, have as-sumed a considerable share of their care. Rare is the man who has taken on equal responsibility for domestic life, but a growing group of men are turning toward family involvement with an enthusiasm hardly seen before.

Housework remains the last frontier that men want to settle, and their resistance here gives credence to what is often called a "stalled revolution."[1] While men's share of domestic work remains on average below that of either employed or nonemployed women, it has risen. This rise is particularly evident in dual-earner households, where a slight increase in men's participation, combined with a larger decrease in women's, has diminished (though far from eradicated) the domestic gender gap.[2] By their own accounts, women report that their husbands make greater contributions to child care than to looking after the home.[3]

But a small group of men has embraced the work of parenthood as perhaps never before. About a third of the men who were interviewed had developed, or planned to develop, significant involvement as a father.[4] While 75 percent of this group were either married or in a committed relationship with a woman, the rest were either divorced, separated, or had never married. About 15 percent were divorced fathers who remained intimately involved in their children's lives after the breakup. In contrast with the estranged fathers, who minimized contact with their offspring after divorce, over 70 percent of these divorced fathers retained either joint or sole residential custody of their children.

Given the social obstacles and disincentives to involved fatherhood, what propelled these men to become involved in caring for children while their peers strove to avoid it? Since the culture of their childhood stressed the virtues of breadwinning and the pleasures of bachelorhood, it is hardly surprising that these men did not imagine, much less aspire to, a nurturant vision of manhood. Like the other men we have met, most expected either to become primary breadwinners or to remain single and childless. Even the few who did hope to share economic duties with a woman did not expect to share child care.

Larry, a limousine driver and father of a young daughter, used to think of fathers as breadwinners—necessary but aloof. He was pleased to have become a major participant in rearing his daughter:

> I would much rather spend time doing the nurturing part that Mother always did. Now Daddy does it too. The whole world is turned upside down.

Lou, a sanitation worker, traded a life of freedom and wild times for a new, "real" identity:

> I thought I was going to be a wild and crazy guy for the rest of my life. I never thought about getting married. But the real me is what's been happening from being married on, not beforehand. Being responsible, getting married, having a child, bringing up a family, becoming responsible for our daughter. This is the real me.

Whether their early outlooks stressed breadwinning or rebellion, these men were pushed by personal experiences at work and at home toward the decision to share the burdens and joys of child rearing. Unlike their breadwinning and autonomous peers, giving up some degree of privilege for more involvement in family life provided them with rewards sufficient to offset their losses. Their experiences offer vital clues about what would promote greater parental involvement among other men.

The Search for Meaning Within and Beyond
the Workplace

Like their autonomous counterparts, involved fathers chose either intrinsically satisfying or less demanding work, even at the expense of lower
pay and prestige. They also chose employment that made it easier to balance family commitments with workplace obligations. Unlike the autonomous men, however, those who became involved fathers did not opt
in large numbers for unstable, insecure jobs. While about 31 percent ultimately chose autonomy at work over job security, the remaining 69 percent settled on secure careers. But their focus was on either a job's enjoyment or its lower demands rather than on the security and pre-
dictability it provided.

Some had become disillusioned with fast-track careers, which appeared to offer many extrinsic rewards but few intrinsic ones. Others
opted at the outset for intrinsically appealing but nontraditional jobs that
didn't necessarily pay well. Still others chose stable jobs that appeared
promising, but found their mobility blocked and became disappointed at
work. Those with college degrees had the luxury of searching for work
satisfaction, while those without them were more likely to become enmeshed in jobs that disappointed. Both middle-class men who chose job
satisfaction over "fast-track" careers and working-class men who met
blocked avenues at work were prompted to turn toward parental involvement.

GETTING OFF THE FAST TRACK: THE MIDDLE-CLASS PATH

Among college graduates who became oriented toward family involvement, 58 percent ultimately chose careers that stressed intrinsic job
characteristics, such as service to society and personal satisfaction, over
extrinsic rewards, such as money and prestige. An additional 23 percent
turned away from demanding, high-pressure careers in search of a looser
commitment to work. In both instances, these men became disillusioned
with traditional male professions and attracted to less lucrative but more
personally satisfying lines of work.

Most found that the traditional, profit-oriented professions, whatever
their advantages, provided a poor fit for their particular talents. This
happened to Rick, a high school teacher who had once considered a
legal career:

> I thought I'd be a lawyer. I knew a number of lawyers and was ap-
> pointed to be a page in the state assembly. I got a pretty good under-

standing of what law was like. I found it not to be my cup of tea at all. Most of that work was really boring. I didn't like that type of thinking. I was always looking for what should be or what could be, rather than what is. I saw that law was not going to be interesting for me. Nor was I likely to be very talented at it. So I just very rationally said, "Forget that."

A few months in business school convinced Craig, an administrator for a dance school, that he was not suited to a business career:

I went off to business school. I didn't have anything better to do and figured it would open a few doors. But it did not appeal. It was something that I found terribly uninteresting.

Those who rejected fast-track careers while still in school were able to bypass a long detour down an unsatisfying road. For others, it took considerable effort to disavow their chosen careers. Brad, a computer programmer, spent years preparing to take over his father's successful small business:

I felt my dad had put me through college and maybe I owed him. I felt I had an obligation to see what the business was like. So I went to insurance school, got my broker's license, and was an insurance broker for three years.

Eventually he realized that making money and pleasing his father were not adequate substitutes for engaging in work he enjoyed:

It was a gradual disenchantment. I'm not a good salesman, and the companies are always making demands on you. I thought, "I just can't do this for the rest of my life." It wasn't an easy decision to leave—I didn't know what I would do—but once I decided, there was nothing my father could do. He tried to get me to stay, offered me higher pay and things like that, but at that point it was really irrelevant.

Rick and Craig rejected traditional careers, even in the face of parental disapproval and the forfeiture of economic security, because they simply didn't like the work. Others veered away from the fast track because they refused to make the moral and lifestyle compromises many high-powered careers demand. For Neil, "Politics has been my consuming passion since I've been a young kid. I thought I'd be in the House of Representatives by the time I was thirty. No joke." But he decided to leave work as a community developer and return to school because

there were all these hot-shot guys who'd lost track of the fact that they were working on projects to help people. And any of the career paths in a place like that are purely political, which means if you want to get an upper management job, you'd better know somebody and kiss a lot of ass, and that didn't really appeal to me. . . . I just realized that for me to keep my principles intact, and to be happy with it, there was no way I could do politics the way I had always envisioned.

Clarence, a freelance consultant and career counselor, opted out of a promising corporate career because moving up the ladder required too many personal sacrifices:

The offers from the pharmaceutical company weren't even tempting, because the requirements of the work didn't appeal to me, nor did the location. It became apparent that they wanted to keep me in the organization and move me up the ladder, but not the ladder that I wanted to move up. So I just turned it down.

At forty-two, Roger, a businessman and divorced, custodial father of two, realized that his employer would never recognize or repay his sacrifices. He decided to take advantage of an early retirement plan designed for much older employees:

For years, I put in astronomical hours. I was leaving the house at seven and getting home at nine or later. I worked my butt off, and I did a damn good job. But there's only so far you can go in a corporation, and I reached that level and realized I can't go past it. I realized I paid too high a price for what I got in return. What I got cannot get me back the time with the kids. . . . So, give me my money and good-bye.

Ernie, a physical therapist, resigned from a managerial position in a large private firm when he discovered his job was damaging his family relationships:

I was working from six-thirty in the morning to seven at night without breaks. I wasn't eating. I was irritable. I couldn't deal with anybody. I was fighting with my wife all the time. We were breaking apart. I wasn't communicating anymore. The job took control of me. I was possessed. I didn't feel patient with my daughter anymore. It was taking a big toll on me, and I didn't like it at all. I decided it wasn't worth it and the only way to stop it was to leave.

Frank was also a self-confessed workaholic, and he nearly sacrificed his marriage for it. To win his wife back, he left a promising career in government to become what he considered "a garden-variety vice president" at a private bank:

I had put myself into a routine that had me at the office at seven every morning and not leaving until seven-thirty or eight in the evening. And I invariably worked at least twelve hours on either Saturday or Sunday, and sometimes both days. I was pleased with my success, but it was never enough from my point of view.

My wife started pointing out to me that I was completely neglecting our personal life. She was absolutely right, but I disputed her at the time and I didn't change my ways. Then one morning she announced that when I got home that evening I wasn't going to find her there.

After remaining alone and preoccupied for a few days, he decided the only way to get his wife back was to resign his job. Although joining management at a bank hardly seems a nontraditional choice or a step toward an undemanding job, it represented a considerable decline in the time and ambition devoted to work for a man who once expected to occupy a powerful government position.

Most of these men found less traditional work more satisfying for various reasons. Some, like Craig, the dance-school administrator, reaped pure pleasure and inspiration from their work:

I had done some dancing in college and enjoyed it tremendously. While I was banging away on some God-awful paper for business school, the woman I was going out with said, "Hey, let's go see a dance concert." So we did, and the world went upside down, and I started talking to people who performed. And I just sort of began from there. Within about two months, I was rehearsing with people.

Similarly, trying to avoid the draft during the Vietnam War provided a fortuitous opportunity for Rick to discover that he loved working with children:

When they took away graduate deferments, I decided, "Well, that gives me a choice of either going to Canada or becoming a teacher." ... I was absolutely the worst-equipped teacher in the world. But I enjoyed the little kids.

Carlos went to a volunteer agency to learn whether he wanted to go into service work. The volunteer work turned out to be more fulfilling than his paid job. He decided to become a social worker. The choices these men made usually involved sacrifices in income and status. Like Carlos, they consciously and willingly chose job satisfaction over money and power:

I knew the field I was going into was not a money maker. You're providing a service, and many of the people you're going to be dealing with are medium- to low-income and have financial limitations. ... But I didn't think making a lot of money, if I was unhappy eight hours a day, was going to help me. I thought it would be more important to have something that I enjoy doing.

The turn away from traditional careers tended to involve rejecting high-pressured jobs in favor of less demanding ones. Some even began to fear they might be offered higher-level jobs in their new situations. After resigning from his job, Ernie "noticed on job interviews that I was even scared of being offered a job. I didn't know if I could do it." He eventually opted for a "safer" one that did not threaten to undermine his self-confidence: "I knew I'd be protected there. I felt secure I could handle it."

In getting off the fast track, involved fathers often made choices that are understandable reactions to genuine conflicts and dilemmas in the nature of paid work. If made by women, they might have been interpreted as "fear of success" or an underdeveloped "need to achieve." These men show that ambivalence about success is not confined to one gender. No matter who experiences it, such ambivalence is really a concern over the high costs that are often attached to success in modern, profit-oriented organizations.[5] Unfortunately, men and women often have to choose between climbing an occupational ladder and seeking a more balanced, morally informed, or satisfying life. By choosing a slower track, these men opted for a personal definition of success rather than one based on economic and social advancement. Concluding that climbing the corporate ladder poses dilemmas not just for mothers, they refused to place work success above all else.[6]

HITTING A DEAD END: THE WORKING-CLASS PATH

A sense of having options, even if they involved trade-offs, made it easier for college-educated men to absorb the economic and social sacrifices their choices entailed. Only 19 percent of this group felt blocked in their careers or expressed disappointment with the occupational paths they ultimately traveled. Men without college degrees, however, were more likely to encounter roadblocks at the workplace that they could not overcome or escape. Thus, 82 percent of those in working-class jobs who moved toward involved fatherhood experienced downward mobility, blocked mobility, or general disappointment at the workplace.

Some hit this dead end when they tried to establish economic independence through self-employment. Dwight, now a computer technician, had built up his own real estate company that then went bankrupt:

> I lost an empire. I always prided myself that very few African-Americans of my age were able to accomplish so much in such a short time, and I had planned to retire by the time I hit thirty-five. I had done a projection on how much money would be coming in. The bankruptcy almost destroyed me, but I learned to be a little bit more cautious in my aspirations.

Others met bureaucratic roadblocks that prevented them from beginning careers they had planned. After a long apprenticeship to become a harbor pilot and "follow in my grandfather's footsteps," Larry found the entry door shut tight by an inscrutable licensing board:

> I worked for seven and a half years at minimum wage, horrible hours. They promised me that I would be a harbor pilot. In the end, they said, "We won't recommend you." After this much time, they told me I didn't meet their criteria. No really hard-core reasons. . . . It was devastating. I felt victimized, ripped off, like I was cheap labor for these swine. I was in shock for months, totally stunned, got very depressed. I'm still very bitter about it.

For Carl, a utilities worker, the declining power of the unions in an occupation buffeted by technological change brought a layoff that ended his lucrative, if uninspiring, career:

> It was a union job, the typographical union. The money was great. I was making a bundle. Financially, the future looked bright. It was eleven years, but to me it was a lifetime.

Todd attributed his inability to realize his dream career to the stigma of being a Vietnam veteran:

> I've always wanted to be a character actor. But after Vietnam, I couldn't find anything. I was a bartender, a mail carrier. I couldn't get anything going, no matter how hard I tried. The guy at the employment agency said I should take Vietnam off my record 'cause nobody would hire me if they knew I had been there. After I had gone over there against my own beliefs, to do the right thing, everybody held it against me.

Difficulty entering or staying in a promising career typically coincided with the choice to "settle" for something else. Bankruptcy sent Dwight reluctantly searching for "survival" instead of fulfillment:

> I was out of work, and I drove a cab, and then I was able to get a regular job. My title is "computer associate," which is a higher title than I started with, but even this is not that great. I kind of figure there has to be more to life than what I'm doing.

Like Larry, these men's aspirations were thwarted:

> I was taught by experts to dock ships, and now I'm a deck hand on a sludge tanker. It's not a very glamorous job, probably one of the easiest jobs in the harbor. I'm working for other people, not using what I was taught. This is definitely a major step down.

All of these men struggled to accept the disparity between their ambitions and their attainments. While some were unable to find or keep desirable jobs, others became disillusioned when they met obstacles to career advancement. The politics of the workplace created one such roadblock.Wesley hoped being a paramedic would combine his desire to help others with his love of medicine. After promises of a promotion were repeatedly broken, however, he lost interest in his career:

> In the beginning, I had hoped for a lot more. They promised me the supervisory position. They had me on the top of the list for promotion. I was counting on it. I was promised it and promised it . . . but it was all political, and I would not kiss anybody's ass. So they said no. It made me sick. If I knew then what I know now, things might have been a lot different.

Estrangement also replaced high expectations when a lack of credentials prevented upward movement. Despite experience, drive, and talent, Keith, a traffic engineer, found himself repeatedly training his new bosses:

> I thought I had a future. I thought I would keep on being able to get bigger and better jobs. But four or five years ago, I started realizing that they were just hiring from the outside. I have as much experience as these other people, but I only have a high school education, and they keep getting put in charge of me. All I know is, I've trained people, and three months later they're my boss. After that happens three or four times, you get down on the job. It's getting to the point where I really don't want to go to work anymore.

Bureaucratic rules that reward seniority over merit also provided a source of blocked mobility. Hank, a nurse's aide, discovered a special joy and skill in helping patients. When superiors failed to recognize and reward his talent and dedication, he felt victimized:

> I worked myself up to the unit coordinator. I was a therapist, supervising other therapists because I was that good. I was Employee of the Year. We did tremendous things. . . .
>
> Then things started going down the drain. . . . I waited three years for a promotion. Finally, they said the promotions were available, but somebody had more seniority than me even though they were not as productive, not doing what I was doing. When I looked around, I saw people who had been there for years. I said, "Thank you very much, good-bye."

Most of these men had chosen work they expected to find fulfilling, but being stuck in a low rung produced growing alienation from the work itself. Keith found it difficult to distinguish the cause of his anger: "I don't know if I really don't like my work as such, or it's just that I think I'm in such a lousy position that I don't like it because of that."

Unlike their middle-class peers, who felt freer to leave dissatisfying jobs, men who lacked college degrees felt stuck in whatever occupation they had chosen. Harvey, an off-track-betting clerk, decided it was "too late" to leave by the time he realized he had hit a dead end:

> I had expectations for the job, that it was going to lead somewhere, and I got sold a bill of goods. I trained two people that are managers today, and I'm still just a clerk. They said, "You'll be manager. Don't worry, your chance is coming." They kept lying, lying. Now, there's no need for managers. There's too many already.

Despite their discontent, then, these men became captives of job security, pensions, and health plans. As Lloyd, a sewage worker, told me: "You can't help but not be satisfied. But where could I go? I'd love to do something else, but how can I turn away that kind of money?" Trapped by the accoutrements of disappointing jobs, they traded career aspirations for a paycheck and an attitude of "putting in my time." Resignation replaced an earlier sense of mission and enthusiasm. Wesley began to feel overworked and unappreciated:

> For so many years, there's no thanks. I have my check every pay period, but it would have been nice to be thanked. I'm on this job fifteen years, and the only thing that's really keeping me on the job is I have tenure, so I don't want to give up my pension, which is only a few years away.

Unsuccessful attempts to enter or stay in preferred occupations forced some to settle for less. Bureaucratic politics, rigid seniority systems, and a lack of educational credentials dashed the hopes of others. Whatever the route, hitting a dead end at work undermined an earlier belief that merit and hard work would be recognized and rewarded, which in turn engendered declining aspirations and rising estrangement from paid work.

CONSEQUENCES FOR MIDDLE-CLASS AND WORKING-CLASS MEN

Hitting a dead end required accepting, with varying degrees of equanimity, limits imposed from without. Deciding to leave the fast track, in contrast, was a voluntary choice. Both paths held similar consequences, largely unintended, for men's work commitment, economic status, self-image, and family involvement.

The most obvious consequences involved changes at work. These men became less willing, for example, to let work infringe on personal and family pursuits. Frank, the "ex-workaholic" who switched jobs to save his marriage, carved out the necessary space and time to devote to his wife and the child they decided to have:

My work habits changed immediately, which is exactly what I expected would happen. And I've never really gone back to my old habits of working all the time. I still work a full day in the office, but I come home to relieve the baby-sitter, and I hardly ever work on weekends, and I don't work at home.

For many, this change meant redefining a career as a job. Dwight, the computer technician, explained:

I started out wanting a decent career, something you can look forward to. I used to have the drive and concept that working on a job, I would try to do my best. Now, I could care less. I come in, do what I have to do, keep it to a minimum, and just look at it as strictly a job.

Work continued to mean more to those who chose to veer off a fast track than to those who met a dead end. Like Roger, these men resisted oppressive work demands in favor of seeking a more balanced life:

I don't mind time and dedication in reasonable amounts, but I've paid my dues. I don't want to work twenty-three hours a day anymore. No more where the company is your life. The company is not my life. The company is a tool for me to use as opposed to the other way around, and if it's not going to be that way, then I won't be there.

Those who encountered blocked mobility had to swallow, with some bitterness, the truncated economic prospects that accompanied thwarted aspirations. Larry mourned the economic implications of his doomed apprenticeship as a harbor pilot: "I should be making ninety grand a year, and I'm making thirty grand a year, and it makes me very bitter all over again."

Those who abandoned the fast track concluded that the money they *could* make was much less important than it had once seemed. Juan, a businessman, left the corporate world because of "cutthroat" competition and dubious moral codes. He had to reassess the importance of money:

Money, for me, is becoming less important. I don't have what I want, but it's less important because I'm beginning to realize that money cannot get you everything.

In both instances, economic sacrifices promoted the search for other sources of satisfaction at work. Russell, a legal aid lawyer, said he hasn't been "guided by maximizing my income." Wesley, the paramedic whose promised promotion never arrived, agreed:

You could be making a million dollars cutting diamonds and not be happy with that pressure. I wouldn't do that type of work. A good job is something that you could look forward to going to work to and coming home from. My own standard of success is having enough money to be happy, but also being happy with what you're doing to get that money.

Getting off the fast track or encountering blocked mobility also reduced the wish for promotions. At times, it fostered an active resistance to moving ahead. For those who rejected traditional professional careers, promotions could appear to threaten job satisfaction. Especially when the work involved delivering a service or working with people, advancement would remove them from the aspects of work they found most meaningful. Carlos, the social worker, discovered:

There's kind of catch-22 where people like to utilize my experiences and bump me up. It's enjoyable, but it's frustrating because the higher you get, the more removed you are from the people that you're serving.

He concluded that these drawbacks outweighed the economic and social benefits:

I don't think I'm goal-oriented towards advancement. It always seems like I'm going in reverse—because I started at a top position running a program, and I've always wanted to get back to do work with people. If I found a job that met my needs perfectly and gave me enough financial backing that I met my other responsibilities, I would be content staying there.

Those who faced blocked or downward mobility also decided that advancement was not worth the price, but they reached this conclusion by a different path. Their disappointment encouraged psychological withdrawal from work. Most reduced the time and effort they devoted to the job; some even declined eventual, if small, promotions. Wesley, the disillusioned paramedic, chose an easier life when years of blocked mobility dampened his enthusiasm for a marginal promotion:

I can still go to supervisor if I want, but nowadays I feel that the higher salary doesn't pay for all the responsibility you have to take. It doesn't bother me now because I enjoy what I'm doing. I work ten minutes away from the house, and it's a lot easier.

These men decided that they did not want what they could not have, a process employed women often undergo when they hit a "glass ceiling" at the office.[7] They also sensed a contradiction between what it takes to get ahead and what it takes to be a caring, morally responsible person. In a world where moving up can mean stepping on others, they felt penalized by their concern for people. Gary, a custodian, quit a promising factory job when he refused to "rat on" the men he supervised. He took pride in defending workers over company profits, but remained angry about the opportunities denied him:

The powers that be want to sacrifice anybody to stay in power. All they care about is how much money they get and how good they look. I've had opportunities to make it, but I can't do that. I'm not totally ruthless, but I'm a little bit tired of breaking my ass trying to do a job, and no one gives a shit. That's my problem; I have very high values and very low esteem.

Their refusal to follow what they considered morally ambiguous standards of behavior undermined the drive to succeed, which led some to doubt their competence or ability. Ernie, the physical therapist, worried about possessing some essential character flaw, but he could not overcome a visceral distaste for the impersonal approach required by the profit-oriented organizations he had once worked for:

Power and control—I'm not that kind of person, although sometimes I wish I were. That's why I don't think I could survive in the business world—because when I had to fire somebody or lay someone off, I got sick to my stomach. I couldn't stand it. I wanted to quit the job before I did that.

Because these men did not place workplace success above all else, they were led to search for other definitions of success and other sources of self-esteem. A deeper involvement in family life helped them move away from traditional notions of primary breadwinning toward a new definition of manhood.[8]

Following such a path forced these men to struggle with the prevailing definition of manly success, which relies heavily on the size of one's paycheck and the social status of one's job. At the extreme, some feared that they were failures in the eyes of others. Patrick, a lifeguard and oc-

154

casional ambulance driver, dreaded explaining his fate to his ex-class-mates at an upcoming high school reunion:

> There's a class reunion coming. When I went to high school, I was doing this job, and now, twenty years later, some people are going to say, "Why? How? What are you doing being a lifeguard at thirty-eight years old?" It's not that I always wanted to do this. It just fell in line with what I was good at.

While most did not judge themselves so harshly, a sense of lost possibilities lingered for many. Lloyd, the sewage worker, lamented his wasted carpentry talents in terms reminiscent of Marx's notion of the alienation of labor:

> At the end of it, you look back at your life and say what a waste. You could have done something, and you never did anything. I would have satisfied myself more making something, building something. I don't do that; I just continually fix things that are broken. I'm a little gear in a big machine. I'm not dying, but always in the back of my mind, I'm saying, "I could have done better. I could have had a better life."

The concern about underachievement falls more heavily on men consigned to dead-end working-class jobs, but some college graduates who eschewed high-powered careers also felt some disapproval and doubt.[9] Even though these men were quite successful compared to most other workers, they made comparisons with "what might have been." Frank, the banker who veered from a government career, surrendered the fantasy of omnipotence when he gave up his political ambitions:

> I have become convinced as a result of working that there are definitely limits to what I can accomplish; there are limits to my talents and creativity. And I used to believe just the opposite of all of those things. . . . Having made that realization, my expectations must be tempered. I can look back on where I've gotten so far, and say, "Well, that's relatively good," but I don't think I'm going to be able to carry myself a great deal farther.

These men could have focused on those with fewer financial resources and lower social status, but their legacy of high aspirations led them to compare themselves with the more successful instead. To temper these misgivings, they searched for other sources of self-respect, other standards for judging their own and others' self-worth.[10] Brad, the ex-insurance salesman who became a computer programmer, repudiated money as the measure of success when he turned away from his father's lucrative business:

It's strange, because there were people who would not consider my modest income as being successful, but I'd say by my own standards I've become successful.

Rick, the teacher who veered away from a career in law, blamed citizens and politics for failing to confer appropriate honor—and sufficient income—on his profession:

The newspapers love to say that teachers have no prestige, and they probably don't in the general public. But I'm not bothered by that at all. I feel I have great prestige. What I don't have, of course, is money, and that I wish I had more of, and I wish that teaching on any level paid more.

Despite his frustration over pay, he felt comparatively fortunate when he listened to the complaints of friends who made plenty of money but hated their jobs:

I have maybe seven or eight friends who are lawyers who were all teachers at one time. All but one are making a decent amount of money, but they don't like it, and in fact are somewhat bitter about being railroaded into a job that they don't find interesting. So I don't have that problem. I probably have more problems balancing my checkbook than they do, but not getting up and going to work every morning.

To affirm their personal worth, all these men chose to focus on noneconomic criteria. Personal character, morality, and the love of others superseded money and social acclaim. Howard, a counselor, argued that honesty, not money, was the ultimate measure of a man:

I think it's very important to be honest because when all else is over and they take all your clothes away and all your wealth, all that you have is your self-esteem and that comes from the kind of person you are.

Even though Carlos, the social worker, felt he could express himself in his work, he did not base his identity on work accomplishments:

I don't think my self-image is as tied into work as maybe someone else's might be. Even if I was a complete failure in the work market, my family would still care for me as a person. They helped me to develop a sense of knowing that anything I did was all right.

Given their choices and experiences, those who remained in highly competitive work settings felt out of place, like William, an accountant:

I'm a different person at work than I am outside work. When I'm in an environment that somehow nurtures, that somehow is cooperative rather than competitive, it enables me to be a different person, to be more myself. So I found out that I really need to be in an environment, if I can find one, that's more cooperative than competitive.

In contrast to those who eschewed family responsibilities in order to preserve their independence at work, these men placed greater emphasis on family commitments as their work commitment eased. After years of not wanting to become a father, Todd, the would-be actor who settled for work repairing pipes, began to see that having a child could compensate for his unfulfilled occupational dreams:

I thought of the thrills of having a little one and bringing it up and influencing it and watching it grow. Maybe it's just a gradual eroding of different illusions, so here was something concrete as opposed to my fantasies, an alternative in life. I knew I had a lot of promise, but it didn't seem to be getting off the ground. I suppose I was making a statement to the powers that be that I was not all bad.

For Timothy, a truck driver (who watched over his toddler as the interview took place), family involvement became preferable to time at work:

Some people feel, "The more I work, the happier I am." I'm not that type of person. I definitely prefer being with the kid. When I get home, my wife disappears and I take care of my son. It's fantastic. I can't wait to get home to see him.

Being out of work convinced Ernie, the physical therapist, that his family, not his job, provided his life's foundation. His wife and daughter became his safety net in an unpredictable and potentially cruel society:[11] "I started realizing that I had to hold on to my family when I was unemployed. I began to see that as long as I have them, it's okay."

The desire to become a father also emerged in response to work disappointment. Arthur, a sanitation worker, explained: "When your dreams fade a little bit, you like to install them in your children." Howard, the financial manager, found that becoming a father rounded out his life: "I just feel that feeling of completion by having a child."

The wish to find fulfillment and completion through parenthood is often attributed to women, but these men looked to family life for similar reasons. Dwight, the disillusioned computer technician, decided that becoming a father would not only provide a rationale for working. More important, it would give his life another, more promising focus:

Having a child might be a financial strain, but it will all pan out. I can say to myself I didn't kill myself working for nothing. I'll be so excited about getting home, seeing my little one. Even right now, the one thing to look forward to in the day is coming home to my wife and my doggie. They're so happy to see me.

As parenthood became a central source of sustenance and self-worth, these men began to welcome the chance to trade time on the job for time with their wives and children. While declining work involvement imposed financial and emotional hardships, they found a silver lining in expanded family involvement. Ernie treasured the chance to participate in rearing his daughter, even though quitting his high-pressured job meant living with financial insecurity:

I quit with no job at all. It was a very hard decision, but it was a blessing in disguise. It was the best thing that ever happened because it gave me a chance to be home with my daughter during the developmental stages. I worked out of the house, and I was able to spend time with my daughter and work later in the evening. I got to do a lot of things that I'll never forget. I got to see her when she first talked and when she first crawled. I was able to *spend* time with her, and she knew it. Not too many fathers get the chance.

Carl felt relief when he lost his uninspiring job. He relished the chance to take care of his daughter as much as he enjoyed not having to work:

When I was unemployed for that year, I was the happiest man in the world. My daughter was two, and my wife would work long hours, so I'd stay with her. . . . I was doing what I wanted to do. The good part was packing my daughter up and taking her everywhere with me. . . . I loved staying home, being around her. I never really got bored.

For most, the decision not to focus on the size of a job's paycheck held unexpected, but not necessarily unhappy, consequences. Neil, the ex-developer, was pleased to trade the burdens of primary breadwinning for the chance to choose more fulfilling work and to share in rearing his children:

When you don't make that much money, you know you can't be much of a breadwinner. It doesn't bother me. I don't want to have to work for a job just to make money to support my family. I just refuse. My idea of sacrifice is that you sacrifice your personal time, and you sacrifice things that you're interested in to have a child. That's worth it. But not yourself. I'm not gonna do that.

Since increased family involvement usually entailed financial sacrifices, the choice to contribute more time but less money meant increasing economic dependence on female partners. Norm, an administrative judge who rejected several offers to join prestigious law firms, appreciated his wife's economic contribution because it allowed him to spend more time at home:

> Maybe I could have pushed myself more, been more ambitious, but I don't think my wife's unhappy because I'm around. I could be making a lot more money, but I wouldn't see my kids, be able to spend time with them. She likes that, so she can't really have it both ways. She makes a good salary. What's enough? We have a nice house, two cars. I want to enjoy my family.

We learned in the preceding chapter that turning from work can also provoke a rising determination in some men to avoid family commitment. Other forces pulled these men toward it. Personal experiences that made commitment and equality in heterosexual relationships and participation in child rearing more attractive were crucial for the men who became involved fathers.

Becoming Committed to a Nondomestic Woman

Among those who moved toward involved fatherhood, almost 90 percent changed their outlook on the kind of relationship they wished to have with a woman. Relinquishing early expectations of either authority over or freedom from women, they came to support more egalitarian ideals and especially the right of women to pursue independent careers outside the home. By no means did all of these men develop thoroughly equal relationships—indeed, most found it easier to support the idea of equality than to behave according to all of its principles[12]—but they did develop a willingness to support egalitarianism, which in turn had important consequences for the kinds of relationships they sought and built.

DEVELOPING AN EGALITARIAN OUTLOOK

Men who developed an egalitarian outlook had experiences that differed from both primary breadwinners and men who moved away from parenthood. While only 19 percent of autonomous men were either married or wished to marry, all involved fathers developed or wished to develop an enduring, exclusive relationship to one woman.[13] In contrast to those who ultimately became primary breadwinners, they developed relationships that stressed a more equal exchange of resources and responsibilities. This change held unforeseen consequences for their commitments to children as well.

Men traveled two routes toward commitment and equality in intimate relationships. Almost half of them developed an egalitarian outlook *before* becoming committed to an enduring relationship. Sexual and other intimate experiences had already pushed or pulled them toward more equality. Others became involved in a committed but relatively traditional relationship that subsequently proved untenable for one or both partners.

Most of those in the former group, like their breadwinning and autonomous peers, grew up believing in men's right to both dominance and independence. Carlos, who felt drawn to social work so that he could help people, recalled:

> When I was in high school, I was more of a traditional Hispanic male—sort of macho. At least, I was playing with that idea. A relationship started that was more of a traditional relationship. I expected that person to give to me more than I gave them. It was almost like a fetch-me type of relationship. I think if we had lived together, she would have cooked, cleaned the house, raised the kids.

A growing sense of discomfort led Carlos to reject this macho image:

> I felt that I wouldn't want to be treated that way, and I shouldn't treat someone else that way. I saw there could be an abuse of the traditional male role, and also I saw limitations in that type of relationship. The woman is limited within the family, and the man gets locked into an image I didn't enjoy. At that point, I pretty much decided that the type of person I wanted to be did not match with the traditional Hispanic role model.

These men also learned that the dynamics of inequality can work in two directions. If intimate relationships based on a woman's economic dependence give power to men, they can also encourage women to adopt a calculating view. They vowed to avoid women who treated them as "success" or "paycheck" objects. Brad, the computer programmer who rejected his father's insurance business, was chastened, but also warned away, when a woman disapproved of his apparent lack of ambition:

> At one point, she said I was the first guy she'd ever dated who didn't have career plans. Career ladders were not something I thought about at all. She said it negatively, although I didn't see it as a negative aspect of myself. I was disappointed to find there are women who would make that judgment and see it in a negative light.

Unexpected pleasure in nontraditional relationships combined with these disillusioning experiences to underscore the costs of dependency. Brad found that he could share more with a woman whose interests did not center on the home:

> In graduate school, I was with a woman I liked very much. She was the first woman I really shared a lot of interests with. It was like discovering something you wished had existed and then found, wow, it really does exist. That was the first time I thought I would really like to marry. She didn't feel that way, but that set a standard for a relationship—that there's this possibility in life. At that point, I never again expected a woman I was going with to drop her plans and sit home.

Such experiences encouraged these men to choose female partners who possessed similar, not "complementary," interests, skills, and resources. More specifically, they became increasingly attracted to work- or career-committed women, who placed nondomestic pursuits on a par with domestic ones. For some, this became a precondition to involvement. Like Brad, they concluded that commitment to work was the best indication that a woman possessed other qualities they deemed important in a mate:

> It's probably that the things that drive a woman to have a career—say the intellectual alertness—is something I appreciate in a woman. I accept that those two things go together.

Neil, the ex-community developer who returned to graduate school, found such women more sexually desirable as well as more mentally stimulating:

> By the time I got through college, I assumed that whoever I married would be working—because the women I was attracted to are clearly gonna have their own careers. If you're gonna spend your life with somebody, there better be a real personal, intellectual, emotional attraction. I wanna have kids, but if somebody was gonna be happy just raising my kids, I just don't see how I could have a life together with someone like that. I just could not see myself living with somebody who was not gonna have the same kind of interest and passion about what they want to do as I did.

Neil also resolved to avoid partners who would treat him as a potential meal ticket:

> It's not that some women expect me to be the breadwinner, but they assume a certain level of material success. I just don't want to be

trapped in a relationship where I'm gonna have to sacrifice things that are so important to me, like my academic career and, particularly, my principles.

These men chose partners who did not want or expect them to carry the full weight of breadwinning. They welcomed the relief from economic pressure, and they concluded that it was worth sacrificing the authority that goes with earning the only paycheck. Todd, the unemployed actor who eventually found work as a utilities repairman, married a professional dancer who was more successful than he:

I almost chose her too precisely for that factor—here's somebody who's going to challenge me. I want to go through life with somebody I don't have to coddle, somebody who's going to challenge me.

It is tempting to attribute this outlook to early childhood experiences in the family. We have seen, however, that as a group, these men did not hold notably different outlooks in childhood than other men. Nor did their relationships with their mothers and fathers differ in significant ways. Instead, these men developed more egalitarian outlooks in late adolescence and early adulthood when their early expectations clashed with real experiences. As the qualities they looked for in a mate shifted, they felt relieved to have avoided the pitfalls that might have accompanied primary breadwinning. Comparing his first girlfriend to his current live-in companion, Claude, a self-employed lawyer, pondered his emerging attraction to nondomestic women:

My first girlfriend—I'm sure she doesn't work, and I don't think that would have worked out. Having her stay home and go off to the country club is not my idea of a shared relationship. She's out having all the fun on my money. I'd prefer to have my kids grow up where everybody chipped in, everybody shared. I like it that my current girlfriend works. She should have her own independence. She likes money. If she didn't spend her own, she'd want to spend mine.

Equality can take many forms, including equal support for remaining single or childless. Indeed, many of the men who eschewed parenthood also supported women's independence, since it aided their own autonomy. Women's sexual and economic independence lessens the economic pressures on men and releases them from the need to marry to enjoy the pleasures of sexual intimacy, as many women from both ends of the political spectrum have noted. (Indeed, the fear that "feminism will free men first" is a common rallying cry among antifeminists.)[14] An egalitarian approach to intimate relationships is thus an important, but not a sufficient, condition for becoming an involved father.

The men who moved toward parental involvement were likely to develop outlooks that *combined* an egalitarian outlook with a desire to be in a committed relationship with a woman or a child. These men decided to seek interdependence, not independence. Like those who became primary breadwinners, but in contrast to those who moved away from parenthood, they tired of sexual and social "freedom." Most found unexpected contentment in a committed relationship.[15] A series of live-in relationships changed Clarence's outlook on marriage:

> At first, the idea of living with someone was kind of threatening, because it was a curtailment of my freedom. But then I got adjusted to living with someone and hated to see it end—just having a companion became very important. I'm really sort of self-sufficient—I can do everything around the house—but it was nice to have someone to share things with. So I'm ready to be committed.

Some men found that sexual freedom was not all it had once appeared. In the wake of AIDS and other concerns, they turned away from casual sexual encounters. Robert, a divorced teacher sharing custody of his two children, decided to remarry when the "bar scene" lost its glow:

> I'd had enough years in between the breakup of one marriage and the beginning of this relationship to lead a fairly dissolute life. And it became rather vacant. Certainly there was the thrill of going out at night and not knowing who you were going to come home with, but it kept making less sense. I wasn't liking it.

Tom, an editor, began searching for a more lasting commitment when he became uneasy with "freer" relationships:

> I always seemed to swing between periods in which I went out with women who weren't interested in anything serious and then becoming involved with someone who was. Then there was a woman I went out with for a short time who was much freer than I was, and that sort of made me evaluate myself. It was harder than it looked to be free. I met my wife not that long afterwards.

The unexpected thrill of a close human encounter overshadowed the attractions of freedom. Hank, the psychiatric counselor who originally felt that he had "never seen a happy marriage," learned that a challenging relationship could be more exciting than a string of one-night stands:

> There was no more challenge at the bars. Everybody knows your name, but when you leave, it's empty. And here she was—we were doing other things, more exciting things. I learned a lot from her, we enjoyed each other, so why not get married? I took a chance.

Being loved and cared for helped others overcome the fear that desirable women would reject them. Rather than giving up freedom, they found they could escape it. Unlike those who turned away from sexual commitment, these men found soothing reassurance in a supportive relationship. Despite early self-doubts, Norm, the administrative judge, gained confidence from his wife's acceptance:

> Self-confidence came from establishing a relationship and knowing that somebody cared for me, that I was important to them and didn't have to try to impress anybody.

Whether they relinquished their "freedom" gratefully or begrudgingly, these men came to focus on creating a lasting, exclusive attachment to one partner. Friendship supplemented erotic desire as the basis of commitment.[16] William, the accountant, discovered:

> As I got older and so much wiser, I learned to value different things about relationships—so that while my love for Linda is not the white-heat kind I had when I was sixteen, I think it's stood the test of time. We've had our ups and downs, but we've weathered it in a way that's been good for both of us.

Unlike those who became breadwinners, involved fathers found satisfaction in relationships based on sharing similar pursuits and interests. Craig, the dancer, overcame a "callous" approach to relationships when he discovered that sharing could be more gratifying than solitude:

> We were each other's best friends and got a lot of pleasure learning things together, doing things together, changing together. We're good together. We try to spend as much time as we can together.

To such men, the struggle for independence becomes one stage on the path toward commitment.[17] This commitment is also a way of attending to a partner's needs. Carlos saw sexual fidelity as part of the mutual respect he sought:

> At the beginning of our relationship, we were both trying to achieve total independence for ourselves. She was a very loving and family-oriented type of person, and she has a lot of those good qualities, which I think rubbed off on me. Fidelity is important to her. And one thing that I've managed to learn through my other relationships is to respect that other person.

The erosion of "traditional" relationships based on complementary roles is often viewed as the triumph of individualism over commitment.[18] Indictments of individualism in American society rarely acknowledge the liberating effects for both women and men of the trend toward women's economic and social independence. The capacity to be independent is not opposed to the ability to make commitments. To the contrary, relationships can be based on sharing strengths rather than compensating for weaknesses.

Equally important, the emergence of egalitarian gender relationships is more complex (and less dire) than the view presented by those who see only the rise of self-interested individualism. Interdependent relationships have emerged alongside individualism, as the sociologist Francesca Cancian has noted.[19] These relationships stress mutual responsibilities as well as individual rights, and they also allow a more equal exchange than one based on "complementary" roles. Although expanded opportunities for women outside the home have given both men and women the option of choosing personal autonomy over lifelong commitment, these new opportunities have also allowed people to create relationships based on mutual commitment and equal exchange.

FACING CHANGE IN MARRIAGE

About half of the involved fathers did not actively choose work-committed partners, however. For these men, a more traditional marriage proved unworkable. Unanticipated events such as an economic squeeze on their households or a wife who became dissatisfied at home pushed them toward a new arrangement. Since events beyond their control provoked change, many did not greet it with the same enthusiasm as those who consciously chose work-committed partners.

Unanticipated economic need changed many traditional relationships, especially for those who had rejected a fast-track career or hit a dead end at work. In the early years of marriage, before they had children, these men had grown accustomed to the higher standard of living afforded by two incomes. By the time children arrived, they were surprised to find that they had unwittingly become dependent on their wives' incomes. Bruce, a paramedic, thus supported his wife's permanent return to work after their child was born, even though he used to think "it was the man's job to support the family and women stayed home with the kids":

> When we first got married, we were both working full-time. Then after April was born, Eileen took a leave of absence. But we realized we couldn't live on my salary because our financial needs had increased, so she said she'd go back to work temporarily to see how things worked out. And it worked out good. So we found a baby-sitter who worked for a reasonable price.

Even if they found it disconcerting to relinquish being the economic heads of the household, these men felt grateful for the support their wives offered. It gave them the chance to choose work they enjoyed and to reject less attractive alternatives. Ernie (the physical therapist) discovered that economic dependence, a state he had always feared, had its silver lining:

All my life, I'd always taken care of myself, taken care of other people. I had a hard time being dependent, but I learned to work on it. I was willing to take every job offered, and she wouldn't let me because she knew that's not what I wanted. I couldn't stand the stigma of being unemployed, and she kept on telling me, "Don't take it, don't take a job unless that's what you want. We'll survive." She was very supportive. She really pulled me through it, because I was falling apart.

As these husbands' ability to earn a family wage eroded, their ideal preferences gave way to economic necessities. Of course, not all wives responded with magnanimity. Robin, a struggling stockbroker, felt helpless to prevent his wife's return to work and her resentment that it was necessary:

When she got pregnant the first time, I basically said, "I'll take care of us," which I did for a while. But when things went against me, she did not understand it. She just decided that I didn't love them as much or that I didn't feel that they were worth it. She's working now. It was a big concession on her part. . . . But I don't have any other choice.

Even when economic squeezes did not force wives into the workplace, other developments could trigger change. Some husbands were surprised to find that their wives were dissatisfied at home. Harold, a tow-truck operator, eventually became the custodial parent when his ex-wife rejected homemaking and caretaking:

I figured that after work all day, I'd come home to a clean house and dinner on the table, but she couldn't get into it. I would come home and things wouldn't be done. I'd have to clean and do the dishes and cook. I used to get up at night to change the kids because she wouldn't get up. I guess after having the baby, it just got to be too much for her. She was unhappy and not responsible. She never took care of the kids or gave me a home life—at least not what I pictured.

When Michael, a therapist and social worker, realized his wife was unhappy, he gave her the courage to seek a new path:

My ex-wife went through a transition from being a full-time housewife and mother to part-time work to full-time work. She was very unhappy being home, obviously depressed about her position, but afraid to do anything else. The first thing I did was encourage her to work part-time. Then I think I really helped get her going. She kept getting better and better jobs, too. I really wanted her to do it because I kept thinking that somehow it would make things better between us if she was happier. But it really didn't, because some of the conflicts were so fundamental. I wanted to be with someone who was more emotionally available, and that was very difficult for her to do. She was very distant.

Even though his support for her emerging independence hastened the end of their marriage, Michael felt few regrets. His ex-wife found a happier life, and he was released from a conflict-ridden relationship. Although he wished to remarry, he vowed to build a different kind of marriage. As he put it, "it's unlikely that I would get involved now with anybody who wasn't very career-oriented."

Other men felt bewildered when their wives did not share their dreams of domestic bliss. Like Gary, the custodian, they did not respond so generously:

My wife was, is, a half-assed mother. It might have been the depression—she would sleep and Katie would be on her own. Then she met a guy she went to school with, and he told her about this job. She decided to try it out and everything really started going down the hill.

Whether prompted by an unexpected economic squeeze or a dissatisfied domestic wife who became increasingly successful or ambitious at the workplace, relationship changes did not typically end in divorce.[20] But they were not always welcomed, either. Dwight, the computer operator who hit a dead end at work just as his wife was promoted, accepted the changed situation but nevertheless longed for what seemed a simpler past:

It used to be the norm that the wife stayed home with the kids, but living in our era, everything is so pathetically high in cost, one person can't pull it. Right now I can't honestly say I could hold all the financial stuff up myself. She likes to work, but if I felt I could afford it, I would definitely prefer for her to stay home.

CONSEQUENCES OF COMMITMENT TO NONDOMESTIC WOMEN

Whether they traveled a path that felt imposed or freely chosen, those who became committed to nondomestic women faced unexpected adjustments. They changed their views of themselves, their partners, and the balance of emotional and economic exchanges between them. They also altered their ties to jobs and children.

Most developed more realistic assessments of their partners' and ex-partners' strengths and weaknesses. Some had to relinquish idealized visions of motherhood. Gary found that a mother's desires and capacities to nurture are neither instinctual nor guaranteed: "I thought that it's in-born in a woman to nurture a family, and it wasn't there."

They realized that their partners were just as aggressive, work-oriented, and self-reliant as any man. Charles, a lawyer and father of a two-year-old son, learned: "My wife is . . . as committed to work as I am. Maybe even more so." Larry, the deck hand and limousine driver who never became a harbor pilot, also came to view his wife, a flight attendant, as more independent, hard-working, and ambitious than he was:

> She's more of a go-getter than I am. I'm a lazy slob! She was more or less thrown out of her household when she was sixteen, and she's been working and going to school ever since. She's very outgoing, aggressive, a doer. She's always had hustle, and she's just so steady.

These men also began to see themselves in less stereotypically masculine ways. Women who offered support and expected equality could call forth more nurturant qualities in their partners. Juan found his self-image changing:

> This relationship has helped me to care for other people. I think through life I've been selfish a lot, thought too much of my own well-being, and I think I'm becoming a better person, more careful with people, more understanding.

They also relinquished their identity as sole or primary breadwinner: "We don't really consider anybody the breadwinner; we're both bread-winners, so we work as a family," Carl, the ex-typographer, explained.

While married women have historically sacrificed career opportunities to preserve an important relationship, men have rarely faced reciprocal pressures. However, an egalitarian commitment implies that men as well as women will make workplace concessions for the sake of their partners. Most men do not face this clash between career and commitment, but those who did had to reassess their occupational ambitions. Recall Frank, the bank vice president, who switched to a less demanding job so that he could devote more attention to his family. He agreed to leave "an institution where I had been quite successful and had no reason to think I wouldn't be more successful in the future and was going into one that was totally foreign to me." William also changed careers rather than accept the frequent trips and moves required by his employer:

They were a good company, and they allowed me to have quite a bit of autonomy, but I would have had to travel a lot and move to another state. Both of us felt that we didn't want to be away from each other that much, and so the combination of things moved me toward another career.

These men gave up more promising, but also more demanding, careers. Relationships with work-committed wives placed some constraints on their job mobility but also gave them more options regarding work. Dean, a park worker, chose to spend more time with his young son instead of taking a promotion:

When Joey was born, I could have taken a promotion, which would have been a pretty good amount of money, but would have changed my lifestyle a whole bunch because of the hours. I decided I wanted to spend time seeing my kid grow up. It was lucky, because Joan worked very hard to get what she has and she said she would like to pursue that. One of the reasons I didn't take the promotion was because she wanted to go back to work. With that the promotion was something I didn't have to do. So it worked out very well, and I would do it again.

Sacrifice, then, is in the eye of the beholder. These men surrendered some opportunities, but weighed this against the advantages of more egalitarian commitment, including less pressure to succeed at work. Hank, the medical technician who hit a dead end as a psychiatric nurse, counted on his wife, a hospital administrator, to protect him against the insecurities of the labor market:

She's my right arm. If I were to lose my job, I know I'd be supported. 'Cause sometimes I feel like, "I quit," and she says, "Okay, do what you want." And the same thing with her if she said, "I can't handle this no more." I see my mother was stuck, my father was stuck. I have the support they didn't have.

For Larry, the would-be harbor pilot, his future wife's emotional and economic support helped him survive career disappointment:

At the end of my apprenticeship, I became real depressed and went into therapy. At the time, I had just started going with Rita, so she really helped me through it. I definitely would have jumped off the deep end without her. She was a life jacket. I never realized it, but it was important for me to marry a strong woman. I'm a better man for it.

The support of a work-committed woman also had important consequences for parenting orientations and decisions. It propelled some toward parenthood despite their skepticism, while encouraging greater participation in child rearing among those who had expected a less engaged kind of fatherhood. Although single and childless, Carlos began to look forward to parenthood as part of his commitment:

> A child is more the need of the person I'm seeing, but I don't think I'll regret it. If I have a child, it's because I've decided that I'm going to give my best effort. I think raising a child is a very large responsibility, and it's something that I wouldn't take lightly. And I know, based on my financial status and things of that nature, I would be the primary person in my child's life.

For men who moved toward more egalitarian relationships, becoming a father had different implications than it did for primary breadwinners: it meant facing significant pressure to participate in child rearing. No wonder those contemplating such a decision were cautious about fatherhood and the changes it would bring. Unlike men who moved away from parenthood, however, this concern was offset by a desire for enduring family commitments. These men also viewed involved fatherhood as part of their support for work- and career-committed partners. Todd, the aspiring actor who worked as a utility repairman, worked the night shift so that he could spend days with his newborn daughter while his wife pursued her dancing career:

> We agreed in the beginning that as much as possible, we share fifty-fifty. What other way can you go nowadays, the whole economy being what it is? But that's also the way it should be. Even if I had the money to take care of things myself, my wife has a calling, a vocation that she needs to fulfill and I want her to fulfill.

As he sat with his infant in his arms, he also concluded that this arrangement had hidden benefits:

> I wouldn't trade it. Tough for her if she's in a sweaty room. She's got to take the responsibility along with the freedom. She *has* to if she wants a man who doesn't mind her being independent.

Adjusting to a wife's nondomestic ambitions could be difficult, however. Warren, an engineering assistant, chafed under the increased demands when his wife first returned to school after the birth of their only child. He accepted his new responsibilities as the price of marital peace:

> After Michelle was born, my wife went back to college. At first, it was very difficult for me. She went nights, and I would be home with the baby. Then came the weekends, and I was cooped up in the house. I didn't have the time to myself I felt I needed. All of a sudden roles

changed, so it was like an upheaval. Then after the Christmas break, I got into the routine.

When his wife returned to full-time work after the birth of their second child, Wesley, the paramedic, surprised everyone by sharing in the work of the household:

It was me taking the initiative, and also Connie pushing, saying, "Gee, there's so much that has to be done." At first I said, "But I'm supposed to be the breadwinner," not realizing she's also the breadwinner. I was being a little blind to what was going on, but I got tired of waiting for my wife to come home to start cooking, so one day I surprised the hell out her and myself and the kids, and I had supper waiting on the table for her.

Most eventually came to believe in the benefits of involvement. For Wesley, the payoff for his work was a strengthened marriage, increased influence at home, and growing personal pride:

Her going to work was a help in a lot of different ways, not just financially. I think it strengthened things between the two of us. It made her realize that I cared enough to share responsibilities, and made me realize there were responsibilities that needed to be shared. We're sharing more, and I really enjoy doing it. We're buying a new stove, and I now have a say in what color comes into the kitchen since I'm here a good portion of the time.

For some fathers, however, the movement toward a more egalitarian relationship ended in divorce. Often, these men preferred to stay married, but their ex-wives decided to leave. Unlike men whose bitter breakups weakened their already fragile parental attachments, divorce unexpectedly pulled these men toward greater involvement. Their wives' lack of interest allowed or forced them to become more involved with their children. Harold, the tow-truck driver, was surprised but happy to retain informal custody of his two daughters after his wife left:

She divorced me. I wanted to keep it together for the kids' sake. I thought I never was going to see them again. I couldn't bear the idea of losing the kids. But after a while, she decided the kids were tying her down. She got a job and started going out every night. The kids were here all the time, and it was like her coming for visitation. There were times when she wouldn't see the kids for months. I'm glad that's what she wanted, because I was devastated for six months. I never did get legal custody, but the kids have lived here the whole time.

Why did these divorced fathers become more involved with their children when most divorced fathers do not? First, when wives were unenthusiastic mothers, fathers were more likely to become either primary or sharing caretakers. Like Harold, Michael, the therapist, became the custodial parent when his ex-wife preferred to leave the children with him:

Initially I was very frightened at the enormity of the responsibility. When I realized how much it would mean to the kids, it felt very important, and I was very eager to take them. For me, it was a good decision. I didn't need to feel that freedom that my ex-wife felt she needed. I'm a very home-oriented, family-oriented person.

When egalitarian relationships ended without extreme rancor, joint custody was more likely to follow. In these cases, work-committed wives promoted, rather than discouraged, fathers' involvement after a breakup. Tom remained a closely involved parent in the aftermath of a friendly divorce:

Compared with what most people go through, I would say the divorce has been terrific. For the most part, everything has been resolved without bitterness. She was very pleased that I wanted to stay so much a part of David's life. And she has actively fostered that. She very much wants him to have a strong sense of me as a father. And most people who know us do think that we have a very strong relationship. He really does have a sense of having two homes. When he comes to my house, he's just totally involved. We have a life together that's just totally ours, and it's never been a situation where he wishes he was at his mama's house.

Although most who found work-committed partners concluded that the benefits of sharing were worth the concessions, some also retained a nostalgic longing for an imagined past of greater male authority. Robert, the divorced teacher with joint custody and a new marriage, acknowledged:

To be able to do it all myself—the traditional man—that's a longing that I sometimes feel. . . . But I wouldn't want to have a housewife, because I simply can't imagine a woman that I'd be attracted to being very happy in that situation.

Amid their ambivalence, however, most chose to emphasize the advantages that modern women's self-sufficiency offers men. As Patrick observed, his parents' pattern had held significant drawbacks for both sexes:

My mother's world, when a woman could just stay home and depend on a man, is gone. Good riddance! My mother just let everybody else take care of her and she did nothing! My wife and I have reached a happy medium. I don't want to lock her out of anything, and I want her to be able to take care of herself.

Fulfilling Experiences with Children

Commitment to a nondomestic woman encouraged men to support the ideals of an egalitarian relationship, including shared breadwinning and caretaking. But coercion or moral decree cannot produce genuinely strong attachments between parents and children. Just as "good enough" mothering cannot be coerced, so "involved fathering" cannot be enforced on purely ideological grounds.[21] Once a belief in egalitarian sharing has emerged, the degree to which it translates into parental involvement depends on experiences with children themselves.

Fathers' genuine pleasure in parenting promotes a willingness to share in caretaking, including some of its least attractive aspects. But it must develop out of the exchanges between men and children and not simply from the bargains struck with female partners. For Robert, intellectual support for feminism bolstered a commitment to involved fatherhood, but it did not fully account for it. Long before divorce and joint custody arrangements required it, sheer enjoyment led him to participate:

> Things going on at that time—the women's movement, consciousness-raising groups—certainly influenced me. And I was in the delivery room with both kids. So from the beginning, we expected that this would be a shared thing. But even more than that, there was something about holding a little baby or changing the diapers that I liked a great deal.

Several paths led toward these men's involvement in child rearing, and each involved encountering unexpected pleasure in relationships with children. For some, experiences with other people's children introduced them to the pleasures of parenting. Caring for their own children changed the lives of others. These experiences undermined earlier skepticism, highlighted the rewards of caretaking, and strengthened both their attachment to their children and their desire for involvement.

Some men learned long before they were in a position to become fathers that they had a special affinity for children and caretaking, as did Vincent, a self-employed businessman:

> In high school I was a tutor, and just teaching those kids was an incredibly worthwhile experience from a very selfish standpoint. There was a great deal that came back to me. I learned I had something for kids, and I expect that to happen with my own, too.

Most, however, did not realize they had nurturing abilities at such an early age. Many did not even wish to have children. Lou, the sanitation worker who ultimately chose to work the night shift so that he could care for his daughter during the day, recalled how rigid and confused his expectations of fatherhood had been:

> I still had these traditional ideas about let the wife take care of the kid, and I'm not going to be the one smelling like A and D Ointment. I didn't know how to be a father. To find out from my parents was difficult, because they could only tell us how to change a baby, not how to be a good father. I thought it was going to be all work and no fun. I really didn't know how much fun it was being a father. I guess I had to find out firsthand.

For Claude, the self-employed lawyer, fears about fatherhood subsided when he got to know his friends' children:

> I didn't think I wanted kids at all. Now I've changed. I see all my friends' kids becoming real people I can talk to. It's something that's new to me, but it's kind of an instinctive thing, a gut thing. I don't think I have to procreate to fulfill my life, but I think I'd be a good father.

For most, transforming experiences with children occurred at home. When Clarence, the freelance job consultant, became the "stand-in" father to his girlfriend's young son, he discovered emotional depths and resources that he had not known he possessed:

> I never envisioned having kids, right up to my middle thirties, and then my relationship with a woman and her son got me to thinking along those lines. I was with her about seven years, and we became a family, and I was sort of instrumental in raising her son, who was about five. I questioned myself for the first year, but then there was a rapport that developed between us, and I really felt good about all the things we'd do every day. I found myself going into his bedroom when he was sleeping and kissing him. I'd look at him in the dark for fifteen minutes. I was really surprised at the things that I would do. I just had to admit how much I loved him. I derived as much satisfaction out of my relationship with him as I did with just about anything in my life.

Even though the end of his relationship with the mother attenuated his involvement with the son, Clarence's new outlook on parenting persisted. Indeed, he felt grateful, not bitter:

> I still miss him, but I really am grateful to both of them because I found that I like being a father, and I realized that I wasn't bad at it. But beyond that, whether I'm the main breadwinner or not, I realized I'd like to share in the caretaking. There's just so much satisfaction that I derived out of being a father when I went through that, so I don't want to miss it.

Most typical of all were those who were drawn toward caring for their own offspring. While their preference for egalitarian commitment led many to anticipate involvement, they agreed with Howard, the financial manager, that the birth of their own children generated feelings they could not have predicted:

Until you're a parent, you don't know emotionally what it is, so there is an emotional change. It was a great feeling. I didn't know how I would react. Like changing diapers: except for my daughter's diaper, I wouldn't think of changing someone's diaper. But when the time comes and the diaper's dirty, you do it. And when the baby came and I had to be there, I was there.

Like Lloyd, the frustrated sewage worker, these men developed a sense of attachment, competence, and ease, despite earlier fears about parenting:

I felt terrible fear. I don't know what I was afraid of, but when I first held her, it was as if I had held her all my life. They handed her to me, and I took her like a pro. I put the diaper on, picked her up, cleaned her. Once I settled right in the groove, I enjoyed it so much.

Participation in the birth itself could plant the first seeds of parental attachment. Ernie found the birth of his child to be a "peak experience":

Thank God that the doctor let me be there, and I participated. I'll tell you, it was probably the most wonderful memory I have, by far. I *loved* it. No matter what the evils of life are, the bad things that go on in this world, something about seeing a life born just knocks you out. It's a tragedy that anyone can miss that experience.

Charles, the lawyer married to a professor, was surprised by his own competence, by how "natural" caretaking became:

I was on such a high when he was born, like I was the first person to have ever had a kid or something. It happened very suddenly because he came five weeks early, and we were totally unprepared for it. And so I was just so busy at the beginning that I just sort of fell into doing everything that had to be done. I had some concerns, like, "How am I going to pick him up?" But it just happens—the baby's there, and you pick him up. And it's just been a very natural thing, the best thing that ever happened.

Involvement in caretaking reinforced this unanticipated sense of exhilaration. When uncontrollable events such as a wife's illness required some to assume caretaking tasks, involved fathers became "mothers" in the same way that widowers become primary caretakers when the death of a spouse turns them into single parents. These "mothering men" learn to parent with as much skill and devotion as any female mother.[22] William found infant care surprisingly easy when his wife developed complications following their son's delivery:

Linda went into toxic shock, and I was Peter's sole parent when he was first born. I've got pictures of myself giving him feedings and stuff. I was sort of brought along as a parent in a way that a lot of parents don't have the benefit of. The nurses showed me how, and it was all a very easy experience. So I always point out the positive aspects to really what was a very traumatic experience.

Tom, who was a student when his son was born, was "scared to death" about becoming a father:

I went through a bad time myself as a child, and I instantly thought of it as a very heavy responsibility. It was fear of failure—what if things don't go right?

His son's birth sparked a love and devotion he had not anticipated:

Once it happened, I was just totally crazy about my son. Then Sarah went back to work after two or three months, which was just about the time I was finishing the school year. So I spent the summer being a househusband, taking care of him every day. And that was a great experience. It just knocked me out. I enjoyed it very, very much.

Even though it is rare for a couple to switch parenting and work duties completely, a wife's rapid return to paid work provided a common trigger for male participation. Since most employed women return to work within six months of childbirth, and half of the returning group do so within three months, new fathers are increasingly likely to face this situation.[23] Ernie's wife's paid job made him the sole parent in the evenings—a responsibility that became a surprising pleasure as well: "I didn't like her working at night, but I liked the fact I had time with Annie alone." In these instances, participation and parental attachment nurtured each other. Unanticipated constraints, such as an employed or ill wife, triggered initial involvement, but the pleasure of active caretaking ultimately became its own reward.

Parental involvement developed more slowly for other fathers. Frank, the banker who left a demanding career to rescue his faltering marriage, had no interest in having a child, much less caring for one. Although he begrudgingly agreed to become a father in order to preserve his marriage, to his own surprise he began to enjoy parenting after his daughter emerged from infancy. By her second birthday, he had become an enthusiastic and involved parent:

When my wife brought the issue up that it was time to have a child, I wasn't too keen on the idea. But I felt I should be amenable because of her deep-seated disappointment over her aborted pregnancy. I agreed, and my attitude shifted from negative to neutral. Then about six months into my daughter's life, something happened. . . . Now I'm delighted to be a parent. It's a form of self-gratification I never imagined.

Finally, the threat of loss provided the catalyst for some to become involved. When his wife's affair led to a separation, Roger realized how much he wanted and needed his children. Using her sexual indiscretion as leverage, he resolved to fight for some form of custody and to take responsibility for rearing his three sons:

I could not conceive of not having my kids with me. This is going to sound very terrible, but when she left, I said, "You can do what you want, but nobody is going to take my kids away from me. I'm not the one out messing around, and I'll be damned if I'm going to be without the kids, too."

While involved fatherhood offers important benefits to women and children, it also challenges twentieth-century notions about the precedence of maternal rights. As some men became more involved, they were also more likely to fight to maintain those ties in the event of divorce. Since rights and responsibilities are inevitably linked in the courtroom just as they are in men's perceptions, the movement of some fathers toward increased parental participation will likely require a reassessment of parental rights as well. Just as custody rights shifted from fathers to mothers at the turn of the last century, we are likely to witness the reemergence of increased paternal rights and joint custody arrangements as the next century approaches. Paternal rights may also encourage paternal involvement. Although this trend challenges some women's presumptive claim to sole maternal custody, research suggests that joint custody can be beneficial for mothers and children as well as fathers.[24]

Participation in parenting promotes emotional attachment and growing attachment makes involvement more pleasurable. This process produces father-child relationships that resemble what we often call mothering or "maternal thinking."[25] These men define parenthood not simply as an extension of their genetic heritage or proof of their manhood, but as a way to express relational and nurturant needs. For Ernie, caring for a child met a desire for attachment:

You feel like you're gifted by having a child, taking care of somebody and being responsible for their growth and development. It was just something I looked forward to ... someone being dependent on me, someone to share life with, to take care of—that was my need, too.

Some believed that caretaking had produced a fundamental change in their personalities. Others felt that it had simply allowed them to express previously hidden, but already existing, emotional capacities. William explained how caring for his child had helped him recover from his own father's neglect. It also affirmed feelings that had gone unnoticed because they are typically deemed a woman's realm:

> People take for granted the interplay between mother and child, and I think there's a bonding between my son and myself. I bring to it also the feelings of not having a relationship with my father that was this close emotionally, and I'm reacting to that in some measure. But in a certain way, it's just me and that's who I am and I've become. I've enjoyed recognizing that in myself. It's made me aware that I'm a very nurturing person.

Whether becoming a caretaking father involved the discovery of once hidden capacities or the development of new ones, children provided all of these men with an emotional base that no other relationship could or would offer. As Tom put it: "It's obviously the basic, the emotional center of my life. I might not have that if I didn't have a child." Like the cliché of the woman who cannot feel fulfilled unless she has a child, Ernie discovered: "I would be empty, incomplete if I couldn't have a child. It would almost be like being punished, because it was something I wanted so badly that if I didn't, I wouldn't feel fulfilled."

In a world where adult relationships can seem dangerous, precarious, and unfathomable, caring for children seemed simpler, less ambiguous, more trustworthy. Michael, the therapist, discovered:

> You bring different needs into a relationship with another adult, a man-woman relationship, than you bring into a relationship with kids. There's something about sexual intimacy that stimulates a lot of unconscious wishes and needs which are very hard to meet. Today, there's such a feeling that we're all entitled to fulfillment and that there must be something wrong if there are fantasies that aren't being fulfilled. But with children, you take care of them, and that's it.

The experience of succeeding as a father provided a new opportunity for growing self-esteem and confidence, especially when work had disappointed (as was often the case among working-class men). These men were proud not simply to have had children but to have contributed actively to their development. Having grown disillusioned with his job driving for the park service, Dean's identity became increasingly lodged in parenting, where he could see the direct effects of his contributions. Like a "proud mother," he felt a "vicarious identification" with his son's scholastic achievements. He concluded that his child represented a far more impressive personal accomplishment than anything he could point to at work:

> Joey's in the first grade, but reading on a fourth-grade level. He's extremely bright, and I tend to think I had something to do with it since I spent the early part of his life with him. I've had teachers tell me, "We don't know what you did, but you did something right," and to me, that's more important than the fifteen years I spent with the job. I hate to say it, but basically my work is just a job. But Joey, to me, is really my greatest accomplishment.

In addition, fatherhood bestowed a new purpose on pursuits that had failed to offer intrinsic meaning. When work for its own sake disappointed, it became instead a means to the end of family well-being. Unlike primary breadwinners, fatherhood did not mean spending more time at work. Rather, even as they redefined work as a way to support children, they began to view employment and parenthood as competing commitments. Work became essential to family survival, but subordinate to family demands. Clarence's attachment to his girlfriend's son gave him new reasons to work, but also new reasons to spend less time at work:

> I'm willing to make a little less money in order to have a little more time. I'm willing to dedicate myself to raising a kid. In other words, I'm working—or I will be working—so that I can be with the family and not so that I can do something else or not so that I can just work. The work is a means to the end. The end is a family.

In a similar way, parenting began to rival, and in some cases, supersede other sources of identity and self-esteem. Even when work provided intrinsic satisfaction, as it did with most of the middle-class fathers, fatherhood began to offer another foundation for a man's self-image. Despite his professional commitment, Michael placed parenthood above all else: "It's the most important component to my identity. Being a father comes first, and being a therapist comes second."

Whether alienated from paid employment or dedicated to it, involved fathers used parenthood to cushion themselves from disappointments and difficulties in other areas. For Frank, the banker:

> It's done something for me that's very important. When I've suffered a setback of some kind—anywhere, anything—I can stop for a moment,

and whoever or whatever causes me to be momentarily set back is unlikely to affect whatever I have relative to my daughter.

Parental involvement also produced some unexpected drawbacks. Rick, the teacher who turned away from a law career, never imagined how much parenting would infringe on the simplest and once-taken-for-granted freedoms:

I knew that it would be an impingement upon time, but I didn't know the extent, nor did I really understand that my freedom would be so curtailed. It was just unbelievably difficult to get used to—not being able to just go to a lecture or a movie or out to eat or even take a walk or visit friends. And it was not that it bothered me; it was that I realized that there was a burden as well as a joy to having children.

As we have seen, the growing importance of parenthood made them less likely to define these demands as sacrifices. Timothy, the truck driver, was surprised to find how little he missed the carousing and camaraderie of his preparental life:

From running around to a completely different lifestyle—staying home and everything—hasn't bothered me at all. I would hope I got it out of my system. I've even cut down on cigarettes. I'm not like the rest of my friends. They go out to party, get drunk. I'd rather stay home and play with my son.

Conclusion

The paths toward parental involvement diverged from both those that led toward primary breadwinning and those that led away from parental commitment. Yet a fine line separates the experiences of the men who traveled these contrasting paths. Involved fathers shared experiences with primary breadwinners that pulled them toward family commitment. They shared other experiences with autonomous men that led them away from primary breadwinning. But a special mix of experiences with work, women, and children encouraged these men to develop a different orientation than either group. Compared to primary breadwinners, those who moved toward parental involvement were more likely either to veer away from high-pressured careers or to hit an occupational dead end. Compared to autonomous men, they were more likely to become committed to one woman or to develop a desire to do so.[26] Compared to both groups, they were more likely to become involved or to seek involve-

ment with a career- or work-committed partner. They were also more
likely to have gratifying experiences with children and caretaking (see
appendix, table 10).

The stories of the men who turned toward family commitment are instructive. The paths they traveled show us how and why a growing proportion of men, though still a minority, become involved in parental
caretaking. Equally important, their experiences make clear how much
pleasure men can and do derive from caring for children when the opportunity and need arises.

The convergence of forces that led men toward a more equal sharing
of breadwinning and caretaking was not obvious to those who traveled
this path. Rather, they generally perceived this unexpected outcome as a
matter of chance. Many of these men (like many of their breadwinning
and autonomous peers) interpreted their family choices as something
that happened *to* them. William, the accountant who shared caretaking
with his wife, a school administrator, expressed such bewilderment: "I
must admit, family life just sort of happened. I never really thought that
much about being a husband or parent."

The perception of being passively swept along by an uncontrollable
process is not wholly incorrect. Larger social forces did create an environment in which unprecedented choices emerged. Yet, although the
outcome may not have been planned, the process was not random. It resulted from an array of labor market and interpersonal experiences, a
combination of constraints and opportunities, that converged in different ways for men who made other choices.

Looking back on choices they could not have foreseen, those who
moved toward parental involvement struggled to make sense of their
lives. They chose two points of comparison: their own original goals and
the fates of others whose paths had led in different directions. Compared
to their original goals, involved fathers tended to see both disappointments and unexpected bonuses along the way. They viewed their career
"mistakes" as a necessary part of the package that ultimately produced
the "payoff" in family attachments. They judged the rewards of family
life as compensating for the roads not taken. Carl, the utilities worker,
explained that, "I guess everybody has a lot of regret as far as what they
should have done, but as I see what I have, who I have, I guess I made
the right decisions. If it was any different, I wouldn't have met Sherry,
wouldn't have had Jenny. If you want to call it second prize—I think it's
first prize."

In trying to understand how they moved so far from where they
began, involved fathers compared their life paths with more conven-
tional ones. Like autonomous men, they viewed breadwinning as a less

ambiguous but also more stifling route to adulthood than their more uncertain, winding paths. Clarence observed that:

> I don't know what heights or depths I might have reached had I gone in the opposite direction. I'm inclined to believe that I would have had a fairly normal life—normal in the sense that I would have moved up the ladder. But I probably would have been frustrated, like my father, about what other things I might have done.

These men relinquished some of the traditional privileges *and* burdens of manhood. Most of them did not go so far, however, as to aspire to become equal caretakers with their wives. Even among this group, equal sharing with a female partner accounted for only about a third of the men.

It may be tempting to focus on the fact that, even among those who support equality, men's involvement as fathers remains a far distance from what most women want and most children need. Yet it is also important to acknowledge how far and how fast many men have moved toward a pattern that not long ago virtually all men considered anathema. Indeed, there is good reason to believe the forces that led these men to value family life are affecting a wide spectrum of American men. One recent survey, for example, found that 73 percent of a group of randomly selected fathers agreed strongly that "their families are the most important facet of their lives"; 54 percent said "a man's most satisfying accomplishment is being a father"; 87 percent agreed that "dad is as vital as mom in raising kids"; and 25 percent strongly supported the women's movement.[27] Another survey found that 72 percent of men felt "torn between the demands of their job and wanting to spend more time with their family."[28] If most men have not upheld these beliefs forcefully enough, then the challenge is to create the social and cultural arrangements that would make it easier for them to do so.

7

DILEMMAS OF BREADWINNING AND AUTONOMY

*One thing that is happening—and I'm not against it—is we're not in com-
plete charge anymore. We probably never were as much as we thought, but
we're realizing it more and more. There is a sharing of responsibility,
more involvement both in the home and in careers. You have to be honest
with it—accept it, be intimidated by it, or attempt to reject it.*

—Zachary, a forty-three-year-old, childless divorcé

While women confront the competing demands of employment and parenthood, men face a related predicament: they must choose between
protecting privileges that can no longer be taken for granted and relinquishing some advantages in exchange for easing some burdens as well.[1]
Primary breadwinners and autonomous men developed different ways of
resisting the forces that would erode men's advantages, while involved
fathers traded some prerogatives for the benefits of more equal sharing.
Each choice offers benefits, but each also presents its own dilemmas.
While their situations are quite different, those who held on to primary
breadwinning and those who moved away from parental involvement
both had to respond to emerging challenges to men's power. Involved fathers had to contend with the consequences of deciding to forgo some of
their advantages. Since no option is entirely without drawbacks, men
must cope with the ambiguities and difficulties of whichever choice they
make.

How did each of these groups respond to the dilemmas they faced?
In this chapter, I examine how primary breadwinners and men with-
out parental ties tried to limit the costs of resisting equality or sharing.
The next chapter will examine how most involved fathers also limited

their concessions, while another became genuinely equal parents.

Primary breadwinners and men who eschewed parenthood opted, often unconsciously and in very different ways, to protect privileges that seemed under assault. In doing so, they enjoyed many anticipated benefits, but they also faced some unexpected difficulties. Breadwinning men found they had to exert sustained effort to maintain and defend their advantages. Even though they were able to limit their domestic participation, they had to contend with the emotional consequences of this strategy. Relationships can become tense and rife with conflict when husbands do not share equitably in the "second shift" of domestic life.[2] As for those who eschewed parental commitments, studies typically find that single men fare poorly on a variety of physical, psychological, and emotional measures.[3] These men had to cope with such perils. Resisting family involvement and domestic participation thus posed dilemmas for breadwinners, childless men, and estranged fathers alike.

Although many men did not consciously recognize these dilemmas, all had to generate some form of response. Some took refuge in traditional beliefs and patterns of behavior, and others developed new ones. Most viewed their reactions as natural and inevitable. However unconscious or unwitting, these actions, feelings, and world views provided ways of coping with unforeseen problems and contingencies. In this sense, all of these men developed coping strategies that helped them to adapt to and partially control their varied situations. Their apparently spontaneous preferences and inclinations are also strategic responses to new social dilemmas—responses that give shape to social change.

Holding On to Separate Spheres

Primary breadwinners had assumed responsibility for the economic security and well-being of their families in exchange for minimizing their participation in domestic work. Whether or not their wives were employed, primary breadwinners believed that they *alone* were responsible for supporting the family. Jesse, an unhappily married construction worker with a young daughter and another child on the way, clung to a traditional definition of manhood:

> I feel that I'm the one who's supposed to go out and make the money to bring it home to support my wife and family. I'm not saying keep her barefoot and pregnant, but I have a responsibility for the wife and child.

Men who saw themselves as breadwinners believed they bore little responsibility for the physical and emotional tasks of running a household.

184

Of performing domestic tasks, George, a forty-two-year-old park maintenance worker with two children, announced:

> I could, but I won't, because I feel I shouldn't have to. I'm just not going to do it. I'm going to provide the money, pay the bills, and she's going to take care of the home.

More important, these men defined their parental responsibilities in largely economic terms. They emphasized money, not time, in calculating their contributions to their children's well-being. For Herbert, a surveyor, being a good father meant being a good provider:

> I always supported my children, fed them, gave them clothes, a certain amount of love when I had time. There was always the time factor. Maybe giving them money doesn't make you a good father, but not giving it probably makes you a bad father. I guess I could have done a little more with them if I wasn't working all the time, but I've never hit my kids. I paid my daughter's tuition. I take them on vacation every year. Am I a good father? Yes, I would say so.

Yet, as we have seen, it has become increasingly difficult even for confirmed breadwinners to maintain their status as sole or even primary economic providers who remain aloof from caretaking. While breadwinning men were relatively insulated from the forces that prompted others to make less traditional choices, they were also affected by the erosion of economic and ideological supports for breadwinning. For example, they also felt the pinch of stagnating wages that have affected all but the top echelons of the labor force over the last decade.[4] As the sole wage earner in his family, George complained that providing for his family had become more difficult than it had been for his father:

> Where my father could support a family of four and pay all his bills, it takes a husband and wife today working two jobs to do the same thing. Today, everybody's in a rat race, and no matter how much they hurry, they can't pay their bills. It's always been hard for a man as a provider, but now it's harder.

Primary breadwinners also found it increasingly difficult to use economic advantage to claim patriarchal control or emotional detachment. In a world where most mothers work and many are reconsidering their beliefs about gender, breadwinners faced an unprecedented challenge to their power at home. George continued: "Men are being emasculated. Nobody respects authority. There's been a total breakdown." In this context, breadwinners actively had to protect advantages they could have taken for granted only a few decades ago. They developed a range of strategies to attain economic security, avoid domestic work, and maintain traditional patterns amid eroding economic and social supports.

Working long hours and having an employed partner are two strate-gies breadwinners used to meet their families' economic needs in an age of stagnant incomes. Indeed, only 14 percent of primary breadwinning men relied solely on the income generated by one forty-hour-a-week job. Of the remaining 86 percent, 27 percent moonlighted and another 45 per-cent held only one job but worked far more than forty hours to bring in extra income. In addition, 55 percent of all men with a breadwinning identity had wives or partners who were employed either part-time (31 percent) or full-time (24 percent).[5] Working long hours, whether at one job or two, and having an employed wife are obviously not mutually ex-clusive, and 39 percent of breadwinners combined a long work week with marriage to (or involvement with) an employed partner. Like most Americans over the last decade, the working hours of these men (and their wives) expanded to compensate for an eroding ability to support their families on a forty-hour-a-week paycheck.[6]

These long hours at work helped to reinforce a breadwinner's posi-tion as the family's central provider, but took an emotional and physical toll on the whole family. An employed wife might relieve some of the economic pressure, but her status as an earner also posed a potential challenge to the breadwinner's authority and identity. In developing an economic strategy to meet their family's financial needs, breadwinners therefore also had to develop interpersonal strategies to cope with the drawbacks of their situations.

LONG HOURS AND SECOND JOBS

Both working-class and middle-class breadwinners spent more time working on average than other men. Whether they worked long hours at one job or moonlighted at a second or even a third job, 72 percent re-ported working more than forty hours a week. Among middle-class breadwinners, the figure rises to 83 percent (compared with 39 percent among men who moved away from parenthood and 22 percent among in-volved fathers). Among working-class breadwinners, the figure is 60 per-cent (compared with 16 percent among autonomous men and 5 percent among involved fathers).

For middle-class professionals, this typically meant building lucrative careers that demanded long hours. Census figures show that in 1989, 44.3 percent of all male executives, administrators, and managers and 37.4 percent of all male professionals were working forty-nine or more hours a week.[7] For Gabriel, a tax accountant and father of three, as for most of these men, leaving work at the office was "a meaningless con-cept":

I work up to sixty hours, and that's probably an understatement. A profession like this is one's entire life. You sleep your profession; you can't put it on and take it off. Anybody who's successful here doesn't even think of it as a job. It is what you do. It's built into you.

Working-class men were less likely to define their primary job as a career, but they were still preoccupied with earning overtime pay and handling second jobs. Like their middle-class counterparts, these men found that only long working hours, often at a second job, would let them reach their economic goals. This strategy appears to be widespread and growing. While moonlighting to supplement a family's income was especially common before the rise in women's employment, the pattern appears to be reemerging in the current era of economic recession and wage stagnation. Thus, while the percentage of men working at more than one job fell between 1970 and 1980, it has risen again over the last decade. In 1989, 6.4 percent of men held at least two jobs, up from 5.8 percent in 1975.[8] These men are likely to be married and facing an economic squeeze. According to one study, those men who held more than one job cited economic hardship as the reason, and 54.9 percent were married and living with their wives. Men with multiple jobs worked an average of 55.8 hours a week.[9] Henry, a construction worker, was one of them. When his wife became pregnant and stopped working,

> I had to make up the difference with another job. At the time we needed two salaries to get a house. I worked day and night, day and night. My wife was a weekend widow. . . . I didn't like it, but there was no choice. I felt strongly that no matter how hard I had to work, I wanted her home.

If the household needed more income than one job could provide, why did these men not ask (or allow) their wives to find outside work? Being determined to hold on to their position as family breadwinner, they preferred to earn a second income on their own, even if it meant personal hardship, rather than undermine their identity as the household head. Brian, a plumber and sanitation worker, worked an average of twelve to fifteen hours a day for eight years to avoid relying on his wife:

> I would rather her be home with the kids and me do the two jobs because that would have been detrimental for the children. A mother's place is at home. I don't want some stranger raising my children. No one else takes care of your children like you do.

Even when a wife was employed, her earnings often did not supply the difference between a primary breadwinner's salary and his perceived financial needs. Brendon, a physical education teacher, moonlighted as a detective four days a week even though his wife worked a full-time week:

> Whatever money she brings home goes to the baby-sitter. There were things we wanted. We were having problems with the car, so she wanted a brand-new car. I said, "Let's buy another used car," but she didn't want it. Plus we ran into some bad luck, and we owe money. So I took on the extra job.

Breadwinners concluded that only by working long hours could they achieve their economic goals, and that these goals mattered more than taking time for family involvement. Glen, an investment analyst with a young child, decided: "I could take a nine-to-five job that would give us a source of sustenance, but that's all. And to me it seems that making a lot of money is what work is for."

This decision gave breadwinners and their families a higher standard of living, but many worried about the price they were paying. Reid, for example, did not feel privileged to work six days a week to keep his small business afloat:

> Six days is starting to get to me now that I have Mollie. There is pressure to keep up. You have to keep up on your job, so what are the priorities? The job, the family, and then yourself. I'd like some more time to myself and my family. But, financially, we'd have to lower our level. I don't know if we could make it.

And Glen was plagued by vague but persistent doubts about his choices:

> I give up a lot of time, and I often wonder, "What am I doing with my life? I'm spending the bulk of my waking hours chasing after this money. What am I accomplishing?"

To justify these costs, breadwinners developed psychological strategies. They argued, for example, that working fewer hours would entail even greater pressures than working long hours. For George, long days at work were preferable to worrying about money:

> If you can't afford to pay your bills, no matter how much time you have to yourself, you're going to be under pressure, and that pressure is going to affect your mental outlook. So, financially, working less would put me under a lot of mental pressure.

In addition, breadwinners concluded that investing a lot of time in work now would enable them to "play" later. Glen explained his preoccupation with money by defining it as a means to another end—future

188

family involvement: "I would like to spend more time with my family, and if I can make a lot of money, then I will have the option of doing that."

Finally, breadwinners also focused on the benefits of having a wife at home caring for their children. As Glen said:

> The trade-off is that I don't have the worry about who is with my baby and are they paying attention to him and is he crying and are they giving him enough stimulation. I know that Will is getting as much care as someone who really loves him can give him, and I don't have to worry about that.

EXPLAINING LOW PARTICIPATION

With their tendency to focus on the issue of employed mothers while ignoring men's absence from the home when they go to work, the media (and the scientific community) have supported and even helped create the view that a father's low level of involvement does no harm. Public discussions are replete with stories of "guilt-ridden working moms" who are endangering their children, even though there is virtually no evidence either that a mother's employment is harmful or that employed mothers experience any more guilt than stay-at-home mothers or, indeed, than employed fathers.[10] Breadwinning men can thus rely on commonly accepted rationales to explain their lack of involvement. They used a variety of arguments to discount the notion that their absence posed a problem.

Believing that long work hours were necessary (and not a voluntary choice) helped dampen concerns. Although Dean, a lawyer, had lost years with his children, he reassured himself that his actions had caused no long-term harm:

> There were plenty of mornings when I would have preferred to stay home with the kids, but I just couldn't do it. It would have been nicer if I could have been around more, but I don't think it's a gigantic tragedy. I never felt guilty about it because I always felt I had to do it. And they seem to be turning out pretty good.

Breadwinners also concluded that if they were more involved in family life, their children would suffer more from a lowered standard of living than they do from a father's absence. Sam, an architect, insisted:

> My son would like it if I worked less because he'd see a lot more of me, but the overall effect would be a lot less of what we're doing as a family. We go to dinner, to the show. I don't deprive anybody of any-

thing, so I always feel I have to generate that extra money. . . . And if my son didn't get what he wanted, he'd be pissed.

In addition, they argued, their devotion to work freed their wives to focus on child rearing. Clint, a bricklayer, was not concerned that his seven-day work week left little time for parenting. Instead, he took pride that his wife could stay home while dual-earner couples were relying on day care: "It gives me a good feeling to be able to get by on one job, even if it is working on the weekends."

Some concluded their children were better off *because* they were not involved. Marvin, a lawyer with three small children, insisted that he would not be a good caretaker and thus there would be no special benefit to his participation:

I really think the children benefit from the absence of their father. If the father's not inclined that way, then what's the point? It doesn't make any progress. I don't think there's any major ethical value to it. People shouldn't do what they don't want to do. And I don't want to do it.

Doug, a thirty-six-year-old sanitation worker, was convinced that his two children preferred freedom from his authority: "If I were around more, the kids would have to toe the line more. They'd hate it. Mommy's a pushover."

Although they found it reasonable to argue that a father should not participate unless he is motivated, these men did not apply the same logic to mothers. Mothers are simply the best caretaking choice, according to them, and cannot substitute "quality time" for long hours of care and supervision—although they themselves could. Single and childless, Julian, an attorney in his mid-thirties, had already formulated this view:

I don't believe I'll be able to be there as much as my father was, but I do think I can minimize the deprivation to the point where it won't affect them. I think that the time I put in will be good-quality time because I will make it count. It's not the amount of time, it's the quality of the time.

But the women they married sometimes posed a challenge to breadwinners' preferences. Not only did some wives object to their husbands' long absences from home, but their near-total responsibility for domestic work also left many feeling overburdened and unfairly constrained. For their part, breadwinning men believed that their wives, like their children, benefited from the economic rewards of their dedication to work. Randall, a physician, coped in this way with his wife's objection to his long working hours:

She leads a very comfortable life. She hasn't had to work. She had that option of not going back to teaching. Now she's working at a job she enjoys where she doesn't even get paid.

George, the park maintenance worker, concluded that enabling his wife to stay at home and run the household released her from the pressures and sacrifice of the workplace:

It's a jungle out there, and here it's not a jungle. It might be depressing to change sheets or whatever, but there's nobody watching you do it, you're not punching a clock, and if you've got a good system, you can get it done fast. I give up seventy-five hours a week, which is more than my wife gives up. I see no problems in running a house today with microwaves and ovens. So it has to be easier on her.

Others, however, recognized what research has confirmed: microwave ovens and other "labor-saving devices" have not lessened but merely changed the burdens of domestic work.[11] They acknowledged that caring for home and family can be a demanding and confining obligation. Many conceded that their wives did not enjoy the "better" part of the bargain. As unwitting beneficiaries of a system they did not create, however, they were able to absolve themselves. Doug admitted that he possessed advantages, but saw no reason to surrender them:

It's easier for me. I've got to go out and work, but I have my own life. I get to come in, play a little, put the check down, and then I'm off again. I have other outlets, so I would say she gives up more of her life and herself. It's not fair, but I didn't make the rules. I'm just living by them but, I have to admit, enjoying them, too. But I don't tell her that because defending myself would be very hard after that.

Breadwinners also argued that their wives could recoup any current losses later. Even though these men placed great importance on their own careers, they did not give equal weight to their partners' work commitments. Rod, an attorney, discounted the sacrifices he expected his fiancée to make when children arrived. He argued that any setbacks to her law career would be only temporary:

She's gonna have to pretty much give up her career. I'm sure it will go straight downhill. But I'm certain that once the children are in school, she'll be able to start working again, and she'll be hired very quickly. I feel bad that she will have to give up more than I will, but not bad enough that I would give it up.

This strategy created the risk that frustrated wives might ultimately erupt with anger. Some breadwinners tried to avoid such collisions and to downplay them when they did occur, but they did not let a wife's misgivings change their behavior. Justin, a forty-year-old teacher, hoped his wife's frustrations would dissipate if ignored:

> I think she feels that she's missed something. She's subject to the same desires and ambitions as anybody else, and I'm sure there are times—maybe there are lots of times—when she feels, "Gee, I could be doing something." She gets those days, and I come home and she's upset. But if I'm smart, I won't say anything. I'll just let her yell and scream and try very hard not to argue with her.

They also concluded that even an unhappy wife has no better alternative. Although his wife was frustrated at home, Paul (the ex-hippie who became director of a social service agency) did not see her staying at home as a sacrifice:

> It's been *very* stressful for her, and it still is. She complains a lot, which I could relate to, because she's doing all this work in the trenches. So she has every right to complain. But I don't know if she's given up anything because it wasn't like she said, "Gee, I want to have a great career, and these kids came along and ruined that."

Most breadwinners, however, felt reassured that their partners preferred to control domestic activities and would not allow their participation if it were offered. Kevin, a paramedic and father of four, concluded:

> She likes to be the homemaker. Since I met her, she has been the classic woman of the house. You may live here, but this is her house. She likes to see everything just nice. If I had lots of money, I could say, "Hey, Suzanne, relax. We'll get a housekeeper." But knowing her, she'd probably clean the house before the housekeeper comes.

MAINTAINING A BREADWINNING IDENTITY WHEN A PARTNER IS EMPLOYED

The rationale for leaving someone else to care for home and children appeared obvious and compelling to breadwinners whose wives were not employed. With two-thirds of mothers with children under six in the labor force, men with homemaking wives took pride in offering their wives the option not to hold down a paid job while also caring for the family. George, the worker for a park service, declared:

> I don't expect my wife to take care of the house and then go work a job like a lot of husbands do. A lot of husbands want her to be God Almighty on the job, come home, and take care of the house, and be supermother. You can really only do one thing well.

Not all breadwinning men could, however, make this claim. Among the married breadwinners (86 percent of all men with a breadwinning outlook), 21 percent had wives who were employed full-time and 35 percent had wives who were employed part-time. Among married breadwinners with children (74 percent of the group), 16 percent had wives employed full-time and 35 percent had wives employed part-time. Among men with a breadwinning outlook who had children living at home, 21 percent of the middle-class fathers, but only 5 percent of the working-class fathers, had wives who were employed full-time. Even if these wives were less likely to be pursuing long-term careers than the partners of more involved men, they nevertheless spent a significant amount of time working outside the home—especially if they worked full-time.

These husbands refused to relinquish their identity as their families' primary economic providers, even though they had wives who worked long hours to bring in income. All employed wives shouldered responsibility for two domains, while their husbands strove to limit their responsibilities to one. Having an employed wife not only posed a challenge to these men's status as breadwinners but also undermined the rationale that excused them from domestic work. They were compelled to develop arguments and beliefs to neutralize these potential threats.

First, they reserved the good-provider identity for themselves alone, deeming their wives' earnings inessential and supplementary. Like Sam, these men did not feel they were sharing the duties of breadwinning. His wife's income from waitressing on the weekends "doesn't affect us at all," he said. "It's not something we need. I guess you'd call her income gravy." Men like Sam didn't wish to face the question of why their wives would work at demanding, but low-paying jobs if they didn't need the income.

Because most of these men had found stable jobs and chosen wives who had not, they were able to command significantly higher incomes than their spouses could hope to earn. For Doug, the sanitation worker, the low pay his wife received as a laundry attendant justified leaving her with exclusive responsibility for raising their two children. It was less a result of their joint decision than "because of how unfair our society is."

Designating their wives' earnings as "extra," such husbands felt their wives enjoyed a choice they themselves did not. Justin "allowed" his wife to accept a job only if it was defined as discretionary and thus did not upset the established division of labor at home:

So long as we were keeping our heads above water, I preferred her not to work. That's why, when this part-time job came in, I thought,

"Here's a good opportunity. Let her do this if she feels it's contributing and gets her out of the house in some way." But it's up to what she wants to do. Whether she works or not, I don't force in any of these things. There's no doubt I'm the breadwinner.

Finally, breadwinners believed that their wives' paid jobs should be subordinated to their unpaid domestic responsibilities. These jobs should not interfere with mothering. Such a stance allowed little room for their wives to develop careers. Jacob, a single businessman, concluded about his hypothetical wife:

I wouldn't mind her working from the house, doing projects in the house, taking courses, or things like that. Or she can schedule work at her leisure; she could do part-time work, which I think would fit in, but not be gone from nine to five. She should plan her work around the child and around the house.

Once a self-described feminist, Sidney, a businessman with a three-year-old daughter, now felt his work demands had to take precedence over his wife's part-time job:

Ellen was making more than I was when we were first married. But now her part-time job really pays enough just for the sitter. The economic influence of her job to the family is nil. So when both of us bring something home in a briefcase to do, my work should have priority because that's really the breadwinning income. I don't think I'm being antifeminist.

The earnings gap also made it easy to devalue the time a wife spent at her paid job. Any hours she might spend at work counted less than his toward determining who did the work inside the home. Despite working full-time for IBM, Julian's wife offset his larger paycheck by performing the major share of the physical and emotional work of the household:

I like it that I make a little bit more than my wife does, frankly. I have taken some pride in the idea that I could be the breadwinner and bring home the bacon. I come home from the jungle every day carrying my prize, and I want to continue doing it. And she does more than hold her own, because she's got a good nine-to-five job. And on top of that she is doing the emotionally compensative work of keeping our household together. So her day doesn't end at five.

These strategies helped men resist involvement in domestic work, and also lessened the misgivings that such an arrangement might generate. Brendon, the teacher who moonlighted as a private detective, argued that because he held two jobs, his wife should do virtually all the housework despite her full-time job and her sense that the arrangement was unfair:

> I refuse to do anything like cleaning the house. I work three nights a week, and I don't feel that I should come home and have to vacuum on the two nights I'm home. In my situation, being out till one at night and then getting up at six-thirty in the morning, I'm not going to come home and have my wife say, "Throw a load of laundry in there."

They were also able to pass the most demanding aspects of child rearing onto their wives, confining their own parental responsibilities to the comparatively fun activities. Although not yet a father, Marshall, a publishing executive, had already decided to excuse himself from the work of taking care of a child: "Not that I wouldn't help, but primarily I see it as her responsibility. I'll be in charge of playing." Dennis, a data-processing manager with two children and a wife "working full-time kind of part-time," acknowledged that such an attitude might not be fair. "I probably shouldn't admit this, but she carries a larger part of the household burden than I do."

While breadwinners with homemaking wives felt that their wives had the luxury of not working at a paid job, those whose wives were employed made the opposite argument, contending that their wives had the best of both worlds. Dennis continued: "I think she feels she has the best of both worlds. She has a job, and she has a family, and she has the time to enjoy them both."

These men discounted the burdens their wives shouldered. In Julian's opinion, his wife "will not miss anything":

> She is very flexible, and she has a very good capacity to encompass a lot of things. I think she will be able to keep all the balls in the air, and those she has to put down will not result in very much of a diminution of her contentment level, because she really does not anticipate that she will rise to the very highest ranks in the company.

Ultimately, primary breadwinners whose wives were also employed left it to their wives to bring them into the work of the household. If wives were reluctant, their husbands could remain uninvolved. Jake, a zookeeper whose wife worked part-time as a saleswoman in addition to caring for their three children, realized:

> What people should do and what they really do are two different things. I know I *should* do more, but I'm not going to do it because she's not forcing me. I'll do it if we're going to fight over it. But she'd have to hit me over the head.

DILEMMAS OF BREADWINNING

Despite these varied coping strategies, most primary breadwinners retained some sense that their choices exacted costs from themselves and their families. In a moment of reflection, George pondered the costs of economic survival in a traditional family:

> I've played the game so long of surviving and working and getting in the system that I can't even really truthfully be honest with myself, whether on the job or at home. Working really helps a lot of people run away from themselves. They lose themselves in their job because they don't want to face themselves.

Most breadwinners nevertheless concluded that the way they chose to live was worth it. The hard work is, ultimately, a means to family stability and closeness. Kevin, the paramedic with four children, found:

> There have been days when I have been so happy to get home to be with my kids. All my problems would just disappear, and I'd realize that the other things were not very important. The really important things were waiting for me to get home, to tell me what happened in nursery school, on the soccer field, in cheerleading.

Yet the strains and rigors of breadwinning also took their toll, leaving some wistful for the attractions of a freer life. Paul, the social service director, acknowledged a persistent ambivalence about his way of life:

> One of my old hippie codes is that one shouldn't work all that much, one should not wake up at five-forty-five every morning and get home at eight at night with a jacket and tie on and be drained and only think about work. That's bullshit, and here I am doing it. So I still have conflicting goals.

But a freer life also has its costs.

Freedom and Its Discontents

Primary breadwinners and men who moved away from parenthood both faced the dilemma of how to protect their privileges in a world where the economic, social, and ideological supports for them are under assault. Both strove to limit their economic dependence on women and their participation in parenting. Breadwinners sought to resist domestic duties, however, while autonomous men sought to bypass parenthood altogether—either by not becoming fathers (about 85 percent of this

196   PATHS OF CHANGE

group) or by limiting their economic and social ties to their children in the wake of divorce (about 15 percent).

Men who eschewed parenthood were caught between their support for some aspects of breadwinning and their opposition to others. As Mark, a single environmental adviser in his early thirties, suggests, they worried both about relying on a woman for economic support and about assuming financial responsibility for a family:

> I can't see how these people with a wife and kids support them. I'm just trying to save up enough money to make ends meet for me. If I have to worry so much just for myself, how am I going to feel about other people too? The only solution is somebody else has to work. I'd have to accept the fact that my wife would have her own job and that's the way she would want to continue it. But . . . I would hate to have to count on that. It really irks me to have to depend on somebody else.

Like breadwinners, autonomous men placed a high premium on being able to pursue personal goals beyond domestic obligations. Many were less willing, however, to condone domestic inequality or to deny the importance of fatherly involvement. This different standard of good fathering clashed with their concern about making sacrifices, whether at work or at play. Dick, a businessman approaching thirty, felt torn between being a good father and being successful on the job:

> I don't believe in stereotypical raising of children because I don't think one should be the mommy and one should be the daddy. As much as possible, there should be even exposure to both parents, in all types of roles—cooking, cleaning, shopping, P.T.A.

He realized he would "have to spend more time at home and less time at work" if he had children, and that was a problem: "It would bother me. I like my work, and I don't like being in the house a hell of a lot."

Morrie, a recreation director and single at thirty-nine, felt he would have to make sacrifices as great as those expected of mothers in order to meet his standards of fatherhood:

> If I make the decision to have children, I must also come to the realization that I must give them all the time, attention, and support that is necessary to make their lives happy. I don't know if it makes it more difficult, but it will regiment me—put me in a position that if I have children, then it may be in conflict with my occupation.

Autonomous men agreed with breadwinners that they did not wish to take on caretaking responsibilities, but they did not find partners to relieve them of these obligations. They were torn between women's rising demands for equality and their own ambivalence about it. Andrew, an interior designer in his mid-thirties, was vaguely aware that he felt caught in a double bind. He was attracted to career-committed women, but he did not wish to share child rearing:

> I would go for the more traditional woman if I had the money, but I also don't like the idea of women not working. I think a woman would become very boring just raising children. I really don't like doting women. I wouldn't want my child to have a mother who didn't have something going on in her mind. But I don't want to have to raise the child, either.

To cope with this ambivalence, autonomous men supported those aspects of equality that make women less economically dependent, but were less comfortable with the "payment" that might be expected of them in return. Mark faced a conflict between his beliefs and his desires: "I agree with the concept, logically, where you have a fifty-fifty relationship. I just honestly don't think I can live with that."

Caught between their rejection of breadwinning and their discomfort with a more egalitarian alternative, they had a better sense of what they wished to avoid than what they wished to affirm. As Andrew declared:

> I don't follow examples very often. I just know what I don't like. . . . And what I don't like is my father having these three children and not really caring whether he had them or not. And what I also don't like is my male friends who have to do half the child rearing and have a job at the same time. I don't like that either, so I would go for something in between.

This "in-between" choice meant avoiding parental commitments and often commitments to women as well. To escape the burdens and restrictions, these men escaped the potential joys as well. Whether they were childless or estranged from their children, autonomous men strove to minimize the importance of children in their lives. Dick explained:

> You don't have that extra burden or responsibility, worrying about them and worrying about the time to spend with them. To a degree, I kind of view being married and having kids like a trap. I'd be very unhappy. So by not having them, I guess I'm not trapped.

In a more extreme view, Toby, a divorced father with three sons, admitted:

> I don't get involved with my children. If they moved across the country, my life wouldn't change. In the beginning, I would miss them. But, you know, I'd get over it.

This "resolution" to the dilemma of protecting advantages in the face of potential threats posed its own dilemmas. By choosing freedom over commitment, autonomous men had to search for social attachments outside the bonds of parenthood and often marriage as well. Ray, a financial officer in his early thirties, acknowledged:

> I've lived on my own for seven years, and it's great to have your own apartment and run your own life. But it's not fun to be alone all the time. There can be many people around and yet the feeling is a very empty one at times. This is typical of most of the single people I know, be they divorced, or not married, or whatever. Some of them, the ones that were married, even have children. It can have a very bad effect on you because there's a void there, and you have to fill that void with something else, and sometimes that's not very easy to do.

And Dick admitted that "I don't know what it is, but I do get a paternal instinct every once in a while":

> There are times when it would be nice to have a little kid around the house—some nights when it's quiet and there's nothing happening. You get all kinds of emotions with children—watching them grow up, watching them take their first step, their first word—a feeling of involvement.

The need of autonomous men to find meaning in other pursuits raised the stakes on other activities. Alex, a gay actor, worried that career setbacks would be even more painful in the absence of an enduring, unassailable personal bond:

> It's very difficult to have a family and to have a career. But what happens to the person who is particularly driven when they don't achieve their goal? What happens to the businessman who goes all his life without a family and at thirty-eight gets fired and can't get rehired because he doesn't have the training for anything else? So that makes me think about family, relationships. What do I want out of life? And are there other things out there that I'm interested in?

Men who moved away from parenthood also had to defend their choice to kin, friends, and acquaintances, many of whom continued to equate manhood with being a father and good provider. They struggled against peer pressure and their own doubts about whether they were "copping out" and "missing out" in important ways. Edward, a single physician, complained:

> It's almost inescapable; it's something you're supposed to do. It's a sense of something missing without it. I guess it makes me feel a little less fitting in with the rest of the world.

But just as breadwinners endeavored to offset the costs of being a good provider, those who eschewed parenthood had to cope with their dilemmas. They searched for other sources of meaning, purpose, and social integration. They strenuously defended themselves against the disapproval of others. And they dampened lingering doubts by downplaying the costs and focusing on the benefits of their choices and by reassuring themselves that their options remained open.

FINDING A PARTNER WITHOUT BECOMING A PARENT

One way to offset or reduce the potential isolation of avoiding parenthood is to find a special partner—a wife or lover, gay or straight, to provide support without subverting the choice. Indeed, 24 percent of the autonomous men were married or in committed relationships with a live-in partner, and most of the single men hoped to find an ongoing relationship. But, consciously or unconsciously, they chose or searched for partners who would provide companionship without pushing for children, thus promising them the greatest amount of freedom. Joel, a forty-year-old married carpenter, and Dick, the single businessman, explained that they wanted a partner who was "independent":

My wife never played mind games. She was a very solid, logical thinker. If we didn't get married, it wasn't going to devastate her. She's very sound; she's got a great head.

I don't like women who cling to me. I like someone who can stand on her own two feet. I don't want somebody who likes to sit around the house and have babies. If she and I have a career, then we don't get in each other's way. If I have to stay late at the office, it won't start jealousy and guilt trips—just an open understanding and acceptance of the other one.

They linked a woman's independence with her willingness to remain childless. Gil, a forty-two-year-old real estate appraiser, only chose sexual partners who accepted his stance toward parenthood. Of his current girlfriend, he said:

When we go out, she pays for herself. She's an independent lady, and I like that.

She knows the way I feel about having children, that I've never had any desire. At this point, *her* not having had kids either, I don't think it's something that she gives much consideration to because *her* life would change, and she's very happy the way it is. Honestly, if she wanted children, I don't think we would have gotten very far.

These men thus did not forgo committed relationships, but they pursued them on terms that were not likely to undermine their independence and sense of autonomy.

FINDING ATTACHMENTS OUTSIDE THE FAMILY

Those who avoided parenthood also had to defend themselves against the allegation that they are selfish or not fulfilling their identities as men. Rejecting such charges, they argued that there are other, equally creative ways to give. Giving to needy children, for example, can be more altruistic than biological procreation. Andrew rejected the notion that bearing children is a selfless act or the only way to nurture others:

> It's easy to say that I'm too self-centered to have children. But I don't think so because I think of myself as a fairly giving person. It just doesn't appeal to me—spending all that time giving in that way. There's plenty of ways to give to other people without having to create your own offspring. There's plenty of kids that need guidance and counseling. Most parents just want somebody to tell what to do, anyway. They're fairly selfish, I think.

They also rejected the notion that enduring and deep attachments are confined to traditional family forms. They developed "surrogate" attachments that offered some of the rewards of parenthood without exacting its possible costs. Work is the most obvious place toward which childless men and estranged fathers can direct their attention. For Zachary, a childless divorcé, work as a financial manager offered an alternative to family life and a way to avoid personal entanglements:

> Work is a very big part of my life because I don't have a family. I have no commitments, so I come in anytime between seven-thirty and nine-thirty and I go home anytime between four-thirty and one at night. If I stay late, I don't have to worry about having to meet somebody.

Gus, a planner, came to see his work accomplishments as "children" he created and then had to set free:

> To develop a business and sell it or maybe take in partners to keep it alive—I think that's when I might feel like I've created a goal or child. Because, really, every project is like a little child, and you have to let it go.

Eliot, being a therapist, had a ready supply of patients who became his "children." From the comparative distance of the psychotherapeutic hour, he was able to become a father figure without getting married or having his own offspring:

To a great degree, my patients could be categorized as my children. They let me participate in their life in a very important way. I like to think I can effect positive change, and part of that is narcissistic, but it's also a humanistic wish to be of some service to mankind.

Others neither derived such satisfaction from work nor wished to pursue it. Instead they turned to leisure, religion, and other voluntary activities. Joel, the carpenter, declared:

Many of my goals are not job-oriented. I love gardening, working on the house, travel. It's becoming more important to me than I ever realized. My wife introduced me to this whole insanity of travel, and it's really very, very important—the ability to travel and being able to do the things I like to do.

Morrie, the recreation director, relied on religion not simply to compensate for the family he did not have but to help him want it less:

At this stage, I am ready to live a single lifestyle. I don't look for rewards anymore. I practice my yoga and Eastern philosophy. Through that, I have learned not to desire worldly goods or things. What I would really like to do is achieve a higher state of consciousness and awareness.

As they turned away from meeting their own or others' needs through family life, these men searched for other goals and purposes. Even though they found a variety of ways to meet this challenge, it was difficult to still their concerns completely. The possibility that some future accomplishment would make a lasting contribution provided an important, if vague, goal. Lester, a sanitation worker who could find little consolation in his occupation, hoped to have the chance to become a hero and thus ensure that his life had not been lived in vain:

There's one thing I would like to do. If I was to pass on, I would like to pass on as a hero, save someone's life. I'd like to leave this world with somebody saying, "He wasn't a bad egg after all."

If childless men turned to work and leisure to fill their time and provide meaningful goals, they turned to friends for intimacy, support, and attachment. Especially if single, they relied on a network of other single men to ease them through difficult situations and particularly lonely times. Since these friends shared their preference for independence and solitude, they supported and reinforced their world views. Zachary looked to men who had made similar choices to bolster his spirits and ease his isolation:

My three closest friends are lifelong friends. None of them have ever been married. They have gone their various ways, but all being single, I've lived through a lot of things with them together. They're important. I influence them; they influence me. They support me; I support them.

Chuck, a systems analyst who is gay, consciously avoided friendships with those whose choices clashed with his own:

I have single, childless friends because I don't have anything in common with married people. Quite frankly, I find most married people boring. If you add stories and pictures about the kids, it's even worse.

These friends provided surrogate families. Indeed, they seemed more dependable and satisfying than their visions of actual families. Chuck continued:

Friends, to me, are extremely important. They're probably more important than family at this point because I have things in common with my friends and I have relatively little in common with my family. My orientation and experience has been that love relationships are transient, but your friend always will be there.

Studies show that men are less likely than women to depend on or recognize the importance of adult friendships for social integration and emotional support.[12] These single and childless men, however, do not fit this view. But work, leisure, and friendships did not give them all the opportunity for nurturance they wanted. Many thus tended to develop connections to other people's children. Never married at forty-two, Alberto, a laborer, volunteered to work with adolescents at his church:

I belong to a very active parish, and I work with the teenage youth group and help out in the Sunday school and play with the kids. I really enjoy the kids. Before I found a parish, I would get very lonely for kids because I get a charge out of just being around kids.

Nieces and nephews provided an especially ready source of surrogate children. By being an involved uncle, a childless man could build a relationship defined by blood with a readily accessible child. He could fulfill nascent parenting desires in a circumscribed context that did not impose the more diffuse, all-inclusive, irrevocable obligations of fatherhood. Harry, a married social service director and childless at forty-four, looked upon his nephew as a substitute child:

Sue says that one day I'm gonna want to share things with a child. But I have a nephew who's fourteen. We see him regularly, so that's really not a missing section for my life. It's been a nice process watching him grow from a baby. It's something that's nice about parenting, I suppose, but I've been able to do that without all of the other stuff.

Single and childless at thirty-seven, Perry, a physician, chose to live close to his divorced sister so that he could help rear his niece:

Sometimes I think it would be nice to have kids. But because I have my niece around all the time, I don't really miss it. I go to the school functions—father-daughter dance, teacher meetings, and all that. It's a very close relationship . . . with no responsibility of discipline and so on.

Some took extraordinary measures to bring children into their lives. After vowing never to remarry, Marty, a thirty-eight-year-old widower, decided to help delinquent children:

After my wife died, I met . . . a priest, and stayed in his prayer group close to a year. Then we had a blowout, and I wound up with the kids that didn't meet his criteria. The word spread from one kid to another. One Christmas I had forty-eight kids.

Though unusual, Marty's choices show the lengths to which some childless men will go to create relationships that mirror the strength of a parent-child bond. He was not interested in assuming the legal obligations of fatherhood, but he came to see himself as a better father than his own father had been to him:

I'm more or less like a father, a super friend, a priest, all rolled into one. There's a feeling there, fulfillment of a need. There's definitely a need on my part, and there's a need on their part. Having been called a "father" by these kids, I feel I'm a real father, and my father's nothing but a biological father.

Most childless men, however, chose relationships with other people's children precisely because they did not imply the legal and social responsibilities of biological fatherhood. "Adopting" child surrogates allowed them to build relatively risk-free relationships that provided some of the benefits of parenthood without imposing its perceived costs. Perry said: "I'm a great uncle, but I never discipline those kids. Never. And that's just the way I like it."

Step-parenthood offers autonomous men another attractive alternative to biological fatherhood. Such men bypass many parental obligations without being consigned to a childless world by marrying a woman who has already raised her children. Zachary hoped to become a stepfather to children already past the most demanding stages:

If I were married to someone like Norma, with two children, it would be no trouble at all. They're sixteen, as opposed to six months old and changing my lifestyle. I'd want to be a close person in their life, but they'll know I'm not their father because they know him and love him. I'm just Mommy's boyfriend, hopefully a real good friend. But their father has a responsibility to be their father, and I won't interfere with that at all. The idea sounds enticing.

These relatively low-risk alternatives to the responsibilities of having a child have been found in other studies as well. One study found, for example, that most infertile and childless men use "child-substitution" strategies. Some of the activities reported in that study, such as developing time-consuming leisure pursuits, are a far cry from parenting; others, such as taking part in the lives of other people's children, serve as more direct "parenting substitutes." Indeed, 19 percent of the men in that sample ultimately adopted a child.[13] Most of these strategies offer a sense of purpose, social integration, and personal fulfillment without involving undue constraints.

Clearly, while commitments to work, leisure, friendships, and other people's children may help ease the difficulties of remaining childless or being estranged from one's offspring, they are not equivalent to being a parent. Indeed, they are chosen precisely because they provide a less absorbing alternative. Autonomous men thus came to view them as a way of having the best of both worlds. Kirk, a forty-one-year-old, married salesman, said of his infant nephews: "When we want them, we have them. It's almost like being grandparents."

These strategies helped quell doubts about rejecting parenthood by providing other sources of meaning, purpose, and giving. They also offered a rationale for abstaining from future commitments. Marty relied on the delinquent adolescents he worked with to protect himself from the pressure to marry again:[14]

I have enough to keep me going. If I did get married again, I wouldn't be able to spend the time with people that I need, whether it be the kids or whoever. I think it's a defense mechanism, but that's me.

These men decided to visit parenthood rather than live it. As Felix, a divorced hospital administrator, put it:

If we go to visit friends who have a child, we both have a wonderful time playing with the child. But when we leave, get back in the car, we say, "That's nice once in a while. A nice place to visit, but I wouldn't want to live there."

CELEBRATING FREEDOM

As we have seen, men who have no children or who are estranged from them used psychological strategies to find comfort in their choices. Just as breadwinners discounted the costs that they and others had to bear for their lack of involvement at home, these men downplayed the costs of eschewing parenthood by focusing on the drawbacks of having children and the advantages of freedom. Zachary, the divorced finance manager, recognized that he relied on such a strategy:

> You see all the negatives when you want to, and you use it, too. If you're not drawn to having a child, it's easy to make up all these reasons—about how difficult it is to raise children—for not wanting to have them.

In the absence of experiences to the contrary, focusing on the negative aspects of parenthood helped autonomous men cope with lingering ambivalence and defend against any disapproval expressed by others. When asked how he thought he would feel if he had had kids, Felix admitted:

> I could give you the answers that people are supposed to say—that I'd feel more fulfilled and rewarded. But I don't know if I'd feel fulfilled. I would be concerned about personal freedom, having those limits on time and money, not being able to do what you want to do when you want to do it. These are the negatives because I don't know the positives. I can't speak for what I'm missing. If it's not there, you don't miss it.

Estranged fathers also downplayed the benefits and emphasized the costs of having children. This helped to defuse any sense of loss and, more important, provided a way to reduce the guilt they might have felt about the obligations they had not honored. Bart, a dump-truck driver and divorced father of two who saw his children sporadically and paid child support grudgingly and inconsistently, had this to say about how he would feel if he had never had kids: "I enjoy them when I see them. But if I never had them, I don't think I'd really miss it."

Walter, a divorced dentist, spent little time with his school-age daughter, who resided with her mother in another city. He nevertheless envied his childless counterparts because they "just seem to have more time to do the things they want to do and don't have to deal with the trials and tribulations of raising a child."

Autonomous men were aware that they paid a price for all this independence: periods of loneliness, worries about fulfilling their identities and concerns about growing old without children. Single and childless at thirty-nine, Morrie, the recreation director, became increasingly concerned about needs and desires unfulfilled:

> There are certain feelings, like loneliness. It's a mood that comes over me. I don't know really how to interpret it, whether it's a desire for a woman or a feeling that I'm not fulfilling myself as a man by having a wife and children. I've measured it over the last several years, and I find it hits me about twice a year and may last a week to a month.

Since they could not totally escape these feelings, autonomous men struggled to contain and endure them when they arose. They defined their loneliness as temporary, manageable, and balanced by more significant advantages. Morrie continued:

> My loneliness doesn't last that long, and it's something I can deal with because I have studied Buddhism and feel that I am in tune. Besides, there are advantages, too. . . . I have a wide range of freedom, going anywhere I choose at any given time.

Mark, the environmental adviser, dreaded holidays, so he emphasized their brief duration:

> I guess it bothers me sometimes, like on Christmas, because I see my brother's kids and they have a good time. I remember what a great time I had opening up all the presents, and sort of wish I had my own little somebody happy like that. But Christmas doesn't last too long.

Men who eschewed parental ties discounted the long-run as well as the short-run dangers of remaining uninvolved. They argued, for example, that parenthood does not guarantee a fulfilling life. Zachary declared:

> I won't have had that love relationship of a father and child. I know that's what I'm giving up, but how important is that? It's not something I feel bad about; it's just something I know I won't experience. But I say no matter what you do, if you're married with children or single and not with children, you can screw your life up and really feel depressed. You've got to make your own moves, your own commitments. It doesn't matter if it's family or friends, you've got to work to keep that relationship.

By the same token, they argued, having children does not guarantee security and companionship in old age—objectively, a sensible opinion: since women tend to outlive men, most men can reasonably expect to be cared for by a female partner in their final years. Women, on the other hand, are less likely to be able to rely on men to nurture them in old age.

Kirk, a salesman, nevertheless argued that he could rely on himself and did not need the help of others:

> People say that you're not going to have anyone to take care of you when you're older, but I've managed to take care of myself up to this point, and I'll manage when I'm older. A lot of our friends are going through the stage where their children are leaving home, and they're much more happy now than when the children were there.

Such men agreed with Tony, childless at thirty-eight, who drew on his experiences as a custodian in a nursing home to confirm his view that parents were no better off in old age than their childless counterparts:

> The idea of children taking care of you in your old age—that way is definitely gone. So I really don't worry too much. I'll be taken care of one way or another.

Childless men took solace in seeing their choices as morally responsible, whatever the price. Chuck, the gay systems analyst, thought that people often had children for selfish reasons, such as hoping to be taken care of by them when they grew old. "That, to me, is not a good reason to have children," he said. "Children should not be an antidote to loneliness."

Autonomous men thus argued that fatherhood is not essential to a man's identity. Married men, however, had to contend with their wives' feelings as well. While some found it simple to reject the traditional equation of manhood with fatherhood, they had a harder time rejecting the equation of womanhood with motherhood. Kirk did not worry that his identity was endangered or his self-esteem diminished by not having a child, but he worried that his wife's might be:

> It doesn't make me feel any less of a man or that I've missed part of my life because I've not had children. I don't see it as a need I have to fulfill. But I sometimes wonder, "Am I depriving Emma?"

Once again, these men emphasized the advantages and discounted the potential costs, arguing that their wives could also find equal or greater fulfillment in other pursuits. Harry, the forty-four-year-old social worker and administrator, recognized his wife's feeling that "there's one part of her life that's missing—childbirth and then having this thing that she created. But you know, she makes pottery, and she's writing a dissertation."

Given their own aversion to parenting, they also recognized that their wives would bear most of the responsibility for child rearing. Arnold, a forty-three-year-old truck driver, knew that his wife would "probably get stuck with the kids all day while I'm doing my thing, and I don't think she'd like that. A lot of people break up because of that." Like Kirk, they all attested:

We're comfortable with each other and the lifestyle we have. When we were both making a lot of money and could have easily afforded to have children, we chose not to because we enjoyed the freedom that we have.

Married men took comfort in knowing that they shared the decision to reject parenthood with another responsible adult who saw things the same way. But estranged fathers faced a much more acute predicament. Their rejection of parental involvement had profound and largely negative consequences for their children, who did not participate in the choice and did not enjoy offsetting benefits. They had to cope with their children's reactions, the disapproval of others, and their own concerns about avoiding parental obligations.

Since most estranged fathers had downplayed financial responsibility as well as intimate involvement, they could not use the breadwinner's argument that economic contributions compensated for their absence. Instead, these men defended their low parental contributions largely by holding "society" responsible. Bart, the divorced dump-truck driver with two children, argued that keeping a family together under current conditions had simply become impossible: "I believe if the family is close, it's better for kids. But nowadays you hardly ever see that. Maybe it's just the times. It's just not possible anymore."

Uninvolved fathers also contended that their ex-wives held ultimate control. By relinquishing authority, they argued, they had also relinquished responsibility. Herman, recently separated, saw his two young children only on Friday nights. Although he wished he could see them more often, in his view:

It's just not possible because of my wife. Sometimes I'd like to spend more time with my kids, be more involved with their life, but sometimes it's good to know that they're all right with somebody else.

Estranged fathers even passed decision-making responsibility along to their children. Even though he had not been involved in their rearing, Bart perceived that his maturing son and daughter—and not he—had made the choice to spend time elsewhere:

They're doing pretty good, I guess. They know my number, so I speak to them pretty regular. They don't come around as much. I'd like to see them a little bit more, but they're at the age where they'd rather stay with their friends than come see Daddy on Sunday afternoon. If they want to come over, they're welcome. If they don't want to, I'm not going to force them. Let them do their thing.

As do countless divorced men who withhold financial support from ex-wives and children, these fathers felt a growing emotional distance as well.[15] This made it easier to discount the negative repercussions. Bart moved from viewing his children as independent to viewing parental investments of money as well as time as expendable. On the topic of his children going to college, he said:

> I don't think it's really necessary. *I* didn't go to college. I've seen people graduate college who can't get jobs either—overqualified or whatever. I think they'll do fine for themselves once they get started.

By viewing parental estrangement as imposed by others, these fathers downplayed the harmful consequences of their choices. Like their childless counterparts, they celebrated the benefits of remaining free while minimizing the costs—even to their children.

KEEPING OPTIONS OPEN

Even the most confirmed bachelors experienced, or thought they might one day experience, second thoughts. Mark, the environmental adviser, admitted:

> I've always been cautious, looking for excuses not to get into a relationship which would end up with children. So with the two relationships that went down the drain, I always wondered, "If they had worked out, how would I feel today? What would I be doing?" So far that doesn't really bother me, but I imagine at forty-five it might.

Such concerns encouraged these men to view their choices, while deeply felt, as "permanently temporary" decisions. This paradoxical outlook was possible because, for both biological and social reasons, these men perceived childlessness (unlike the choice to have a child) as reversible—at least in principle. Unlike childless women in their thirties and forties, childless men did not worry about impending biological deadlines. Lester, the sanitation worker, knew "a man who told me his uncle got married and started a family for the first time when he was eighty-six."

By itself, however, men's biological capacity to procreate throughout adulthood does not fully explain why they sense few age deadlines regarding marriage and parenthood. After all, a biological potential can be realized only if social circumstances permit. A man's ability to become a father depends on finding a woman willing and able to join in such a pursuit. Depending on whether they were married or single, childless men thus adopted one of two stances to keep their parental and family options open.

Married men had to confront the limits on their wives' childbearing years. Convinced that his physical youth would continue indefinitely, Vern, a gardener in his mid-thirties, was aware that his wife did not feel so complacent:

Physically, I feel like I'm eighteen. Even if I'm forty-five, I hope I'll feel like when I was eighteen. So as long as I'm physically fine, I'll be able to have a child, play with the child, and bring it up properly. I'll feel great. But my wife is thirty-three now. She feels if she wants one, it should be soon because of her age.

As married men faced this clash between their own wish to postpone final decisions and their partners' approaching biological deadlines, some kept their options open by considering adoption later. Despite the great financial and emotional reserves necessary to undertake such an option, Felix viewed that possibility as a "safety valve" to use "if and when I ever feel more comfortable, and if and when Linda should ever agree."

Single men had easier ways to postpone final decisions. As these men age, they encounter women who are concerned about the ticking clock. In an ironic twist, Andrew linked his own sense of not feeling pressure to the mounting pressure felt by his female companions:

I don't feel pressured at all. I think the chances are that I won't have a child because it's not important to me. I'm not going to go out of my way for it. But if I change my mind, I know a lot of women who don't have any husbands who are dying to have children. They're thirty-six, thirty-seven, and they're just crazy because they don't have children.

He also looked to divorced mothers as a source of "ready-made" families if he ever desired one.

Single men also enjoyed a growing advantage over single women because they are more likely than women to choose younger partners. As men age, they thus face an expanding pool of potential partners (while the pool for women shrinks). So single men's perception that they would be able to choose younger women with whom to start a family was even more important than their sense of gaining leverage over women their own age.[16] Jonathan, a paramedic, told me:

When I was twenty-five, I wasn't ready. Now, at thirty-five, I don't really envision myself wanting a child in the *near* future. The trouble is, if I change my mind, I'd have to have a younger wife. But I've always wanted to marry someone in their early twenties because I've never mentally aged from the early twenties.

The prospect of sharing middle or old age with a younger woman also helped dampen fears about growing old without children. While breadwinners and involved fathers found that children helped them to recapture the pleasures of youth, childless men and estranged fathers relied on younger women to fulfill similar hopes. Marty, the widowed paramedic, looked to younger women as a consolation for growing older: "I prefer young women because I would say that I'm after the youth, the springtime that is no longer here, being a little poetic."

Autonomous men also viewed younger women as a reward for economic success. Victor, a single engineer in his mid-thirties, asserted:

> If having children was something that was a burning desire, I probably would have had them already. I don't need companionship, at least till I get to be sixty or sixty-five, and then hopefully I'll be rich and I can have a nice eighteen- or nineteen-year-old model.

Obviously, the men who hoped to choose a younger woman were stressing the physical attributes of these potential partners. Taken to its extreme, this perspective defined any particular woman, indeed any specific relationship, as disposable. Women could be seen as interchangeable, individual women as replaceable. By comparing his live-in companion to an automobile, Stan, a thirty-five-year-old mechanic, boldly expressed a sometimes unspoken assumption among those who avoided commitment:

> I ain't interested in kids at no point, at no time. Someday, when push comes to shove, I'll have to deal with Julia wanting one. But if I sold that car, I'd just get another one. The same with her. I wouldn't want her to hear me say that, but I'm telling you the truth.

In these ways, men who eschewed parenthood reserved the option to change their minds. They were able to ward off doubts about earlier mistakes and future unknown consequences by viewing change as a continuing possibility. This sense of options remaining perpetually open made it easier to discount the long-run costs of rejecting parenthood. It also promoted a kind of aimlessness regarding personal relationships. Change remained possible, but it was not actively sought, planned, or anticipated. Even though he worried about the implications of rejecting marriage and children, Stuart, a teacher approaching forty, remained staunchly opposed to seeking change in an active way. This choice not to act took the form of a moral code:

> I suppose as I get older, I could become very lonely and disappointed about not having a family. That's something that has occurred to me as a possibility. But I don't feel a burning need for it,

and I certainly don't feel that one sets out to get married. It seems to me, one doesn't—this one doesn't—plan a marriage and a family the way he plans a career. Maybe I have a very romantic conception, but I refuse to go out and find someone to marry. In that sense, I'm very passive.

PROTECTING AGAINST THE RISKS OF "GETTING CAUGHT"

Since autonomous men left open the possibility of changing their minds (thereby assuming the very costs they had endeavored to escape), it is not surprising that they also considered ways to protect themselves against the risks of commitment. For most, protection lay in defining commitment as contingent and reversible.

Some chose cohabitation as a way to enjoy the advantages of marriage with fewer risks. Stan, the mechanic, hoped to avoid a legal bond:

> The way I figure it, marriage is a piece of paper. It's somebody screaming at a VFW hall, a couple of photograph albums, and shit like that. Why do I gotta? It's easier just to live together—easier to break up. If you're married and you change your mind, there's all this legal stuff involved. But if the girl lives with me and if I get tired of the girl or the girl gets tired of me, we don't have to go through all this legal stuff.

Others were not so sanguine about their ability to resist the social and personal pressures to marry and procreate. These men acknowledged, with an air of resignation, that they would probably "get caught" sooner or later. Although he had successfully avoided marriage and defined family life as a trap, Victor was preparing to accept his "fate":

> When people ask me why haven't you gotten married, normally what I say is, "Marriage is a fine institution. I'm just not crazy enough to be locked up in an institution." But, more or less, I have accepted the fact that it probably will happen. I've accepted the fact that I will be locked up in an institution one of these days. I probably will accept my fate in society.

Accepting the inevitability of marriage, however, did not necessarily mean accepting the costs of commitment. Those who were resigned to getting married searched for ways to lower the risks by developing psychological and social protections. Divorce, like cohabitation without marriage, provided a crucial escape route. Arnold, the truck driver, was willing to marry only because he had the option of divorce. When asked why, he replied:

It sounds like a woman referring to a man, but I said to myself, "She has a good job, is the right age, a good girl, a good cook, let's go." I figured if it didn't work, I'd get a divorce. That wouldn't bother me at all. I never feel I'm getting trapped in anything.

Some thought more seriously about the dangers of divorce, however. Fred, a real estate developer, admitted:

One thing that definitely bothers me about marriage is the fear of divorce. My main concern is getting married, inheriting a large sum of property, and having a woman walk away with half of it. It would kill me to drag through the courts in a messy divorce and lose half the assets. I would feel a lot more secure and a lot happier if there were something in writing. So if I do get married, I feel I have to be somewhat protected.

The perception among some autonomous men that they will ultimately marry is not ill founded, since the vast majority of men do eventually marry and, in the event of divorce, remarry. Nevertheless, in the last several decades there has been a decline in the marriage rate as well as a rise in the average age of first marriage. In 1990, 10.5 percent of white men aged forty to forty-four had never married, up from 7.1 percent in 1980. Recent research suggests, moreover, that the chances of a never-married man eventually marrying decrease significantly after the age of forty.[17] For better or worse, many of these men may leave their options open so long that they disappear.

SEARCHING FOR PRIVILEGE WITHOUT A PRICE

Those who eschewed parental and family involvement felt relieved to have bypassed the burdens and pitfalls of breadwinning. Joel, the carpenter, felt fortunate to have escaped the "traps" to which breadwinners succumb:

I grew up with one very good friend—my best, closest friend. It's depressing. He's like a mummy almost. He has a nice house, a great wife, a good job, two kids. But he doesn't do any of the things he used to do. He can't anymore, and it's taken its toll. He keeps plugging along, but it really shows. It's like life is to survive rather to enjoy.

Indeed, some began to feel not just fortunate, but special. They took pride in their resistance to the prevailing demands of breadwinning, with its emphasis on material success and obeisance to social rules. Stan, the mechanic, declared:

People try to brainwash me into it, but I'm *very* happy with what I got, and not many people think like that. I more or less operate on my own. I don't need other people around me, like crutches. My life could be complete if it was just me. People with a wife, two kids—they're not happy. That's for someone else—having to pay the bills and always trying to keep up with the Joneses. The Joneses can keep up with me.

Jeremy, the divorced computer consultant, was proud that, at forty, he retained a youthful zest for risk taking long after others his age had traded such pleasures for the demands and strictures of "maturity":

As you get older, you start to say, "Well, there's certain things that I shouldn't be doing. I'm too old or too mature to do that." Which is stupid. You start to put limitations on yourself. I find I do a lot less of that than most people.

Given the demands and difficulties of primary breadwinning, this sense of having escaped an unpleasant fate is understandable. Yet heightened individualism and avoiding commitment are not the only alternatives to the burdens of primary breadwinning. Sharing both economic and emotional responsibility for family life offers a different way to escape the dilemmas of becoming a good provider. But autonomous men also found this route unattractive and unattainable. They rejected both breadwinning and more equal sharing. Married to a career-committed woman, Joel did not want to be a "superdad":

I see a lot of my friends with children, and it's tough to have to come home and be a loving daddy after a lot of aggravation at work. There's just so much I can handle. A lot of people can cope with it. I can't.

These men adopted strategies to minimize both the costs of commitment and the costs of freedom. They built "bounded" social ties; they searched for meaning and social integration without feeling overburdened and constrained; and they kept their options open without actively seeking change.

Both primary breadwinners and uninvolved men engaged in an effort to defend certain privileges against increasing erosion. While these reactions were effective, they were necessarily imperfect and incomplete. Whether the problem is for a primary breadwinner to meet his economic obligations in a changing economy or for an unencumbered man to find social and emotional ties outside of marriage or parenthood, these men faced a price for their choices. Given the difficulties, it is not surprising that another group of men rejected both of these alternatives, opting instead to forgo some privileges in exchange for sharing some burdens.

8

DILEMMAS OF INVOLVED FATHERHOOD

Work's a necessity, but the things that really matter are spending time with my family. If I didn't have a family, I don't know what I would have turned to. That's why I say you're rich in a lot of ways other than money. I look at my daughter and think, "My family is everything."
—Carl, a thirty-four-year-old utilities worker

As they looked for commitments beyond the workplace and became involved with women who desired and expected help in child rearing, involved fathers found unexpected pleasure in parenting. Spending time with their children became as important to them as contributing money. Becoming an involved father, however, meant trading some historically male advantages for the chance to ease some historically male burdens.

While all involved fathers wished to participate in family life more than their breadwinning and autonomous peers did, most resisted full equality in parenting. Almost 40 percent of all involved fathers became (or planned to become) genuinely equal or primary parents, but the remaining men are better described as "mothers' helpers." This chapter takes a close look at all involved fathers, with an eye toward understanding their dilemmas and conflicts, their strategies for limiting their burdens, and the differences among them. What helped or hindered a father's involvement once a desire to participate had emerged? Why did some involved fathers become mothers' helpers, while others became equal or primary caretakers? The answers to these questions help us to identify the social and ideological barriers that suppress equality as well as the social conditions that foster equal or primary parenting among men.

The Shape and Limits of Involved Fatherhood

Involved fathers rejected distinct boundaries between supporting a family and nurturing one, and defined neither as one person's domain. Carl, a utility repairman with a young daughter and a wife employed as a marketing manager, insisted:

> It's not like "Give me your money, and or you take my money." We put it in one pot and take care of whatever we need. . . . We pull the same weight. . . . As far as time and being around the house is concerned, I can stay home more than my wife can stay home. I come home in the afternoon, and I'm here with my daughter after school. My wife can come home at night to be with her. She likes her job, and she likes the sharing. She's got both worlds. So it's worked out good.

Some men in dual-earner marriages take little responsibility for child rearing, defining their parental commitments in terms of breadwinning despite being married to women who work outside the home. Similarly, while most caretaking fathers were married to (or planned to marry) work-committed women, about 5 percent of them had nonemployed wives and another 20 percent had wives or partners who were employed part-time.[1] It is his participation in caring for his children that determines whether a man is an involved father, not the shared breadwinning that typically accompanies it.

How do I define *participation?* The type and degree of activity varied greatly among the involved fathers, but they all emphasized sharing and flexibility in parenting and domestic tasks. Lou, a sewage worker and father of a young girl, and Theodore, a planner who is married but not yet a father, sound remarkably similar despite differences in class and life stage:[2]

> Patricia and I know how the other works. If one of us has a bad day, the other person will pick up the slack. If it's getting Hannah ready, teaching her writing, spelling, or such, it's whoever is in a better frame of mind that day that handles it. We feed off each other's vibes. If we both have bad days, then whoever had the better day takes care of her.

> One thing I learned: you can't take domestic jobs and say, "You do this, and I do that. You're the one who does the vacuuming and washing and ironing, and I'm the one who does the car and cleans the bathroom." I don't think that's right, and I think the same way with children. It's not going to be, "You're the one who changes the diapers while I burp the child." You do it together. If she's too tired, then I'll do it; and if I'm too tired, then she'll do it.

Involved fathers are flexible. Just as they decline to accept a rigid division between breadwinning and caretaking, they also reject rigid divisions in parenting itself. They do not distinguish "mothering" from "fathering." Vincent, a businessman in his early thirties who planned to become involved when he had children, explained:

I think you have obligations to your kid not as a husband or a father but as a parent. There is nothing as a male that I would not do. I never really changed a diaper before, but I'm sure I can learn how to do it.

Clarence, a self-employed consultant, added:

It doesn't have to be fifty-fifty. It may be seventy-five–twenty-five where I do seventy-five and she does twenty-five, or where she does seventy-five and I do twenty-five. But there's nothing in the raising of a child that I can't see myself doing—changing diapers, getting up, or whatever has to be done—all of that I'm ready to do.

Autonomous men could make work choices without taking the economic needs of children into account. Primary breadwinners faced pressure to maximize their economic contribution, but they could also make choices about work without concern for spending time at home. Men who wished to care for their children, however, faced hard choices between freedom and commitment, career and parenthood, time spent with children and time spent making money or pursuing leisure. In the past, such trade-offs appeared to be the sole preserve of employed mothers; today they confront any adult who tries to be both a committed parent and a committed worker.[3]

First, involved fathers faced a conflict between spending time making money and spending time caring for their children. They felt torn between an ideal of good parenting that stresses providing emotional sustenance and one that stresses providing economic support. Michael, a therapist, had become the custodial parent of his adolescent son and daughter. He worried about how to meet both his emotional and economic obligations:

I think there's an ideal in my head that I should be around more than I am. I try to be as available as I can be with the amount of time that I work, but there's something to be said for quantity, not just quality, of time.

The sense that good parenting means devoting a lot of time to children inevitably clashed with the equally urgent desire to provide a decent standard of living by working hard. Michael continued:

It's tough to maintain a standard of living in today's world—to live in a nice place and be able to send your kids to college or take vacations. And nobody pays you for doing nothing. They don't pay you unless you bust your neck. So it's difficult for me to make a choice, to spend the time I think I should with them. It makes the choices complicated, because you frequently are in situations where you're damned if you do and damned if you don't.

Another dilemma for involved fathers revolves around the contrasting demands of nurturing a family and nurturing a career. Unlike the previous problem, this one concerns how these men can meet their own needs as well as their children's. Ernie, a physical therapist, explained how:

You always feel like you have to make a choice between a career versus family, and that's so unfair. I want a higher position where I can grow and be financially okay, but I don't want to have to travel or be away on weekends. I don't want to sacrifice time with my family; it isn't worth it. I want my cake and eat it too. So that's why I have to struggle all the time, why I always have problems making a decision.

Third, even in the absence of a perceived conflict between family and career, involved fathers faced trade-offs between freedom and commitment, privilege and participation, the ability to pursue personal interests and the demands of family involvement. Neil, a graduate student, anticipated that he would have to sacrifice many treasured leisure activities when he became a father:

I think I can balance my career and a child, but it's the other personal things that will obviously suffer—leisure time, political activity. That's definitely starting to concern me.

Involved fathers felt these conflicts more acutely than other men precisely because they defined "good fathering" in terms of active involvement. Benjamin, a social worker, and his wife faced the same overloaded schedule in caring for their toddler:

It's very exhausting to be a man today, especially a man with a young child. It's exhausting for everybody because if you're going to share the responsibility, which my wife and I have always done, it means there's just a lot to do. I don't want to make it sound too depressing, because you get into the rhythm of it, but I wonder now, "How do I do it? How do I get up at six-fifteen every morning when I used to love to sleep late? How do I get through the day on only six hours sleep?" The fact is that I do, and I'm not falling over, but it's tiring.

How did these involved fathers cope with the responsibilities of parental participation and the attendant loss of privileges that other men retained?

Containing the Costs of Involvement

Involved fathers were flexible about what they would do, but their commitment not to rule anything out did not necessarily include a commitment to rule everything explicitly in. The stress on fluid, interchangeable responsibilities left unresolved the question of how much time they would commit and how much responsibility they would assume. They could use this vagueness to avoid certain tasks. Indeed, most were able to limit or pass on some of the costs of child rearing. These efforts eased involved fathers' personal binds, but they also reduced the chances that their parental involvement would take the form of full equality.

One way to limit the demands of parenthood and still play a significant role in child rearing is to keep the family small. Many involved fathers pushed for this, sometimes amid a wife's ambivalence. Norm, an attorney, insisted on stopping after he and his wife had two children:

> I don't want another child. My wife does and doesn't. If we had another one, it would be too much of a burden. We had a lot of time with Becky. We were able to give her a lot, and I want to be able to do the same thing for the little one, not have a third child in there where they really have to share that.

Some, like Frank, a banker, concluded that the work of rearing one child was more than enough:

> My wife brings the matter up from time to time, "Aren't we foolish not to have another one? The first one has been such a joy and a pleasure." And she has been. But I take a more tempered view and say, "Well, as great a joy as she is, she still requires a great deal of time on both of our parts. Isn't our time spread pretty thin already?" She agrees with that logic.

On the other hand, some involved fathers found themselves settling for fewer children than they would have preferred. Warren, an engineer with an eight-year-old daughter, reluctantly accepted his wife's decision:

> I want more children. She doesn't. She just feels one's enough. She's satisfied. I don't like it, but I've learned to live with it. I can't force her, and even if it were to come down to that, I wouldn't want her to carry

a kid just for me. I feel she might be resentful, taking something away from her career.

Given the convergence of demands on both partners, it makes sense that involved fathers had fewer children than breadwinning fathers. Among primary breadwinners with children, 34 percent had at least three, 49 percent had two, and only 17 percent had only one child. In contrast, only 6 percent of involved fathers had more than two offspring, while 42 percent had only one. Even more telling, taking both current and planned fertility into account, 24 percent of involved fathers planned to limit their family size to one child, while only 10 percent of primary breadwinners held similar expectations. While 36 percent of breadwinners hoped to have at least three children, only 17 percent of involved fathers did. For almost a quarter of those who were (or planned to be) significantly involved in caretaking, one child appeared to be the best compromise between a desire to be involved and a countervailing desire to keep down the costs of involvement. Paradoxically, the men most oriented toward child rearing—those who expressed the most pleasure from taking care of children—were also the least likely to have a lot of them. Carlos, a social worker, said of his and his fiancée's plans:

> Unless there was a radical change in our work style, having a second child would be an extreme hardship on both of us. And I don't think we would want to bring a child in and not be able to really meet that child's needs. I think having one child would meet our needs.

Although the one-child strategy helped resolve the dilemma of how to be an involved father without relinquishing too much freedom, this choice could also produce a sense of unfulfilled desires.[4] To cope with concerns about having a small family, caretaking fathers focused on the potentially dire consequences of having a larger one. In rejecting his sister's suggestion that he and his wife consider adoption when they discovered she could not bear another child, Ernie emphasized the toll a second child might take on his career, his family's financial security, and the time available for his daughter:

> I wouldn't do it now because I feel we struggle as it is with one. There are times that I feel like I don't give enough to Annie, and I don't feel I can provide enough to her. She gets a lot of attention; she gets a lot of love, which to me is primary, and materialistic things are secondary. But I don't feel I could take in another person. I feel we're just managing with one.

The decision to have one child, then, also promoted greater involvement by limiting a father's financial burdens and allowing more time for family life.[5] For Dean, a park worker married to a waitress, having one child allowed him to avoid his father's pattern of working too much and parenting too little:

I always say, "It would be nice to have another one." I enjoy Joey so much. A couple of times I kid my wife, "Maybe tonight's the night." She'll say, "Don't talk crazy." The thing always crosses your mind, but it's really not feasible. I would rather have one child and really devote time to him than have three and be like my father, where he had to work and not get much time.

Limiting family size may seem an ironic response to the desire to be involved, but it lowered parenthood's emotional, physical, and financial demands. It did not, however, resolve all the dilemmas of involved fatherhood. As Benjamin found, even one child can take a significant toll: "Karen . . . sleeps through the night; she's a really good baby. But it is still exhausting to have a child—just exhausting."

Since only a small proportion of involved fathers shared parental responsibilities with a nonemployed partner, most (over three-fourths) of these households relied on paid or unpaid help from an additional caretaker. Involved fathers knew this help was essential for their own well-being, but they tended to view paid baby-sitters, housekeepers, and even relatives as substitutes for their wives (or, in some cases, ex-wives) and not for themselves. Since even the most involved fathers did not consider their paid work responsibilities to be negotiable, the wife's decision to remain at work (or her absence from the home altogether) triggered the search for a "substitute mother." Nevertheless, Norm found that hiring a caretaker after the birth of his second daughter relieved him of many of the duties he had assumed with his first child:

Before the housekeeper, I got my older daughter ready every morning, fed her breakfast, made her lunch—because my wife left earlier than me. Now when my wife and I have to get ready for work, we bring the baby downstairs. The housekeeper'll give the baby breakfast, take care of her, dress her or whatever. So she does a lot of things I used to do.

Of course, the willingness and ability of parents to rely on "parent substitutes" vary. Working-class households were less likely than middle-class ones to use help. While 88 percent of middle-class families with involved fathers relied on some form of paid or unpaid help from a third party, 62 percent of the working-class families did so; 73 percent of middle-class families relied exclusively on paid help, while only 14 percent of working-class families did. But working-class families were more likely to rely on a web of interdependent relationships than were middle-class households.[6] Almost half of working-class involved fathers (and their wives) had help from relatives or friends (or, in the case of those who had not yet had a child, planned to do so).

Scott, a paramedic, and his wife, a nurse, "adopted" his mother-in-law to help with their two children while they both worked full-time:

> We moved in with her mom, and she helped a lot with raising both children. She's been an integral member of the family right from the beginning. I feel she's more my mother than my mother-in-law. She even treats me like her son. I don't think we could exist as a family without her help.

Extended kin allowed working-class fathers to get help without adding a significant new expense to an already strained family budget. It also allowed them to rely on someone they trusted. Todd, a construction worker married to a dancer, conceded the need for an extra caretaker, but did not wish to entrust his newborn daughter to a "stranger":

> Looking for somebody to watch her or even a day-care center—it's expensive and a risk, too. It takes a great amount of awareness to take care of a child. But without some sort of child care, we would inevitably get on each other's nerves. We have to have some time, or our relationship would deteriorate. Luckily her folks are going to be retiring, so we can depend on them.

In some cases, a friend became a caretaker. These arrangements eased concerns about the quality of a child's care; they also offered flexibility and economic savings. Larry, now a limousine driver, was relieved to find a friend to care for his daughter:

> So many people have problems about baby-sitters, and some of them are real expensive, too. We're very lucky. We hired a friend and bring the baby to her house. She doesn't care if we drop the baby off at six in the morning or if we pick her up at night. I don't know any other baby-sitter we could do that with.

Since involved fathers, by definition, wished to participate in child rearing, it is not surprising that they were ambivalent about depending on others, paid or unpaid, strangers or friends. While breadwinners gave little thought to the possible drawback of their daily absence, involved fathers were more likely to worry that the time they had to spend at work might not be good for their children. After Michael acquired custody of his son and daughter, he felt a nagging sense of guilt about relying on someone else to help care for them:

> For the first couple of years, I had to have help in. I had an aunt, and then when she got sick, I had to hire a stranger. I didn't like it. It just

exacerbated my guilt feelings that, "Why wasn't I there? You're the absent man." And, you know, it wasn't realistic. The kids liked it. They were together. If I came home late, there was a regular dinner.

To assuage these concerns, involved fathers looked to the benefits of such arrangements. Housekeepers, baby-sitters, and day-care centers, they argued, exposed their children to a range of experiences that parents alone cannot offer. Charles, a lawyer married to a professor, had nothing but praise for his son's day-care center:

> He's in the center three days a week in addition to the baby-sitter. He loves it. I don't know if it would work with every kid, but it's certainly worked with him. I think there's a need for social interaction besides the mother. It can be bad if the kid ends up being isolated, so the center is very important.

Some involved fathers rejected the argument that either parent's daily absence is cause for concern. Rather, they felt able to parent better precisely because caretaking "backups" relieved the pressures on them. Like less involved fathers, they also focused on the quality of the time they spent with their children. Russell, a legal-aid attorney married to a public relations director, concluded that having an extra caretaker gave his two children more attention than they could receive under different circumstances:

> We've had two housekeepers. The first one was wonderful; the current one is even better. If it were *just* our responsibility to take care of them, things wouldn't happen to the same extent. They get out and play; they're read to; they don't have problems with separating from their parents. And because we're not with them all the time, we're fresher when we are; we're able to spend productive time with them. They have plenty of exposure to their parents. I think it's a wonderful arrangement. It's definitely agreeing with them.

Ultimately, of course, nonparental caretakers could provide involved fathers and their wives only limited assistance. To some extent, this stemmed from the scant social supports for child rearing. Neil complained:

> I have no problems with day care. I don't think there's anything destructive at all. In fact, I see a lot of positive things. I'd like to see my child exposed to people of different racial, ethnic, religious backgrounds. Unfortunately day-care systems are one of the things that nobody spends money on in this country.

Yet involved fathers, like Clarence, wished to keep reliance on an "extra" parent within limits: "Raising a kid is like an investment, and I

224

want to protect my investment. That means being involved as much as I can."

As any mother can attest, a great deal of caretaking work remains even after baby-sitting help is taken into account. As Benjamin put it, there are "countless errands in just the day-to-day running of a household. You throw a child in and, housekeeper or not, it's very tiring." And, while all involved fathers did more caretaking than breadwinning and autonomous men, most still relied on a woman to be the primary parent. Frank, the bank vice president, pointed out how he "helped" his wife, a public relations officer, in caring for their young daughter:

My participation is very extensive. I thoroughly enjoy my daughter's company. I regularly take her out on my own to allow Sharon time without the interruptions of a young child. And when she has got to go out of town on business—often for as much as a week or ten days at a time—I'm perfectly capable of stepping into her shoes.

Some fathers, however, became genuinely equal—and, in rare cases, primary—parents. Thirty-nine percent of involved fathers (or 13 percent of the entire sample) went beyond being mothers' helpers, reflecting a limited but growing trend. Although it is not possible to know exactly what proportion of couples share equally, even conservative estimates suggest that it is on the rise. One study found that about twenty percent of dual-earning couples shared "the second shift" equally.[7] Todd, the construction worker, was one of them:

With the baby, we do everything even steven. We're in this together; we both want to be an influence on the child. The next step is for both of us to spend time with her. It's not just a case of doing what you call extra things because you're taught to think in role models. I'm not doing extra things. This is what has to be done when you have a baby.

While all involved fathers faced trade-offs that other men do not, the degree and consequently the price of parental involvement varied among the group.[8] Why and how did some men become equal, or even primary, parents, while most remained mothers' helpers?

Resisting Full Equality: The Strategies of Mothers' Helpers

Mothers' helpers managed to evade what they considered the dirty work of child care even while embracing the more enjoyable activities. They tended to treat child care and housework as separate domains, so that even when they divided the former equally, the latter remained primarily their wives' duty. And, as I will explain, they avoided *responsibility* for domestic arrangements even when participating equitably in carrying out the tasks. Like breadwinning fathers and autonomous men, they also developed rationales for their selective involvement. In doing so, they contained the costs of involved fatherhood and reduced their unease about passing such costs onto their partners.

AVOIDING THE DIRTY WORK

Mothers' helpers devoted much time and energy to their children, but they avoided those activities that they deemed least attractive. Although Howard, a financial manager, spent his evenings and weekends sharing child care with his employed wife, he let himself off the hook when it came to certain responsibilities:

> I wouldn't say either of us expends ourselves greater in time or emotion. We have a baby-sitter who comes in full-time, but when she's not there maybe Marcia does a little bit more physically. She'll probably get up at night more than I will. I sleep heavier. I don't even hear the baby, and she's up in a snap, and I won't even know it in the morning.

Though still single, Barry, a church organist, anticipated the pleasures of having a child one day, pleasures he associated with affection, not work:

> I'd probably hog certain parts of it—the rocking, the cuddling, and that sort of thing. I like children that much. I probably wouldn't care for changing diapers too much.

What is deemed fun and what is deemed work is, of course, subjective. But the option to choose between desirable and undesirable tasks, which their wives did not possess, allowed most of these mothers' helpers to pass to someone else much of what they preferred not to do.

When they did share child care equally, these men did not share housework in the same way. William, an accountant, and Charles, the lawyer married to a professor, agreed:

> With Danny, I'd say it's pretty shared. It's really whoever happens to be there. He feels very comfortable with both of us. In the evening, I'll give him a bath and put him to bed, change him. We share responsibilities for Danny probably more equally than household chores.

> It's much more equal in what I do with Pete than in the house. I enjoy looking after him; it's more fun than washing dishes or even than putting them in the dishwasher, which I'm still not very good at. I'm lazy about housework and stuff like that, and Rachel is compul-

sive enough that if it doesn't get done, she'll do it. And I take advantage of that.

The pattern of men's avoiding housework while participating in child care appears to be widespread. One study of two-career families found that some men became equal sharers, but that others avoided housework even when they became involved in caretaking. In another, men's share of child care was shown to be substantially higher than their share of housework. And a third found that women do 83 percent of the housework in breadwinner-homemaker households and 70 percent of the housework in dual-earner families (with no significant differences between classes).[9]

PARTICIPATING WITHOUT RESPONSIBILITY

Mothers' helpers were also reluctant to take responsibility even though they participated. Dean, the park driver, conceded that despite his extensive involvement in domestic work, he relied on his wife to assign the tasks: "Joan does a little more of the housework. We never actually sat down and said who should do what, but if she asks me to do something, I'll pretty much gladly do it."

Warren, the engineer, relied on his employed wife to make last-minute arrangements during unexpected emergencies, even when caused by his job:

Sometimes, like if I get stuck working overtime, she'll have to make arrangements for getting a baby-sitter. She always complains to me that I'm working the overtime and she gets stuck finding the baby-sitter because she has to go to work that night. So the pressure is put on her.

Participation without responsibility placed mothers' helpers in the role of reactor rather than initiator. The job of seeing that tasks are distributed equitably—or of making sure they get done at all—fell to the mother. Yet mothers' helpers, unlike breadwinners, did acquiesce to requests for help. Frank, the banker, explained:

My wife sought out commitment from me in terms of how involved I would be, and I gave the commitment to do whatever was assigned. My own attitude was that whatever was reasonable for me to do I would do it. And I think I've been pretty much behaving myself.

The husband who remained a helper placed limits on his wife's ability to secure equality. Ultimately, he decided if and when to participate, knowing that she would make up for his absence. The struggle to secure domestic equality became her job, not his.

EXPLAINING UNEQUAL PARTICIPATION

All involved fathers took pride as well as pleasure in their participation, but those who remained mothers' helpers faced a contradiction between their beliefs and their behavior. Since they supported the ideal of gender equality, they harbored concerns that their resistance clashed with their ideological commitments. Scott, the paramedic married to a nurse, conceded:

> What my opinion is and what we do are two different things. I feel that it should be shared equally, and if the situation warranted it, I could do more housework. I'm not afraid of getting my hands dirty.

To reconcile their behavior with their egalitarian beliefs, mothers' helpers developed rationales to explain the domestic gap that remained even after their participation was taken into account. Their most prevalent rationale centered around housework: they argued that their wives had different standards of cleanliness and different timetables for getting chores done. From this perspective, inequality in housework resulted as much from their wives' choice to do more as from their own choice to do less. Having lived alone before marriage, Keith, a traffic engineer, felt comfortable cleaning.[10] His wife did more housework, he concluded, because she insisted on a "spotless" home:

> As far as washing dishes, taking care of the kids, anything, it really doesn't bother me in the least. I lived alone for a number of years, so I know how to do things. But Barbara's more into cleaning— everything's got to be spotless. She irons my shirts; I never used to do that. If she wants to do it, it's okay with me. She doesn't have to, but that's the way she is.

In these instances, the party willing to tolerate a messy home held the upper hand in any negotiation over domestic labor. The person with the higher standards necessarily lost, either by doing more work or by living with conditions she (or he) did not like. But this impasse could also discomfit the benefiting party. Tom, an editor, found his wife's lack of patience more decisive than his own reluctance, but he was nevertheless uncomfortable with the result:

> I wish I did more, but our time reference is quite different. I'll say, "Okay, I'll do that, but let me do this first." But she will frequently get

frustrated and just not be able to stand the thought that it's not done, and then go ahead and do it.

Another way to cope with the unease that accompanied domestic inequality was to attribute the imbalance to differences in skills and capacities. Since involved fathers rejected the belief that men cannot nurture children, the mothers' helpers among them tended to rely on a version of the skills argument that isolated the specific tasks they wished to avoid. Wayne, a comptroller for a large company, contended that changing diapers, unlike cuddling and playing, required an ability he lacked: "I would try, but I think she'd wind up taking the diaper away from me. I'm not skilled at that."

This argument also helped draw attention to the work that mothers' helpers performed unassisted. For Howard, the financial manager, being responsible for household maintenance offset his reluctance to perform daily chores:

I have things around the house that Marcia doesn't do—yard work, painting, carpentry, repairs, or whatever, so there's still things that I do and still things that she does, and it isn't chauvinism. It's just practicality and experience.

Whatever the reasons, the wives of these men assumed the larger share of domestic work. Men who became mothers' helpers thus discounted the costs to their partners, emphasized their partners' willingness to pay them, and avoided the question of who paid the higher price. Russell, the legal-aid attorney with two children and a live-in caretaker, downplayed his wife's greater career concessions:

Everything I've given up she's given up, plus she's had more at home and her career is more affected than mine. So I guess she's given up more, but with full knowledge of what she was doing and pleasure in doing so.

Mothers' helpers also concluded that their involvement did not fall very far short of equality. By comparing themselves to other men rather than to their partners, they could and did view their participation as admirable and their sacrifices as significant. Considering how much less the average man contributes, it is hard to disagree with Dwight, a computer technician who planned to share caretaking with his wife, an upwardly mobile manager at a utilities company:

I guess we both have to do some sacrificing; that's basically what it is to be a parent. It's probably not going to be fifty-fifty. . . . I think the mother would have a tendency to do a little more. But even sixty-forty is pretty good compared to the average.

While few of these men denied that their partners bore the larger share of family responsibilities, they attributed the gap to situational pressures more than personal preferences.

Tom was in graduate school when his first child was born. He was thus able to take primary responsibility for his infant son's care when his first wife returned to work. Since he was now employed full-time, however, he did not expect to be able to re-create that arrangement when he and his second wife had a child:

> I think ideally the father should be just as responsible as the mother, should have just as much a share. So I think if it worked some other way this time, it is simply because of circumstances. Roz happens to work at home. If she had an office job, then it would be as equally shared as possible.

Because a man's participation emerges from fragile social contexts rather than an "inherent" ability or desire, he may become an equal father in one situation and a mother's helper, a breadwinner, or even an autonomous father in another. If some fathers did become equal participants in child rearing, it is because they faced stronger incentives and met fewer obstacles than other men.

Beyond Helping: What Leads to Equal Parenting?

If most involved fathers resisted equal participation, a substantial minority did not. These "equal parents" shared what mothers' helpers eschewed (see appendix, table 11). Ernie shared responsibility for making arrangements for the care of his young daughter:

> I wanted to be there for the good times and the bad times. I wanted to share in making decisions, which was good for my wife, too. I don't want her to decide on a nursery school; let's decide together.... How can I say I want children and not take that kind of responsibility?

Equal fathers also shared the dirty work of child care and housework. Lloyd, a sanitation worker with three children, drew few boundaries in dividing daily tasks with his wife, a chiropractor:

> We've always shared breadwinning and caretaking right down the middle. That's from washing the floor, changing diapers, washing clothes, cleaning the house. I don't draw any lines as to what is men's work and women's work; work is work.

Ernie and his wife specialized in certain household tasks, but did not divide them in a stereotypical way:

It's got to be done, so at least we try to divide up the things that we are better at. She couldn't deal with shopping, and I'm much better shopping because I do the cooking and know what we use, so I do the shopping. One time I used the washing machine and it broke, so I stay away from that now. We split on the cleaning. We split on Annie. We're pretty balanced.

Some childless men planned to become equal fathers when they had children.[11] Carlos kept an immaculate apartment while living alone. He also cared for many nieces and nephews in his large, close-knit Hispanic family. He thus did not doubt he would share these aspects of domestic life once he married:

> I've changed diapers, baby-sat, rocked children. I'm not afraid of infants. I've fed children, burped them, and got thrown up on. I don't think I would be the type of person to say, "Well, the baby's crying. Go take care of it." And I don't want one person to accept a load that would tire them out to the point that they can't respond to anything else. It's my responsibility as well as the other person's—a fifty-fifty deal.

In rare but significant cases, a father's contribution exceeded his partner's.[12] Rick, a teacher, assumed the lion's share of caretaking when his wife, a librarian, returned to a more highly structured, nine-to-five job shortly after the birth of their first daughter:

> For those first five years, I got the kids dressed and fed and everything. I always got up in the night with the first one. Always. It was ninety-nine percent me with the older one. With the second one, it was shared. We have experimented and continued to do so—not really much thinking of it as an experiment anymore.

For many years, he also did the larger share of the housework:

> I have always done about ninety percent of the grocery shopping and about half of the cooking. For five years, I did most of the laundry, which I hate. Housecleaning, to the extent it gets done, is now probably half and half.

In these families, mothers became "fathers' helpers." Michael, the divorced therapist, explained:

> We had joint custody, but I had the primary residence. They were with me all the time. I was very eager to take the kids. I knew that she would help out, in the sense of being somewhat available. They visit her when they want.

By rejecting the path of least resistance, these men illumine the unusual circumstances that allow and promote equality and even primary parenting for men. They also underscore what deters most involved fathers from choosing full equality even when they might wish to do so.

WHEN MOTHERS ARE MORE COMMITTED THAN FATHERS TO WORK

Among most dual-earner couples, men enjoy higher earnings, better prospects for occupational mobility, and a wider range of career opportunities than do women. Most fathers thus believe their employment should and must take precedence over their partners'. They also conclude that it is both practical and fair to rely on their wives or partners as primary caretakers. For most dual-earning parents, including men who became mothers' helpers, inequality in career and economic opportunities constricts the options of both parents, dampens a father's incentive to become an equal parent, and provides a justification for domestic inequality.[13] Frank's wife adjusted her work schedule when their daughter's child-care arrangements changed:

> Amy is at school two mornings a week, and Sharon takes those days off now. And on the other days, Amy is with the neighbor down the street in a great environment.

When asked whether he would consider part-time work himself, he said:

> As somebody with some training in economics, I happen to believe in specialization and comparative advantage. And my time spent working is more rewarded than hers.

Indeed, many economists, especially those who employ a "human capital" perspective, use precisely this argument to explain domestic inequality.[14] They argue not only that income inequality makes domestic inequality a rational choice but that economic inequality arises from differences in men's and women's tastes or preferences. This perspective assumes that men prefer to maximize their earnings while women prefer to balance domestic and paid work.

In reality, economic and occupational opportunities are far more rigidly divided by gender than are the tastes and preferences of individual men and women. Not only do a large and growing proportion of women wish to enhance their economic and occupational chances by developing their "human capital," but a significant proportion of men would clearly prefer to work less if they could.[15] Those men whose tastes do not place unquestioned preeminence on paid work still face severe constraints on "choosing" to focus less on work and more on domestic pursuits. Although social incentives and constraints tend to push men out of the home and leave women responsible for it, both groups face conflicts between the demands of employers and the noneconomic needs of their families. Claude, a self-employed lawyer, agreed that his superior earnings potential meant that his live-in girlfriend, rather than he, would become the primary parent when they had a child. Ironically, he was uneasy because his higher earnings foreclosed the option of working less:

> I don't think we could consider role reversal because she doesn't have the capability to earn as much as I can, strictly because of job positions. If there came a time when she was, I'd be more than happy to stay home. I'd love it if I could. Unfortunately, I have to work. She's got the luxury of a choice.

In spite of the general pattern of occupational inequality, cases in which a woman finds equal or better career opportunities than her partner's are becoming more widespread. The Census Bureau reports that the number of wives who earn more than their husbands increased from 4.1 million in 1981 to 5.3 million in 1987. The ratio of wives' mean earnings to husbands' mean earnings also increased during those years, from 0.41 to 0.45. For couples in which both partners work full-time, the ratio increased from 0.50 to 0.54. And the proportion of married women working full-time rose from 44 percent to 50 percent.[16]

Even when a wife's current earnings do not outpace her husband's, her long-term career prospects might. Thus Todd watched his wife's dancing career flourish as his acting career came to a standstill:

> We agreed in the beginning that whichever career was taking off at the moment, the other one would take up the slack. And with her dancing, it's easier to get some employment in that if you're good. You can teach dancing, so she can always work. Theoretically, I could teach acting, but when you do that, people want to know, "What have you been in?"

Hank, a paramedic married to a hospital administrator, knew that his wife's long-run chances of pursuing an emotionally rewarding and well-paid career exceeded his own:

> My skills and lifestyle always came with a flippant attitude. I'm a jack-of-all-trades, a master of none, and Connie is a master at something. Financially, she makes more than me, and she has more potential. She has more degrees, and she's going for another one now, so she'll always have that potential. So if I can make arrangements—because financially we're not there yet—I'll stay home and raise the kids.

When a man's partner became more committed to a career than he did, neither parental equality nor a reversal of parental duties was assured. Social and ideological pressures to conform to a different pattern made equal parenting an unlikely outcome even in conducive circumstances. In the rare instances when a reversal of occupational trajectories did occur among parents, however, a more equal arrangement became more likely. There is good reason to believe this dynamic occurs across a broad spectrum of couples. One study found, for example, that when a woman's career commitment is high, her share of domestic labor drops substantially. A comparison of nonemployed wives with those who worked fifty hours a week and earned at least $25,000 a year showed that the employed women's share of domestic labor dropped from 75 percent to 56 percent as their husbands and children took on more. While just being employed may not make much difference for married women's domestic burden, full-time employment in better-paying jobs clearly does.[17]

Not only did economic factors make domestic equality a more practical choice, but the relative career prospects of mothers and fathers had ramifications that extended beyond and superseded economic considerations. The logic of economic advantage could be used to promote parental equality and role reversal in much the same way that it provided a rationale for most men's resistance, but the calculus of decision making involved more than money.

The relative degree of work commitment and satisfaction among parents was more decisive than strict economic accounting. Thus the percentage of equal fathers and mothers' helpers who earned about the same as their partners is roughly equal (44 percent to 38 percent), but equal fathers were more likely to be involved with a woman who faced better *long-term* career prospects (28 percent compared with only 7 percent for mothers' helpers). While neither pure economics nor pure ideology accounted for their decisions, the career trajectories and long-term economic prospects of both partners had subtle but important effects on how they negotiated their current family arrangements.[18] If an involved father became alienated from his job while his partner developed a strong attachment to her career, her expanding occupational commitment provided him with expanding domestic options. In these cases, men viewed equal parenting not as a burden but as an opportunity. As Clark said:

> I don't know how long I would be home, but however long it is, it would be a rest from my job. She knows I'm not too happy with what I'm doing, and I have told her I can't see doing this for the rest of my life.

Choosing parental equality—or role reversal—contradicts the complex array of social pressures that push men to choose another path. Achieving this fragile outcome depends on consent from both parents. To be willing to take equal responsibility, fathers had to derive more from caretaking than just pleasure. The promise of a happier marriage and the hope of expanding their own occupational options provided equal fathers with additional incentives to take on the less pleasant tasks of parenthood as well. For Carlos, being willing to share caretaking and breadwinning gave him the freedom to work in a more satisfying, but less highly paid, profession:

> It's become very expensive to raise a child . . . even with both incomes. So both of us would have to work . . . unless I decided to make a radical change and go into business to make money, like my aunt told me I should.

A father's personal commitment needed to be bolstered by economic circumstances and by a partner's willingness to support his choice. Hank knew that his staying home with a child would depend on his wife's support—which in turn depended more on her preferences than his own:

> If it made me happy, she'd go for it, and she knows the kids would be looked after. It's better than a sitter, day care, something like that. But if she feels the need to be home with Junior, then she'll be home with Junior. I'm only jealous because she has that option, and I don't.

Circumstances that permitted and promoted egalitarian or primary fathering were thus fragile and rare. When a father's dissatisfaction with work combined with a mother's growing commitment to it, however, their job trajectories converged to make equality or primary parenting by a man more attractive—certainly not guaranteed, but more likely.

WHEN FATHERS TAKE ADVANTAGE OF FLEXIBLE WORK

Men who became mothers' helpers often perceived that differences in work arrangements allowed their partners, but not themselves, to integrate work and parenting. Craig, once a dancer and now an educational administrator frustrated in a nine-to-five job, longed for the relative flexibility of his wife's dancing career:

> A good deal of her work is either in the home or in a location where she could have a child with her. In terms of sheer time, hers is something that can be adjusted up and down. Whereas the things I'm doing now and envision doing in the near future are much more time-specific, like nine to five.

A wife with more flexible work helped some men to explain the discrepancy between their ideals and their behavior. Charles, the lawyer married to a professor, saw scheduling differences as the reason why his wife was responsible when emergencies arose:

> When Pete is sick and a major adjustment has to be made, if I'm able to do it, I do it. But I think she's made more adjustments than I have. She is much more able to work at home. I can't bring my law library home with me. And the courts refuse to hold hearings in my living room. But so much of her stuff is self-generated—reading, writing, whatever—she is much more able to make the adjustments in her schedule than I am. So it's partly sexism and partly that she really does have more flexibility.

Lack of job flexibility provided a genuine reason as well as a justification for unequal participation. Whatever their desires, most fathers were constrained by rigid work schedules, which make equal parenting less attractive and easier to avoid, if not impossible. In a recent Census study of child-care arrangements for dual-earning couples with children under five, when both parents worked during the day, only 4 percent of mothers reported that their husbands were the primary caretakers when they were at work. When both parents worked at night, however, 31 percent relied on their husbands as primary caretakers. When the father worked during the day and the mother worked at night, 32 percent relied on their husbands. And when the mother worked during the day and the father worked at night, 18 percent relied on their husbands.[19] Caretaking by fathers is thus more likely to occur when at least one parent works an unconventional shift.

We have seen that some workers who had the option of working unconventional hours did not choose to do so. Still others chose to spend the time made available by flexible work to engage in leisure pursuits rather than care for their children. About 30 percent of breadwinners had work schedules that offered flexibility (through shift work or self-employment), but these men did not use this flexibility to increase their parental participation. Instead they chose either to bolster income by working longer hours or to enjoy leisure activities.[20] Without the motivation to become more involved with his children, a father's job flexibility bears no relation to his parenting. But the proper motivation enhanced the chances that an involved father would use a flexible work schedule to become an equal parent. This was especially so when his partner's work schedule was more rigid. For Rick, the teacher, shorter hours at the workplace and summers off allowed him more family time than his wife, a librarian, could muster. For many years he was the primary parent; now that the children are in school, he and his wife share child care "about equally." He explained how this arrangement came to pass:

> I always got out of work sometimes at noon, sometimes at one o'clock, two o'clock, three o'clock, and she always worked till between five and six. So I also was the one who did most of the shopping and the laundry and straightening up in the house. And I took care of the kids the lion's share of the time.

Work choices made by both parents long before the birth of their children could promote this outcome. Neil chose academia for other reasons, but valued the opportunity to work at home:

> One of the great things about being in academia is that you are around your kid a lot more than if you have a nine-to-five job. If my wife was working nine-to-five and I was gonna be home a few days a week, I'd take care of the kid. I would want to, and I see it as essential for my kid.

For some, flexible work schedules had the unintended consequence of promoting equality or primary caretaking by a man. Others consciously chose to reject a nine-to-five schedule so that they could be more involved. Todd opted for the evening shift at his construction job so that he could spend his days with his newborn daughter while his wife pursued her dancing career:

> I take care of her in the morning and until I have to leave for work. I wake up with the morning ahead of me, and that's important with a little one. Even if I'm pretty tired when I get up, all I have to do is look at that little face, and I feel good.

Flexible work schedules could exact costs. They sometimes came at the expense of other work rewards, such as opportunities for advancement and a higher income. Equal fathers were willing to pay this price in order to spend more time with their children. Carl, the utility repairer, left a job as a court clerk and took a less promising job to take advantage of a shorter commute and an earlier quitting time:

> I had to start as low man on the totem pole. But it's a great job because I get home early. I used to get home around six-thirty. Now I'm home at twenty to four and spend a lot of time with my daughter.

When job flexibility converged with a desire to seek rewards outside work, fathers were more likely to become equal parents. Although rare, some men chose this arrangement in spite of the toll it might take on their work careers. They saw offsetting benefits. Practical and emotional support from a partner was also important. Carl explained how his wife's schedule and personal desires meshed with his own:

> She took a night job. If I had a night job, she would be working days. As far as being around the house, I can stay home more than she can. I told her, "Look, when you're tired of it, let's sit down and have a talk, and we'll change." She seems to like this way, and she's got both worlds. If you're both in agreement, there's nothing wrong.

Flexible work provided the opportunity for equal parenting, but more subtle psychological incentives allowed and encouraged men to take advantage of it.

WHEN FATHERS DON'T HAVE A WOMAN TO RELY ON

Although divorce typically separates fathers from their children, fathers can become more involved if they retain joint or sole custody. Of course, men seek custody precisely because they wish to participate in rearing their children. Nevertheless, retaining custody can have unintended as well as planned consequences.

Both one-parent families headed by men and joint-custody divorces remain rare, although the size of both groups is growing. The percentage of male custodial households has grown from 1.9 percent in 1970 to 3.1 percent in 1989. The number of divorces that produce joint-custody arrangements is harder to ascertain, but it is clearly growing at a much faster pace than male custody alone.[21] The number of divorced fathers in my study is small (only fourteen), but 43 percent of them retained some form of joint or sole custody, albeit not always legally.[22]

Robert, a divorced high school teacher and father of two, is typical of these men, who chose involvement long before getting divorced:

> It was pretty equal before the divorce, including during times when she was seeing other people and I was seeing other people. It was as equal as it could be, since I couldn't nurse. But certainly, as far as everything else, it was equal. We both had daytime jobs, and I did most of the cooking and things with each child.

When a father has become close to his children, divorce, even when it is welcomed, threatens to undermine or even destroy that attachment. If the bond between father and child is to survive after the bond between husband and wife is severed, the father must acknowledge the importance of being involved and make an effort to retain that status. Tom, the editor, sought joint custody to allay fears of losing his one-year-old son:

I was terrified that I would lose contact with my son. There was never the kind of hostility that made me think she was gonna try to prevent me from seeing him. I just became very afraid of what being a part-time father might do—that it might not be enough to have the kind of relationship that I certainly wanted.

Paternal custody, although unusual, shows how a mother's helper can become an equal or primary parent. Michael became the custodial parent when his ex-wife became increasingly frustrated being a housewife and mother:

I think it was something we both wanted. Her need for freedom—I didn't need to feel that. I'm a very home-oriented, family-oriented person. And times have changed. You can make different decisions now. Once we agreed on all that, that was it.

Expanding opportunities for women outside the home have made it easier for frustrated wives and mothers to acknowledge their feelings and act on them. An "abandoned husband" may find himself unexpectedly assuming the chief duties of child rearing. Even before his divorce, Harold, a tow-truck driver, found parenting thrust on him when his wife rejected the role:

It was amazing to me how, after her being home all day, nothing was done. I would come home and do the dishes, clean the house, do whatever had to be done. There were times when she wouldn't even get up to give them a bottle. I would get up at night and find Dawn soaking wet, change her, change the crib, and go sit in the living room with her in my arms until we fell asleep.

Whatever the path, retaining some form of custody held unforeseen consequences for fathers who, though involved, were formerly able to rely on a woman to do a large share of the parental work. Divorce shattered some men's belief that a woman would always be there. Michael grieved for the past he had lost:

When you get divorced, you have to give up a fantasy that there's always going to be somebody there for you to rely on. It was very difficult for me to give up a dream of building something with another human being. If I want to build something, I've got to do it myself. And even if I get married again, it's not the same thing.

The loss of a female partner may also have more felicitous consequences. It forced once-complacent fathers to confront the previously unnoticed tasks required to rear a child. Fathers who did not have a woman to rely on had little choice but to develop what some call "maternal thinking."[23] Roger, a businessman, was converted from a primary breadwinner into a primary caretaker of three young sons when his wife left him for another man:

> I went from having to do almost nothing except playtime to having to do virtually everything. . . . You sit down, and where do you start? From scratch. You start by writing a list of everything that comes to your mind that you need to do. You realize the list goes from the floor to the ceiling a half-dozen times.

These divorced men came to realize how much their freedom and independence had depended on their former wives' presence. They learned what their ex-wives already knew: involved parenting requires personal sacrifices. Michael discovered that his children's needs could and often did conflict with his own desires:

> I always felt responsible, but it's gotten worse since I got divorced. When my ex-wife was at home, that was her job, and my job was to go out and make money. And I think our relationship suffered from that situation. Now, I feel more responsible—which is a little conflict in the sense that it's a choice between doing what I want for myself and being the parent I really want to be.

When the shock wore off, however, custodial fathers discovered the capacities to meet this new challenge. Like women who succeed after being thrust unexpectedly into motherhood or the workplace, custodial fathers became successful parents despite initial fears, doubts, and resistance. They learned what research has confirmed: they could parent as successfully as any woman.[24]

If divorce did not diminish or sever a father's bond, some form of shared or sole parenting ensued. Even in joint-custody arrangements, parental separation could intensify paternal involvement. The strict apportioning of parenting time in the aftermath of divorce made these men more aware of what it takes to build a relationship. Those who wanted to preserve or strengthen their bonds to their children had to become more committed. Although Tom feared that divorce would steal his child from him, he found instead that it forced him to become more involved:

> It's one of those things where, since I do see him on a restricted basis, I think the time we spend together is more intense than it was or would be. Instead of me just taking him for granted, being around the house, I see to it that we're always doing everything together when he's here.

Like other equal fathers, custodial fathers were likely to search for less demanding and more flexible jobs. Roger found himself making unexpected work sacrifices to accommodate his new job as a primary parent:

> The boys remained with me from the beginning, and I needed stability. I couldn't start a new job and rearrange my home schedule, so I stayed. I was making enough money, the hours fit, and it was convenient. I could be home at five-fifteen, have dinner on the table by six-fifteen. I was bored, but it was convenient for what else I was dealing with at the time. It's a seesaw. You've got to keep things balanced.

This strategy brings things full circle, as custodial fathers, like other equal parents, struggled to combine work and parenthood. It also tells us what many fathers want and need. These men were willing to trade money for fewer demands and more control over the conditions of work. But finding a job that provides flexibility and control is more easily wished for than accomplished—for a woman or a man.

Coping with the Costs of Equality

Equal fathers are rare because it takes rare circumstances for them to emerge. These men make it clear that, when those circumstances demand, men are able to express love in a variety of ways, including the "expressive" forms so often assumed to be the preserve of women. A range of studies report that a man can become a nurturing parent in a variety of situations, but especially when he loses his wife or when his wife is a "mainstay provider."[25]

Among the men in these pages, those who became equal parents did so as a last resort when other alternatives were unavailable, unacceptable, or too costly. When a father's occupational prospects were dimmer than his wife's, when his job was more flexible or less demanding, or when his wife was absent altogether, an involved father moved beyond helping to sharing equally or becoming the predominant parent (see appendix, table 12). It took these unusual opportunities and constraints on both parents to overcome the heavy social and ideological barriers to equal participation. Since social arrangements make equal parenting both unlikely and difficult, "male mothering" emerged only when it became easier to choose it than to avoid it. When this happened, men developed parenting skills and attachments that rival those more often imputed to women. Indeed, when the opportunity arose, these men became "mothers" with apparent ease.

Said Todd, the pipe repairer and aspiring actor, as he cradled his daughter in his arms:

Sometimes I do it a little more than Sally just because I like to. It's a thrill to watch the various senses start to come into play. She'll make a gurgling noise that's close to a vowel sound or syllable, and I'll repeat it. I love the communication. The baby smiles more around me than around her mother. So I benefit, too.

Equal fathers had worries similar to those of mothers. The strength of their emotional attachment could make them concerned about being overprotective and too indulgent, like Michael:

I lean in the direction of being more nurturing than maybe is good for them . . . too overprotective and being there to smooth out the rough spots in life, which doesn't really teach kids that smooth functioning is more a rarity than an everyday occurrence.

Like women who place a large emphasis on mothering, they worried about the loss and separation that would come with an empty nest. Michael and Harold discovered:

I can understand how women feel about empty nests. It's really like I put all this time and energy into something, and all of a sudden it's, "Whoosh, what am I going to do with myself now that I don't have to be home tonight?"

My daughter is seventeen, and she just took off to the university. I miss her so much, it's unbelievable. I've had her with me so long. Thankfully, she's been home almost every weekend.

Just as equal and primary fathers acted and thought like caretaking mothers, they faced similar conflicts. While mothers' helpers strove to justify the inequality that remained after their participation was taken into account, equal and primary fathers had to cope with the difficulties of juggling heavy work and family demands. The similarities between equal fathers and work-committed mothers are unmistakable. While most men may not trade off between family and work as women do, those men who face similar constraints are likely to make choices in similar ways. Michael, for example, worried about the toll his working took on his children:

Probably the thing I dislike the most has to do with my being hard on myself for being so career-oriented. I am very ambitious, and it's a conflict that's still unresolved. I get the guilts about how much time I spend away.

Equal fathers also worried about the personal costs of their choices. Like employed mothers, they could feel overwhelmed by the magnitude of all they had to do. Michael continued:

Because I have custody of the children, because I have very responsible positions, because I'm doing so many things—trying to do all of
that is hard. When I tell friends what I do, they say, "Oh my God, you
poor guy. You must be overwhelmed." And it's true. Sometimes I feel
that way.

To cope with the conflicts and the costs of their choices, fathers who
became equal or primary parents focused on the benefits and discounted
the costs to themselves and their children. They emphasized such personal rewards as a greater sense of domestic control, the intrinsic pleasure of being close to their children, and even the advantages of receiving credit for a job well done. Robert, the high school teacher with joint
custody, acknowledged:

> I take a little late-twentieth-century pride in being a single parent be-
> cause I know I succeeded. And when things are running smoothly,
> like clockwork, I can take the credit. I'm proud of the fact that, yes,
> I'm a good parent. I'd feel incomplete without my kids.

Equal parenting increased a father's work load, but it also increased
his say in running the household. Michael felt relief—not just concern—
when his wife left him in charge of rearing their daughter and son:

> Well, for one thing, there was less conflict around child-rearing issues.
> So in some ways, there was less pressure because we didn't have to
> fight about that anymore. I was in control; it was my ball game; and as
> long as I kept her informed about important decisions, that was okay.

For those men who wished to have more control over how things got
done, even housework did not seem unduly onerous. Lloyd, the sanitation worker with three children, explained how his wife, a chiropractor,
agreed to adopt his standards and rules in exchange for his increased
participation:

> I like cleaning. I'm a neatnik, and I can't help it. I'm very organized.
> When I see what has to be done, when I come up with a routine, it's
> usually the quickest and most efficient way of doing things. Doing the
> wash every day is a lot easier than waiting for two hundred pounds of
> laundry. She would rather go with the two hundred pounds of laun-
> dry, but we do it my way.

Most, however, found it hard to see the benefits of doing the laundry
every day. They argued, rather, that the long-term rewards of close relationships with their children offset the short-term drawbacks. Rick explained:

It doesn't seem like it at the time, when they get up five times in the middle of the night crying, or when you're constantly having to diaper, or when you're exhausted and you still can't go to sleep.... But it doesn't last forever. The kids do grow up, are able to take care of themselves. So I feel very good about that.

Egalitarian fathers also downplayed the costs of their choices. Rick put his doctoral degree on hold to attend to his daughters' needs:

My fear was always that I would never be able to finish my doctorate, and I might add that was not very irrational. That was a very wise, a very understandable fear because I always gave that the back seat. I always paid more attention to the kids, which is why it took me nine years to get my Ph.D.

These fathers discounted personal concessions much the way that mothers' helpers discounted their wives' heavier burdens. Rick defined his "sacrifices" as a temporary delay rather than a permanent setback:

It required sacrifices, but the joys far outweigh it.... It was worth it. I'm embarrassed that it took so long to finish my doctorate, but it *did* finally get done. So the fact that it took longer—well, I just write that off.

Equal fathers also downplayed the importance of their work or career in comparison to their children's well-being. They took as much or more pride in their parental accomplishments as in their work achievements. Deriving a vicarious identity from parenting, they were prone to identify with their children and their children's accomplishments. Roger, the businessman with custody of three sons, decided that giving his children stability was more important than climbing his career ladder:

After my wife left, I didn't want to take away the kids' support system. That's why I didn't move—so their whole life wasn't disrupted. In that sense, it restricted me. I turned down a very good position because I didn't want to do that to them. People say, "What about your career?" Screw my career. I can fix that later.

Carl, the utility repairer who left a job as court clerk, also felt that spending time with his daughter compensated for lost career opportunities:

I felt good going to work in a suit and a tie. It was a new thing for me. But life goes on. As long as my family's together and I'm happy at home, the rest is secondary. I had the opportunity to spend a couple of years with my daughter. You can't have that back.

Finally, when these psychological strategies fell short, equal fathers became fatalistic. Things could be worse, they reasoned; in any case, they could not avoid the costs they bore. Single fathers who felt abandoned were especially likely to develop a fatalistic world view. When his wife moved out, leaving him to care for their school-age daughter, Gary, a custodian, took solace by comparing his current situation to less fortunate times:

> It's a big deal, and it isn't. It's more work, but I've lived in a house with no heat and no hot water. I've worked in shit. Compared to some of the things I had to do, it's nothing. When the going gets tough, the tough get going.

Like employed mothers who struggle to be "superwomen," equal fathers tried to be "superdads" who could juggle the demands of full-time work and parenting. They made trade-offs between family and career that other men did not have to face. Ernie worried:

> I've had opportunities, but maybe I've sacrificed and not pushed for certain things—things that might have required more traveling, more nights, and more time away. So maybe I traded off for my family. But I tell you, I never second-guessed, I never had any hesitation. I certainly would rather have what I have than trading off the family for a career.

Their sacrifices, moreover, were rarely noticed or applauded, as Rick learned:

> There was one time when one of these doyens of the junior league was sitting in her shop, and I walked in with the two kids. And she said, "Oh, I have seen you at the school many times. I always thought you were a nonworking parent, that you stayed home." At the time, I was furious because I was holding down a job and taking care of the kids and writing a dissertation, and she thought I just hung around the playground all the time.

Given that equal fathers perform a juggling act with as few social supports as employed mothers possess, it is hardly surprising that so few men choose equality. Most involved fathers concluded that being a mother's helper holds fewer drawbacks and offers enough rewards to make it the more attractive option.

The Suppression of Fatherhood: Social and Ideological Obstacles to Equality

Among those men who became involved in caretaking, only a minority embraced full equality. But more men wished to participate equally than actually did. Even when they wished it otherwise, men's parental involvement was systematically suppressed.

Contrary to the stereotype of the work-obsessed man, most involved fathers preferred to work less and parent more. Most, and especially those who held full-time jobs organized around rigid schedules (the situation obtaining for the majority), desired a significantly different work situation than the one they were in (see appendix, table 13). Were it not for economic necessity, they would have chosen a more flexible or less time-consuming full-time job, a part-time job, or no job at all. Bruce, a paramedic, explained:

> If I was making the same or more and only working part-time, I'd definitely enjoy it more. . . . If I came into a lot of money, a sufficient amount to where I didn't have to work, I wouldn't. There's a lot of things I'd like to do—gardening, woodwork, making things.

As Howard, the financial manager, revealed, most did not equate a "classic job" with creativity, accomplishment, productivity, or fulfillment. To the contrary, paid work stood in the way of accomplishing the goals that many deemed more important:

> A lot of people say, "If I won the lottery, I'd keep my job." If *I* won the lottery, I'd stop tomorrow. If I didn't have to work at the classic job, I wouldn't. That doesn't mean I wouldn't be productive, but I would have the ability to be productive in whatever way that I wanted.

Given the right conditions, many men would forgo traditional jobs in favor of more control over the conditions of work and the ability to spend less time at it. For involved fathers, more flexibility and control meant more time for family life, not just more time for leisure. The right conditions rarely obtain for those who would choose to spend less time at work and more with their families, however. The obstacles that constrain men's domestic participation not only make parental equality an elusive option; they also perpetuate the belief that all men prefer it that way. These obstacles are varied, widespread, and deeply embedded in how work, the economy, and domestic life are organized. Given these obstacles, it is not surprising that few men become equal parents.

Fathers and would-be fathers rarely enjoy the option to withdraw from paid work, even temporarily, to care for a child. Although full-time domesticity has declined as an option for women, it has not emerged as an option for men. Involved fathers were keenly aware that others frowned on the choice *not* to pursue a career. Even independent wealth did not entirely excuse a man from the cultural imperative to prove himself through work. Carlos imagined the disapproval he would face if his desire to quit work ever became a real option:

Personally, if I had an independent source of money and didn't have to work, I would enjoy it. But at the same time, a lot of people associate who they are through their jobs. When I wasn't working and met other people, it seemed very difficult to tell people who you were if you couldn't talk about what type of work you did.

Even more important than social disapproval, however, were personal circumstances that put domesticity or part-time work out of reach. The systematic depression of women's earnings and the gender gap between men's and women's incomes made it impractical and, indeed, impossible for most men to consider staying home while their wives went to work. Even if social change has made switching places more ideologically palatable, the persistence of economic inequality renders it a largely hypothetical option. Clarence, the self-employed career consultant, could not imagine finding a woman willing or able to support him as a full-time parent:

I have gotten away from the idea of role playing, so that if there's someone who's comfortable out there in the job market and really making enough money to maintain us, then I could have my role be to take care of the family. I haven't ruled that out, but I haven't met a woman who's been willing to take care of me.

Most involved fathers supported the ideal of an egalitarian exchange in which each partner shared both economic and domestic responsibilities, but they were less comfortable with the idea of depending on their partners for financial survival. Unable to accept an arrangement in which his wife worked and he did not, Carl wished that both could escape the world of paid work. The ideal job for him would be no job:

But it's just not possible. I wouldn't ask Sherry to be the only worker. I couldn't just quit and say, "You work, and I'll stay home." But if we were put into the situation where we didn't have to work, I could tell her we could both quit.

Economic inequalities between women and men underlay and reinforced cultural measures of manhood that stress work and earnings over parental dedication. However devoted, few fathers had the option to give their undivided attention to their children. Choosing domesticity required extraordinary economic circumstances and the strength to resist prevailing ideologies. Like Roger, the businessman who used his "golden parachute" to rear his three sons full-time, the few who chose domesticity had to overcome huge hurdles:

Instead of looking for a job, I'm going home to see my son's wrestling match. How many wrestling matches is he going to have in his life? But I wouldn't be doing that if I didn't have the financial package.

Social disapproval and economic inequality put full-time domesticity out of reach for almost all men. Yet most also found that economic necessity and employer intransigence made anything less than full-time work an equally distant possibility. Few employers offered the option of part-time work, especially in male-dominated fields. Arthur, a married sanitation worker planning for fatherhood, complained:

> If it was feasible, I would love to spend more time with my child. That would be more important to me than working. I'd love to be able to work twenty-five hours a week or four days a week and have three days off to spend with the family, but most jobs aren't going to accommodate you that way.

Yet, even if part-time work were available, involved fathers still needed the earnings that only full-time and overtime work could offer. Lou, the sewage worker who worked the night shift in order to spend days with his young daughter, could not accept lower wages or fewer benefits:

> If I knew that financially everything would be set, I'd stay home. I'd like to stay more with my daughter. It's a lot of fun to be with a very nice three-year-old girl. But if I work less, I would equate it to less money and then I wouldn't be taking care of my family. If it meant less work and the same or more money, I'd say, "Sure!" I'd be dumb if I didn't.

Dean, the driver for a city department of parks, agreed that his economic obligations could not take a backseat to his nurturing ones:

> It always comes down to the same thing: I would like to have more time to spend with my children, but if I didn't have money, what's the sense of having time off? If I could work part-time and make enough money, that would be fine and dandy.

Since involved fathers tried to nurture as well as support their children, they made an especially hard choice between money and time. Like many mothers, they had to add caretaking onto full-time workplace responsibilities, but employers are generally reluctant to recognize male (or female) parental responsibility as a legitimate right or need.[26] Worse yet, paternal leaves are rarely considered a legitimate option for men even if they formally exist. Involved fathers wished to take time off for parenting, but like most men they were reluctant to do so for fear of imperiling their careers.[27] And even though most employers allow health-related leaves with impunity, they have not been so flexible when it comes to the job of parenting. Workers receive the message that illness is unavoidable, but parenting is voluntary—an indication of a lack of job

commitment. Our current corporate culture thus makes parenting haz-
ardous to anyone's career, and choosing a "daddy track" can be just as
dangerous as the much-publicized "mommy track." Juan, a financial analyst, knew he could not pull back from his job for more than a few days
or a week without jeopardizing his job security. To parental leave,

> I'd say yes, but realistically no. It would be a problem because it's very
> difficult for me to tell my boss that I have to leave at such a time. I
> have deadlines to meet. If I leave the office for two or three months,
> my job is in jeopardy.

Because employers did not offer flexible options for structuring work
on a daily basis or over the course of a career, some involved fathers
looked to self-employment or home-based work for more flexibility and
control. Craig, the ex-dancer currently working in an office, hoped he
would be able to integrate work and parenting by working at home:

> I would like to find myself in the situation where I'm not locked into a
> nine-to-five schedule. Ultimately, I hope I'm doing consulting on my
> own at home, which means time close to the family. So that in the
> middle of my own workday, at the house, I'm available. I can just put
> my work aside and play Daddy.

Most could not even entertain this option. They had to fit parenting in
around the edges of their work lives.[28]

Domestic arrangements also impeded full equality. Child rearing remains an undervalued, isolating, and largely invisible accomplishment
for *all* parents. This has fueled women's flight from domesticity and also
dampened men's motivation to choose it. Russell, the legal-aid attorney
and father of two, recognized that child rearing was less valued than employment:

> I think I would feel somewhat meaningless to not be engaged in any
> form of productive work—although certainly raising children is pro-
> ductive work. But I couldn't be responsible for that on a full-time basis.
> While I love my guys, I don't think I could be around them all the time.

Child rearing can be invisible as well as undervalued. Unlike the size
of a paycheck or the title one holds at work, there are few socially recognized rewards for the time a parent devotes to raising a child or the results it produces. This made only the most dedicated, like Hank, willing
to consider full-time parenting:

> Nobody will know the time and the effort I put in the family. They will
> look down on it. I would devote time, hours, and nobody will be
> happy with it except me because I'll know what I was trying for.

The forces pulling women out of the home are stronger than the forces pulling men into it. Since the social value of public pursuits outstrips the power and prestige of private ones, men are likely to resist full-time domesticity even as women move toward full-time employment. This process is similar to the one pulling women into male-dominated occupations while leaving men less inclined to enter female-dominated ones. In addition, just as women in male-dominated occupations face prejudice and discrimination, fathers who become equal or primary parents are stigmatized—treated as "tokens" in a female-dominated world.[29] Roger shied away from the pervasive questioning about his life as a custodial parent:

> I think I've become somewhat more introverted than I used to be—because I get tired of explaining my situation at home. . . . The thing that blows all the kids' minds—they're all living with Mommy and my kids are living with Daddy.

In the face of such disincentives, most involved fathers rejected staying home for the same reasons many women do and more. Female breadwinning and male homemaking did not seem acceptable even when they made economic sense. Robin, a stockbroker, rejected domesticity precisely because his poor work prospects left him in no state to bear the additional stigma of becoming a househusband. Although he was making a lot less money than his wife was, he felt too "demoralized" to consider staying home. "I'm not secure enough, I guess, to stay home and be a househusband."

Of course, involved fathers actively resisted the discrimination they encountered. They asserted their nurturing competence and insisted on being taken as seriously as female parents are. The prevailing skepticism about men's parental abilities, however, made this an uphill battle. Ernie complained:

> I believe I have as much right in raising the child as she does, but I found a lot of reverse discrimination—people assuming that the mother takes care of the child. It's a lot of stereotyping, a lot that's taken for granted. Like pediatricians: they speak to my wife; they won't speak to me. I say, "Hey, I take care of her, too." They look at me like I'm invisible. The same thing with the nursery school. I went out on all the interviews. They looked at me like, "What're *you* doing here?"

Economic, social, and ideological arrangements thus made involved fatherhood difficult. The lack of workplace and domestic supports diluted and suppressed the potential for involvement even among the most motivated men. In the absence of these hurdles, fathers who wished to be involved might have participated far more than they actually did.

They might, in fact, have made choices that now remain open to a rapidly diminishing number of women. Ernie wished he had options that only full-time mothers enjoy:

> I'm not the type that has career aspirations and is very goal-oriented. If I didn't have to work, I wouldn't. But I would volunteer. I would work in a nursery school. I would do a lot more volunteer work with my daughter's school. I would love to go on trips like the mothers who don't work, be more active in the P.T.A. I would *love* that. But I can't.

As the supports for homemaking mothers erode, supports for equal and primary fathers have not emerged to offset the growing imbalance between children's needs and families' resources. Fathers have had to depend on paid help, relatives, and already overburdened wives even when they did not wish to do so.

These obstacles not only left mothers giving up more. They also made involved fathers appear heroic about *whatever* they did. Comparisons with other men could be used to ward off complaints and resist further change. Ernie maintained:

> Sometimes she didn't think I did enough. I couldn't stand that because I thought I was doing too much. I really felt I was doing more than I should, whatever that means. I told her to go talk to some of her friends and see what their husbands are doing.

Nurturing fathers faced deeply rooted barriers to full equality in parenting. Social arrangements at work and in the home dampened even willing men's ability to share equally. The truncated range of choices open to most of these men limited the options of their wives, ex-wives, and partners as well. We can only guess how many mothers' helpers would become equal parents if these obstacles did not exist or, better yet, were replaced by positive supports for involved fatherhood.

Benefiting from the Loss of Privilege:
Incentives for Change

If full equality remained beyond the reach of most involved fathers, they nevertheless moved a notable distance toward it. They were not simply forced to make concessions; nor were they just being altruistic. They also perceived offsetting, if unheralded, benefits. After all, parenting can be its own reward—offering intrinsic pleasures and a powerful sense of accomplishment. Rick explained:

I have an extremely close relationship with my kids, and that makes me feel good. The fact that they're both doing very well in school—I know that at least a little bit of that comes from having been with them when they were young. So there's all those interactions in seeing them on their way to being healthy and vibrant kids.

These feelings took on added significance when other avenues for building self-esteem were blocked. Todd, the aspiring actor who became a construction worker, hoped his talents could be channeled toward his daughter instead of his job:

If there's any Creator at all up there, She or It or They're going to ask for some sort of accounting at the end. They're going to be pleased if they gave you a certain amount of gifts and you were able to do something with them. I'd still like to be a part of something more meaningful than putting in a new fire hydrant—I guess through my influence on this little one's life.

If children offered a source of pride for those whose workplace aspirations had not been met, this was not just a concern for passing on genes or the family name. Contributions of time and emotions counted more. Carl, who chose utility repair work so that he could care for his daughter after school, saw his "investment" reflected in her talents and achievements:

I've had a lot of compliments on her, and I take them as a compliment also. It's something that became part of you—teaching them different things, helping them grow up. They'll do something, and it's like seeing a reflection of you.

As work opportunities stall in an age of stagnant economic growth, parenting offers men another avenue for developing self-esteem. But economically successful fathers also reaped benefits from involvement because it balanced lives that would otherwise have been more narrowly focused on paid work. For Charles, the attorney with a young son, caretaking provided a legitimate reason for limiting the demands of work: "I'm working a little less hard, taking on fewer responsibilities. . . . But I think it's great. I don't need all the other shit."

Children also provided the hope of permanence in an age of divorce. Even happily married fathers came to see their children as the bedrock of stability in a shaky world, the one bond that could not be severed or assailed. Having been reared by a single mother, Juan viewed his children rather than his wife as the best chance for enduring emotional ties: "What if one day my wife and I get sick of each other after so many years? So I would like to have children."

Involved fatherhood also provided emotional supports by creating a bond between husbands and wives. Married men were less likely to feel rejected by their wives and excluded from the new relationships that form with the birth of a child. Timothy, the worker at a city dump, could not understand why less involved fathers complained of being rejected when a new baby arrived:

> They have these books about how fathers are supposed to go through blues because the wife is giving her attention to the child. Is this some kind of maniac that wrote this? I take care of him just as much as she does.

Sharing the load of caring for a newborn also seemed to decrease the chances that a mother would feel overwhelmed and alone during a critical, and trying, turning point in a marriage.[30] Carlos hoped that sharing the caretaking would help him avoid the hostility that he felt unequal arrangements would generate:

> I think it's a great burden to have one parent do all the caretaking. It would burn out that person, and they're not going to be able to respond to you. Then I would start feeling resentment towards her and possibly the child. So the only way I could see avoiding that is by sharing the responsibility.

Since involved fathers believed that a satisfying relationship depended on both partners being able to meet their needs, thwarting a partner's dreams by refusing to participate seemed to be a Pyrrhic victory. The costs of *not* sharing appeared greater than the costs of sharing. Carl was pleased to escape his parents' pattern:

> My parents are the old school. He never really touched a dish. I like what I'm doing better. The older way, I feel the woman will think, "I never really had an opportunity to do things." She will become resentful later on. Where my wife can't say nothing because she's had her freedom, she's worked, she's not stayed in the kitchen barefoot and pregnant, and I did what I had to do. I feel in the long run it pays off. The other way, maybe she would have left.

Involved fatherhood thus offered two ways of coping with the risks of marriage in an era of divorce. It provided another source of emotional sustenance in the event that the marital bond did not survive. And it offered a way to build less rancorous relationships by reducing wives' resentment. Indeed, there is growing evidence that egalitarian relationships do provide benefits to husbands and wives. In one report, wives whose husbands participate in domestic duties showed lower rates of depression than those with husbands who don't, while another found that the more housework a husband does, the lower are the chances that his wife has considered divorce.[31]

Emotional gratification and marital peace were not the only payoffs. In agreeing to share the domestic load, men can also share the economic load. Their wives' income lessens the pressure to work long hours and take on second jobs. Wesley was pleased to exchange extra hours at work for domestic sharing:

> If Cindy wants to be home, she can stay home. But that would proba- bly mean I would have to either get myself another job or work over- time on the job I have. I would do it. She knows that. But she doesn't want me to. We spend more time with each other this way.

Involved fathers also believed their children would benefit in both the short and long runs—perceptions that research on both married and di- vorced fathers supports.[32] Larry observed:

> Having spent a lot of time with both of us, she's not really dependent on either one of us. Mommy's like daddy; daddy's like mommy. At times I *am* her mother. It's good to switch roles. She don't run to mommy or run to daddy. She runs to both of us.

They hoped their example would help their daughters and sons de- velop a flexible approach to building their own lives. Ernie decided his involvement created a better domestic environment for his daughter:

> The sharing—it's a good role model for her. She sees me cook. I'm try- ing to teach her baking, and I think it's nice my daughter is learning baking from her father. So I'm hoping she sees that it's split and not that just the wife does this and the man does that.

He also hoped his participation would give his daughter a sense of self-reliance, agreeing with a growing group of psychologists who argue that girls no less than boys need their fathers. Both sexes identify in varying degrees with both parents, and girls look to fathers as well as mothers to provide models for living:[33]

> Raising my child, that is my priority—seeing that she's raised well in the sense of preparing her to face the world, trying to get her exposed as much as possible, so she may find out what she likes to pursue. I hope she has a career. I hope she finds something she really likes and works for it.

These men concluded that their domestic arrangements would also benefit their sons, echoing recent research showing that sons of involved fathers are likely to show a more developed capacity for empathy.[34] Wesley thus concluded that his two sons "feel close to the two of us. Maybe when they get married, they'll share in the house."

Just as these fathers created families that differed from the households in which they were reared, so their children will take the lessons of their childhood into unknown futures. Involved fathers' belief in the advantages of domestic sharing cannot guarantee a similar response in their children, but it can and did strengthen their own resolve to create a more egalitarian household. As more fathers become involved, their growing numbers should prompt wider social acceptance of egalitarian households, bolstering the option to make such choices.

Ultimately, however, men's movement toward domestic equality will depend on their ability to overcome the obstacles to change and their desire to resist the social pressures to conform. Equal fathers were willing and able to defy social expectations, to overcome social constraints, and to reject the pathways of the past. There is good reason to believe that their outlooks and choices reflect a simmering mood among many American men, who long for more work flexibility and fewer work demands. There is even reason to believe many would be willing to relinquish some earnings in exchange for spending more time with their families. A *Time* survey found that 56 percent of a random sample of men said they would forfeit up to one-fourth of their salaries "to have more family and personal time," and 45 percent "said they would probably refuse a promotion that involved sacrificing hours with their families."[35] Carl reflects this mood:

> It's amazing how many people don't understand the way I feel. I would prefer to be home than work overtime, where they would kill to get it. They say, "What are you, rich?" No, but you only need a certain amount of money to live. God forbid you walk down the street and get struck by a car, or whatever, and it's over. I don't want to say, "Why didn't I spend more time with my family?" It's not going to happen to me. You can control it.

By focusing on the advantages and discounting the drawbacks of their choices, men are able to overcome some of the social and ideological barriers to equal parenting. In adding up the sacrifices and the gains, Larry spoke for the group: "I've given some things up, sure, but the changes in my lifestyle are eighty or ninety percent in the positive."

Though few in number, equal fathers demonstrate that men can discover or acquire nurturing skills and find pleasure in using them. Those men who did find support for being an equal father made contingent choices just like those who did not. In both instances, different circumstances could easily have produced different outcomes. It is not surprising that Rick found his rare and unexpected path to be a matter of chance:

> I have very conservative attitudes in many respects. The fact that we got married and had children was very conservative. The fact that within those parameters, we shared, co-shared, work and family— that was not conservative. We've never discussed it, but I feel that the outcome is built much more on chance. I may not have always felt that way, but my own experiences confirmed it.

Chance, however, is just another way of saying that his choice was based on unusual and unexpected opportunities. Given how rare are the supports for involved fathering and how pervasive the obstacles, its rise is even more significant than its limited nature. For the potential of the many men who wish to be more involved to be realized, however, the unusual circumstances that now prompt only a small fraction of men to become equal parents must become real for a much larger group.

PART III

THE CAUSES AND
CONSEQUENCES OF CHANGE

9

THE MYTH OF MASCULINITY

To me, the key to being a man is the same as being a woman. It's being a good human being. I could stay home and be happy and have a lot of, quote, feminine characteristics. In some situations, it helps to be macho, but that just reflects stereotypes. If it's a guy, he's aggressive; if it's a woman, she's a ballbuster. And it can be the same behavior. Sometimes I wish it were a little clearer, but basically there's nothing that really defines being a man.

—Edward, a single physician

My father ruled the house. He wouldn't touch a diaper or a dish. He supported the family, and that was it. When he finished supper, he walked with his friends and read the newspaper. You didn't bother your father. Mama didn't ask where he was going, when he was coming home. She was not like the women today. My father answered to no one. The men were men in those days.

—George, a married park maintenance worker

The changes now occurring in men's lives are limited and contradictory, leading in several directions at the same time. If the future remains uncertain, it is clear that there will be no return to the brief period in American history when most men assumed the responsibilities and claimed the privileges of primary breadwinning.

The decline of the male breadwinner has prompted confusion and discomfort because it calls into question many of our most deeply held beliefs about manhood and masculinity. If men no longer share a distinctive identity based on their economic role as family providers, then what is a man? If men can no longer claim special rights and privileges based on their unique responsibilities and contributions, then how can they justify their power? If men can no longer assert patriarchal control by being the heads of their households, then what kind of relationships will they establish with women and children? The no man's land they now occupy undermines the legitimacy of male power and privilege.

Searching for a new definition to replace the old one, some essential quality that binds all men together and separates them from women, leads us in the wrong direction, for it cannot take into account the complexity of men's choices or the growing diversity among them. The shifts now taking place in men's lives give us an ideal opportunity to broaden our understanding of American men—to develop a fuller conception of how they behave, why they resist change, and what will induce them to support equality.

The Paths of Change

The life stories of the men we have met show that while men need not choose between having children and succeeding at the workplace, they face other hard choices—between freedom and sharing, between independence and interdependence, between privilege and equality. In responding to these dilemmas, men, like women, have developed new ways of balancing work and family. Despite the prevailing image of men as independent actors in control of their lives, the social world has molded their lives as much as they have molded it. Their choices show a rich variety of outlooks and adaptive strategies. Yet the interplay between social change and personal choice has also provided a uniting thread.

While some were able to sustain their early outlooks, most encountered unanticipated constraints and opportunities that prompted them to change the expected direction of their lives. Over time, all of these men built or rejected personal commitments in response to a mix of experiences. Differences in workplace opportunities, in relationships with women, and in experiences with children combined in diverse ways to promote divergent orientations to family and work. The men traveled a range of paths, ultimately becoming divided among those who developed or sustained a breadwinning identity (including some whose wives were not employed and others who had partners employed outside the home), those who chose to affirm autonomy over parental commitments (including some who planned to remain childless and others who had become estranged from their offspring), and those who became or planned to become substantially involved in rearing their children (including some who saw themselves as helpers and others who were equal or primary parents). (See appendix, table 14, for a summary of these paths and patterns.) Although college-educated men were slightly more likely to develop an involved outlook, the differences between classes are small and far less important than the diversity within each. Indeed, the range of patterns that emerged—not the number of men in any particular group—is most telling.

Taken together, these men forged a variety of strategies that can also be found in national trends. Those who held tightly to a primary bread-winning outlook, even when their wives were employed, reflect the "stalled revolution" in which men remain aloof from domestic work even as women become increasingly committed to paid work. Those who chose autonomy over parenthood resemble the "male rebels" and "estranged dads" who have left increasing numbers of women and children on their own. Those who became involved fathers represent the growing group of men who have become more integrated into the work of family life.[1] We may not know the size of these various groups, but we can be sure that they are developing side by side. (Table 15 in the appendix presents an overview of the living situations of American men.)

Men are traveling not only diverse paths but fragile and ambiguous ones. Increasingly, men (and women) move in and out of different family forms over the course of their lives, altering their domestic and work commitments along the way. Over time, any individual man may find himself moving from one pattern to another in unexpected ways. These "mixed" cases are especially instructive, for they illuminate the importance of social circumstance for explaining men's choices.

Several men did not participate in rearing the children of a first marriage, but became intimately involved in caring for the children of a later marriage. In these cases, divorce and remarriage created contrasting contexts for decision making. For Todd, a contentious divorce left him estranged from a son, while his subsequent marriage brought him deeply into the process of rearing his daughter.

In a world where divorce and remarriage are common, such men comprise a fast-growing group.[2] Yet it is also possible to be more involved in rearing a first child than a second, especially if the original conditions fostering involvement undergo change. Thus, Tom, the editor, found that a change in his job situation—more than a change in his marital partner—was decisive. When his son was born, he was a graduate student who stayed home while his first wife went to work. Years later, as he and his second wife planned for a child, his nine-to-five job required his daily absence.

These cases show clearly how circumstances shape men's parental choices, either evoking or suppressing involvement. They also show that men's work and family commitments are fragile. The trade-offs among domestic work, paid work, and leisure vary among men and also over the course of individual men's lives. Indeed, vacillation and change are likely responses to changes in life circumstances. It is thus understandable that many men feel confused, wary, and ambivalent.[3] Having experienced unexpected turns in their lives, they recognize the possibility of future change as well.

These changes suggest that it is time to reconsider some of our most accepted assumptions about how men behave. Experts have tended to invoke "masculine personalities," a "culture of masculinity," or "male dominance" as the prime cause of men's behavior, but these customary ways of making sense of men's lives cannot account for the rise of such diverse and shifting patterns.

MASCULINE PERSONALITY

We have seen that men's childhood experiences bear a complex relationship to their choices as adults. Many encountered experiences in the adult world that led them to reassess the meaning of their parents' lives and their own early outlooks. Childhood provided a point of departure, but most men found that their early aspirations were difficult, and sometimes impossible, to achieve. As they grew, many men confronted unexpected situations for which childhood experience had left them ill prepared. They adjusted their outlooks, changed the direction of their lives, and discovered emotional resources they did not know they had.

The capacity for change over time dilutes the power of childhood socialization to explain adult outcomes.[4] Even among those who did not experience significant change in outlook or life direction, the context of adulthood mattered. It supported stability in some lives while encouraging or forcing change in others. Ultimately, how men evaluate, respond to, and resolve the conflicts and ambiguities established in childhood depends on experiences encountered later in life.[5]

The variety of men's outlooks, motives, and choices cannot be explained by a shared complex of psychological qualities commonly labeled "masculine personality." While a minority of men do fit the stereotype of the distant father, the patriarchal husband, or the work-obsessed breadwinner, this image does not capture the range or complexity of men's emotional capacities or behavioral styles. As a group, men display a wide variety of psychological orientations and proclivities, including those typically considered feminine. Many are rejecting work achievement as a supreme value and finding gratification in relationships of nurturance and intimacy.

The diversity in men's temperaments and outlooks undermines the power of approaches that stress a shared will to achieve, desire to dominate, or resistance to establishing intimate, deeply bonded relationships with others. Personality approaches, which rely on the notion that men share a complex of personality traits that binds them together and separates them from women, cannot explain the rich variety and complexity of men's work and family choices. Childhood socialization approaches, which stress the determining role of childhood experiences in producing adult outcomes, cannot account for men's widespread experience of change over time.[6]

A full account of men's lives needs to acknowledge and explain a fuller range of psychological patterns and emotional possibilities for men. As diversity in men's life choices, personal outlooks, and psychological capacities grows, we will stand on safer ground by rejecting evaluative accounts that label nonstereotypical behavior as psychologically deviant. Just as we now understand that classical notions of femininity, however defined, are misleading and oversimplified, so it is time to acknowledge that large numbers of men do not conform to the prevailing view of masculinity.[7] Beyond the gender stereotypes there lies a more interesting and complex story about diversity among men and declining differences between men and women.

MASCULINE CULTURE

The notion of a "culture of masculinity" cannot explain men's diverse paths and strategies, either.[8] This approach argues that men share a distinct cluster of values, beliefs, and behavioral styles and that more widely held social and cultural values encourage men to behave in distinctly masculine ways. The meaning of manliness varies with different theories, but "masculine" values usually include a stress on independence, rationality, and aggression; the admiration of emotional control over emotional attachment and the open expression of feelings; and a glorification of physical strength and even violence. Regardless of which value is stressed, these approaches argue that cultural beliefs and expectations produce male behavior and that cultural change produces change in behavior.

While compelling, the "culture of masculinity" argument is actually no better equipped than personality theories to explain the variety of paths and strategies men are forging. First, our values, norms, and beliefs concerning manhood have deeper historical roots than the changes now taking place in men's lives. The cultural tradition that idealizes male flight from commitment is as old as American culture itself. Our literary tradition amply demonstrates that cultural models have long included heroes—Huckleberry Finn, Captain Ahab, and the Lone Ranger, to name only a few—who earn and maintain their manhood by eschewing the bonds of domesticity, commitment, and familial love.[9] The American idealization of the lone man extends back at least to the period of the frontier and Manifest Destiny. A set of cultural values that emerged long before the current period cannot explain why dramatic changes in behavior are occurring *now*.[10]

Second, the cultural tradition of masculinity is too complex to provide a simple blueprint for individual behavior. Men are exposed to an ambiguous, paradoxical cultural legacy that stresses conflicting, even mutually exclusive, values. American culture idealizes both the responsible good provider and the loner who remains free of obligations to work and family. It is impossible for any one man to live up to these contradictory cultural ideals. Men have to respond to several sets of competing values and choose among opposing ideals as they endeavor to make personal choices and develop their own identities. The "culture of masculinity" does not provide clear-cut guidelines for behavior.[11]

Amid new social realities, new cultural ideals can also emerge to compete with long-standing cultural traditions. Alongside the breadwinner ethic and the ideal of the unfettered loner, another vision of manhood has arisen that stresses interdependence and emotional openness.[12] This new vision contrasts with the cultural tradition that poses freedom and responsibility as competing masculine ideals, but it also goes further: it rejects the views that manhood is the opposite of womanhood, that *masculine* means *not feminine*, and that the values associated with women necessarily threaten men.[13] It stresses the similarities between men and women and asserts that gender differences are smaller, more malleable, and less desirable than traditional views suggest.

But older patterns persist while new ones emerge, including both male disengagement from familial bonds and greater male involvement in family life. If change in men's lives is paradoxical and multifaceted, then so are the cultural constructs that surround it. Since older cultural values cannot account for the rise of new ones, creative cultural change poses the question: Even if values and beliefs affect behavior, where do they come from and how are new ones created? More fundamental social changes in the economy, the workplace, and the home are producing changes in the culture of masculinity along with changes in men's behavior. Indeed, these changes have prompted cultural confusion and a growing debate over the meaning of manhood. This confusion is more a result than a cause of change.

Finally, the widespread discrepancy between preferred ideals and actual choices weakens the power of cultural explanations. There is rarely a simple, one-to-one relationship between what people value and what they choose. Some may face circumstances that allow them to enact their highest ideals, while others may change their ideals to fit their circumstances more closely. But many face circumstances that leave them coping with a gap between options and ideals, between what they do and what they feel they should do.

The disparity between values and behavior can take a variety of forms. However deep the cultural tradition of masculine independence, it alone does not produce behavior. More often, it provides an escape fantasy for those leading more mundane lives. How many of the men who read *Playboy* are actually driving sports cars, living in glamorous bachelor pads, and being pursued by numerous women? More likely, they are working men who steal a few moments from their daily routines to imagine the pleasures of this unattainable world. Life choices should not be confused with erotic fantasies, and "values" are rarely reflected so straightforwardly in behavior.

In any case, competing cultural visions and fluctuating values are more likely to produce ambivalence and confusion than strict adherence to cultural injunctions. Culture is not static, consistent, or determining. "Masculine culture" provides a contradictory context for decision making, and most choices require giving up some ideals in order to attain others. Men's behavior should not be confused with cultural ideals. Men either sustain old ideals or invent new ones in order to make sense of actions that can never be entirely free. They use, create, and selectively call upon culture in the process of making choices.[14]

MALE DOMINANCE

If neither masculine personality nor masculine culture can account for the social transformation in men's lives, it is tempting to conclude that male dominance, or what has come to be called *patriarchy*, does. Theories that stress the role of male dominance, or patriarchy, focus on how institutional arrangements bestow power and privilege on men and how, in turn, men behave as a group to perpetuate these advantages. In the public sphere, men enjoy economic and occupational advantages, and in the domestic sphere, they are excused from the least pleasant and most time-consuming tasks. Men's advantages in one sphere contribute to their advantages in the other. Workplace advantages give men the economic and social power to avoid domestic work, and the avoidance of domestic work gives men advantages in a competitive marketplace. Male power and privilege is thus re-created via a mutually reinforcing and self-sustaining cycle.[15]

Clearly, many men continue to benefit from and to perpetuate a patriarchal system. And if the persistence of patriarchy were the whole story, this approach might suffice. But the pattern of men's lives, as well as the contours of male dominance, have taken a more varied and complex form. Male dominance, whether conceived as an institutional arrangement or an ideological stance, is incomplete, double-edged, and under assault. This places limits on men's ability and desire to dominate.

First, the legitimacy of male power and privilege is increasingly subject to questioning and debate, and the institutional bases of male dominance are eroding. Certainly, most men continue to enjoy social, political, and economic advantages because they are men. Nevertheless, the closing decades of the twentieth century have witnessed important changes in the degree as well as the nature of patriarchal control. The expansion of women's legal rights, employment opportunities, sources of economic support, and capacity to live independently has undermined men's ability to control them, as wives or as workers. And although male privilege persists, it no longer reigns uncontested. The advantages men once took for granted are now open to debate and challenge.[16]

This context of erosion and dispute has given male dominance a double-edged quality. It continues to offer considerable rewards, but it also entails mounting costs. As the costs of breadwinning have grown, even the most "traditional" men have confronted new pressures to change and new challenges to their authority. These developments have undermined men's capacity and desire to dominate completely.

Male dominance has become increasingly variable as well. On average, men possess disproportionate power and privilege, but beyond these group advantages lie important variations. Male power "is not spread in an even blanket" across all men or "every department of social life."[17] What's more, differences among men matter. Diversity in social resources generates diversity in behavior and outlook as well. Just as men have encountered different occupational and family opportunities, so they have developed different views about where their interests lie. Because social change has different consequences for different groups of men, they do not all share the belief that they have a large stake in perpetuating gender inequality. Rather, men's stances toward patriarchy and male dominance are diverse and, increasingly, opposed.

Breadwinners, for example, have good reasons to defend male power and privilege in the face of increasing opposition. As women have fought for equal rights and other men have moved away from family patterns that emphasize male control, those who remain committed to the good-provider ethic feel embattled and threatened. They fear the erosion of advantages that their fathers could take for granted. It is thus no surprise that many of these men have concluded that control in marriage and distance from child rearing are not only justified but in everyone's best interest.

Those who have rejected breadwinning hold different stances toward male dominance. Whether they have moved away from parenthood or become involved fathers, nonbreadwinners see less advantage and much disadvantage to authoritarian control over wives and girlfriends. Not only does it produce economically dependent women; it also subverts the chances for an emotionally satisfying relationship. The desire for personal freedom and mutual support makes dominance seem, at least to some extent, counterproductive.

While those who have rejected breadwinning may still enjoy the benefits of male privilege, they are more likely to question its legitimacy. Both those who have moved away from parenthood and those who have become involved fathers support equality in the public sphere, but they do not agree about private commitments.

Autonomous men support women's economic self-sufficiency because it enhances their own ability to remain independent, free of the obligations that accompany breadwinning. This vision of economic and social equality does not extend to the domestic sphere, however, where their desire for personal freedom produces an ideological paradox: they espouse the equal right to be free while resisting the equal responsibility for domestic work and child rearing.

This separation of public rights and private obligations explicitly rejects a traditional ideology of dominance, but it replaces it with a different kind of advantage. Since dominance via primary breadwinning entails too many economic obligations, this strategy replaces overt control with a more subtle form of power, indifference. These men argue that they will neither stand in a woman's way *nor* offer her much help. Women thus have the "right," if they choose, to be superwomen who work, raise a family, and take care of the home.

Involved fathers, in contrast, are uncomfortable with male dominance in the home as well as the workplace. They may not always live up to their ideals, but they have concluded that men and children as well as women benefit from more equal sharing.

Men do not retain a monolithic interest in dominance, and not all men are able or willing to impose their desires on a woman against her will. Because they enjoy different opportunities and face different constraints, they also have developed different outlooks on dominance and control. Separated by varied life experiences, men have constructed contrasting interests in the process of reaching different conclusions about the benefits and costs of dominance itself.[18]

Whether conceived as a social institution or a set of beliefs and attitudes, male dominance cannot explain why the legitimacy of male privilege is being challenged or why men increasingly disagree among themselves about whether to preserve or surrender it. Men do not make choices in a context of unbridled freedom. They enjoy many significant advantages, but their ability to control is not complete and their desire to do so varies.[19] Indeed, the unspoken assumption that men do not face conflicts and dilemmas is deceptive and shortsighted. We can build a

world where women do not have to choose between work and family
and where men are not systematically excluded from parenting only by
understanding the dilemmas men face and the varied ways they are responding to them.

The Social Transformation of American Manhood

Even taken together, masculine personalities, male dominance, and a
culture of masculinity cannot explain the changes in men's family and
work ties. The shared focus on uniformity among men and continuity
over time makes it difficult to identify, much less explain, the diverse
pathways men are forging.[20] Instead, we need to examine the contours of
large-scale institutional change, the social geography of men's exposure
to change, and their strategic responses to new options and pressures.

Changing social circumstances have confronted men with new freedoms and new constraints. The most important social shifts include a decline in men's economic resources, a rise in women's attachment to paid
work, an expansion of alternatives to permanent marriage, and a growing separation between marriage and parenthood. These changes are
closely connected and deeply anchored.

THE DECLINE OF ECONOMIC ENTITLEMENT

Compared to women, men as a group continue to enjoy higher average wages, superior access to higher-paying and more prestigious jobs,
and less responsibility for domestic tasks.[21] Nevertheless, over the last
several decades, changes in the economy and the labor market have undermined many men's economic security and eroded their occupational
entitlements. The degree of change is circumscribed, but the direction of
change is clear. Although male executives and professionals in the upper
echelons of the occupational structure have enjoyed soaring incomes,
the vast majority of male workers have experienced stagnant or declining economic fortunes and contracting prospects for secure, highly rewarded jobs.

This has been true since the early 1970s, when the United States
emerged from the burst of post–World War II economic expansion and
faced, instead, a lower rate of economic growth. Men's average hourly
wages fell by 5.1 percent between 1979 and 1989 and by 2.1 percent between 1989 and 1991. Although less educated men have suffered the
steepest declines, all but the best-educated and most highly paid workers have lost ground. Among men who did not finish high school, average hourly wages dropped 18.2 percent from 1979 to 1989 and 6.2 per-

cent from 1989 to 1991; among high school graduates, they dropped 12.7 percent and 3.8 percent; among men with one to three years of college, they dropped 8.3 percent and 1.4 percent; and among men with four years of college, they rose only 0.3 percent from 1979 to 1989 and then dropped 2.6 percent from 1989 to 1991. Only those with at least six years of college enjoyed rising earnings over this period.[22] Similarly, except for men in the upper 10 percent of the wage ladder, male workers across the wage hierarchy have suffered declining or stagnant earnings.[23] Men under forty-five working year-round full-time, and white men serving as their family's only breadwinner, have been especially hard-hit. The median inflation-adjusted income for men who were sole breadwinners fell 22 percent between 1976 and 1984.[24]

This reduction in wages is linked to changes in the occupational structure—that is, the number and types of jobs available to men. Over this same period, the percentage of jobs in highly rewarded, male-dominated economic sectors such as industrial production has declined, while the share of jobs in less rewarded and secure economic sectors has grown. Between 1950 and 1989, the percentage of nonagricultural employees working in manufacturing dropped from 38.9 percent to 21.6 percent, and the percentage holding jobs in transportation and public utilities dropped from 10.3 percent to 6.3 percent. At the same time, the percentage working in the services rose from 13.7 percent to 29.6 percent; in wholesale and retail trade from 24 percent to 28.4 percent; and in finance, insurance, and real estate from 4.8 percent to 7 percent.[25] Since jobs in manufacturing, transportation, and public utilities provide higher earnings on average than jobs in retail, wholesale, and finance, the transfer of jobs from the former economic sector to the latter has contributed significantly to the overall decline in wages.[26]

These changes in the job structure have also promoted a rise in the percentage of workers who are self-employed, including freelancers, contract workers, and temporary workers. The percentage of self-employed workers rose from 8 percent of the labor force in 1980 to 10 percent in 1990.[27] Men who are self-employed do not enjoy company-sponsored benefits, do not have the assurance of continued employment, and on average earn a third less than wage and salaried employees. Thus, "the growth of male self-employment means depressed earnings" and a decline in job security for many men.[28]

These economic setbacks have not been confined to the poor or to racial minorities, nor do they show signs of abating.[29] Since they are based on structural changes in the economy over which individual men have little control, they are likely to continue for the foreseeable future. "[D]espite the widely held assumption that higher-paying white-collar jobs are the wave of the future, there is little evidence that the deterioration of job quality and wages that took place in the 1980s will be reversed in the 1990s. . . . [I]t is unlikely that wages will be greater in the year 2000 than they were in 1980."[30] Moreover, there are indications that the erosion of economic security may spread to the higher echelons of workers.[31]

The stagnation of wages and the decline in job security have eroded men's ability to earn a so-called family wage on a consistent, predictable basis. Thus, despite the persistence of occupational sex segregation and a gender gap in wages, changes in the occupational structure have undermined most men's economic resources as well as the ease of maintaining primary breadwinning. The economic support of wives and children has become more difficult and less attractive to a growing proportion of men.

THE RISE OF COMMITTED EMPLOYMENT AMONG WOMEN

As men's labor force participation has dropped below 80 percent, women's has risen to almost 60 percent. Among women between the ages of twenty-five and forty-four, the ages when women once dropped out of the work force to bear and rear children full-time, that rate has climbed to around 75 percent.[32] More important, women's attachment to paid work had grown increasingly strong. In 1990, only 23 percent of employed women worked part-time (down from 63.1 percent in 1960), and 5.6 percent of these part-time workers would have preferred full-time work if they could find it.[33] Among full-time employed women, moreover, 46 percent thought of their work as a career rather than a job.[34]

The causes of women's increasing attachment to paid work are manifold, including the enticements of expanding workplace opportunities and the economic pressures created by eroding male incomes, high divorce rates, and rising rates of singlehood.[35] Whatever the causes, women's growing commitment to paid work has given them increased economic independence and a growing incentive to challenge men's privileges at the workplace and in the home.

It has also undermined men's once-uncontested access to the best jobs. Women committed to full-time, uninterrupted work increasingly vie with men for employment rewards and increasingly demand that they share them more equally. Although inequality remains pervasive, the push for workplace equity undermines the legitimacy, if not the reality, of male privilege at work. Legal challenges, such as affirmative action, comparable worth, and sexual harassment initiatives, are only the tip of an iceberg. Discrimination in pay and employment persists, but modest improvements have taken place in women's average earnings and access to better jobs. Thus, between 1979 and 1989, when men's average wages were falling, women's were rising an average of 6.7 percent.[36] The pay gap between women and men continues, to be sure, but it has improved from about 63 percent in 1979 to about 72 percent in 1990.[37] Similarly, although most women continue to work in lower-paying, female-dominated jobs, a notable proportion have made inroads into professional and managerial positions dominated by men. In 1989, for example, 29 percent of all M.B.A.'s, 22.2 percent of all lawyers, and 17.9 percent of all physicians were women; and women held 40 percent of all entry-level and middle-management jobs.[38]

These trends appear to be "solid" and "enduring."[39] As younger generations of women enter and remain in the labor force, their stronger work commitment compared to earlier generations is likely to push the gains for women higher. For example, in 1979, 74 percent of young women reported that they expected to be in the labor force when they were thirty-five. In 1988, 53 percent of all B.A.'s, 52 percent of all M.A.'s, 37 percent of all Ph.D.'s, and 36 percent of all professional degrees were awarded to women. Women accounted for 33.6 percent of all new M.B.A.'s and 40.4 percent of all those receiving law degrees in 1989. These younger cohorts of women appear to be keeping pace with their male counterparts. Fewer are dropping out of the work force, and, when they do, it is for a shorter period of time. In terms of years of work experience, women in their thirties in 1987 showed a 90 percent equivalence to a comparable group of men. Yet women born between 1946 and 1955 (who were between thirty-five and forty-four in 1990) earned sixty-nine cents for every dollar earned by a man in the same age group.[40]

Women's expanded ability to survive on their own is as important as their more modest labor market gains. Amid the persistence of workplace inequality, a growing group of work-committed women can claim economic and social independence. Employment gives women an income of their own, even if it is likely to be lower than a man's. Most women no longer have to marry for economic reasons; and if they do marry, they are more likely to make important contributions to their families' economic welfare. Indeed, as men's average earnings have fallen, women's earnings have provided the means by which average family income has remained stable over the last two decades.[41] Women's growing commitment to paid work has given them increasing economic clout, expanding their options regarding marriage and parenthood and making their families more financially dependent on them.[42]

This fundamental change in women's situation has important, but paradoxical, implications for men. On the one hand, women's declining economic dependence has given men greater freedom to eschew commitment or to sever the bonds of a relationship without feeling economically responsible for the person left behind; on the other hand, an independent source of income gives an employed woman more leverage in a relationship. She, too, has the option to leave. If she stays, she has the incentive to expect her partner to participate in the running of the household. As women become less dependent on men, men are both less and more constrained.

THE RISE OF ALTERNATIVES TO PERMANENT MARRIAGE

The rise of fluid sexual and marital partnerships has similarly ambiguous implications for men's choices. Divorce, remarriage, cohabitation outside of marriage, serial monogamy, and permanent singlehood all have grown in popularity since the 1950s, when permanent marriage predominated. High divorce rates are the most obvious indicators of this trend. The divorce rate climbed upward during the late 1960s and the 1970s, reaching a peak in the years between 1979 and 1981. It then decreased slightly, but it has remained stable since 1986. Currently, about half of the marriages of those people now in their thirties are likely to end in divorce, or have already ended that way.[43]

As the divorce rate has stabilized, the rates of people living alone and cohabitating outside of marriage have grown. By 1991, 10 percent of American households consisted of a man living alone and 15 percent consisted of a woman living alone, up from 5.6 percent and 11.5 percent in 1970. An additional 4.7 percent of households were made up of unrelated adults living together (without children), up from 1.7 percent in 1970.[44] A 1987–88 survey found that over 40 percent of heterosexuals between the ages of twenty-five and thirty-nine had lived with a person of the opposite sex outside of marriage.[45] Legal marriage has clearly become more discretionary, one of a number of alternatives for living, sharing intimacy, and meeting sexual needs. And more adults are also moving in and out of different family and household arrangements over the course of their lives.[46]

The expansion of legitimate alternatives to permanent marriage, like the rise in women's economic resources, has given men new freedoms and confronted them with new constraints. Men are freed from the obligation to maintain a lifelong economic and emotional commitment to one woman, but women have more discretion about when and whether to marry as well as when and whether to stay married.

THE SEPARATION OF MARRIAGE AND PARENTHOOD

As marriage has become more fluid and discretionary, parental ties have become increasingly distinct from marital bonds. The rise in divorce and, to a lesser but rising extent, out-of-wedlock births has loosened the connection between childbearing and child rearing—especially for men.[47] Three of every ten marriages are likely to end in divorces that involve young children.[48] Although a growing number of divorced fathers retain some form of custody of their children, the overwhelming majority of children remain with their mothers in the event of divorce or an out-of-wedlock birth. While about 17 percent of white one-parent families and about 7 percent of black one-parent families are headed by a father, all those remaining are headed by a divorced, separated, or never-married woman.[49] In 1988, 21.2 percent of all families with children were headed by women, up from 9.4 percent in 1960. In 1987, 16.5 percent of white mothers and 50.3 percent of black mothers with children under eighteen were not living with a husband (up from about 5.8 percent and 21.7 percent in 1960).[50] Under current conditions, at least half of all American children will likely spend at least part of their childhood in a single-parent family, most likely headed by a woman.[51]

A growing proportion of men now find parental ties, like marriage itself, voluntary and discretionary. Fatherhood as an economic, social, and emotional institution is increasingly based on what men want and find meaningful rather than on what they are constrained—by women and social regulations—to do. The implications for men's lives are, again, ambiguous. Certainly, the rise of divorce and out-of-wedlock childbearing make it easier for men to avoid parental responsibilities if they prefer. On the other hand, biological fatherhood no longer routinely gives men power over or access to their children. Fathers who wish to sustain strong parental attachments may find that they have to work harder than they anticipated to keep their children in their lives.

CONTRASTING ENCOUNTERS WITH CHANGE

These shifts in the economy, marriage, and parenthood reinforce each other and are beyond the capacity of any individual or group to prevent. While their combined effect is to reduce the incentives and constraints for men to choose good providing as a way of life, it is less clear which alternatives they are promoting in its place. The ultimate outcome is uncertain for three reasons. First, institutional change is ambiguous and paradoxical, leading in different directions at the same time. Second, men's exposure to institutional change is uneven, leaving some searching for new ways of life and others defending older ones. Third, these institutional changes have created new dilemmas of masculinity, compelling men to develop creative responses.

Since institutional change is neither consistent nor complete, different groups of men have been affected in different ways. While some have retained patriarchal control in so-called traditional households, others have found their range of control over women and children diminished. They have faced good reasons to relinquish some control in exchange for greater freedom or more sharing. Differences in men's exposure to change have promoted differences in their strategies for coping with these new dilemmas.

The Dilemmas of Change

Men's divergent choices are reasonable, if often unexpected and unconscious, reactions to changing personal experiences and circumstances. Yet these responses are more than purely rational choices calculated to maximize self-interest. When social change sets up contradictory options, it becomes impossible to discover one's "best interests" by means of a simple rational calculation. Before men can act on their interests, they must first decide how to value goals that may be conflicting.[52]

As the difficulties of being a primary breadwinner increase, men are caught on the horns of a dilemma: Do they resist the pressures for change in an attempt to preserve historical privileges or, instead, embrace the expanded opportunity to ease or escape the burdens that privilege entails? How can they keep down the costs of either strategy? Men, like women, find it increasingly difficult to "have it all," although "all" has decidedly different meanings for each group. If women find it difficult to combine a sustained work career with motherhood, men face a conflict between maintaining their privileges and easing their burdens. They must choose among opposing interests: autonomy, power, and control, on the one hand, and sharing and support in relationships with women and children, on the other. They have little choice but to develop new ways of negotiating the uncharted territories of change.

A range of social shifts has spawned confusion, ambivalence, and disagreement over the guidelines, models, and definitions of manhood.[53] If institutional change requires individual change, then individual change adds another element of uncertainty to social change. Eroding economic opportunities, for example, may spark diverse reactions. Those who are able to forge stable marriages with a woman who prefers domesticity may decide to work harder to bolster their position as family breadwinners. Those who become committed or attracted to a work-committed woman may opt to share breadwinning and caretaking. Those whose intimate relationships with women or children have been dissatisfying and difficult may decide to go it alone and keep their earnings to themselves.

The cross-cutting pressures on men thus provide the underpinnings for many different futures. Indeed, diversity in men's choices is probably here to stay. While some men may continue to find well-rewarded, secure jobs, a growing group will not. While some men will marry early and stay married to the same woman for life, others will postpone marriage, get divorced, or stay single. While some men will marry women who are willing and able to do the bulk of domestic work whether or not they hold a paid job, a growing group will find that the women they meet and become involved with are committed to working outside the home and unwilling to perform two jobs while their partners perform only one. In the face of these changes, some men will find that equality and sharing offer compensations to offset their attendant loss of power and privilege, but others are likely to conclude that maintaining power or eschewing commitment are more attractive options. We are living through a protracted period when no one pattern predominates and no one set of values is shared by all, or even most.

Although some sort of change is inescapable, the future can take many forms. Indeed, these changes in men's lives offer opportunity and danger. The ultimate outcome remains open because it depends on how we, as individuals and as a society, respond to the challenge.

10

MEN AND THE POLITICS OF GENDER

A central paradox of the human condition is that our species possesses the capacity to carry sexual inequality to its greatest known extremes, but we also possess the potential to realize an unusual social equality between the sexes should we choose to exercise that potential.
—Sarah Hrdy, *The Woman Who Never Evolved*

We are in a period of sustained and deeply rooted diversity in men's lives—one in which breadwinners, involved fathers, and single and childless men are contending for economic and social support. This transformation extends well beyond the confines of the so-called underclass or other minorities pursuing "alternative lifestyles." The fundamental social and economic changes propelling this revolution have affected most men, and especially those under the age of forty. Even if they have not personally experienced declining economic fortunes or been involved with work-committed women, men have felt the ripple effects of changes that have spread outward in unforeseeable ways.

Men are facing new dilemmas as well as new choices. Those who withdraw from work or share economic obligations with a woman face being labeled inadequate providers. Those who decide not to have children are seen as irresponsible or selfish. Those who become primary breadwinners confront the charge that they are male chauvinists. Diversity has thus generated ambivalence and disagreement about the appropriate obligations and legitimate rights of men. It is time for the national debate to address the cultural, political, and social policy implications of changes in men's lives.

Contending Visions of Manhood

The decline of a cultural consensus on the meaning of manhood—along with the demise of a predominant pattern of behavior for most men—has opened the door to political debate. As men have chosen different paths, they have also reached different conclusions about the kind of world they would like to see created. While all men share certain advantages because they are men, they disagree about how privileged they are and what they are prepared to do to retain those privileges.

Men with primary breadwinning responsibilities face convincing reasons to retain a belief in the justice and inevitability of male advantages, but nontraditional men are tentatively and ambivalently considering the attractions as well as the dangers of gender equality. One nontraditional vision stresses the equal right to be free but fails to take account of men's domestic responsibilities as women assume breadwinning ones. Another vision of equality faces the harder challenge of accepting sacrifices as well as enjoying gains. This third vision recognizes that genuine equality can be achieved only through mutual support and a shared commitment to nurturing and providing for children.

These contending visions of manhood have important political ramifications. Even if only a small percentage of men live up to each, they help define what is considered legitimate behavior and are likely to shape a growing debate over men's needs, rights, and duties. The varied directions of change have thus encouraged a complicated array of competing political ideologies about the proper role of men in society. Listen to how some of the men whose lives I have traced expressed them.

DEFENDING INEQUALITY

The decline of primary breadwinning, along with the rise of new alternatives for men, poses a threat to those who have maintained an allegiance to the good-provider ethic. The erosion of supports for their choices leaves them feeling nostalgic about the past, embattled in the present, and worried about the future. Breadwinners are thus prone to argue that nontraditional arrangements pose dangers to them, to society, and to other men and women. Although they tend to believe that men—and especially breadwinning men—have endured serious setbacks, they do not automatically construe men's losses as women's gains. Rather, they contend that both men and women have suffered from social change:

> I'm not a male chauvinist, but I think somebody should be more or
> less in control in the marriage. I don't think you can have a democ-

racy—clashing all the time. And I don't think people today are as happy as they were years ago. Men are under so much pressure to produce and to pay these bills. It just shows in the statistics. Men are dying younger.

Since women's assuming of the male's responsibilities, the women are getting the cancer and the heart attacks and the ulcers. They're not adjusting to this as well as they thought they would. Women who are successful are absolutely miserable. They have no children; they're not satisfied with the men they meet. Their marriages, if they are married, are in trouble.

These men are inclined to view "career women" as both the agents and victims of change. Since being a successful breadwinner requires access to the most secure jobs with the highest pay, even modest gains made by women can seem a serious threat. Breadwinning men are thus likely to overestimate women's gains, to view them as unfair, and to claim that they exact an excessive cost from the women who achieve them:

Women have it a little easier as far as job-related matters are concerned. The tests are getting easier. Classifications are going down to let women in.

In this place where I work now, I can't think of any man who's not married, but there are a number of women in their thirties and forties who are not married and don't have children. I really feel sorry for them. It's indirectly very selfish. Even though they may themselves not be responsible for the situation, it's symptomatic of a very selfish age.

Work-committed women are not the only group that may appear to pose a danger. Breadwinning men fear that their own choices will lose legitimacy and support as other men follow different paths. They are thus likely to view nontraditional men with suspicion. These men, they claim, are shirking their manly responsibilities:

If a man is home part of the time with the baby, it would probably lower my opinion, because I would tend to think, "Why couldn't this guy make a good enough living so his wife doesn't have to go out and leave him with the kid? Is he not smart enough? Did he not work hard enough?"

Breadwinners thus tend to define their interests not just in terms of being a man but in terms of being a good provider who needs protection in a world grown increasingly hostile to his plight. They also conclude that there is more at stake than their own self-interest. Equality, they argue, robs women of protections rather than giving them rights:

I think that the woman should be protected, the woman should have a higher place. A mother is the most cherished thing you could be on this earth, and the woman should be respected and cared for. Equality would reduce that.

Discomfited by the loss of once-secure advantages, breadwinning men face strong incentives not just to protect themselves but to oppose the changes taking place around them. Their arguments about the dangers of change are firmly rooted in a concern for their own security, but these arguments also speak to many women's fears. As long as men remain distant partners in the work of child care and women remain disadvantaged at the workplace, then change can pose palpable risks to women and children as well as to men.[1]

FREEDOM VERSUS SHARING AS VISIONS OF EQUALITY

Those who have moved away from primary breadwinning also believe that the privileges of manhood are endangered, but they are less inclined to feel nostalgia for a waning pattern. If breadwinners would like to turn back the clock to a time when male advantages were uncontested and supporting a family was an easier task, nontraditional men have little desire to resurrect a system they doubt ever worked very well. In their view, traditional arrangements are rife with drawbacks for men and women:

The woman is getting all the sympathy for her desperate position in the home by herself, lonely and isolated, taking care of these kids. I also have sympathy for the guy who has to be out getting his ass kicked by industrial tyrants and corporate assholes and the whole competitive complex. I think it's a tough life.

When I look at people whose wives don't work, I think they're making a big mistake. There's really nothing a housewife can do for eight hours a day in the house—just sit in front of the TV and watch soap operas. To me, it's a waste of a person.

Rather than defending a system in decline, nontraditional men are drawn to other visions of gender and of family life. They are more likely than breadwinners to reject the view that men and women are fundamentally different, arguing instead that the qualities the sexes share far outweigh the differences:

I think I can do everything a woman can do except have a child. I believe there's a lot of women out there that can do anything a man can do without a problem.

Women are just as much of a human being as I am. They've got the same intellect, the same ideals and goals. There's absolutely no difference in that respect. And that's all that counts.

I have some feelings about human beings being a lot more amorphous, androgynous. And I think this caretaking experience, if men get more involved, is going to bring out their more feminine feelings. We'll see how it works over the long run. Maybe it wasn't meant to be that way, but I can't see why not.

This vision extends beyond a rejection of difference to include support for equal rights, especially on the job, and support for the view that men and women should uphold the same ideals:

If a woman is strong enough to become a fireman, a police officer, a paramedic, let her do it. If a man is sensitive enough to become a nurse, fine. Anybody who fills the bill can have it.

An ideal woman has the same qualities I associate with a man—truthful, sensitive, willing to go that extra yard, to do more, to be more concerned for the other partner than they would be for themselves. All that good stuff.

Rejecting the moral supremacy of a social order based on gender differences and separate spheres, nontraditional men support more equal arrangements between women and men. In their ideal world, women would be more like men and men would be more like women. The shape of this new world, however, can assume several forms. In one, equality is affirmed, but defined more in terms of equal freedom than in terms of equal responsibility. In another, equality means equal sharing of responsibilities as well as equal access to freedom and opportunity. This latter vision involves bringing men into the home as well as allowing women to leave it.

For men attracted to autonomy, equality tends to mean freedom and independence for both women and men. An ideal woman, like an ideal man, is, as one man put it, "someone that is independent, that can rely on herself, take care of herself, function within her personal life and at the workplace as an individual entity." This focus on independence can also mean a concern that women face the dangers and difficulties as well as the advantages once reserved for men:

If women want equal rights, let them pay child support, alimony. Let them get drafted. You want to be equal, you do everything equal, not just certain things.

I'm not really big on women who stay home and just raise kids. I think everybody should be a fully functioning, self-supporting adult. In terms of women's issues, if they prepared themselves for the idea that they have to assume their financial burdens and responsibilities, they won't have to be emotional hostages to toxic relationships. And men won't either.

Support for equality is thus grounded in the conviction that equality cuts both ways and offers advantages to both sexes. Yet this vision of equality does not necessarily include acceptance of the idea that men will assume new responsibilities as they agree to share old ones. When it comes to parenthood, autonomous men are more likely to conclude that men and women have an equal right *not* to have children rather than an equal responsibility for rearing them. Indeed, they may conclude that not having children is the most responsible choice:

As far as I'm concerned, there's generations of parents out there who have no business being parents. I joke about believing there should be a parental aptitude test. Especially in this day and age when there is *not* enough to go around, I am extremely pro–birth control, zero-population growth, and all those things.

The expansion of everyone's freedom and range of choice is a compelling reason for men to support gender equality. Yet by down-playing the price to be paid, those who uphold the value of autonomy without facing the implications for caretaking offer a vision that is incomplete. If it does not include a concern for equal caretaking as well as for equal rights, the struggle for equality runs the same risks that breadwinning men (and domestic women) dwell upon: that women and children will lose social, economic, and legal "protections" while failing to achieve either genuine equality or a better life.[2] As one autonomous man put it, "I guess an ideal woman would be one who could hold a job, and raise a family, and cook and do all those things."

If women are to gain opportunities rather than lose supports, and if children are to be assured parental attention in a world where mothers cannot do it all alone, nontraditional men need to face the costs as well as the benefits of change. Such a vision of equality would extend beyond the ideal of every man and woman for him- or herself.

A vision that takes account of mutual responsibilities as well as expanded choice can be found in the views of those men who have turned toward parenting and domestic involvement. These men have learned that equality includes a man's responsibility to help bake the bread as well as a woman's responsibility to help earn it. They have also rejected any argument suggesting that men lack the emotional capacities to parent as well as women:

I don't see any natural biological relationship or emotional reason why the father shouldn't take just as active a role in child care. And if somebody's wife does all the cooking, I always feel very uncomfortable about that too.

While breadwinners look askance at men who are not the primary family earners, these men argue that preoccupied, disinterested, or uninvolved fathers are the ones who are truly shirking their duties:

> My best friend has two boys, and he doesn't do anything with the children. To me, it's not healthy because the kids are not close to their father. He doesn't see it—he sees it as he's busy—but I can see it.

> Men who work all day, come home late, support the family, but don't have time with children—I personally think that they're crazy. Spending *time* at home is more important. If what you feel is important is making money—that's almost like they've got their values a little messed up.

Men who moved toward family involvement are thus able to fashion a reciprocal vision of equal rights and equal responsibilities. By stressing the personal advantages to shared caretaking, they are also able to reconcile the apparent conflict between sacrifice and self-interest. The ideal of reciprocity allows these men to transform costs into benefits. Yet they, too, believe that women cannot achieve equality for free. If men are to relinquish workplace and domestic advantages, then women must give up the presumption of parenting superiority:

> Women have got to pay the price for equality, and that price is that I won't assume you don't know anything about cars because you're a woman, and you won't assume that I don't know anything about babies because I'm a man.

> One of the things that I get angry about is when there's the emphasis that the mother-child relationship only seems to be important, that there's not really a nurturing need for men, that if the child loses the father, it's not as traumatic as the child losing a mother. Obviously, a man can't duplicate pregnancy and breast-feeding, but after that, the relationship between the child and the father can be as intense as the mother and child.

Yet involved fathers are left facing the same conflicts that most women face. Denied viable avenues for balancing earning a living and caring for others, they fear that equality may simply mean that no one can "have it all." They hope for a world in which a range of choices is more widely available to everyone:

> I want the best of both worlds. I want to make a lot of money and spend time with my daughter, but obviously I can't have both.

I think it would be ideal if there could always be someone at home doing the child rearing. The only other step is that whichever parent wants to be home should be able to be there without any restrictions about it being a mother or a father.

In truth, women can never have the best of both worlds until men share equal responsibility for the worst of both worlds. Making that option more accessible depends on more than the support of men. It requires social policies that allow a truly reciprocal ideal of equality to become common practice. A young father put it eloquently:

It would be ideal if I could go to work half the time and Rita could go to work half the time. Then each of us would be home half the time. It would be great for us, and it would be great for Jimmy. But society isn't organized that way. Society just said, "No, it wouldn't be great for society." So it just isn't going to happen.

THE PROMISE AND DANGER OF THE FUTURE

The ambiguities of change suggest three different possibilities for the future. In the first scenario, the imagined past is regained: primary breadwinning once again becomes the predominant pattern for men, and male privilege and control are restored as legitimate and widely supported social values. Yet the clock cannot be turned back to a golden era that never was, even if men agreed (and they do not) that it were desirable to do so. The institutional changes in the economy, marriage, and parenting that have undermined breadwinning and produced diversity in men's choices are widespread, long in the making, and far beyond the capacities of either individuals or governments to halt or reverse. Wishing it were not so or proclaiming it wrong will not make change disappear. Nor can men resurrect a misplaced nostalgia for a simpler, more "primitive" life when manhood was earned by surviving physical challenges. Gathering in the forest in an attempt to find manly support and commune with nature does not provide a viable answer to the challenges of modern life. Moreover, anthropologists have found that male separation rituals are strong indications of highly unequal societies, while male participation in child rearing is one of the best indications of greater gender equality.[3]

The second vision of the future recognizes that change is inevitable, but leaves it dangerously incomplete. Rather than balancing greater freedom for men with greater responsibility, it grants men new freedoms from the burdens of breadwinning without allowing or expecting them to assume new responsibilities for their children. This version of change has alarming implications for women and children. Women are granted new opportunities outside the home, but face the loss of supports within it; and children face an erosion of time with one parent without gaining the attention or support of the other.

Each of these visions is problematic. The first upholds the importance of commitment and sacrifice, but at the expense of gender equality and women's legitimate rights; the second offers the promise of individual freedom and equality, but at the expense of interpersonal commitment and children's needs. All too often, the future is posed in these dichotomous, unpalatable terms. Yet there is an alternative to the Scylla of male dominance and the Charybdis of obsessive individualism. It is the vision offered by that group of men who wish to be genuinely equal partners in the work of caring for and supporting their families. It rests on the twin principles of equal opportunity and equal responsibility. In this vision, commitment, sharing, and sacrifice are integral, rather than antithetical, to equality.[4]

As social change continues to transform the division of moral labor, women can no longer be counted on to be the exclusive repositories of caretaking values while men alone are sanctioned to pursue self-interest. The vacuum created in the division of moral labor cannot be filled by asking women to sacrifice the self for the sake of men's continued privilege, whether it takes the form of control within the family or freedom from family obligations. The answer to this predicament is not to stifle or condemn women's fight for individual rights, but to hold men equally responsible for the moral work of caring for others. Only then can the crisis of caretaking be truly and fairly resolved.[5]

If men are to accept equal responsibility for caretaking, however, they need more opportunities for family involvement. The men who have spoken in these pages provide more reasons to be optimistic about men's desire to nurture children than about their opportunity to do so. Social barriers, not just individual resistance, limit men's family participation and thwart even the most motivated men's ability to become equal parents. Even those who resist taking care of children can imagine its attractions if the opportunity were truly available. As one man put it, "One of my friends can work on a flexible schedule and does probably fifty percent of the nurturing. That does bring out feelings in me because he seems to have it all."

While many women grapple with the choice between parenting and committed employment, men are generally denied such a choice. Even when a man wishes to be involved, he is rarely able to trade full-time employment for parental involvement. Social barriers to involved fatherhood suppress feelings as well as actions. We can only guess how many more men might wish to nurture if they could more easily express and enact these desires. Yet social change has made it more difficult for women to parent without making it much easier for men. Given the *lack* of change in men's options to choose parenting over work, it is not surprising that most men resist equal participation. More remarkable, perhaps, is how strongly some men have asserted their need, desire, and right to care for children.

Men's Parenting and Social Policy

The decline of male breadwinning poses significant dangers, but it also offers an unprecedented opportunity to bring greater equality to family and work life while expanding men's and women's range of choice and enhancing the well-being of children. Accomplishing these ends, however, requires more than the efforts of ordinary men. Just as individuals develop strategies to respond to unavoidable change, so must societies. While changes in the organization of the economy, marriage, and child rearing make the decline of breadwinning inevitable, social policies can help shape the forms that emerge to take its place. We have seen how opportunities and barriers at work and in the home can either thwart or encourage men's family involvement. Since men's choices are shaped by social circumstances, the challenge is to build social institutions that support the best aspects of change (such as the expansion of equality, choice, and family involvement) and discourage the worst (such as the abandonment of children and the overburdening of women). In the best American tradition, we need to build policies that respect diversity, encourage responsibility, and create equal opportunity.

Diversity in men's choices is here to stay. A new cultural consensus on the meaning of manhood appears no more imminent than the emergence of a new dominant pattern of behavior. In light of these new realities, we need to avoid replacing one dogma with another. Tolerance for diversity is central to American political culture. On the other hand, a cultural politics of division and blame draws attention away from the social challenge to adapt to inevitable change. It is time to abandon the search for one, and only one, correct pattern for all men. It is time not only to accept diversity but to respect it.

In rejecting rigid definitions of manhood, we need to include new responsibilities along with an expanded range of choice. Among men who retain a breadwinning identity, there is a difference between those who are actually supporting nonemployed wives and those who refuse to admit that their wives are breadwinners, too. Among men who have moved away from parenthood, there is a difference between those who have decided that the responsible choice is to remain childless and those who have abdicated responsibility for their children. Among involved fathers, there is a difference between those who have accepted equal responsibility for domestic work and those who remain helpers. Clearly, some choices are more responsible than others.

We can uphold the ideal of diversity and choice without sacrificing responsible standards of behavior. In a world where marital and parenting commitments have become fragile, this does not mean that everyone should get married or have children. It does, however, mean that choosing marriage or parenthood implies assuming serious responsibilities and making necessary sacrifices. If a man chooses to marry, he is agreeing to uphold the principles of justice and fairness. If he chooses to become a father, he is making a lifelong commitment to caring for his children.

Upholding standards of justice and sharing in personal commitments is neither a punishment nor an unmitigated loss to men. We have seen that men have much to gain from more equal relationships with women and more caring connections to children. Economic and social changes may require men to relinquish some long-standing privileges, but they also offer men a chance to claim new rights and surrender old burdens. No longer held solely responsible for the economic health of their families, men can look forward to sharing the obligations of breadwinning and enjoying the pleasures of care. Moreover, if men become more involved in the care of their children, they gain the moral authority to fight for parental rights inside and outside of marriage. Not only do involved fathers have a greater claim to parental rights in the event of divorce, but they are also less likely to abandon their children.[6] If marriage becomes more just and equal, then so can divorce. On the other hand, if men want parental rights, they must earn them the way women do—by being responsible, caring, sharing parents who meet their children's needs in myriad ways every day.

Institutions can foster or discourage responsible choices. If we want men to behave responsibly, then we must build social policies that support and encourage such an outcome. Effective social supports could transform men's family involvement from a latent, incipient possibility to expected, unremarkable behavior. Given the growing proportion of women struggling to balance work and family obligations and the growing proportion of children living without the economic or emotional contributions of men, men's commitment to care and equality has become greatly needed as well as morally desirable. Such a profound transformation in men's lives will require equally fundamental changes in the organization of the workplace and the economic opportunities available to women.

Women's movement into the labor force has made it clear that the home and the workplace are interacting rather than separate spheres. Yet conflicts between work and family have typically been viewed as a woman's problem. The current organization of the workplace makes it difficult for any parent, regardless of gender, to combine employment and parenting. Work also poses obstacles to men's family involvement, and to ignore these obstacles is to leave the problem unfairly resting on women's shoulders.

In addition, the historical bargain between employers and families has broken down. When employers paid their male workers enough to support a homemaking wife, they could argue that children's needs were not their concern. Since employers are now less likely to pay men a family wage that subsidizes female caretakers, the time has come to admit that most families depend on either two earners or one parent. These revolutionary changes in gender and family life require a new bargain between employers and workers based on the principle that parenthood is a right, not just a privilege, for all.

What does this mean in practical terms? At the least, it means no longer penalizing employed fathers or mothers for providing the care and attention that children require. Even more, it means offering workers greater flexibility in how they choose to balance work and family contributions over the course of the week, the year, and the career. Caretaking demands ebb and flow in unpredictable ways that cannot be addressed via rigid work schedules and career tracks. We need to create a more flexible boundary between family and work. Yet only about 3,500 companies address family policy issues at all, and most do so in a piecemeal fashion. Only about 50 companies have developed fully integrated work/family benefits, including appointing someone with designated responsibility to develop and oversee a package of policies.[7]

Bringing the workplace into a new partnership with family life will require more than the goodwill of employers, most of whom are unlikely to institute change unless compelled to do so. And it will require more than de jure policies that formally allow family involvement but informally penalize those who choose it. If involved parenting remains a formal option that few feel entitled to take without great sacrifice to their careers, the most ambitious among us—women as well as men—will resist involved parenthood and reject the programs that exist on paper but punish those who utilize them.[8] Instead, we need "family support" policies that allow involvement for all parents. If men and women unite to fight for the parental rights of all workers, then the conflicts between work and family may begin to dissolve.

Creating genuine family support policies to replace the patchwork of company-initiated programs that now exist will require political and legislative action. The federal family leave law that requires larger firms to offer their workers three months of unpaid leave in the event of a child's birth or a family medical emergency is certainly an important start, but it needs to become the floor on which we build more fundamental programs rather than the ceiling above which family policies cannot rise. Sweden, for example, guarantees all workers six weeks of paid vacation each year, three months paid leave when children are sick, the right to work part-time without losing one's job until one's children are seven years old, and eighteen months of parental leave to fathers as well as mothers. A quarter of Swedish fathers take paternity leave.[9] To move beyond family leave to secure the broader range of parental rights that many Europeans now take for granted may ultimately depend on a "parents' movement" comparable to the movements for workers' rights that once secured limits on the length of the work week, safer working conditions, and minimum wage guarantees. This means bringing men into the fight that women have pioneered in pursuit of a more family-supportive workplace.

A reorganized workplace is necessary, but not sufficient, to bring men into family life. Men's family involvement also depends on equal economic opportunities for women. Women's economic resources give them the leverage to insist that men parent more. They also make it possible for men to work less. A father's involvement depends on economic opportunities for his female partner. Thus, policies that promote economic opportunity for women also promote men's parental involvement.

Of course, economic opportunity and family obligation are related. Women cannot enjoy equal employment opportunities until men shoulder equal family obligations, and men are not likely to become equal parents until women enjoy equal economic opportunities. Indeed, when parenthood becomes as costly to men's work careers as it is to women's, then men, too, will have a stake in reducing the economic and social penalties for taking care of children.[10]

Equal opportunity and a reorganized workplace will be difficult to achieve, and the struggle to achieve them will surely remain politically controversial.[11] But the costs of *not* creating family-friendly workplaces, equal economic opportunities for women, and equal family opportunities for men will be much worse. Even if these were not worthy goals in themselves, our economic and social health depends on achieving them. The costs of a system that has put parenthood, along with women and children, last have already proved to be far too high.[12]

Why should men support institutional changes that respect diversity and promote responsibility and equality? Because policies that offer men an equal opportunity to parent and offer women an equal opportunity to support their families will reduce the dilemmas and expand the range of choices for all. Even more important, the long-run fates of men, women, and especially children will depend on how our political and social institutions respond to the spreading dilemmas of family life that have been created in no small measure by changes in the lives of men.

Revolutionary change has produced confusion and disagreement among men and dilemmas for which there are few clear resolutions. Some men are opposing challenges to their power and privilege, labeling them threats to the social order and moral fabric. Others are welcoming the chance to escape the narrow and stringent demands of twentieth-century masculinity. Inevitably, conflicts are emerging between those who see change as a threat and those who see it as an opportunity, and between those for whom opportunity means more freedom and those for whom it means more sharing. As new conflicts develop among men, new alliances may also develop between men and women who share a similar vision of the future they would like to create.[13] Indeed, men and women face a historic opportunity to forge new alliances based on their common ground as parents and workers.

Will future generations of men—the children of those who have created and coped with the current transformation—emulate, rebel against, or ignore the choices made by this one? Will they steadfastly declare themselves to be the only breadwinners and breadwinners only, even as they watch their female friends and partners build strong work commitments? Will they eschew family obligations in ever-rising numbers, deciding not to father children or to care for those they have? Or will they join with women to create a more equal and flexible balance between family and work, caretaking and breadwinning? These are all ways for men to claim the no man's land created by social change. Which vision becomes predominant in reality depends on which alternatives men are offered. Either we create the conditions for equality and caring or we live with the consequences of failing to do so.

NOTES

Preface

1. Mills, 1959: 143.
2. Although domestic activities are an important form of work, I use the term *work* to refer to activities performed outside one's home for pay. Using another term that might be technically more precise would be cumbersome.
3. As names were selected, potential respondents were contacted first by mail and then by telephone. During the phone call, potential respondents were screened, and those who fell within the specified age range were asked to participate in the study. Seventy percent of those who were eligible agreed to be interviewed, and there were no significant differences in the demographic attributes of those who agreed and those who declined.
4. For example, the U.S. Bureau of the Census (1991) reports that approximately 88 percent of American men between the ages of thirty and forty-four have either completed four or more years of college (27 percent) or have completed four years of high school or one to three years of college (61 percent).
5. I personally conducted seventy-two interviews, relying on two research assistants for the rest. Both assistants were women, and there is thus no way to assess the effect of the sex of the interviewer on the respondent's willingness to disclose. Research on interviewer effects suggests, however, that men as well as women are more likely to confide in a woman than in a man. Certainly, the vast majority of our respondents disclosed openly and with enthusiasm.

6. Those who would like to see a similar version of the interview schedule can refer to the one published in my earlier book, *Hard Choices: How Women Decide About Work, Career, and Motherhood* (1985). That book also uses life-history analysis to explore divergent paths and to discover the pushes and pulls, constraints and opportunities, that promote different choices among members of one gender group.

7. Connell, 1991a, discusses the use of transition points as pegs for memory when using the life-history method to study varieties of masculinity.

8. Gerth and Mills, 1953, present the classic discussion of the relationship between personal biography and what they term "vocabularies of motive."

Chapter 1: Introduction

1. See Cherlin, 1981, and Gerson, 1983.

2. Gerson, 1985: 237. Stacey, 1991, provides an excellent discussion of how these earlier signs of alternative family structures, which at that time were more prevalent in minority and working-class communities, were precursors of more widespread social change. See also Mintz and Kellogg, 1988.

3. See Bernard, 1981, and Ehrenreich, 1983.

4. U.S. Department of Labor, 1980 and 1991.

5. U.S. Department of Labor, 1980 and 1991; U.S. Bureau of the Census, 1992b.

6. Smith, 1979, coined the phrase "the subtle revolution" to describe the social shifts caused by women's movement into the labor force. Although one kind of revolution consists of a revolt from below that overthrows an established government or political system, I use the term to refer to a more general process of social upheaval that produces a rapid and fundamental restructuring of the organization and social relations of a society.

7. U.S. Bureau of the Census, 1990, and U.S. Department of Labor, 1991.

8. More recently, popular books on men and manhood—especially Bly, 1990, and Keen, 1991—have climbed to the top of the best-seller lists. These books are more concerned with lamenting the current state, and purported decline, of manhood than carefully analyzing the lives of real men. Their popularity suggests not only a deep unease about current change but also a widespread cultural confusion about how men should behave in the wake of the gender revolution. Kimmel, 1992a, presents an incisive critique of these recent books. In discussing Bly's book, Connell worries that it is "a disturbing index of current sexual politics [that] significant numbers of middle-class North American men are attracted to a view of masculinity which is nativist, separatist, homophobic, and expressed through concocted myths of ancient men's rituals" (1992: 19).

9. See Hochschild, 1989. Other studies that describe both the rise in men's domestic participation and the persistent gap between what men and women do include (among others) Gershuny and Robinson, 1988; Goldscheider and Waite, 1991; Pleck, 1983 and 1985; Robinson, 1988. See La Rossa, 1988, for an example of a strong version of the view that men's behavior has not changed despite cultural change.

10.   Fuchs, 1988: 78.
11.   Ehrenreich, 1983, argues that men, not women, were the first to leave the family as cultural change transformed the meaning of manhood from responsible breadwinning to freedom from commitment. In many ways, this is a brilliant, incisive work. Its power is marred, however, by several logical flaws. First, Ehrenreich stresses the role of culture in allowing and propelling men to flee the home in the decades following World War II. Historians and literary scholars can attest that the cultural theme of men's flight from domesticity to achieve manhood in a world without women extends back as far as American history itself. Surely this cultural theme cannot explain why a trend toward family flight emerged and gained momentum in the last several decades. Second, Ehrenreich ignores a second, and equally profound, dimension of change. While some men have moved away from family commitments, others have taken on new ones—becoming *more* involved in family life. Surely a full consideration of the "hearts of men" should include this trend as well.
12.   Barringer, 1992a.
13.   Slade, 1991.
14.   Barringer, 1992b, and U.S. Bureau of the Census, 1991.
15.   Fuchs, 1988: 16.
16.   Slade, 1991.
17.   That figure includes 20 percent for white children and 58 percent for black children. See Barringer, 1992a.
18.   Suro, 1992.
19.   Brody, 1991.
20.   According to Dugger, 1992, only 14 percent of unmarried mothers collected any child support in 1989. She also reports that the percentage of children born to unwed parents has leapt from 5 percent in 1958 to 25 percent in 1988.
21.   Weitzman, 1985, argues that "no fault" divorce laws have contributed to this trend. Others who stress men's estrangement from family life after divorce include Arendell, 1986; Hewlett, 1986; and Wallerstein and Blakeslee, 1989.
      There is little question that divorce provides a powerful disruption that often drives a wedge between men and their children. However, the extent of the damage is far less clear. Critics have pointed out that both Weitzman and Wallerstein report findings that are exaggerated and based on flawed analyses. By reanalyzing some of Weitzman's reported findings, Hoffman and Duncan, 1988, report, for example, that the decline in women's economic status after divorce is probably closer to 33 percent than the 73 percent Weitzman reports. Their figure is consistent with others' findings as well. Moreover, others have shown that the long-run consequences of divorce are even less severe, since most divorced women get back on their feet economically by establishing a work career and/or remarrying. (See, especially, Peterson, 1989.)
      In Wallerstein's study, the lack of a control group makes it impossible to separate the effects of divorce from the effects of having parents who are or were unhappily married.

294   NOTES

22. U.S. Bureau of the Census, 1991; U.S. Department of Labor, 1991.

23. U.S Bureau of the Census, 1991.

24. Mishel and Frankel, 1991: 46–47.

25. Robinson, 1988.

26. Goldscheider and Waite, 1991.

27. U.S. Bureau of the Census, 1992a, tables 1 and 4.

28. Pleck, forthcoming: 7.

29. More divorced fathers retain *legal* custody, which involves retaining decision-making rights in child rearing, than retain *residential* custody, which
includes specific arrangements for a child to reside at least part-time with
her or his father. A study of divorce in two California counties between
September 1984 and March 1985 reported that joint legal custody was
awarded in three-fourths of the divorces involving dependent children, but
joint residential custody was awarded in only 20 percent of the cases
(Fuchs, 1988: 69).

30. Brody, 1991.

31. Excellent studies of involved fathers and how they participate include
Beer, 1983; Lamb, ed., 1982; Lamb, Pleck, and Levine, 1987; Levine, 1976;
Lewis and Sussman, eds., 1986; Pleck, 1985; Pruett, 1983 and 1988; Risman,
1985 and 1986.

32. Several analysts have described this multidimensional change. See, especially, essays by Furstenberg, 1988, and Pleck, 1987a. Furstenberg points
out that the emerging variety among men includes not only contrasting
strategies for different groups of men but also a variety of strategies for the
same man. For example, some men become estranged from their children
after divorce, only to remarry and become deeply involved in rearing the
children in their new partnership. Chapter 9 considers the theoretical implications of such changes over the life course of individual men.

33. Barringer, 1992b.

34. These percentages add to more than 100 percent due to rounding.

35. For discussions of how gender is an important category of social analysis,
see Scott, 1988. Unfortunately, the study of men as gendered human beings
rather than prototypical humans has been slow in developing. As early as
1976, Komarovsky studied the "dilemmas of masculinity," but few followed
her lead at that time. Over the last decade, however, social scientists have
paid increasing attention to men *as men*. The growth of gender as a field of
study and the emergence of feminism as an intellectual perspective have
invigorated the study of men. A partial list of those who have contributed
to the study of men and masculinity includes Brod, 1987; David and Brannon, 1976; Fine, 1987; Franklin, 1984 and 1988; Hanson and Bozett, 1985;
Jardine and Smith, 1987; Kimmel, 1987 and 1992a,b; Kimmel and Messner,
1989; Lamb, 1976, 1986, and 1987; Levine, 1976; Lewis, 1986; Lewis and
O'Brien, 1987; Lewis and Salt, 1986; Pleck, 1981 and 1987a,b; Pleck and
Sawyer, 1974; Pruett, 1988; Segal, 1990; Weiss, 1990.

36. Determinist arguments can rely on biological or social imperatives to assert the inevitability of inequality. Goldberg, 1973, provides a classic socio-
biological analysis of what he calls "the inevitability of patriarchy." The clas-

sic functionalist position on the inevitability of gender inequality can be found in Parsons, 1942, 1954, 1958, and Parsons and Bales, 1955. Some highly influential feminists, such as Chodorow, have also adopted a neofunctionalist framework that comes close to implying that gender differences are so pervasive and deep-seated that they may be inescapable (1978).

37.   Connell (1987), Epstein (1988), and Tavris (1992) present convincing discussions of the limitations of a framework that assumes "dichotomous distinctions" between women and men. They point out that most observed gender differences in psychological capacity are small and that variation within each gender group far exceeds variation between women and men. If the capacities men and women share outnumber those that separate them, then why is the assumption of "dichotomous distinctions" so tenacious despite the lack of scientific support? Epstein argues that making "dichotomous distinctions" between women and men acts as an ideology of social control that helps to keep men in power. Faludi's analysis of the "backlash" against women (1991) makes a similar point. However, as both Epstein and Faludi note, many women also subscribe to this position. Most likely, a perspective that emphasizes dichotomous distinctions persists because it serves different ends for different groups. Men may find comfort in the power it confers on them, while women may seek refuge in its view that they hold special qualities that men do not possess.

38.   Goode, 1982, points out that few men feel as privileged as they are told they are. They take their historical privileges for granted, assuming they are either justly earned or biologically bestowed. They overemphasize the costs and burdens of privilege, and they overestimate their losses in times of change.

39.   Scott, 1985, analyzes the process by which subordinate groups carve out strategies of resistance, which he calls "weapons of the weak."

40.   In reviewing the recent spate of books on manhood, Kimmel points out that

> [t]hese books often use the analogy of the chauffeur to describe men's plight. He's in the driver's seat, wearing the uniform, so you'd naturally assume he has the power. But from his perspective, someone else is giving the orders. Brilliant, no? But only half right. What's missing from the analogy is the observation that the one giving the orders is also a man. By removing individual men from the social world in which men continue to give the orders, we miss the systemic, social context for an individual's experience within it (1992a: 170).

In short, men are more likely to feel powerless in relation to other men than in relation to women. The erosion of men's economic resources is a greater threat to their power than the rise of women's claims.

41.   See Weiss, 1990, for a thorough analysis of the dilemmas and adjustments facing "traditional breadwinners" in an era of change.

42.   See, for example, Komarovsky, 1962; Goode, 1963; and Hochschild with Machung, 1989.

43.   As Faludi, 1991, and Tavris, 1992, clearly document, this view has become

surprisingly popular even among those who define themselves as feminists. Coltrane notes:

> Depicting rigid gender-based divisions of household labor as normative and invariant poses a danger. Focusing on gender as the universal primary determinant of household labor allocation masks diversity and disregards exceptions to normative patterns. Treating gender or "sex" as an "independent variable" predisposes researchers to underestimate the importance of the meaning of the situation for social actors and to neglect the influence of specific situational constraints. To treat gender as the "cause" of household division of labor overlooks its emergent character and fails to acknowledge how it is in fact implicated in precisely such routine practices (1989: 489).

Chapter 2: The Changing Contours of American Manhood

1.   For discussions of the history of fatherhood and masculinity, see Bernard, 1981; Bloom-Feshbach, 1981; Demos, 1986; Eggebeen and Uhlenberg, 1985; Friedman, 1992; Gerzon, 1982; Kimmel, 1987; Parke and Tinsley, 1983; and Rotundo, 1985. For overviews of historical changes in American family patterns, see Bane, 1976; Evans, 1989; Gerstel and Gross, 1989; Laslett and Brenner, 1989; Mintz and Kellogg, 1988; Skolnick, 1991; Stacey, 1990, 1991; and Ryan, 1979, 1981.

2.   Zelizer, 1985, analyzes the transition from the "useful" child to the "priceless" child in the United States around the turn of the century. Aries, 1962, presents the classic study of childhood before the Industrial Revolution. See also Tilly and Scott, 1987.

3.   As life expectancy has expanded, divorce and fluid sexual partnerships have merely replaced death as the primary sources of family breakup. For analyses of changes in rates of divorce and their relationship to changing life expectancies in the United States and the Western world, see Bane, 1976; Cherlin, 1981; Glick and Norton, 1977; Levinger and Moles, 1979; Phillips, 1988; Riley, 1991; and Stone, 1990.

4.   Connell, 1992, points out that these two visions of masculinity—the "brawling single frontiersman" and the "settled married pioneer farmer"—are common cultural images that have persisted as "a characteristic part of sexual ideology" in disparate national settings, including such former colonies as South Africa and Australia as well as the United States.

5.   For analyses of the emergence of occupational sex segregation and the norm of the male family wage, see Hartmann, 1976; W. Seccombe, 1986; and Zaretsky, 1982. For discussions of the creation of female domesticity during the emergence of industrialism, see Oakley, 1974; Ryan, 1981; and Smelser, 1959.

6.   See, for example, May, 1982.

7.   See Jones, 1985; Kessler-Harris, 1981; Skolnick, 1991; Stacey, 1991.

8.   Zelizer, 1985.

9. Kessler-Harris, 1981.

10. Welter, 1966, discusses the emergence of the "cult of true womanhood" during the mid-nineteenth century.

11. See Cohn, 1987, for a trenchant analysis of how some occupations that originally employed men became "feminized" while others did not.

12. Smith, 1979.

13. U.S. Department of Labor, 1991.

14. For discussion of the rise of poverty among women and children, see Eggebeen and Lichter, 1991; Ellwood, 1988; Garfinkel and McClanahan, 1986; Moynihan, 1986; Sidel, 1986; and Weitzman, 1985.

15. Although the earnings among high-wage male earners, those in the upper 10 percent, "have grown modestly since 1973, including a 0.4 percent annual growth since 1979" (Mishel and Frankel, 1991: 78–81).

16. Phillips, 1990: 18.

17. During the same period, the median hourly wage for women rose 5.8 percent (Frankel and Mishel, 1991: 81).

18. As shown in appendix, table 1, the percentage of "nonfamily households" (composed of a "primary individual" not living with a spouse or a child related by blood or law) rose from 10.8 percent in 1950 to 29.2 percent in 1990. Among men living alone in 1990, 47 percent were between the ages of twenty-five and forty-four, up from 26 percent in 1970. Only 22 percent of men living alone in 1990 were over sixty-five, down from 33 percent in 1970—when widowhood accounted for a larger proportion of single men (U.S. Bureau of the Census, 1991).

19. Stacey, 1991, refers to this rediversification of households and families in the late twentieth century as the "postmodern family" (p. 19). She uses the term *postmodern* "to signal the contested, ambivalent, and undecided character of contemporary gender and kinship arrangements." Skolnick, 1991, p. 19, shows how these changes are not surprising from a long-term historical perspective. She reiterates the finding of most analysts of the family that the domestic model of the 1950s provides a poor model for understanding change since it was atypical. See also May, 1988.

20. Swidler, 1980, discusses the tension between freedom and commitment in American cultural definitions of adulthood.

21. See Weiss, 1990, for an in-depth consideration of breadwinning men who "stayed the course" in these difficult times.

Chapter 3: The Child and the Man

1. Nine percent reported either that they had no father or that they could not tell how their father felt about his work.

2. Although the concept of "fear of success" was developed to explain women's ambivalence toward careers, subsequent research has demonstrated that men are as likely to fear success as are women. For a critique of this much-publicized but never demonstrated thesis, see Kaufman and Richardson, 1982.

3. Among those whose mothers were full-time homemakers or held part-time employment, 53 percent and 63 percent, respectively, developed a bread-winning orientation in childhood. Only 40 percent and 26 percent, respectively, were oriented toward breadwinning in adulthood, however. Among those whose mothers worked full-time before their sons started school, only 29 percent developed a breadwinning orientation in childhood, and only 21 percent held such an outlook in adulthood.

4. See Weitzman, 1984, for an excellent summary of the "sex-role socialization" perspective. For psychoanalytic and developmental accounts of gender socialization, see Chodorow, 1978; Gilligan, 1982; and Johnson, 1988. A number of writers have pointed out that these theories elevate a stereotypical description of gender difference to a "standard normative case." See, for example, Connell, 1987; Epstein, 1988; Pleck, 1981; and Tresemer, 1975.

5. Recent results from the Harvard Valliant study, which is tracing the life paths of a sample of Harvard male graduates who recently turned sixty-five, suggest that even difficult childhood experiences can be transformed into positive sources of change and survival in adulthood. According to Goleman, 1990, the study found that childhood trauma and other experiences have virtually no predictive power for well-being in later life. For especially insightful discussions of the indeterminate effects of child-rearing practices, see Kagan, 1984 and 1989.

6. See Waller, 1937, for the classic discussion of marriage as a market in which men and women compete for the best partner they can obtain. See Collins, 1971, for a consideration of how men, like women, in advanced industrial economies must use physical attractiveness as a resource for nabbing a mate.

7. All of the men who served in the armed forces were from a working-class background. For an excellent analysis of how working-class boys went to war and middle-class boys went to training for professional careers during the Vietnam War, see Baskir and Strauss, 1978.

8. See Eisenstadt, 1956, and Elder, 1987, for classic theoretical considerations of the transition to adulthood in modern societies. Among the many who have traced historical changes in the structuring of the life course and found choice points to be increasingly less predictable, see Buchman, 1989; Demos, 1986; Modell, Furstenberg, and Hershberg, 1976; Hareven, 1977; Kett, 1977.

9. The finding of change in adulthood is a common one in contemporary research. My earlier study of women's work and family choices found a similar dynamic to be typical of contemporary women. Others who have focused on the change process in adulthood include Brim, 1992; Furstenberg, Brooks-Gunn, and Morgan, 1987; and Jacobs, Karen, and McClelland, 1991. Jacobs, et al., found that young men's occupational aspirations are highly unstable. In general, they tend to decline with age and become more stable later on, when inequality in educational attainments forces men from the lower classes to settle for less.

Chapter 4: Turning Toward Breadwinning

1. Among all married breadwinners (including those who moved toward breadwinning and those who followed stable paths) with children living at home, 21 percent of the middle-class men and 5 percent of the working-class men had full-time employed partners. But for these men, an employed wife did not mean a work-committed wife. They viewed their wives' income as expendable, unpredictable, and discretionary.

2. This process worked both ways: labor force experiences affected marital and childbearing decisions, and experiences in private life affected employment decisions. See Merton, 1957, for the classic statement on the unintended consequences of human action.

3. Granovetter, 1973 and 1974, shows how important even "weak ties" are for securing a good job. See also Granovetter, 1985, for an excellent discussion of how economic action is "embedded" in social networks.

4. Peterson and Gerson, 1992, show that work constraints affect the ability of both men and women to take responsibility for making child-care arrangements.

5. Chinoy, 1955, found that the dream of self-employment was a common reaction to stifled opportunities on the assembly line. Steinmetz and Wright, 1989, report that self-employment is on the rise in late-twentieth-century America.

6. The argument that American men wish to remain young forever was popularized by Dan Kiley in *The Peter Pan Syndrome* (1983). The problem with this argument, of course, is that most men do not remain perpetually free and many man do not even wish to do so. See Weiss, 1990, for an in-depth analysis of men who choose instead to "stay the course" of breadwinning.

7. Chapter 7 examines how primary breadwinners whose wives are employed denigrate and downplay the importance of their wives' paid jobs in order to maintain their own breadwinning identity.

8. My study of women's choices found that blocked opportunities at the workplace led many women to relinquish career ambitions and choose domesticity instead. See Gerson, 1985 and 1987b, for a fuller analysis of why some women become domestically oriented (and seek good-provider husbands) despite holding nondomestic aspirations in childhood. Pittman and Orthner, 1988, discuss the conditions under which wives are likely to support their husbands' careers.

9. As the psychological literature on cognitive dissonance points out, people commonly face strong incentives to convince themselves that they want what they have chosen and do not want what they cannot have. See Hochschild, 1983, for a more sociological treatment of the ways in which people perform "emotion work" to bring their feelings into line with their situations.

10. About two-thirds of the reluctant breadwinners purposefully chose a domestically oriented spouse, but the remaining third became involved with women whose career prospects and aspirations declined after the relationship was established.

11. See, for example, Bernard, 1972; Gove, 1972 and 1979; and Kessler, Brown, and Broman, 1981.

12. What appears to be chance to an individual is usually part of a more determined process. For example, a small percentage of plane crashes are inevitable, but we chalk it up to bad luck if anyone we love happens to be on one. Groups are subject to probabilities, but individuals appear lucky or unlucky. For an excellent analysis of how "accidents" are really "determined," see Perrow, 1984.

13. Although anthropologists originally coined the term *patriarchy* to refer to father rule, modern feminists and others use it to refer to social systems that grant authority, power, and control to men. See G. Rubin, 1975.

14. See Fowlkes, 1987, for an excellent discussion of the "myth of merit" in male professional careers. Kanter, 1977, Papanek, 1973, and Hochschild, 1975, analyze how the structure of the corporation and the life cycle of the "male career" make it easier for men than women to build professional careers.

Chapter 5: Turning Toward Autonomy

1. See Bernard, 1981, for an analysis of the rise and fall of the "good provider." For a general discussion of these trends, see Goldscheider and Waite, 1991. See Ehrenreich, 1983, for an analysis of men's "flight from the family" in late-twentieth-century America. See Weitzman, 1985, and Wallerstein and Blakeslee, 1989, for discussions on estrangement between divorced fathers and their children. Although Weitzman argues that liberalized divorce laws have allowed and encouraged men to avoid economic responsibility for children and ex-wives, it appears that legal changes in divorce are more a consequence than a cause of the growing demand for divorce among women and men alike. Whatever the cause, there is little doubt that rising rates of divorce and single motherhood have contributed to the growing proportion of women and children living in poverty.

2. See Steinmetz and Wright, 1989.

3. See Hunt and Hunt, 1987b, for an analysis of how men trade off between leisure and paid work. See Wilensky, 1960, for one of the earliest discussions of the "uneven distribution of leisure" across social groups.

4. Connell, 1987, uses the term *hegemonic masculinity* to refer to the dominant or prevailing ideals of manhood in any cultural epoch.

5. See Wilson, 1987, for a discussion of how a scarcity of "marriageable men" plays a role in the dynamics of poverty and family formation. Bernard, 1972, was probably the first analyst to demonstrate systematically that single men rank lower than married men or single women in most measures of mental and physical health. Her findings have been replicated by numerous others over the last two decades. See Faludi, 1991; Gove, 1972; Kessler, Brown, and Broman, 1981.

6. Waller, 1937, and Rubin, 1973, discuss how power accrues to the person who "cares least" in a love relationship.

7. Blakeslee, 1991.

8. The 57 percent of uninvolved divorced fathers includes two men who be-
    came estranged from the children born in their previous marriages, but in-
    volved in rearing children of subsequent marriages.
9. For analyses of the postdivorce relationships between fathers and their
    children, see Furstenberg, 1985; Furstenberg, Morgan, and Allison, 1987;
    Seltzer, 1991; Seltzer and Bianchi, 1988; Kline, Johnston, and Tschann,
    1991. Arendell, 1986, explores the estrangement of divorced fathers primar-
    ily from the perspective of women and children.
10. In a rare discussion of men who feel rejected by their ex-wives, Myers,
    1986, looks at the syndrome of the "angry, abandoned husband."
11. See Suro, 1991 and 1992. For discussions of the uncoupling of marriage
    and motherhood, see Furstenberg, 1985; Furstenberg, Brooks-Gunn, and
    Morgan, 1987a; Garfinkel and McLanahan, 1986; Lewin, 1992; and Luker,
    1991.
12. Brody, 1991. Analyses of the economic consequences of divorce for
    women and children can be found in Hoffman and Duncan, 1988; Peterson,
    1989; Weitzman and Dixon, 1980; Weitzman, 1985; and Wikler, 1981.
13. Both Arendell (1992: 562) and Coltrane and Hickman (1992: 400) use the
    term *rhetoric of rights* to describe the strategies men use to control con-
    flict and dampen personal doubts about father-child relations after divorce.
14. Chodorow, 1978, argues that men have more "rigid ego boundaries" than
    women. Gilligan, 1982, extends this argument by contrasting a hypothe-
    sized male "ethic of justice" with a female "ethic of care."
15. Only two of these estranged fathers had remarried. An additional divorced
    father is not included here because he became involved in rearing a child
    born in his second marriage. He developed an increasingly common
    "mixed pattern," in which a father becomes estranged from the children of
    a first marriage but becomes involved in rearing the children of a second
    one. For an excellent discussion of this mixed pattern, see Furstenberg,
    1988.
16. See Hirschhorn, 1977, and Schor, 1992. For an interesting analysis of the
    relation between "disorderly careers" and social integration, see Wilensky,
    1960. It is notable that 27 percent of those who became autonomous, but
    only 9 percent of the stable breadwinners, opted for self-employment.
17. The view that men are rejecting commitment to emphasize self-fulfillment
    and personal autonomy is part of a larger debate on whether close bonds
    of attachment are declining in America. Bellah et al., 1985, have argued
    that individualism is on the rise in late-twentieth-century America. Lasch,
    1977 and 1979, provided an earlier version of this argument. Gans, 1988,
    and Cancian, 1987, have responded that narcissism is not rampant and that
    there is scant evidence that "community" is declining.

Chapter 6: Turning Toward Family Involvement

1. Hochschild with Machung, 1989.
2. See Hochschild with Machung, 1989, for a summary of the voluminous lit-
    erature on the gender division of household labor, especially among dual-

earner couples. See also Aldous, 1982; Berk, 1980 and 1985; Coverman, 1983 and 1985; Coverman and Sheley, 1986; Geerken and Gove, 1983; Hertz, 1986; Hood, 1983 and 1986; Huber and Spitze, 1983 and 1988; Pepitone-Rockwell, 1980; and Rapoport and Rapoport, 1977. For insightful analyses of how and why men's participation has changed in recent decades, see Coltrane, 1989a, 1989b; Gershuny and Robinson, 1988; Jump and Haas, 1987; Pleck, 1985 and 1993; Robinson, 1988; and Spitze, 1986. For a more pessimistic perspective, see La Rossa, 1988, and Nock and Kingston, 1988.

3.   Goldscheider and Waite, 1991, find that, on average, men are far more involved in child care than housework. Coltrane, 1989a and 1989b, presents an excellent analysis of how and why some fathers become equal domestic partners.

4.   For studies of caretaking fathers, see Beer, 1983, and Pruett, 1983 and 1988.

5.   For a critique of Horner's much-publicized but never demonstrated thesis, see Kaufman and Richardson, 1982.

6.   A recent cover story in *Fortune* magazine was entitled, "Why Grade 'A' Executives Get an 'F' as Parents." Recognizing that most of these "failing" parents are men, the editors pictured on the cover a set of keys to a Porsche wrapped in a red ribbon and attached to a note that read, "Dear Son, Enjoy the Gift! Sorry I won't be around for Christmas. Love, Dad" (O'Reilly, 1992).

7.   Kanter, 1977, provided the classic analysis of how hierarchical work structures inhibit women's job aspirations. See Chinoy, 1955, for another classic analysis of how hitting a dead end on the assembly line prompted auto workers to turn toward home, family, and leisure as alternative sources of identity and gratification. Ferree, 1987, found that poor jobs lead both women and men in the working class to look to family for emotional sustenance and meaning. On the other hand, Komarovsky, 1940, found that unemployed men in the Great Depression resisted domestic involvement, which they viewed as undermining their identities.

8.   Men who choose caring over rational self-interest call into question the power of economic approaches that analyze labor market and family choices in terms of maximizing economic self-interest (see, for example, Becker, 1976 and 1981; Stigler and Becker, 1977). They also call into question approaches that posit a different moral perspective for women and men. Analyzing the limits of economic determinism, Zelizer (1989a and 1989b) argues that economic life is itself a cultural construct.

9.   Sennett and Cobb, 1973, vividly illustrate the "hidden injuries" of not succeeding in a culture where so much value is placed on work success.

10. Henry, 1965, presents an intriguing analysis of how American culture promotes a sense of insecurity and failure even among the most successful. Brim, 1992, analyzes how people cope with failure and success by lowering or raising their standards accordingly.

11. Lasch, 1977, discusses the role families can play as a "haven in a heartless world." While many continue to count on their families for sustenance and

protection, others have found such a vision to be an empty promise. Mounting evidence of widespread family violence and abuse suggests that many women and children live in families that more closely resemble battlefields or prisons than safe havens. See, for example, Herman, 1992.

12. Research suggests that middle-class men are more likely to pay lip service to gender equality while resisting it in their behavior, and working-class men are more likely to oppose equality verbally but to uphold it to a surprising degree in their behavior (see Goode, 1963, and Hochschild with Machung, 1989).

13. This figure represents all of those who avoided parenthood, including "stable avoiders" whose orientation never changed as well as those who developed an autonomous outlook in adulthood. Comparisons among all autonomous men, all primary breadwinners, and all involved fathers are presented in the appendix, table 10.

14. See English, 1983; Mansbridge, 1986; and Ehrenreich, 1983.

15. Only three involved fathers did not follow this pattern. These men retained custody of their children after divorce, but never remarried.

16. Goode, 1959, discusses the process by which romantic love becomes "routinized" in a long-term relationship.

17. Erikson, 1963, was one of the first psychologists, and certainly the most influential one, to delineate the stages of human development. Although he focused on childhood, the transition from a concern with autonomy to intimacy may be repeated and reaccomplished in adulthood. For discussions of the stages of adult development, especially among adult men, see Levinson, 1978, and Gould, 1978. See also Smelser and Erikson, 1980.

18. See, especially, Bellah et al., 1985, and Lasch, 1977.

19. Cancian, 1987, makes this argument most convincingly. Collins, 1971, argues that advanced market economics encourage men and women to exchange similar rather than different resources. Parsons, 1942, 1954, and 1958, and Parsons and Bales, 1955, present the classic functionalist argument that modern families require differentiated roles.

20. Only 17 percent of this group were divorced fathers, and half of these men had already remarried.

21. Chodorow, 1978, is surely correct that coercion alone cannot produce "good-enough" parenting. Her approach nevertheless fails to recognize that a significant proportion of women do not find pleasure in parenting and that a significant proportion of men do. Jackson, 1989, and Epstein, 1985 and 1988, offer incisive critiques of the presumption that parenting motivations and capacities are divided so strictly according to gender.

22. See Risman, 1985 and 1986. See also O'Brien, 1982.

23. See Noble, 1993.

24. See Friedman, 1992; Kingston, 1988; and O'Toole, 1991.

25. Ruddick, 1989.

26. Even among divorced men, two-thirds of those who become involved fathers had either remarried or hoped to do so, while only one-third of those who moved toward autonomy had remarried or established another long-term, stable commitment.

27.   See Peterson, 1988. Other polls have found similar levels of support among men for so-called feminist goals (see Dionne, 1989).

28.   Belkin, 1989. This *New York Times* poll found that 83 percent of the women who were interviewed (all of whom were employed) also felt torn.

Chapter 7: Dilemmas of Breadwinning and Autonomy

1.   For an analysis of the differences between women's and men's work/family choices, see Bielby and Bielby, 1989.

2.   Hochschild with Machung, 1989, presents a penetrating analysis of the price of domestic inequality at home. Goode, 1982, utilizes a "sociology of dominant groups" to explain "how men resist" equality and why they also face good reasons to move toward it.

3.   The classic study reporting single men's plight is Bernard, 1972.

4.   See, especially, Levy, 1987; Levy and Mishel, 1991; and Mishel and Frankel, 1991.

5.   Among breadwinning men with children living at home, 51 percent had an employed wife, but only 13.5 percent had a wife who was employed full-time.

6.   Schor, 1992.

7.   Kilborn, 1990.

8.   See Kilborn, 1990, and Wilensky, 1963.

9.   Mischel and Frankel, 1991: 141–43.

10.   For example, a 1992 series in the *New York Times* on "The Good Mother: Searching for an Ideal" included articles entitled "New Realities Fight Old Images of Mother" (Chira, 1992), "Rise in Single Parenthood Is Reshaping U.S." (Lewin, 1992), "Learning If Infants Are Hurt When Mothers Go to Work" (Eckholm, 1992a), and "In Family-Leave Debate, A Profound Ambivalence" (Barringer, 1992c). The series focused entirely on the "ideal mother" and never raised questions about the "ideal father" or whether infants are harmed when their fathers go to work.

The vast preponderance of research, however, does not support this cultural preoccupation with the dangers of maternal employment. Rather, most careful research has shown that two factors—how a mother feels about her situation and the quality of caretaking arrangements—are far more important in determining a child's well-being than whether a mother is employed. (See, for example, Hoffman, 1987.) Moreover, Crosby, 1987, shows that the multiple "roles" of spouse, parent, and worker can provide life-enhancing challenges that offset the difficulties of "doing it all." In sum, under supportive circumstances, a mother's employment provides tangible benefits to children in the form of increased economic resources, a more fulfilled parent, and a positive role model.

11.   Cowan, 1983, shows that the development of "labor-saving devices" has not lowered the work load for homemakers, but rather raised the standard to which they are held.

12.   Gerstel, 1988, found that men and women tend to approach the task of developing relationships in the wake of divorce in different ways. Women are

more likely to turn to relationships that are old and enduring, while men are more likely to seek new or recent ones. In addition, men are more likely to have "instant networks" that cushion the potential isolation of divorce and provide new pools of relationships. For studies of differences in men's and women's friendships, see also Bell, 1981; Fischer, 1982; Oliker, 1989; and Rubin, 1976, 1983.

13. Snarey, 1988.

14. Scott and Lyman, 1968, argue that "excuses" and "justifications" provide ways that people account for behavior that is either unanticipated or not considered completely legitimate either by themselves or by others. Justifications of this sort can be considered sociological analogues to the psychoanalytic concept of defense mechanisms.

15. See, for example, Arendell, 1986; Duncan and Hoffman, 1985; Furstenberg, 1985, 1988, 1990; Hoffman and Duncan, 1988; Peterson, 1989; Wallerstein and Blakeslee, 1989; and Weitzman, 1985.

16. Despite other changes, the pattern of older men marrying younger women remains predominant. This pattern of mate selection, which gives men a growing advantage as they age and enjoy an expanding pool of potential partners, depends on two social factors. First, variation in the size of adjacent birth cohorts affects the opportunities for mate selection. When a large group of older men must choose from a smaller group of younger women, women's leverage is improved. Similarly, when a small group of older men confront a large group of younger women, the pool of mate choices expands for men. The importance of birth cohort size depends, however, on the persistence of the age norm that promotes older men–younger women liaisons. Since age norms are socially constructed and subject to change, the older man–younger woman pattern may decline in popularity as women gain power and economic advantage. Powerful older women may attract and select younger men for the same reasons that powerful older men now choose younger women. If this occurs, the advantage that age confers on men will decrease. (See Bell, 1970; Easterlin, 1980; Neugarten and Datan, 1973; and Riley, 1971.)

17. Bernard, 1991. For overviews of trends in marriage, divorce, and staying single, see Blakeslee, 1991; Cherlin, 1981; Glick, 1990; Glick and Norton, 1977; and Goldscheider and Waite, 1991.

Chapter 8: Dilemmas of Involved Fatherhood

1. Eighty percent of involved fathers were married or in a committed relationship.

2. As table 7 in the appendix shows, 36 percent of the college-educated men became involved fathers, while 31 percent of the working-class group did so. Given the small size of the sample, these differences are not significant.

3. My research on women's choices (Gerson, 1985) found that both domestic and work-committed women confronted conflicts and social disapproval. Hertz, 1986, also explores the dilemmas that both mothers and fathers face in dual-career marriages.

4. Before the rise of breadwinning, potency was considered an important measure of manhood. This made sense in a preindustrial context, where children contributed to their families' economic survival and large families meant more people to rely on. As children became economic liabilities, however, family size declined and bearing many children receded as a measure of a man's masculinity. Today, procreative measures of manhood persist mainly in poor communities and "traditional" cultures, where men have little chance of meeting more modern standards based on economic and work success. As women join men in the labor force, usurping their hold on economic power, men may turn to sexuality to reassert a separate masculine identity. Connell, 1991a, points out that men use physical attributes such as size, strength, and sexual potency to assert power when economic control eludes them.

5. Even though dual-career couples may wish to keep family size down, Peterson and Gerson, 1992, found that dual-earner couples who have large families are more likely than those with small families to share child-care responsibilities. In these cases, the larger workload makes it harder for a husband to avoid domestic work or pass it on to his wife.

6. A large body of research has found that working-class and poor communities are more likely to depend on informal networks of kin and friends to help care for their children. See, for example, Stack, 1974, and Zinsser, 1990. Hertz, 1986, presents an excellent analysis of how dual-career professional couples use hired caretakers to lighten their child-care load.

7. Hochschild with Machung, 1989.

8. Bielby and Bielby, 1989, argue that family-oriented men do not make trade-offs in their identity as women do because men can combine family and work more easily. This is the case when involved fathers remain mothers' helpers, but not when they become equal or primary parents.

9. Berardo, 1987; Gilbert, 1985; Goldscheider and Waite, 1991. Brines, 1990, explores the factors that encourage men to participate in housework.

10. Goldscheider and Waite, 1991, report that men and women who lived on their own before marriage were more likely to choose nontraditional family arrangements.

11. Among all involved fathers, the percentage of childless men who planned to become equal parents was 35 percent, not quite as high as the 41 percent of fathers who had already done so. This is a small difference, which is not significant for such a small number of cases.

12. Five men, four of whom were divorced, became the primary parent to their children.

13. See Shelton and Firestone, 1989. Coverman, 1983, also shows that time spent in domestic labor reduces the wages of both women and men. It is thus reasonable for men to fear that family participation will have negative consequences for their earnings and careers.

14. The economic literature, and especially the "human capital" approach to explaining family life outlined by Becker, 1981, argues that men become breadwinners because of a "taste" or "preference" for market work while women become domestic caretakers because of a "taste" for family care.

Both reluctant breadwinners and involved fathers show that tastes may follow necessity, but they are not always consistent with actual choices. Clearly, social arrangements, not simply tastes and preferences, limit men's choices as well as women's. If tastes and preferences were the most powerful determinants of what men did, far fewer would work full-time or, for that matter, at all. But most men face economic and social constraints that deny them the choice to work less in order to parent more.

15. There is ample evidence that the human-capital perspective does not explain women's disadvantaged position in the labor market. Many studies have shown that women earn lower economic returns for their investment in education and that they earn lower wages even after controlling for skills, amount of hours working, and length of time in the labor market. See Amsden, 1980. Hirschhorn, 1977, and Jencks, 1992, show a downward shift of male labor-force participation, with the slack being take up by employed wives.

16. U.S. Bureau of the Census, 1989b: 1.

17. Goldscheider and Waite, 1991. Wright et al., 1992, found that economic leverage helps women to balance the domestic division of labor; and Coltrane, 1989a, and Coltrane and Ishii-Kuntz, 1990, found substantial participation among fathers in dual-career couples. Coltrane also distinguishes between "helping fathers" and "co-parents." Although Hochschild with Machung, 1989, asserts that women who are more successful than their husbands feel they need to reassure their husbands by doing more at home, there is little evidence for this position.

18. Surveys that measure income alone—thus overlooking the importance of the nonmonetary aspects of job rewards—often fail to demonstrate a relationship between relative labor-market position and a couple's household division of labor. These surveys ignore the importance of relative work commitment, focusing only on short-term economic calculations that do not explain why people make choices over the long run. Despite the emphasis on economic accounting in "rational-choice" approaches, "economic" and "rational" are not the same. In making so-called rational choices, people take many noneconomic factors into account. As Zelizer, 1989a, points out, economic decisions, like other social processes, are culturally and socially structured.

19. U.S. Bureau of the Census, 1992a.

20. Hertz and Charlton, 1989, found that shift work has ambiguous consequences for the division of labor between spouses. They argue that while many shift workers rely on "father care," the mothers tend to retain responsibility for making arrangements and seeing that things get done around the house. Presser, 1988, also argues that shift work per se does not reduce inequality between employed parents. Barnett and Baruch, 1987, found no significant effect when they examined the effects of a father's work schedule on a variety of measures of involvement in household labor, but they studied a small sample and did not distinguish among different types of men. Staines, 1986, also explores the relationship between men's work schedules and their family participation.

21.   U.S. Bureau of the Census, 1991.

22.   Of the 57 percent who became estranged from their children after divorce, 14 percent became involved fathers in *new* marriages. Those cases in which the same father became estranged from some offspring while becoming involved in the rearing of others suggest that the circumstances of marriage and divorce are crucial in encouraging or impeding a father's involvement with his children.

23.   See Ruddick, 1989 and 1991.

24.   Risman, 1986, and Risman and Park, 1986. Other studies of fathers parenting alone include Chang and Deinard, 1982; Defrain and Elrich, 1981; Furstenberg, 1985; Greif, 1985; Hipgrave, 1981; and Smith and Smith, 1981.

25.   Zavella, 1989, reports that Hispanic men become actively involved in child care when their wives are the "mainstay providers." Risman and Atkinson report that men become "mothers" when "they do not have wives to do it for them . . . when men are custodial single fathers they develop the kinds of relationships with their children similar to those relationships children usually share with their mothers" (1990: 6). See also Levine, 1976; Pruett, 1988; Robinson, 1986; and Russell, 1986.

26.   See Lawson, 1991. The Family Leave Act that finally became law in 1993 is an important first step, but much more will be needed for men to feel able to choose equal parenting, as I will discuss in chapter 10.

27.   Pleck, 1993.

28.   According to Risman and Atkinson: "No matter how involved 'new feminist' fathers become in child-care, they . . . are expected to work harder and are constrained from leaving less than optimal jobs because of their economic responsibilities. When they do care for their children after work, they are praised highly by friends, family members, and wives as wonderful, modern, 'involved' fathers" (1990: 15–16).

29.   Men who become primary parents face barriers similar to those faced by the first female managers, who had to cope with being "tokens." Strauss, 1989, discusses the stigmatization and social isolation of househusbands. Kanter, 1977, analyzes how the first female managers were tokens in the corporation. Robinson, 1986, reports that male caregivers who work in nursery schools and day-care programs also faced discrimination and stigma from employers, co-workers, and even parents.

30.   See Rossi, 1960.

31.   Huber and Spitze, 1983; Ross, Mirowsky, and Huber, 1983. See also Lamb, Pleck, and Levine, 1987, and Hochschild with Machung, 1989.

32.   See Furstenberg, Morgan, and Allison, 1987b; Hanson, 1986; Lamb, 1976; Santrock and Warshak, 1979; and Santrock, Warshak, and Elliot, 1982.

33.   Secunda, 1992.

34.   Goleman, 1990.

35.   Reported in Stacey, 1991. See also Moen and Dempster-McClain, 1987. If Chinoy, 1955, found that automobile workers in the 1950s dreamed about retiring, inheriting wealth, or opening their own businesses as an alternative to dead-end factory jobs, then the decline of well-paying, secure manu-

facturing jobs over the last decade has given this dream of independence through self-employment new life.

Chapter 9: The Myth of Masculinity

1. Hochschild with Machung, 1989, coined the phrase "the stalled revolution," and Ehrenreich, 1983, coined the term "male rebels."
2. Furstenberg, 1988, discusses this "mixed" pattern.
3. Jacobs, 1989a and 1989b, points out that high rates of individual change do not necessarily reflect a high degree of social change. When changes among individuals offset each other, the overall patterns may remain stable. For social change to take place, individual change must stem from changes in social institutions and practices. See also Stinchcombe, 1968.
4. Perhaps the most widely accepted approach to explaining men's behavior emphasizes how processes of childhood socialization create adult men who have a "masculine personality." Although important differences exist between classical "sex-role identity" theories and more recent feminist revisions of the psychodynamic and moral development models, these approaches share a focus on the processes and consequences of psychological development and personality formation in early childhood. Sex-role learning theories argue that boys "learn" to be men by identifying with their fathers and other male role models. They also stress the role of rewards and punishments in shaping boys who behave in appropriately "masculine" ways. (See Maccoby, 1966, and Maccoby and Jacklin, 1974.)

   Psychoanalytic theories, including the feminist revisions pioneered by Chodorow (1974, 1978, 1990), point to the importance of unconscious dynamics that take place between parents, especially mothers, and children in the earliest years of life. (Johnson, 1988, argues for the importance of fathers.) This perspective rejects the significance of intentional role learning, arguing instead that men repress their emotional capacities and establish rigid ego boundaries in a struggle to separate from already distant mothers.

   Classical and feminist approaches place different values on the desirability and inevitability of the socialization processes that produce a masculine personality. Classical theories argue that these processes are natural, healthy, and probably inevitable. They imply that when deviations occur, the consequences will be unpleasant (and even dire) for men, women, and children. In contrast, feminist theories argue that these processes are not only socially constructed but also organized to confer power and privilege on men rather than women. Alternative socialization processes, especially those that dampen the differences between men and women, are not only possible but socially desirable.

   Despite these ideological differences, classical and feminist personality theories explain men's behavior in similar ways. Both argue that men share personality attributes that bind them together as a group and distinguish them from women. Both argue that childhood is the decisive period and the family the crucial arena in which a masculine personality is forged. And both conclude that once created, a masculine personality leads adult men to make similar work and family choices. Men's behavior, like gender inequality, is thus reproduced across generations via a closed circle of links among family structure, childhood experience, and personality formation. These models have different ideological agendas, but they reach similar conclusions about the nature of male psychology and its effect on social arrangements.

Wrong, 1961, presents a classic and still peerless critique of the "oversocialized" view of human action, and Giddens, 1979, provides an equally trenchant and critical assessment. Pleck, 1981, offers an insightful analysis of the "myth of masculinity" upon which gender-personality theories are built. For an excellent critique of feminist revisions of psychoanalytic theory, and especially how they fail to account for the complexity of women's psychology and inner life, see Grosskurth, 1991.

5. A rich literature on human development over the life course focuses on how changes in adult opportunities produce changes in the process of adult development. For example, Buchman, 1989, found that the adult life course has become "individualized" and "destandardized." See also Brim, 1968; Elder, 1974 and 1978; Gerth and Mills, 1953; and Rindfuss, Swicegood, and Rosenfeld, 1987. Gould, 1978, and Levinson, 1978, provided some of the first discussions of men's adult transitions, but they used successful, white, middle-class men as the model for all men.

6. In studying widowers who became single fathers, Risman and Atkinson found that a lack of socialization for nurturance did not inhibit the development of intimacy and caring when structural contingencies demanded that men become their children's primary nurturers.

7. Tavris, 1992, provides a powerful critique of prevailing ideas about a distinctly feminine psychology.

8. For a debate on the significance of men's "inexpressiveness," see Balswick, 1979; Balswick and Peek, 1971; and Sattel, 1976. Easthope, 1990, analyzes the masculine myth in popular culture. Willis, 1977, analyzes how working-class masculine culture, which stresses rebellion against authority and the superiority of physical to mental prowess, actually serves to keep working-class boys at the bottom of the class hierarchy.

Jasper, 1990, discusses the conflicting ways of defining and conceiving *culture*. He points out that culture operates in at least two domains: as ideologies (the stated tenets of individual and collective actors) and as policy styles or distinct clusters of images, symbols, and behaviors that an individual or group can use approaching problems and developing responses.

9. For the classic literary analysis of this tradition, see Fiedler, 1966.

10. Ehrenreich, 1983, uses a cultural explanation for the decline of the male breadwinner in postwar America. She argues that popular culture, through such disparate vehicles as *Playboy* magazine, the hippie counterculture, and the modern health movement, has promoted men's flight from commitment by making singlehood and the pursuit of leisure socially legitimate choices for men. A "male revolt" against the family thus preceded the rise of both feminism and antifeminism, social movements that are responding

in different ways to the same cause: men's abandonment of breadwinning obligations. As noted in chapter 1, this argument is compelling, but flawed. Ehrenreich ignores the cultural tradition of extolling male flight that began long before the current trends emerged. She also oversimplifies the contours of change. Along with a rise in men's abandonment of family ties, the decline in the breadwinner ethic has also promoted the rise of the sensitive man and the nurturing father as cultural ideals.

11. Swidler, 1980, discusses how the American cultural tradition stresses both freedom and commitment as competing definitions of maturity. Komarovsky, 1976, analyzes the dilemmas and contradictions of the "male role."

12. See Cancian, 1987.

13. Kimmel, 1987, and Jardine and Smith, 1987, provide evidence that there is a historical tradition of support for feminism among men. This legacy of feminist men belies the notion of dichotomous male and female cultures, demonstrating that a convergence of men's and women's values is not only possible but actually occurs when conditions support it. Kimmel, 1992a, points out that the two most important factors contributing to women's higher status are men's participation in child care and women's ownership of property.

14. Swidler, 1986, argues that people use values as a "tool kit" from which to fashion responses to new situations. Used in this way, culture provides the tools for shaping action, but the substance or content of action remains open and subject to change.

15. See Craib, 1987; Hartmann, 1976; Hearn and Morgan, 1990; Polatnik, 1973; Reskin, 1988; and Rubin, 1975.

16. It is important to make a distinction between the degree of change and the direction of change. Although inequality persists with tenacity, the long-term historical trend is clearly in the direction of declining patriarchal control. Collins, 1971, thus argues that advanced market economies, which are marked by high female labor-force participation rates and strong state structures, provide women with sufficient economic resources and legal protections to challenge male control. Men often resort to desperate means to retain power, but these efforts meet increasing opposition from women and the state. For example, men continue to use violence and physical force to enforce their will, but it is no longer deemed a legitimate use of patriarchal authority. Indeed, the recent interest in studying patriarchy may well be a signal that it is declining. As Myles points out, "institutionalized relations of power [commonly] become visible only when they are in decline. When these relations are most effective, they tend to be invisible, since the ideologies that support them dominate people's everyday common sense understandings. The feminist critique of male dominance, for example, appeared when that dominance was beginning to weaken" (1989: 219).

17. Connell, 1987: 109.

18. Giddens proposes three types of consciousness: unconscious motivation; practical consciousness, which is used to make sense of taken-for-granted,

routine acts; and discursive consciousness, which is required when new circumstances make it necessary to justify new actions. Rapid social change has compelled many men to move from "unconscious motivation" and "practical consciousness" to "discursive consciousness." See Risman and Atkinson, 1990.

19.   Arguments based on the premise that male power, dominance, and privilege assure their own reproduction and transmission, even when social institutions are changing, suffice *neither* as an explanation of men's behavior *nor* as a universal outcome to be explained. The more interesting task is to discover the circumstances that make dominance easier or harder to attain. As Zaretsky, 1982, makes clear, patriarchy is not an explanation but a social institution that needs to be explained.

20.   Whether they stress processes of psychological development, the cultural construction of social norms and values, or the creation and reproduction of male dominance, all of these approaches make similar assumptions about the nature of manhood. By focusing on differences between men and women, they all imply that differences among men are either insubstantial or inconsequential and that men and women possess opposite, mutually exclusive attributes. They overestimate the similarities and discount the differences among men.

      These perspectives also focus on how men's personalities, values, and abilities to dominate remain stable (or are reproduced) over time. This logic, which takes the form of "the more things change, the more they remain the same," implies that *significant* change is impossible. By proposing a closed circle of causality in which male power, culture, and psychology are reproduced across historical time and despite large-scale social change, they imply that men possess some innate quality that does not change in different social contexts. Thus, despite the expressed concern with social factors, they come close to assuming an "essential" masculine quality that is universal, innate, and impervious to change. To this extent, they present a picture reminiscent of biosocial approaches (for example, Rossi, 1977, 1984).

      To account for the dynamics of change as well as persistence, theories must first allow for "the constant possibility that structure will be constituted in a different way" (Connell, 1987: 45). Powerful groups will surely endeavor to reproduce their power and privilege, but their strategies and ultimate success are not preordained. Social theories need to allow for the possibility of progressive change, even if it does not often occur. See Connell, 1987, Epstein, 1988, and Gerson, 1990, for overviews and critiques of these approaches. For critiques of biological models, see also Fausto-Sterling, 1987, and Hrdy, 1981.

21.   Even though the wage gap between men and women has narrowed slightly over the last two decades, on average women earn 72 percent of what men do. Similarly, members of younger cohorts of women have made significant inroads into previously all-male occupational preserves, especially in managerial and professional job categories, but most women continue to work in female-dominated fields, and a only a small percentage of men are

employed outside male-dominated fields. See Reskin and Roos, 1990; Jacobs, 1989a, 1989b, and 1991; and U.S. Department of Labor, 1991.

22. Uchitelle, 1992b.

23. Between 1973 and 1988, all but the top 25 percent of the male work force experienced wage reductions (Mishel and Frankel, 1991: 78–79; see also Levy, 1987; Levy and Michel, 1991; and Newman, 1988).

24. Phillips, 1990: 18; Kosters and Ross, 1988: 11.

25. Barringer, 1990.

26. Uchitelle, 1990b.

27. Uchitelle, 1992a. See also Steinmetz and Wright, 1989.

28. Mishel and Frankel, 1991: 150.

29. Sherman and Sherman conclude that "the dominant trend . . . during the 1980s has been for low-paying jobs to replace those which provided a middle-class standard of living. [This trend has affected] full-time and part-time workers, white and nonwhite workers, and was felt particularly by men." Sherman and Sherman, 1988. See also Harrison and Bluestone, 1988 and 1990; and Bowles, Gordon, and Weisskopf, 1988.

30. Mishel and Frankel, 1991: 119, 125, 127.

31. Greenhouse, 1992.

32. U.S. Department of Labor, 1991; Cowan, 1989. According to Schor (1992: 27), men's labor-force participation rate dropped from 89 percent in 1948 to 78 percent in 1987.

33. U.S. Department of Labor, 1991; Mishel and Frankel, 1991: 43.

34. Belkin, 1989.

35. My earlier book (Gerson, 1985) considers the multiple pushes and pulls that have sent a growing number of women into the workplace in late-twentieth-century America. Seeing these choices as voluntary or involuntary creates a false distinction. For most women, choice and necessity have become wedded by social circumstance.

36. They also rose 1.1 percent between 1989 and 1991 (Uchitelle, 1992b).

37. U.S. Department of Labor, 1991. Mishel and Frankel report that "48% of the reduction in inequality is due to falling real wages among men and 52% is due to rising real wages among women" (1991: 81).

38. Jacobs, 1991, shows that women's movement into management positions is not illusory—that is, an artifact of the relabeling of jobs—but represents real gains made by women into the ranks of management. See also Jacobs, 1989b, and Reskin and Roos, 1990.

39. Nasar, 1992.

40. Ibid. These findings were originally reported by Goldin, 1990, and Blau and Ferber, 1986.

41. Kilborn, 1992.

42. For analyses of the emerging economic independence of women, see Bergmann, 1986; Davis, 1984; Fuchs, 1988; Sorenson and McLanahan, 1987; and South, 1988.

43. Glick, 1990; Barringer, 1989.

44. U.S. Bureau of the Census, 1992b.

45. Barringer, 1989; Bumpass, 1990.

46.   For overviews of changes in patterns of marriage, divorce, and cohabitation, see Anderson and Silver, 1991; Bane, 1976; Bumpass, 1990; Cherlin, 1981; Espenshade, 1985; Furstenberg, 1990; Glick and Norton, 1977; Hacker, 1987 and 1988; Levinger and Moles, 1979; Santi, 1987; Sweet and Bumpass, 1987; and Stone, 1989 and 1990.

47.   According to Jencks (1992: 195), 14.5 percent of white women and 62.6 percent of black women were unmarried when they became mothers (up from 5.1 percent and 35.1 percent in 1969). According to Pear (1991), 17.2 percent of white mothers and 56.7 percent of black mothers who had a child in 1990 were not married.

48.   Glick, 1990.

49.   Among whites, about 60 percent of one-parent families are headed by a divorced or separated woman. Among blacks, over 50 percent of one-parent families are headed by a never-married woman (Suro, 1992).

50.   Jencks, 1992: 195.

51.   Luker, 1991, and Bumpass, 1990.

52.   Coleman, 1990, uses rational-choice theory to blend economic and sociological models. Friedman and Diem, 1990, and Hechter and Friedman, 1990, make compelling use of a rational-choice framework to analyze gender inequality and childbearing decisions. Insightful discussions of the limits of a rational-choice approach include Cook and Levi, 1990, and Mansbridge, 1990. England and Kilbourne, 1990, show how feminist critiques of rational-choice theory have enlarged our vision of human nature beyond a "separatist model of self." Zelizer, 1989a and 1989b, shows that even economic relations cannot be entirely reduced to rational-choice principles. See also Pescosolido, 1992.

53.   While the historical context limits the range of potential responses, men must respond to the ambiguities and contradictions of manhood in creative ways that cannot be entirely determined by the context itself. It is no surprise that this context has also witnessed the emergence of a plethora of best-selling books on men. In addition to Robert Bly's *Iron John* (1990) and Sam Keen's *Fire in the Belly* (1991), other recent books that convey a deep discomfort with the changes that imperil men's prerogatives include Astrachan, 1986; Farrell, 1986; and Osherson, 1986.

Chapter 10: Men and the Politics of Gender

1.   The argument that women will lose from equality was used by opponents of the Equal Rights Amendment in their successful campaign to block its ratification. As Faludi (1991) points out, this is a common reaction to even small gains in women's position. It is reminiscent of the argument made by plantation owners that blacks would lose from the abolition of slavery. For penetrating analyses of the social and political bases of antifeminism among women, see English, 1983; Klatch, 1987; Klein, 1983 and 1985; and Mansbridge, 1986.

2.   Formal equality in the absence of de facto equality can, of course, have unfortunate consequences. But women's fight for equality is not the cause of

these problems, despite the suggestions of Hewlett (1986) and others. Women's loss of traditional protections results from inevitable social and economic changes, which would have occurred whether or not there had been an organized attempt on the part of women to secure their rights. Blaming the women's movement for women's continuing disadvantages is akin to blaming the messenger for the message. Since change of some sort is inevitable, the real danger to women lies in *not* achieving their rights.

3.   See Kimmel, 1992b, for an excellent reply to Robert Bly's (1990) vision of achieving manhood through rituals of male separation.

4.   As women have pressed for equal rights, they have been criticized for affirming the value of individual freedom at the expense of children's needs. This argument is closely linked to the "decline of community" thesis, which claims that close-knit bonds of moral reciprocity have declined in postindustrial America. (See Bellah et al., 1985, and Lasch, 1977.) Cancian (1987) notes, however, that self-development and commitment are not mutually exclusive. While some men and women have chosen to pursue personal development by eschewing commitment, others have affirmed their individuality by forging commitments based on the principle of equality. Women need not sacrifice equality for the sake of commitment.

5.   Gilligan's work on women's moral voice (1982, 1989) has drawn attention to the tension between a morality of "rights" and a morality of "care." Her focus on different types of moralities provides a powerful critique of developmental theories that posit the superiority of a rationalist perspective. However, it is inaccurate to draw dichotomous distinctions between men's and women's moralities. Both sexes draw on a variety of moral perspectives and use diverse moral voices. See, for example, Kittay and Meyers, 1987; Melson and Foge, 1988; and Ruddick, 1991.

6.   Numerous studies have noted that when divorced fathers are estranged from their children or from making decisions about their children's lives, they are likely to withhold or withdraw economic support as well. By allowing and encouraging fathers' participation, we increase the chances that children will also receive economic support. (See Hanson, 1986; McLanahan et al., 1992; Wallerstein and Blakeslee, 1989; and Weitzman, 1985.)

7.   These estimates are based on a study by the Families and Work Institute reported in Smith et al., 1990. Smith et al., 1990, and Schor, 1992, argue that social policies need to redress the time imbalance caused by "greedy" work institutions.

To imagine a more flexible integration of family and work, we need only look to the world before the advent of industrialism, when work and family were more closely integrated and parenthood was not rigidly divorced from other productive activities. (See Stacey, 1990 and 1991, on the "postmodern family" and Hochschild with Machung, 1989, on modern women as "urbanized peasants.")

8.   Schwartz, 1989, proposed that employers offer women a "mommy track." By relegating mothers, and mothers only, to a second tier in the managerial structure of organizations, this proposal provides a remarkably regressive

response to new family dilemmas. It allows employers to avoid addressing the twin dilemmas of gender inequality and work/family conflicts; it reinforces an unequal division of labor between women and men; it forces women, but not men, to make wrenching decisions between employment and parenting; and it maintains the historic obstacles to male parental involvement. In other words, the idea of a mommy track perpetuates the idea that work and parenthood are in conflict and that caring for children is an indication of low work commitment. As Capek (1990: 1) notes: "The issues for a viable, competitive workforce—ultimately the same issues for a viable, competitive American economy—are not 'mommy tracks' but managing diversity; not 'letting in a few women without rocking the boat,' but radically rethinking the future American workplace in an increasingly multiracial, multicultural global economy." Other critiques of the mommy-track approach include Smith et al., 1990, and Rodgers and Rodgers, 1989.

9. Hobson (1991: 846–48). Studies that document the comparative lack of family and child-care policies in the United States include Hofferth, 1990; Hofferth and Phillips, 1987; Kamerman and Kahn, 1987; Moen, 1989; and Pleck, 1989 and 1993.

10. Okin, 1989, argues that our notions of justice should encompass themes of both care and abstract rights. For women, care has all too often meant relinquishing rights and becoming dependent on men within marriage. Since marriage can no longer offer women economic security, the philosophy of individual rights must encompass women and the obligation to care for others must include men.

11. Some feminists have expressed discomfort with those aspects of change that require women to forfeit some privileges in order to obtain other rights. For example, Smart and Seven-Huijsen, 1989, and Chesler, 1988, argue that women should retain priority in child custody decisions, even though redefining men's and women's parental rights is a logical consequence of the movement toward gender equality (Kingson, 1988). Other feminists have argued that equality requires recognizing diversity among men and women rather than perpetuating a principle based on gender difference. See Vogel, 1990.

12. The heavy social costs of *not* implementing family support policies have been well documented by Edelman, 1987; Folbre, 1987; Hewlett, 1991; and Sidel, 1986 and 1990. Less obvious is the mounting evidence that companies also incur higher costs by denying family support, such as parental leave, than by offering it. See Spalter-Roth and Hartmann, 1990, and Roel, 1991.

13. The development of political divisions among men may also involve the emergence of coalitions between men and women who share similar world views. Numerous studies have found that a "marriage gap" in voting behavior is larger than the more highly publicized gender gap. Breadwinners and homemakers tend to vote in similar ways, while single men and women also show similar voting patterns. See Brackman and Erie, 1986; Fleming, 1988; Gerson, 1987a; Goertzel, 1983; Greenberg, 1985; Kingston and Finkel, 1987; Klein, 1985; Luker, 1984; Mansbridge, 1985 and 1986; Mason and Lu, 1988; and Weisburg, 1987.

APPENDIX

Tables

Table 1 Composition of U.S. Households, 1950–1990

	Married Couples		Other Households		
	Wife Not Employed	Wife Employed[a]	Female-Headed	Male-Headed	Single Individuals
1950	59.4%	19.6%	8.4%	1.8%	10.8%
1960	51.2	23.2	8.5	2.5	14.9
1970	41.6	28.9	8.8	1.9	18.8
1980	30.3	30.6	10.8	2.2	26.1
1990	23.3[b]	32.7	11.7	3.1	29.2[c]

Sources: Compiled from Lawrence Hirschhorn, "Social Policy and the Life Cycle: A Developmental Perspective," Social Service Review 51 (September 1977): 435; U.S. Bureau of the Census, Current Population Reports, ser. P-20, no. 336, Household and Family Characteristics: March 1980 (Washington, D.C.: U.S. Government Printing Office, 1981); U.S. Bureau of the Census, Current Population Reports, Special Studies, ser. P-23, no. 173, Population Profile of the United States, 1991 (Washington, D.C.: U.S. Government Printing Office, 1991).

a. Including wives employed part-time. In 1990, wives worked part-time in 7.5% of U.S. households, and less than full-time year-round in 16%.

b. This figure includes 9.4% of households in which neither spouse was employed. When these couples are subtracted from the total, the percentage of American households consisting of a married couple with only the husband employed drops to 13.9%.

c. This figure includes 12.4% men and 16.8% women.

Table 2   Fathers' Employment and Parental Characteristics

Father's Occupation	Percent Who Worked More Than 40 Hours/Week[a]	Percent Reporting High Work Satis-faction	Percent Reporting Daily Partici-pation in Child Care[b]	Percent Sole/Main Wage Earner When Son Lived at Home[c]
Blue Collar[d] (n = 61)	31	39	30	71
Lower White Collar (n = 61)	13	25	50	63
Middle or High Management[e] (n = 17)	65	53	24	77
Professional (n = 24)	25	63	42	79
Self-Employed (n = 16)	81	50	31	75
Total[f] (n = 134)	38	45	34	72

a.   On average.

b.   Available at night and on weekends on a regular basis.

c.   Married to a homemaking or part-time-employed wife.

d.   Six fathers had extended periods of unemployment.

e.   Including three fathers in the military.

f.   Four missing cases.

Table 3   Percentage of Men with a Breadwinning Orientation,
by Perception of Father's Work Satisfaction

Perception of Father's Work Satisfaction	Breadwinning Orientation in Childhood	Currently Oriented Toward Breadwinning
Very Satisfied (n = 61)[a]	59	30
Moderately Satisfied (n = 46)[b]	43	46
Dissatisfied (n = 19)[c]	42	32
Can't Say (n = 12)[d]	33	42
Total (n = 138)	49	36

a.   Job or career was fulfilling; father would not have chosen a different line of work.

b.   Job or career was not unpleasant, but it offered little fulfillment.

c.   Father would have preferred a different job or career or would have preferred not to work.

d.   Had no father or had no perception of father's work satisfaction.

Table 4   Men's Current Orientation, by Perception of
Father's Participation in Child Rearing

Perception of Father's Participation in Child Rearing	Current Orientation Toward Child Rearing		
	Involved Fathering	Breadwinning	Autonomy
Participated Daily (n = 45)	38%	31%	31%
Participated on Weekends (n = 35)	26	40	34
Participated Occasionally or Not at All (n = 53)[a]	36	36	28
Total (n = 133)[b]	34	35	31

a.   Four respondents reported no participation.

b.   Five missing cases.

Table 5   Men's Perception of Mothers' Employment Preferences, by Mothers' Employment Patterns (within class groups)

Mother's Employment Pattern	Preferred Not Working	Preferred Being Employed	Had Mixed Feelings	Could Not Tell
Not Employed[a]				
Middle Class (n = 27)	74%	—	4%	22%
Working Class (n = 26)	54	12%	4	31
Total (n = 53)	64	6	4	26
Employed Part-time or Intermittently				
Middle Class (n = 21)	29	38	24	2
Working Class (n = 14)	36	29	21	14
Total (n = 35)	31	34	23	11
Employed Full-time After Respondent in School				
Middle Class (n = 18)	17	61	22	—
Working Class (n = 15)	13	53	20	13
Total (n = 33)	15	58	21	6
Employed Full-time When Respondent a Preschooler				
Middle Class (n = 6)	17	83	—	—
Working Class (n = 8)	13	87	—	—
Total (n = 14)	14	86		
Total (n = 135)[b]	39	34	13	15

Note: Some rows total more or less than 100% due to rounding.

a.   While respondent lived at home.

b.   Three missing cases.

Table 6   Percentage of Men with a Breadwinning Orientation,
           by Mother's Employment Pattern

Mother's Employment Pattern	Childhood Orientation	Current Orientation
	Percent Breadwinning	Percent Breadwinning
Domestic Mothers (n = 88)	57	33
Never Employed[a] (n = 53)	53	40
Employed Part-time or Intermittently (n = 35)	63	26
Work-Committed Mothers (n = 47)	38	40
Employed Full-time After Son Entered Grade School (n = 33)	42	48
Employed Full-time Before Son Entered Grade School (n = 14)	29	21
Total Sample (n = 135)[b]	49	36

a.   While respondent lived at home.

b.   Three missing cases.

Table 7   Men's Current Orientation, by Their Childhood
Orientation (total sample and within classes)

	Current Orientation:		
Points of Departure	Primary Breadwinning	Autonomy	Involved Fathering
Breadwinning Orientation			
Middle Class (n = 40)	40%	25%	35%
Working Class (n = 28)	36	43	21
Total (n = 68)	38	32	29
Nonbreadwinning Orientation			
Middle Class (n = 33)	24	39	36
Working Class (n = 37)	43	19	38
Total (n = 70)	34	29	37
Total Sample			
Middle Class (n = 73)	33	32	36
Working Class (n = 65)	40	29	31
Total (n = 138)	36	30	33

Note: Some rows total more or less than 100 due to rounding.

Table 8   Comparisons Between Reluctant Breadwinners
and Stably Autonomous Men

	Reluctant Breadwinners (n = 24)	Stably Autonomous Men (n = 20)
Life Events		
Unexpected Job Stability/Opportunity	75%	45%
Unexpected Marital Commitment	88%	25%
Commitment to Domestic Partner	67%[a]	0%[b]
Unexpected Parenthood	71%	0%
Demographics		
Average Age	36.3	36.5
Percent College Graduates	33%	65%

a.   Remaining 33% included 25% with full-time employed partners; 4% with student partner; and
     4% with no partner.

b.   65% were not married or involved with a steady partner; 35% had a partner who was career-
     committed.

Table 9 Comparisons Between Men Who Moved Toward
Autonomy and Stable Breadwinners

	Unexpected Autonomy (n = 22)	Stable Breadwinners (n = 26)
Life Events		
Unexpected Dissatisfaction with Stable Job	59%	0%
Unexpected Instability in Relationships:		
Divorce, Separation, and		
Widowhood Among the Ever Married[a]	90%	0%
Rejection and Loss Among		
the Never Married	92%	—
Dissatisfying Experiences with Children:[b]		
Among Childless Men	40%	0%
Among Fathers	86%	0%
Demographics		
Average Age	36.5	35.2
Percent College Graduates	45%	62%

a. 86% of Autonomous Men and 12% of Stable Breadwinners were never married.

b. 68% of Autonomous Men and 23% of Stable Breadwinners were childless.

Table 10   Comparisons Among All Involved Fathers, All Primary
Breadwinners, and All Autonomous Men

	Involved Fathers (n = 46)	All Breadwinners (n = 50)	All Autonomous Men (n = 42)
Fluid Employment Trajectories			
Veered Off Fast Track	46%		
Hit a Dead End	48%		
Total	94%	12%	57%
Satisfaction in a Committed Relationship			
Got Married	67%		
Not Yet Married	5%		
Total	72%	86%	24%
Attraction to a Career-Oriented Partner			
Before Marrying	43%		
After Marrying	46%		
Total	89%	14%	na[a]
Fulfilling Experiences in Caretaking			
With Own Children	63%		
With Other People's Children	11%		
Total	74%	12%	5%
Demographics			
Average Age	36.1	35.8	36.5
Percent College Graduates	57%	48%	55%

a.   Of the 24% in a satisfying, committed, heterosexual relationship, 90 percent (or 21% of all autonomous men) had a career-oriented partner.

Table 11   Differences in Domestic Participation—Comparisons Among
Equal Fathers, Mothers' Helpers, and Breadwinners

Percent Who Say They Share Equally or Are Primarily Responsible:	*Equal Fathers*	*Mothers' Helpers*	*Breadwinners*
Selected Child-Care Times (for current parents only)	(n = 12)	(n = 18)	(n = 39)
Morning	92	39	8
Afternoon	50	44	13
Evening	83	100	44
Night	100	78	38
Weekends	100	89	74
Percent Who Cite Four or More Time Periods:	83	44	5
Selected Child-Care Activities (for current parents only)	(n = 12)	(n = 18)	(n = 39)
Feeding	100	44	21
Shopping	92	44	21
Bathing	58	33	18
Dressing	58	33	13
Playing	100	100	51
Disciplining	83	89	62
Percent Who Cite Four or More Activities:	100	50	10
Selected Household Chores (for those not living alone)	(n = 12)	(n = 26)	(n = 45)
Grocery Shopping	67	35	29
Housecleaning	58	46	11
Cooking	58	38	4
Laundry	42	35	18
After-Meal Cleaning	75	46	38
Percent Who Cite Three or More Activities:	67	31	11

Table 12 Exposure to Circumstances Promoting Parental Equality—
Comparisons Between Equal Fathers and Mothers' Helpers

	Equal Fathers (n = 18)	Mothers' Helpers (n = 28)
Percent Whose Wives Face Better Career Prospects	28	7
Percent with Flexible Job Schedules	72	29
Percent Without a Partner to Rely On	33	—
Percent Exposed to Two Factors	44	11
Percent Exposed to at Least One Factor	100	39

Table 13 Employment Preferences Among Involved
Fathers, by Current Employment Status

	Employment Preference		
	Full-time, Rigid Schedule	Full-time, Flexible Schedule	Part-time or Fewer Hours[a]
Current Employment Status			
Full-time, Rigid Schedule (n = 27)	22%	37%	41%
Full-time, Flexible Schedule (n = 17)	—	59%	41%
Part-time or Not Employed (n = 2)	—	50%	50%
Total (n = 46)	13%	46%	41%

a. Includes 3 respondents who prefer not to work at paid employment.

Table 14   Men's Alternative Developmental Paths (with sample percentages)

Childhood Orientation	Current Orientation

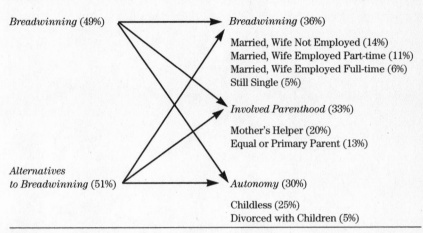

Breadwinning (49%) → Breadwinning (36%)

Married, Wife Not Employed (14%)
Married, Wife Employed Part-time (11%)
Married, Wife Employed Full-time (6%)
Still Single (5%)

Involved Parenthood (33%)

Mother's Helper (20%)
Equal or Primary Parent (13%)

Alternatives to Breadwinning (51%) → Autonomy (30%)

Childless (25%)
Divorced with Children (5%)

Note: Some rows total more or less than 100% due to rounding.

Table 15   Living Situations of American Men, 1970–1990

	1990	1980	1970
Married, Nonemployed Wife	32.7%	40.8%	52.8%
Husband Employed	19.5		
Neither Employed	13.2		
Married, Employed Wife	45.7	41.5	36.6
Both Employed	42.0		
Wife Only	3.7		
Single Head of Family Household	4.3	2.9	2.5
With Own Children Under 18	1.7		
Without Own Children Under 18	2.6		
Single Adult	17.4	14.8	8.1
Lives Alone	13.5		
Lives with Unrelated Person	3.8		

Source: U.S. Bureau of the Census, *Current Population Reports, Special Studies,* ser. P-23, no. 173, *Population Profile of the United States, 1991* (Washington, D.C.: U.S. Government Printing Office, 1991).

BIBLIOGRAPHY

Aldous, Joan, ed. 1982. *Two Paychecks: Life in Dual-Earner Families.* Beverly Hills, Calif.: Sage Publications.

Amsden, Alice H., ed. 1980. *The Economics of Women and Work.* New York: St. Martin's Press.

Anderson, Barbara A., and Brian D. Silver. 1991. "Recent Changes in Cohabitation, Marriage, and Fertility in Cross-National Perspective." Proposal to Social Science Research Council (December), New York.

Arendell, Terry. 1986. *Mothers and Divorce.* Berkeley and Los Angeles: University of California Press.

———. 1992. "After Divorce: Investigations into Father Absence." *Gender and Society* 9 (4) (December): 562–86.

Ariès, Philippe. 1962. *Centuries of Childhood: A Social History of Family Life.* New York: Knopf.

Astrachan, Anthony. 1986. *How Men Feel.* Garden City, N.Y.: Anchor Press.

Balswick, Jack O. 1979. "The Inexpressive Male: Functional-Conflict and Role Theory as Contrasting Explanations." *The Family Coordinator* (July): 331–35.

Balswick, Jack O., and Charles W. Peek. 1971. "The Inexpressive Male: A Tragedy of American Society." *The Family Coordinator* (October): 363–68.

Bane, Mary Jo. 1976. *Here to Stay: American Families in the Twentieth Century.* New York: Basic Books.

Barnett, Rosalind, and Grace K. Baruch. 1987. "Determinants of Fathers' Participation in Family Work." *Journal of Marriage and the Family* 49: 29–40.

Barringer, Felicity. 1989. "Divorce Data Stir Doubt on Trial Marriage." *New York Times* (June 9): A1, A28.

———. 1990. "What America Did After the War: A Tale Told by the Census." *New York Times* (September 2): E1, E5.

———. 1992a. "Rate of Marriage Continues Decline." *New York Times* (July 17): A20.

———. 1992b. "Census Reveals Changes as It Paints a Picture of Metropolitan America." *New York Times* (August 1): 7.

———. 1992c. "In Family-Leave Debate, A Profound Ambivalence." *New York Times* (October 7): A1, A22.

Bart, Pauline. 1975. "The Loneliness of the Long-Distance Mother." In *Women: A Feminist Perspective* (1st ed.), pp. 156–70. Edited by Jo Freeman. Palo Alto, Calif.: Mayfield.

Baruch, Grace K., and Rosalind Barnett. 1981. "Fathers' Participation in the Care of Their Preschool Children." *Sex Roles* 7: 1043–55.

Baskir, Lawrence M., and William A. Strauss. 1978. *Chance and Circumstance: The Draft, the War, and the Vietnam Generation.* New York: Knopf.

Bauerlein, Monika. 1991. "Why Doesn't the U.S. Have a Family Leave Policy?" *Utne Reader* (September/October): 17–19.

Becker, Gary. 1981. *A Treatise on the Family.* Cambridge, Mass.: Harvard University Press.

———, ed. 1976. *The Economic Approach to Human Behavior.* Chicago: University of Chicago Press.

Beer, William R. 1983. *Househusbands: Men and Housework in American Families.* New York: Praeger.

———. 1988. "New Family Ties: How Well Are We Coping?" *Public Opinion* 10 (6): 14–15, 57.

Belenky, Mary Field, Blythe McVicker Clinchy, Nancy Rule Goldberger, and Jill Mattuck Tarule. 1986. *Women's Ways of Knowing: The Development of Self, Voice, and Mind.* New York: Basic Books.

Belkin, Lisa. 1989. "Bars to Equality of Sexes Seen as Eroding, Slowly." *New York Times* (August 20): A1, A26.

Bell, Inge P. 1970. "The Double Standard: Age." *Trans-Action* (November/December): 75–80.

Bell, Robert R. 1981. *Worlds of Friendship.* Beverly Hills, Calif.: Sage Publications.

Bellah, Robert N., Richard Madsen, William M. Sullivan, Ann Swidler, and Steven M. Tipton. 1985. *Habits of the Heart.* Berkeley and Los Angeles: University of California Press.

Benhabid, Seyla. 1987. "The Generalized and the Concrete Other: The Kohlberg-Gilligan Controversy and Moral Theory." In *Women and Moral Theory.* Edited by Eva F. Kittay and Diana T. Meyers. Totowa, N.J.: Rowman and Littlefield.

Benin, Mary Holland, and Joan Agostinelli. 1988. "Husbands' and Wives' Satisfaction with the Division of Labor." *Journal of Marriage and the Family* 50 (May): 349–61.

Benson, Leonard. 1968. *Fatherhood: A Sociological Perspective.* New York: Random House.

Berardo, Donna H. 1987. "The Housework Gap." *Journal of Marriage and the Family* 49: 381–90.

Bergmann, Barbara R. 1986. *The Economic Emergence of Women.* New York: Basic Books.

Berk, Sarah F. 1985. *The Gender Factory: The Apportionment of Work in American Households.* New York: Plenum Press.

———, ed. 1980. *Women and Household Labor.* Beverly Hills, Calif.: Sage Publications.

Bernard, Jessie. 1972. *The Future of Marriage.* New York: Bantam Books.

———. 1981. "The Good Provider Role: Its Rise and Fall." *American Psychologist* 36 (1): 1–12.

Bernard, Joan K. 1991. "Male, Single, and over Forty." *New York Newsday* (October 5): 15–17.

Bianchi, Suzanne M., and Daphne Spain. 1986. *American Women in Transition.* New York: Russell Sage Foundation.

Bielby, Denise D. 1992. "Commitment to Work and Family." *Annual Review of Sociology* 18: 281–302.

Bielby, Denise D., and William T. Bielby. 1988. "She Works Hard for the Money: Household Responsibilities and the Allocation of Work Effort." *American Journal of Sociology* 93 (5): 1031–59.

Bielby, William T., and Denise D. Bielby. 1989. "Family Ties: Balancing Commitments to Work and Family in Dual Earner Households." *American Sociological Review* 54 (5): 776–89.

Blakeslee, Sandra. 1991. "Confirmed Bachelorhood: It May Be a State of Mind." *New York Times* (August 21): C1, C10.

Blau, Francine D., and Marianne A. Ferber. 1986. *The Economics of Women, Men, and Work.* Englewood Cliffs, N.J.: Prentice-Hall.

Bloom-Feshbach, J. 1981. "Historical Perspectives on the Father's Role." In *The Role of the Father in Child Development* (2nd ed.). Edited by Michael E. Lamb. New York: Wiley.

Blumberg, Rae L., and M. Coleman. 1989. "A Theory-Guided Look at the Gender Balance of Power in the American Couple." *Journal of Family Issues* 10 (2) (June): 225–50.

Bly, Robert. 1990. *Iron John: A Book About Men.* Reading, Mass.: Addison-Wesley.

Bowles, Samuel, David M. Gordon, and Thomas E. Weisskopf. 1989. "Business Ascendancy and Economic Impasse: A Structural Retrospective on Conservative Economics, 1979–87." *Journal of Economic Perspectives* 3 (Fall): 107–34.

Brackman, Harold, and Steven P. Erie. 1986. "The Future of the Gender Gap." *Social Policy* (Winter): 5–11.

Brim, Gilbert G., Jr. 1968. "Adult Socialization." In *Socialization and Society*, pp. 182–226. Edited by John A. Clausen. Boston: Little, Brown.

———. 1992. *Ambition: How We Manage Success and Failure Throughout Our Lives.* New York: Basic Books.

Brim, Gilbert G., Jr., and Stanton Wheeler. 1966. *Socialization After Childhood.* New York: Wiley.

Brines, Julie. 1990. "What Makes Housework Men's Work? The Politics of Change and Its Lessons for Current Family Policy." Paper presented at the 85th Annual Meeting of the American Sociological Association (August), Washington, D.C.

Brod, Harry, ed. 1987. *The Making of Masculinities: The New Men's Studies.* Boston: Allen & Unwin.

Brody, Jane E. 1991. "Children of Divorce: Steps to Help Can Hurt." *New York Times* (July 23): C1, C9.

Buchman, Marlis. 1989. *The Script of Life in Modern Society: Entry into Adulthood in a Changing World.* Chicago: University of Chicago Press.

Bumpass, Larry L. 1990. "What's Happening to the Family? Interactions Between Demographic and Institutional Change." *Demography* 27: 483–90.

Burawoy, Michael, et al. 1991. *Ethnography Unbound: Power and Resistance in the Modern Metropolis.* Berkeley and Los Angeles: University of California Press.

Cancian, Francesca M. 1987. *Love in America: Gender and Self-Development.* Cambridge and New York: Cambridge University Press.

Capek, Mary E. 1990. "Beyond Parent Tracks: Alliances for the '90s." Newsletter of the National Council for Research on Women. New York.

Chafetz, Janet S. 1990. *Gender Equity: An Integrated Theory of Stability and Change.* Newbury Park, Calif.: Sage Publications.

Chang, Pi-Nian, and Amos S. Deinard. 1982. "Single-Father Caretakers." *American Journal of Orthopsychiatry* 52: 74–80.

Cherlin, Andrew. 1981. *Marriage, Divorce, Remarriage.* Cambridge, Mass.: Harvard University Press.

———, ed. 1988. *The Changing American Family and Public Policy.* Washington, D.C.: Urban Institute Press.

Chesler, Phyllis. 1988. *The Sacred Bond: The Legacy of Baby M.* New York: Times Books.

Chinoy, Eli. 1955. *Automobile Workers and the American Dream.* New York: Random House.

Chira, Susan. 1992. "New Realities Fight Old Images of Mother." *New York Times* (October 4): 1, 18.

Chodorow, Nancy. 1974. "Family Structure and Feminine Personality." In *Woman, Culture, and Society*, pp. 43–66. Edited by Michelle Z. Rosaldo and Louise Lamphere. Stanford, Calif.: Stanford University Press.

———. 1978. *The Reproduction of Mothering: Psychoanalysis and the Sociology of Gender.* Berkeley and Los Angeles: University of California Press.

———. 1990. *Feminism and Psychoanalytic Theory.* New Haven, Conn.: Yale University Press.

Christensen, Bryce J. 1988. "The Costly Retreat from Marriage." *The Public Interest* 91: 59–66.

Cohen, Susan, and Mary F. Katzenstein. 1988. "The War over the Family Is Not over the Family." In *Feminism, Children, and the New Families*, pp. 25–46. Edited by Sanford M. Dornbush and Myra H. Strober. New York: Guilford Press.

Cohn, Samuel. 1987. *The Process of Occupational Sex-Typing: The Feminization of Clerical Labor in Great Britain, 1870–1936.* Philadelphia: Temple University Press.

Coleman, James S. 1990. *Foundations of Social Theory.* Cambridge, Mass.: Harvard University Press.

Collins, Randall. 1971. "A Conflict Theory of Sexual Stratification." *Social Problems* 19: 3–21.

Coltrane, Scott. 1989a. "Household Labor and the Routine Production of Gender." *Social Problems* 36 (5) (December): 473–90.

———. 1989b. "The Social Construction of Shared Parenting: Social Networks and Parental Discourse." Paper presented at the Annual Meeting of the American Sociological Association (August), San Francisco.

Coltrane, Scott, and Neal Hickman. 1992. "The Rhetoric of Rights and Needs: Moral Discourse in the Reform of Child Custody and Child Support Laws." *Social Problems* 39 (4) (November): 400–20.

Coltrane, Scott L., and Masako Ishii-Kuntz. 1990. "Men's Housework: A Life Course Perspective." Paper presented at the Annual Meeting of the American Sociological Association (August), Washington, D.C.

Connell, R. W. 1987. *Gender and Power.* Stanford, Calif.: Stanford University Press.

———. 1990a. "A Whole New World: Remaking Masculinity in the Context of the Environmental Movement." *Gender and Society* 4 (4) (December): 452–78.

———. 1990b. "The State, Gender, and Sexual Politics: Theory and Appraisal." *Theory and Society* 19: 507–44.

———. 1991a. "Live Fast and Die Young: The Construction of Masculinity Among Young Working-Class Men on the Margin of the Labour Market." *Australian and New Zealand Journal of Sociology* 27 (2) (August): 141–71.

———. 1991b. "Men of Reason: Themes of Rationality and Change in the Lives of Men in New Professions." Unpublished manuscript.

———. 1992. "The Big Picture: Masculinities in Recent World History." Unpublished manuscript.

Cook, Karen S., and Margaret Levi. 1990. *The Limits of Rationality.* Chicago: University of Chicago Press.

Coverman, Shelley. 1983. "Gender, Domestic Labor Time, and Wage Inequality." *American Sociological Review* 48 (October): 623–27.

———. 1985. "Explaining Husbands' Participation in Domestic Labor." *Sociological Quarterly* 26: 81–97.

Coverman, Shelley, and Joseph Sheley. 1986. "Change in Men's Housework and Child-Care Time, 1965–1975." *Journal of Marriage and the Family* 48: 413–22.

Cowan, Alison L. 1989. "Women's Gains on the Job: Not Without a Heavy Toll." *New York Times* (August 21): A1, A14.

Cowan, Ruth Schwartz. 1983. *More Work for Mother: The Ironies of Household Technology from the Open Hearth to the Microwave.* New York: Basic Books.

Craib, Ian. 1987. "Masculinity and Male Dominance." *Sociological Review* 35 (4): 721–43.

Crompton, Rosemary, and Michael Mann. 1986. *Gender and Stratification.* Cambridge: Polity Press.

Crosby, Faye, ed. 1987. *Spouse, Parent, Worker: On Gender and Multiple Roles.* New Haven, Conn.: Yale University Press.

David, Deborah S., and Robert Brannon. 1976. *The Forty-nine Percent Majority: The Male Sex Role.* Reading, Mass.: Addison-Wesley.

Davis, Judith B. 1990. *Family Size and Achievement.* Berkeley and Los Angeles: University of California Press.

Davis, Kingsley. 1984. "Wives and Work: A Theory of the Sex Role Revolution and Its Consequences." *Population and Development Review* 9 (3): 397–417.

Davis, Kingsley, and Amyra Grossbard-Schectman, eds. 1985. *Contemporary Marriage: Comparative Perspectives on a Changing Institution.* New York: Russell Sage Foundation.

Defrain, J., and R. Elrich. 1981. "Coping as Single Parents: A Comparative Study of Mothers and Fathers." *Family Relations* 30: 265–73.

Demos, John. 1986. "The Changing Faces of Fatherhood." In *Past, Present, and Personal: The Family and the Life Course in American History*, pp. 41–66. Edited by John Demos. New York: Oxford University Press.

Dinnerstein, Dorothy. 1976. *The Mermaid and the Minotaur: Sexual Arrangements and Human Malaise.* New York: Harper & Row.

Dionne, E. J., Jr. 1989. "Struggle for Work and Family Fueling Women's Movement." *New York Times* (August 22): A1, A18.

Dornbusch, Sanford M., and Myra H. Strober. 1988. *Feminism, Children, and the New Families.* New York: Guilford Press.

Dugger, Celia W. 1992. "Establishing Paternity Earlier to Gain Child Support Later." *New York Times* (January 3): A1, B6.

Duncan, Greg J., and Saul D. Hoffman. 1985. "A Reconsideration of the Economic Consequences of Marital Dissolution." *Demography* (22): 485.

Easterlin, Richard A. 1980. *Birth and Fortune: The Impact of Numbers on Personal Welfare.* New York: Basic Books.

Easthope, Anthony. 1990. *What a Man's Gotta Do: The Masculine Myth in Popular Culture.* Cambridge, Mass.: Unwin, Hyman.

Eckholm, Erik. 1992a. "Learning If Infants Are Hurt When Mothers Go to Work." *New York Times* (October 6): A1–2.

———. 1992b. "Solutions on Welfare: They All Cost Money." *New York Times* (July 26): 1, 18.

Edelman, Marian W. 1987. *Families in Peril: An Agenda for Social Change.* Cambridge, Mass.: Harvard University Press.

Eggebeen, David J., and Daniel T. Lichter. 1991. "Race, Family Structure, and Changing Poverty Among American Children." *American Sociological Review* 56 (6) (December): 801–17.

Eggebeen, David J., and Peter Uhlenberg. 1985. "Changes in the Organization of Men's Lives, 1960–1980." *Family Relations* 34 (2): 251–57.

Ehrenreich, Barbara. 1983. *The Hearts of Men: American Dreams and the Flight from Commitment.* Garden City, N.Y.: Anchor Press.

Eisenstadt, S. N. 1956. *From Generation to Generation: Age Groups and Social Structure.* New York: Free Press.

Elder, Glen H., Jr. 1974. *Children of the Great Depression: Social Change in Life Experience.* Chicago: University of Chicago Press.

———. 1978. "Approaches to Social Change and the Family." In *Turning Points: Historical and Sociological Essays on the Family*, pp. S1–S38. Edited by John Demos and Sarane S. Boocock. Chicago: University of Chicago Press.

Ellwood, David T. 1988. *Poor Support: Poverty in the American Family.* New York: Basic Books.

England, Paula, and George Farkas. 1986. *Household, Employment, and Gender: A Social, Economic, and Demographic View.* New York: Aldine.

England, Paula, and Barbara S. Kilbourne. 1990. "Feminist Critiques of the Separative Model of Self: Implications for Rational Choice Theory." *Rationality and Society* 2 (2) (April): 156–71.

English, Dierdre. 1983. "The Fear That Feminism Will Free Men First." In *Powers of Desire: The Politics of Sexuality,* pp. 477–83. Edited by Ann Snitow, Christine Stansell, and Sharon Thompson. New York: Monthly Review Press.

Epstein, Cynthia F. 1985. "Ideal Roles and Real Roles or the Misplaced Fallacy of the Misplaced Dichotomy." *Research in Social Stratification and Mobility* 4: 29–51.

———. 1988. *Deceptive Distinctions: Sex, Gender, and the Social Order.* New Haven, Conn.: Yale University Press.

Erikson, Erik H. 1963. *Childhood and Society,* 2nd ed. New York: Norton.

Espenshade, Thomas J. 1985. "Marriage Trends in America: Estimates, Implications, and Underlying Causes." *Population and Development Review* ll (2) (June): 193–245.

Evans, Sara M. 1989. *Born for Liberty: A History of Women in America.* New York: Free Press.

Faludi, Susan. 1991. *Backlash: The Undeclared War Against American Women.* New York: Crown.

Farrell, Warren. 1986. *Why Men Are the Way They Are.* New York: McGraw-Hill.

Fausto-Sterling, Anne. 1987. *Myths of Gender: Biological Theories About Women and Men.* New York: Basic Books.

Ferree, Myra M. 1987. "Family and Job for Working-Class Women: Gender and Class Systems Seen from Below." In *Families and Work,* pp. 289–300. Edited by Naomi Gerstel and Harriet E. Gross. Philadelphia: Temple University Press.

Fiedler, Leslie A. 1966. *Love and Death in the American Novel,* rev. ed. New York: Stein & Day.

Fine, Gary A. 1987. *With the Boys: Little League Baseball and Preadolescent Culture.* Chicago: University of Chicago Press.

Fineman, Martha L. 1986. Review of *The Divorce Revolution,* by Lenore J. Weitzman. *American Bar Foundation Research Journal* 4: 781–90.

Fischer, Claude S. 1982. *To Dwell Among Friends: Personal Networks in Town and City.* Chicago: University of Chicago Press.

Fleming, Jeanne J. 1988. "Public Opinion on Change in Women's Rights and Roles." In *Feminism, Children, and the New Families,* pp. 47–66. Edited by Sanford M. Dornbusch and Myra H. Strober. New York: Guilford Press.

Fogel, Gerald I., Frederick M. Lane, and Robert S. Liebert. 1986. *The Psychology of Men: New Psychoanalytic Perspectives.* New York: Basic Books.

Folbre, Nancy. 1987. "The Pauperization of Motherhood: Patriarchy and Public Policy in the United States." In *Families and Work,* pp. 491–519. Edited by Naomi Gerstel and Harriet E. Gross. Philadelphia: Temple University Press.

Fowlkes, Martha R. 1987. "The Myth of Merit and Male Professional Careers." In *Families and Work*, pp. 347–60. Edited by Naomi Gerstel and Harriet E. Gross. Philadelphia: Temple University Press.

Franklin, Clyde W. II. 1984. *The Changing Definition of Masculinity*. New York: Plenum.

———. 1988. *Men and Society*. Chicago: Nelson-Hall.

Freudenberger, Herbert J. 1987. "Today's Troubled Men." *Psychology Today* (December): 46–47.

Friedman, Debra. 1992. *The Social Origins of Maternal Custody*. Unpublished manuscript, Department of Sociology, University of Arizona.

Friedman, Debra, and Carol Diem. 1990. "Feminism and the Pro- (Rational) Choice Movement: Rational Choice, Feminist Critiques, and Gender Inequality." In *Theory on Gender/Feminism on Theory*, pp. 91–114. Edited by Paula England. New York: Aldine.

Fuchs, Victor R. 1988. *Women's Quest for Economic Equality*. Cambridge, Mass.: Harvard University Press.

Furstenberg, Frank F., Jr. 1985. "Parenting Apart: Patterns of Childrearing After Marital Disruption." *Journal of Marriage and the Family* 47: 893–904.

———. 1988. "Good Dads/Bad Dads: Two Faces of Fatherhood." In *The Changing American Family and Public Policy*, pp. 193–218. Edited by Andrew J. Cherlin. Washington, D.C.: Urban Institute Press.

———. 1990. "Divorce and the American Family." *Annual Review of Sociology* 16: 379–403.

Furstenberg, Frank F., Jr., and Andrew Cherlin. 1991. *Divided Families: What Happens to Children When Parents Part*. Cambridge, Mass.: Harvard University Press.

Furstenberg, Frank F., Jr., Jeanne Brooks-Gunn, and S. Phillip Morgan. 1987. *Adolescent Mothers in Later Life*. New York: Cambridge University Press.

Furstenberg, Frank F., Jr., S. Phillip Morgan, and Paul D. Allison. 1987. "Paternal Participation and Children's Well-Being After Marital Dissolution." *American Sociological Review* 52 (5): 695–701.

Gans, Herbert. 1988. *Middle American Individualism*. New York: Free Press.

Garfinkel, Irwin, and Sara S. McLanahan. 1986. *Single Mothers and Their Children: A New American Dilemma*. Washington, D.C.: Urban Institute Press.

Geerken, Michael, and Walter R. Gove. 1983. *At Home and at Work: The Family's Allocation of Labor*. Beverly Hills, Calif.: Sage Publications.

Gershuny, Jonathan, and John P. Robinson. 1988. "Historical Changes in the Household Division of Labor." *Demography* 25 (4) (November): 537–54.

Gerson, Kathleen. 1983. "Changing Family Structure and the Position of Women: A Review of the Trends." *Journal of the American Planning Association* 49 (2) (Spring): 138–48.

———. 1985. *Hard Choices: How Women Decide About Work, Career, and Motherhood*. Berkeley and Los Angeles: University of California Press.

———. 1987a. "Emerging Social Division Among Women: Implications for Welfare State Politics." *Politics and Society* 15 (2): 213–21.

———. 1987b. "What Do Women Want from Men? Men's Influence on Women's

Work and Family Choices." In *Changing Men: New Directions in Research on Men and Masculinity*, pp. 619–34. Edited by Michael S. Kimmel. Beverly Hills: Sage Publications.

———. 1990. "What's Wrong with 'Mommy Tracks'? Lessons from Research." Paper presented at the 60th Annual Meeting of the Eastern Sociological Society (March), Boston.

———. 1991. "Coping with Commitment: Dilemmas and Conflicts of Family Life." In *America at Century's End*, pp. 35–57. Edited by Alan Wolfe. Berkeley and Los Angeles: University of California Press.

———. 1992. "Families and Change: Where We Stand and What We Need to Know." *Contemporary Sociology* 21 (4) (July): 444–45.

Gerstel, Naomi. 1988. "Divorce, Gender, and Social Integration." *Gender and Society* 2 (3): 343–67.

Gerstel, Naomi, and Harriet E. Gross. 1989. "Women and the American Family: Continuity and Change." In *Women: A Feminist Perspective*, 4th ed., pp. 89–120. Edited by Jo Freeman. Mountain View, Calif.: Mayfield.

Gerstel, Naomi, and Harriet E. Gross, eds. 1987. *Families and Work*. Philadelphia: Temple University Press.

Gerth, Hans, and C. Wright Mills. 1953. *Character and Social Structure: The Psychology of Social Institutions*. New York: Harcourt, Brace, and World.

Gerzon, Mark. 1982. *A Choice of Heroes: The Changing Face of American Manhood*. Boston: Houghton, Mifflin.

Giddens, Anthony. 1979. *Central Problems in Social Theory: Action, Structure, and Contradiction in Social Analysis*. New York: Basic Books.

Giele, Janet Z. 1988. "Gender and Sex Roles." In *Handbook of Sociology*. Edited by Neil J. Smelser. Newbury Park, Calif.: Sage Publications.

Gilbert, Lucia A. 1985. *Men in Dual-Career Families: Current Realities and Future Prospects*. Hillsdale, N.J.: Lawrence Erlbaum.

Gilligan, Carol. 1982. *In a Different Voice: Psychological Theory and Women's Development*. Cambridge, Mass.: Harvard University Press.

Gilligan, Carol, Janie V. Ward, and Jill M. Taylor. 1989. *Mapping the Moral Terrain: A Contribution of Women's Thinking to Psychological Theory and Education*. Cambridge, Mass.: Harvard University Press.

Gilmore, David D. 1990. *Manhood in the Making*. New Haven, Conn.: Yale University Press.

Ginsberg, Faye. 1989. *Contested Lives: The Abortion Debate in an American Community*. Berkeley and Los Angeles: University of California Press.

Glaser, Barney, and Anselm Strauss. 1967. *The Discovery of Grounded Theory*. Chicago: Aldine.

Glenn, Norval D., and Charles N. Weaver. 1988. "The Changing Relationship of Marital Status to Reported Happiness." *Journal of Marriage and the Family* 50 (May): 317–24.

Glick, Paul C. 1990. "American Families: As They Are and Were." *Sociology and Social Research* 74 (3) (April): 139–45.

Glick, Paul C., and Arthur J. Norton. 1977. "Marrying, Divorcing, and Living Together in the U.S. Today." *Population Bulletin* 32 (October): 2–39.

Goertzel, Ted G. 1983. "The Gender Gap: Sex, Family Income, and Political Opinions in the Early 1980's." *Journal of Political and Military Sociology* 11: 209–22.

Goldberg, Steven. 1973. *The Inevitability of Patriarchy: Why the Biological Difference Between Men and Women Always Produces Male Domination.* New York: Morrow.

Goldin, Claudia. 1990. *Understanding the Gender Gap: An Economic History of American Women.* New York: Oxford University Press.

Goldscheider, Frances K., and Linda J. Waite. 1991. *New Families, No Families? The Transformation of the American Home.* Berkeley and Los Angeles: University of California Press.

Goleman, Daniel. 1990a. "Men at 65: Surprising Findings About Emotional Well-Being." *New York Times* (January 16): C1, 12.

———. 1990b. "Surprising Findings About the Development of Empathy in Children." *New York Times* (July 10): C1.

Goode, William J. 1959. "The Theoretical Importance of Love." *American Sociological Review* 24 (1) (February): 38–47.

———. 1963. *World Revolution and Family Patterns.* New York: Free Press.

———. 1982. "Why Men Resist." In *Rethinking the Family: Some Feminist Questions*, pp. 131–50. Edited by Barrie Thorne with Marilyn Yalom. New York: Longman.

Gould, Roger L. 1978. *Transformations: Growth and Change in Adulthood.* New York: Simon & Schuster.

Gove, Walter R. 1972. "The Relationship Between Sex Roles, Marital Status, and Mental Illness." *Social Forces* 51 (September): 34–44.

———. 1979. "Sex, Marital Status, and Psychiatric Treatment: A Research Note." *Social Forces* 58 (September): 89–93.

Granovetter, Mark. 1973. "The Strength of Weak Ties." *American Journal of Sociology* 78 (6): 1360–80.

———. 1974. *Getting a Job.* Cambridge, Mass.: Harvard University Press.

———. 1985. "Economic Action and Social Structure: The Problem of Embeddedness." *American Journal of Sociology* 91: 481–510.

Greenberg, Stanley B. 1985. "Recapturing Democratic Majorities: Housewives and Their Men." Prepared for the Michigan Democratic Party, May 21. New Haven, Conn.: Analysis Group.

Greenhouse, Steven. 1992. "Income Data Show Years of Erosion for U.S. Workers." *New York Times* (September 7): 1, 39.

Greif, Geoffrey L. 1985. "Single Fathers Rearing Children." *Journal of Marriage and Family* 47: 185–91.

Grosskurth, Phyllis. 1991. "The New Psychology of Women." *New York Review of Books* 38 (October 24): 25–32.

Hacker, Andrew. 1987. "American Apartheid." *New York Review of Books* (December 3): 26–33.

———. 1988. "Getting Tough on the Poor." *New York Review of Books* (October 13): 12–17.

Hall, Trish. 1991. "Time on Your Hands? It May Be Increasing." *New York Times* (July 3): C1, 7.

Halle, David. 1984. *America's Working Man: Work, Home, and Politics Among Blue-Collar Property Owners*. Chicago: University of Chicago Press.

———. 1987. "Marriage and Family Life of Blue-Collar Men." In *Families and Work*, pp. 316–37. Edited by Naomi Gerstel and Harriet E. Gross. Philadelphia: Temple University Press.

Hanson, Shirley M. H. 1986. "Father/Child Relationships: Beyond *Kramer vs. Kramer*." In *Men's Changing Roles in the Family*, pp. 135–50. Edited by Robert A. Lewis and Marvin B. Sussman. New York: Haworth Press.

Hanson, Shirley M. H., and Frederick W. Bozett, eds. 1985. *Dimensions of Fatherhood*. Newbury Park, Calif.: Sage Publications.

Harding, Sandra. 1986. "The Instability of the Analytical Categories of Feminist Theory." *Signs: Journal of Women in Culture and Society* 2 (4): 645–64.

Hareven, Tamara. 1977. "Family Time and Historical Time." *Daedalus* 106 (Spring): 57–70.

Harrison, Bennett, and Barry Bluestone. 1988. "Who's Who in the Lower Half: The Changing Composition of the Lower-Wage Workforce in the U.S. Since 1963." Unpublished manuscript.

———. 1990. *The Great U-Turn: Corporate Restructuring and the Polarizing of America*. New York: Basic Books.

Hartmann, Heidi. 1976. "Capitalism, Patriarchy, and Job Segregation by Sex." In *Women and the Workplace*. Edited by Martha Blaxall and Barbara Reagan. Chicago: University of Chicago Press.

Hayes, Cheryl D., John L. Palmer, and Martha J. Zaslow, eds. 1990. *Who Cares for America's Children?* Washington, D.C.: National Academy Press.

Hearn, Jeff. 1987. *The Gender of Oppression: Men, Masculinity, and the Critique of Marxism*. New York: St. Martin's Press.

Hearn, Jeff, and David H. J. Morgan. 1990. *Men, Masculinities, and Social Theory*. Cambridge, Mass.: Unwin, Hyman.

Hechter, Michael, and Debra Friedman. 1990. "Valuing Children." Paper presented at the Annual Meeting of the Public Choice Society (March 16–18), Tucson, Ariz.

Henry, Jules. 1965. *Culture Against Man*. New York: Vintage Books.

Herman, Judith L. 1992. *Trauma and Recovery: The Aftermath of Violence*. New York: Basic Books.

Hertz, Rosanna. 1986. *More Equal Than Others: Women and Men in Dual-Career Marriages*. Berkeley and Los Angeles: University of California Press.

Hertz, Rosanna, and Joy Charlton. 1989. "Making Family Under a Shiftwork Schedule: Air Force Security Guards and Their Wives." *Social Problems* (36) 5: 491–507.

Hess, Beth B. 1990. "Beyond Dichotomy: Drawing Distinctions and Embracing Differences." *Sociological Forum* 5 (1) (March): 75–94.

Hetherington, I. Mavis, and Josephine D. Arasteh, eds. 1988. "Divorced Fathers: Stress, Coping, and Adjustment." In *The Father's Role: Applied Perspectives*, pp. 103–34. Edited by Michael E. Lamb. New York: Wiley.

Hewlett, Sylvia A. 1986. *A Lesser Life: The Myth of Women's Liberation in America*. New York: Warner Books.

———. 1991. *When the Bough Breaks*. New York: Basic Books.

Hipgrave, Tony. 1981. "Child Rearing by Lone Fathers." In *Changing Patterns of Childbearing and Child Rearing*, pp. 149–66. Edited by R. Chester, Peter Diggory, and Margaret B. Sutherland. London: Academic Press.

Hirschhorn, Lawrence. 1977. "Social Policy and the Life Cycle: A Developmental Perspective." *Social Service Review* 51 (September): 434–50.

Hobson, Barbara. 1991. "Reply to Popenoe." *American Journal of Sociology* 97 (3) (November): 846–48.

Hochschild, Arlie R. 1975. "Inside the Clockwork of Male Careers." In *Women and the Power to Change*, pp. 47–80. Edited by Florence Howe. New York: McGraw-Hill.

―――. 1983. *The Managed Heart: Commercialization of Human Feeling.* Berkeley and Los Angeles: University of California Press.

Hochschild, Arlie R., with Anne Machung. 1989. *The Second Shift: Working Parents and the Revolution at Home.* New York: Viking.

Hofferth, Sandra L. 1990. "Employer Benefits and Parental Leave Policies in the U.S." Paper presented at the 85th Annual Meeting of the American Sociological Association (August), Washington, D.C.

Hofferth, Sandra L., and Deborah A. Phillips. 1987. "Child Care in the United States, 1970 to 1995." *Journal of Marriage and the Family* 49 (3): 559–71.

Hoffman, Lois. 1983. "Increased Fathering: Effects on the Mother." In *Fatherhood and Family Policy*, pp. 167–90. Edited by Michael E. Lamb and Abraham Sagi. Hillsdale, N.J.: Lawrence Erlbaum.

―――. 1987. "The Effects on Children of Maternal and Paternal Employment." In *Families and Work*, pp. 362–95. Edited by Naomi Gerstel and Harriet E. Gross. Philadelphia: Temple University Press.

Hoffman, Saul D., and Greg J. Duncan. 1988. "What *Are* the Economic Consequences of Divorce?" *Demography* 25 (4) (November): 641–45.

Hood, Jane C. 1983. *Becoming a Two-Job Family.* New York: Praeger.

―――. 1986. "The Provider Role: Its Meaning and Measurement." *Journal of Marriage and the Family* 48 (May): 349–59.

―――, ed. Forthcoming. *Work, Family, and Masculinities.* Newbury Park, Calif.: Sage Publications.

Hrdy, Sarah B. 1981. *The Woman That Never Evolved.* Cambridge, Mass.: Harvard University Press.

Huber, Joan, and Glenna Spitze. 1983. *Sex Stratification: Children, Housework, and Jobs.* New York: Academic Press.

―――. 1988. "Trends in Family Sociology." In *Handbook of Sociology*, pp. 425–48. Edited by Neil J. Smelser. Newbury Park, Calif.: Sage Publications.

Hunt, Janet G., and Larry L. Hunt. 1987a. "Male Resistance to Role Symmetry in Dual-Earner Households: Three Alternative Explanations." In *Families and Work*, pp. 192–203. Edited by Naomi Gerstel and Harriet E. Gross. Philadelphia: Temple University Press.

―――. 1987b. "Labor and Leisure: Toward a New Formulation of Gender Roles." Paper presented at the 57th Annual Meeting of the Eastern Sociological Society (May), Boston.

Isherwood, J. Thomas. 1983. "The Male Role: Limitations and Interventions." *Free Inquiry in Creative Sociology* 11 (2) (November): 227–30.

Jackson, Robert M. 1989. "The Reproduction of Parenting." *American Sociological Review* 54 (2): 215–32.

Jacobs, Jerry A. 1989a. *Revolving Doors: Sex Segregation and Women's Careers.* Stanford, Calif.: Stanford University Press.

———. 1989b. "Long-Term Trends in Occupational Segregation by Sex." *American Journal of Sociology* 95 (1): 160–73.

———. 1991. "Women's Entry into Management: Trends in Earnings, Authority, and Values Among Salaried Managers." Unpublished manuscript, Department of Sociology, University of Pennsylvania.

Jacobs, Jerry A., David Karen, and Katherine McClelland. 1991. "The Dynamics of Young Men's Career Aspirations." *Sociological Forum* 6 (4) (December): 609–40.

Jardine, Alice, and Paul Smith. 1987. *Men in Feminism.* New York: Methuen.

Jasper, James M. 1990. *Nuclear Politics: Energy and the State in the United States, Sweden, and France.* Princeton, N.J.: Princeton University Press.

Jencks, Christopher. 1992. *Rethinking Social Policy.* Cambridge, Mass.: Harvard University Press.

Johnson, Miriam. 1988. *Strong Mothers, Weak Wives.* Berkeley and Los Angeles: University of California Press.

Jones, Jacqueline. 1985. *Labor of Love, Labor of Sorrow: Black Women, Work, and the Family from Slavery to the Present.* New York: Basic Books.

Jump, Teresa L., and Linda Haas. 1987. "Fathers in Transition: Dual-Career Fathers Participating in Child Care." In *Changing Men: New Directions in Research on Men and Masculinity*, pp. 98–114. Edited by Michael S. Kimmel. Newbury Park, Calif.: Sage Publications.

Kagan, Jerome. 1984. *The Nature of the Child.* New York: Basic Books.

———. 1989. *Unstable Ideas: Temperament, Cognition, and Self.* Cambridge, Mass.: Harvard University Press.

Kamerman, Sheila, and Alfred J. Kahn. 1987. *The Responsive Workplace.* New York: Columbia University Press.

Kanter, Rosabeth M. 1977. *Men and Women of the Corporation.* New York: Basic Books.

Kaufman, Debra R., and Barbara L. Richardson. 1982. *Achievement and Women: Challenging the Assumptions.* New York: Free Press.

Keen, Sam. 1991. *Fire in the Belly: On Being a Man.* New York: Bantam Books.

Keller, Evelyn Fox. 1985. *Reflections on Gender and Science.* New Haven, Conn.: Yale University Press.

Kessler, Ronald C., R. L. Brown, and C. L. Broman. 1981. "Sex Differences in Psychiatric Help-Seeking: Evidence from Four Large-scale Surveys." *Journal of Health and Social Behavior* 22 (March): 49–63.

Kessler-Harris, Alice. 1981. *Women Have Always Worked: A Historical Overview.* Old Westbury, N.Y.: Feminist Press.

Kett, Joseph F. 1977. *Rites of Passage: Adolescence in America, 1790 to the Present.* New York: Basic Books.

Kilborn, Peter T. 1990. "As Americans Push Harder to Keep Up, Work Dominates." *New York Times* (June 3): E1, E3.

———. 1991. "Part-Time Hirings Bring Deep Change in U.S. Workplaces." *New York Times* (June 17): A1, A12.

———. 1992. "The Middle Class Feels Betrayed, But Maybe Not Enough to Rebel." *New York Times* (January 12): sec. 4, pp. 1–2.

Kiley, Dan. 1983. *The Peter Pan Syndrome: Men Who Have Never Grown Up.* New York: Dodd, Mead.

Kimmel, Michael S. 1987a. "Men's Responses to Feminism at the Turn of the Century." *Gender and Society* 1 (3): 261–83.

———. 1987b. "Rethinking 'Masculinity': New Directions in Research." In *Changing Men: New Directions in Research on Men and Masculinity*, pp. 9–24. Newbury Park, Calif.: Sage Publications.

———. 1992a. "Reading Men: Men, Masculinity, and Publishing." *Contemporary Sociology* 21 (2) (March): 162–71.

———. 1992b. "Weekend Warriors: Robert Bly's *Iron John* and the Masculine Retreat." Unpublished manuscript, Department of Sociology, State University of New York at Stony Brook.

Kimmel, Michael S., and Michael A. Messner, eds. 1989. *Men's Lives.* New York: Macmillan.

Kingson, Jennifer A. 1988. "Courts Expand the Rights of Unmarried Fathers." *New York Times* (October 28): B9.

Kingston, Paul William, and Steven E. Finkel. 1987. "Is There a Marriage Gap in Politics?" *Journal of Marriage and the Family* 49: 57–64.

Kittay, Eva F., and Diana T. Meyers. 1987. *Women and Moral Theory.* Totowa, N.J.: Rowman and Littlefield.

Klatch, Rebecca E. 1987. *Women of the New Right.* Philadelphia: Temple University Press.

Klein, Ethel. 1983. *Gender Politics.* Cambridge, Mass.: Harvard University Press.

———. 1985. "The Gender Gap: Different Issues, Different Answers." *The Brookings Review* (Winter): 33–37.

Kline, Marsha, Janet R. Johnston, and Jeanne M. Tschann. 1991. "The Long Shadow of Marital Conflict: A Model of Children's Post-divorce Adjustment." *Journal of Marriage and the Family* 53: 297–309.

Komarovsky, Mirra. 1940. *The Unemployed Man and His Family.* New York: Dryden Press.

———. 1962. *Blue-Collar Marriage.* New York: Random House.

———. 1976. *Dilemmas of Masculinity: A Study of College Youth.* New York: Norton.

Kosters, Marvin H., and Murray N. Ross. 1988. "A Shrinking Middle Class?" *The Public Interest* 90 (Winter): 3–27.

Lamb, Michael E., ed. 1976. *The Role of the Father in Child Development.* New York: Wiley.

———. 1982. *Nontraditional Families: Parenting and Child Development.* Hillsdale, N.J.: Lawrence Erlbaum.

———. 1986. *The Father's Role: Applied Perspectives.* New York: Wiley.

———. 1987. *The Father's Role: Cross-Cultural Perspectives.* Hillsdale, N.J.: Lawrence Erlbaum.

Lamb, Michael E., Joseph H. Pleck, and James A. Levine. 1987. "Effects of Increased Paternal Involvement on Fathers and Mothers." In *Reassessing Fatherhood: New Observations on Fathers and the Modern Family*, pp. 103–25. Edited by Charlie Lewis and Margaret O'Brien. Newbury Park, Calif.: Sage Publications.

La Rossa, Ralph. 1988. "Fatherhood and Social Change." *Family Relations* 37: 451–57.

Lasch, Christopher. 1977. *Haven in a Heartless World: The Family Besieged.* New York: Basic Books.

————. 1979. *The Culture of Narcissism: American Life in an Age of Diminishing Expectations.* New York: Norton.

Laslett, Barbara, and Johanna Brenner. 1989. "Gender and Social Reproduction: Historical Perspectives." In *Annual Review of Sociology*, vol. 15, pp. 381–404. Edited by W. Richard Scott and Judith Blake.

Lawson, Carol. 1990a. "Hope for the Working Parent: Company Care Plans Slowly Spread." *New York Times* (March 15): C1, C10.

————. 1990b. "Tracking the Life of the New Father: Children vs. Career." *New York Times* (April 12): C1, C6.

————. 1990c. "Class of '90 on the Family: Who Will Mind the Children?" *New York Times* (June 7): C1, C6.

————. 1990d. "Like Growing Number of Companies, I.B.M. Is Building Child-Care Centers." *New York Times* (December 12): A20.

————. 1991. "Baby Beckons. Why Is Daddy at Work?" *New York Times* (May 16): C1, C8.

Levine, James A. 1976. *Who Will Raise the Children? New Options for Fathers (and Mothers).* New York: Lippincott.

Levinger, George, and Oliver C. Moles, eds. 1979. *Divorce and Separation: Context, Causes, and Consequences.* New York: Basic Books.

Levinson, Daniel J. 1978. *The Seasons of a Man's Life.* New York: Ballantine Books.

Levy, Frank. 1987. *Dollars and Dreams: The Changing American Income Distribution.* New York: Russell Sage Foundation.

Levy, Frank, and Richard C. Michel. 1991. *The Economic Future of American Families.* Washington, D.C.: Urban Institute.

Lewin, Tamar. 1992. "Rise in Single Parenthood Is Reshaping U.S." *New York Times* (October 5): A1, B6.

Lewis, Charlie, and Margaret O'Brien, eds. 1987. *Reassessing Fatherhood.* Newbury Park, Calif.: Sage Publications.

Lewis, Robert A. 1986. "Men's Changing Roles in Marriage and the Family." In *Men's Changing Roles in the Family*, pp. 1–10. Edited by Robert A. Lewis and Marvin B. Sussman. New York: Haworth Press.

Lewis, Robert A., and Robert E. Salt, eds. 1986. *Men in Families.* Newbury Park, Calif.: Sage Publications.

Lockwood, David. 1986. "Class, Status, and Gender." In *Gender and Stratification*, pp. 11–22. Edited by Rosemary Crompton and Michael Mann. London: Polity Press.

Luepnitz, Deborah A. 1982. *Child Custody: A Study of Families After Divorce.* Lexington, Mass.: Lexington Books.

Luker, Kristin. 1984. *Abortion and the Politics of Motherhood.* Berkeley and Los Angeles: University of California Press.

———. 1991. "Dubious Conceptions: The Controversy over Teen Pregnancy." *The American Prospect* (Spring): 73–83.

Maccoby, Eleanor E., ed. 1966. *The Development of Sex Differences.* Stanford, Calif.: Stanford University Press.

Maccoby, Eleanor E., and Carol Jacklin, eds. 1974. *The Psychology of Sex Differences.* Stanford, Calif.: Stanford University Press.

Mackey, Wade C. 1985. *Fathering Behaviors: The Dynamics of the Man-Child Bond.* New York: Plenum.

Macklin, Eleanor D. 1983. "Effect of Changing Sex Roles on the Intimate Relationships of Men and Women." *Human Sexuality and the Family.* New York: Haworth Press.

McLanahan, Sara, Judith Seltzer, Tom Hanson, and Elizabeth Thomson. 1992. "Child Support Enforcement and Child Well-Being: Greater Security or Greater Conflict?" Paper presented at the Annual Meeting of the American Sociological Association (August), Pittsburgh.

Mann, Michael. 1986. "A Crisis in Stratification Theory? Persons, Households/Families/Lineages, Genders, Classes and Nations." In *Gender and Stratification,* pp. 40–56. Edited by Rosemary Crompton and Michael Mann. London: Polity Press.

Mansbridge, Jane J. 1985. "Myth and Reality: The ERA and the Gender Gap in the 1980 Election." *Public Opinion Quarterly* 49: 164–78.

———. 1986. *Why We Lost the ERA.* Chicago: University of Chicago Press.

———, ed. 1990. *Beyond Self-Interest.* Chicago: University of Chicago Press.

Marciano, Teresa Donati. 1986. "Why Are Men Unhappy in Patriarchy?" In *Men's Changing Roles in the Family,* pp. 17–30. Edited by Robert A. Lewis and Marvin B. Sussman. New York: Haworth Press.

Marini, Margaret M. 1990. "Sex and Gender: What Do We Know?" *Sociological Forum* 5 (1) (March): 95–120.

Marriott, Michel. 1992. "Fathers Find That Child Support Means Owing More Than Money." *New York Times* (July 20): A1, A13.

Marsiglio, William. 1988. "Commitment to Social Fatherhood: Predicting Adolescent Males' Intentions to Live with Their Child and Partner." *Journal of Marriage and the Family* 50 (May): 427–41.

Mason, Karen O., and Yu-Hsia Lu. 1988. "Attitudes Toward Women's Familial Roles: Changes in the United States, 1977–1985." *Gender and Society* 2 (1): 39–57.

May, Elaine Tyler. 1988. *Homeward Bound: American Families in the Cold War Era.* New York: Basic Books.

May, Martha. 1982. "The Historical Problem of the Family Wage: The Ford Motor Company and the Five-Dollar Day." *Feminist Studies* 8 (2) (Summer): 399–424.

Melson, Gail F., and Alan Foge. 1988. "Learning to Care." *Psychology Today* (January): 39–45.

Merton, Robert K. 1957. *Social Theory and Social Structure.* New York: Free Press.

Messner, Michael. 1989. "Masculinities and Athletic Careers." *Gender and Society* 3 (1): 71–88.

Milkman, Ruth. 1987. *Gender at Work: The Dynamics of Job Segregation by Sex During World War II*. Urbana: University of Illinois Press.

Miller, Joanne. 1988. "Jobs and Work." In *Handbook of Sociology*, pp. 327–59. Edited by Neil J. Smelser. Newbury Park, Calif.: Sage Publications.

Millman, Marcia. 1991. *Warm Hearts and Cold Cash: How Families Handle Money and What This Reveals About Them*. New York: Free Press.

Mills, C. Wright. 1940. "Situated Actions and Vocabularies of Motive." *American Sociological Review* 5: 904–13.

——. 1959. *The Sociological Imagination*. New York: Oxford University Press.

Mintz, Steven, and Susan Kellogg. 1988. *Domestic Revolutions: A Social History of American Family Life*. New York: Free Press.

Mishel, Lawrence, and David M. Frankel. 1991. *The State of Working America*. Armonk, N.Y.: M. E. Sharpe.

Modell, John, Frank F. Furstenberg, Jr., and Theodore Hershberg. 1976. "Social Change and Transitions to Adulthood in Historical Perspective." *Journal of Family History* 1 (Autumn): 7–32.

Moen, Phyllis. 1989. *Working Parents: Transformations in Gender Roles and Public Policies in Sweden*. Madison: University of Wisconsin Press.

Moen, Phyllis, and Donna I. Dempster-McClain. 1987. "Employed Parents: Role Strain, Work Time, and Preferences for Working Less." *Journal of Marriage and the Family* 49 (3): 579–90.

Morrison, Peter A. 1986. "Changing Family Structure: Who Cares for America's Dependents?" Santa Monica, Calif.: Rand Corporation.

Moynihan, Daniel P. 1986. *Family and Nation*. San Diego and New York: Harcourt, Brace, Jovanovich.

Myers, Michael F. 1986. "Angry, Abandoned Husbands: Assessment and Treatment." In *Men's Changing Roles in the Family*, pp. 31–42. Edited by Robert A. Lewis and Marvin B. Sussman. New York: Haworth Press.

Myles, John. 1989. "New Productive Forces, Old Social Relations: The Political Economy of Postindustrialism." *Contemporary Sociology: An International Journal of Reviews* 18 (2): 219–21. (Review of Fred Block, *Revising State Theory: Essays in Politics and Postindustrialism* [Philadelphia: Temple University Press, 1987].)

Nasar, Sylvia. 1992. "Women's Progress Stalled? It Just Isn't So." *New York Times* (October 18): sec. 3, pp. 1, 10.

Neugarten, Bernice L., and Nancy Datan. 1973. "Sociological Perspectives on the Life Cycle." In *Life-Span Developmental Psychology: Personality and Socialization*, pp. 53–69. Edited by Paul B. Baltes and K. Warner Schaie. New York: Academic Press.

Newman, Katherine S. 1988. *Falling from Grace: The Experience of Downward Mobility in the American Middle Class*. New York: Free Press.

New York Times. 1991. "It's Cheaper to Give Unpaid Leave Than to Dismiss, U.S. Study Says." (March 25): A13.

Noble, Barbara P. 1993. "An Increase in Bias Is Seen Against Pregnant Workers." *New York Times* (January 2): 1, 39.

Nock, Steven L., and Paul W. Kingston. 1988. "Time with Children: The Impact of Couples' Work-Time Commitments." *Social Forces* 67 (1): 59–85.

Nye, F. Ivan. 1988. "Fifty Years of Family Research, 1937–1987." *Journal of Marriage and the Family* 50 (May): 305–16.

Oakley, Ann. 1974. *Woman's Work: The Housewife Past and Present.* New York: Random House.

O'Brien, Margaret. 1982. "Becoming a Lone Father: Differential Patterns and Experiences." In *The Father Figure*, pp. 184–207. Edited by L. McKee and Margaret O'Brien. London: Tavistock Publications.

Okin, Susan Moller. 1989. *Justice, Gender, and the Family.* New York: Basic Books.

Oliker, Stacey. 1989. *Best Friends and Marriage.* Berkeley and Los Angeles: University of California Press.

O'Reilly, Brian. 1992. "Why Grade 'A' Executives Get an 'F' as Parents." *Fortune* (January 1): 36–46.

Osherson, Samuel. 1986. *Finding Our Fathers: The Unfinished Business of Manhood.* New York: Free Press.

O'Toole, Kathleen. 1991. "Joint Custody Can Work." *Stanford Observer* (September–October): 6.

Papanek, Hannah. 1973. "Men, Women, and Work: Reflections on the Two-Person Career." In *Changing Women in a Changing Society*, pp. 90–110. Edited by Joan Huber. Chicago: University of Chicago Press.

Parke, Ross D. 1981. *Fathers.* Cambridge, Mass.: Harvard University Press.

Parke, Ross D., and Barbara R. Tinsley. 1983. "Fatherhood: Historical and Contemporary Perspectives." In *Life Span Developmental Psychology: Historical and Cohort Effects*, pp. 203–48. Edited by K. A. McCluskey and H. W. Reese. New York: Academic Press.

Parsons, Talcott. 1942. "Age and Sex in the Social Structure of the United States." *American Sociological Review* 7: 604–16.

———. 1954. "The Incest Taboo in Relation to Social Structure and the Socialization of the Child." *British Journal of Sociology* 5: 101–17.

———. 1958. "Social Structure and the Development of Personality: Freud's Contribution to the Integration of Psychology and Sociology." *Psychiatry* 21: 321–40.

Parsons, Talcott, and Robert F. Bales. 1955. *Family, Socialization, and Interaction Process.* Glencoe, Ill.: Free Press.

Pear, Robert. 1991. "Larger Number of New Mothers Are Unmarried." *New York Times* (December 4): A20.

Pepitone-Rockwell, Fran, ed. 1980. *Dual-Career Couples.* Beverly Hills: Sage Publications.

Perrow, Charles. 1984. *Normal Accidents: Living with High-Risk Technologies.* New York: Basic Books.

Pescosolido, Bernice. 1992. "Beyond Rational Choice: The Social Dynamics of How People Seek Help." *American Journal of Sociology* 97 (January): 1096–1138.

Peterson, Karen S. 1988. "Today's Man Loves Family, Being a Dad." *USA Today* (March 24): 1A.

Peterson, Richard R. 1989. *Women, Work, and Divorce.* Albany, N.Y.: State University of New York Press.

Peterson, Richard R., and Kathleen Gerson. 1992. "Determinants of Responsibility for Child-Care Arrangements Among Dual-Earner Couples." *Journal of Marriage and the Family* 54 (3) (August): 527–36.

Phillips, Kevin. 1990. *The Politics of Rich and Poor: Wealth and the American Electorate in the Reagan Aftermath.* New York: HarperCollins.

Phillips, Roderick. 1988. *Putting Asunder: A History of Divorce in Western Society.* Cambridge: Cambridge University Press.

Pittman, Joe F., and Dennis K. Orthner. 1988. "Predictors of Spousal Support for the Work Commitments of Husbands." *Journal of Marriage and the Family* 50 (May): 335–48.

Piven, Frances F. 1987. "Women and the State: Ideology, Power, and the Welfare State." In *Gender and the Life Course*, pp. 265–87. Edited by Alice S. Rossi. New York: Aldine.

Pleck, Joseph H. 1981. *The Myth of Masculinity.* Cambridge, Mass.: MIT Press.

———. 1983. "Husbands' Paid Work and Family Roles: Current Research Trends." *Research in the Interweave of Social Roles: Jobs and Families* 3: 251–333.

———. 1985. *Working Wives, Working Husbands.* Beverly Hills: Sage Publications.

———. 1987a. "American Fathering in Historical Perspective." In *Changing Men: New Directions in Research on Men and Masculinity*, pp. 83–97. Edited by Michael S. Kimmel. Newbury Park, Calif.: Sage Publications.

———. 1987b. "The Contemporary Man." In *Handbook of Counseling and Psychotherapy with Men.* Edited by Murray Scher, Mark Stevens, Glenn Good, and Gregg Eichenfield. Newbury Park, Calif.: Sage Publications.

———. 1989. "Family-Supportive Employer Policies and Men's Participation." Paper presented at workshop of Panel on Employer Policies and Working Families, Committee on Women's Employment and Related Social Issues, National Research Council (March 20–21).

———. Forthcoming. "Are 'Family-Supportive' Employer Policies Relevant to Men?" In *Work, Family, and Masculinities.* Edited by Jane C. Hood. Newbury Park, Calif.: Sage Publications.

Pleck, Joseph H., and Jack Sawyer. 1974. *Men and Masculinity.* Englewood Cliffs, N.J.: Prentice-Hall.

Plutzer, Eric. 1988. "Work Life, Family Life, and Women's Support of Feminism." *American Sociological Review* 53 (4): 640–49.

Polatnik, Margaret. 1973. "Why Men Don't Rear Children." *Berkeley Journal of Sociology* 18: 45–86.

Popenoe, David. 1988. *Disturbing the Nest: Family Change and Decline in Modern Societies.* New York: Aldine de Gruyter.

Presser, Harriet B. 1988. "Shift Work and Child Care Among Young Dual-Earner American Parents." *Journal of Marriage and the Family* 50 (1): 133–48.

Preston, Samuel H. 1984. "Children and the Elderly: Divergent Paths for America's Dependents." *Demography* 21 (4): 435–57.

Pruett, Kyle D. 1983. "Infants of Primary Nurturing Fathers." In *The Psychologi-*

cal Study of the Child, pp. 257–77. Edited by Lottie Maury Newman. New Haven, Conn.: Yale University Press.

———. 1988. *The Nurturing Father*. New York: Warner Books.

Quindlen, Anna. 1990. "Out of the Trunk." *New York Times* (November 8): A35.

Radin, N. 1982. "Primary Caregiving and Role-Sharing Fathers." In *Nontraditional Families: Parenting and Child Development*, pp. 173–204. Edited by Michael E. Lamb. Hillsdale, N.J.: Lawrence Erlbaum.

Rapoport, Rhona, and Robert Rapoport. 1977. *Dual-Career Families Re-examined*. New York: Harper & Row.

Reskin, Barbara F. 1988. "Bringing Men Back In: Sex Differentiation and the Devaluation of Women's Work." *Gender and Society* 2 (1): 58–81.

Reskin, Barbara F., and Patricia A. Roos. 1990. *Job Queues, Gender Queues: Explaining Women's Inroads into Male Occupations*. Philadelphia: Temple University Press.

Rexroat, Cynthia, and Constance Shehan. 1987. "The Family Life Cycle and Spouses' Time in Housework." *Journal of Marriage and the Family* 49 (4): 737–50.

Riley, Glenda. 1991. *Divorce: An American Tradition*. New York: Oxford University Press.

Riley, Matilda W. 1971. "Social Gerontology and the Age Stratification of Society." *Gerontologist* 11 (Spring): 79–87.

Rindfuss, Ronald R., C. Gray Swicegood, and Rachel A. Rosenfeld. 1987. "Disorder in the Life Course: How Common and Does It Matter?" *American Sociological Review* 52 (6): 785–801.

Risman, Barbara J. 1985. "Intimate Relationships from a Microstructural Perspective: Mothering Men." Revised version of paper presented at the Annual Meeting of the American Sociological Association (August), Washington, D.C.

———. 1986. "Can Men 'Mother'? Life as a Single Father." *Family Relations* 35 (January): 95–102.

Risman, Barbara J., and Maxine P. Atkinson. 1990. "Gender in Intimate Relationships: Toward a Dialectical Structural Theory." Paper presented at the National Council on Family Relations Theory, Construction, and Research Methodology Workshop (November), Seattle, Wash.

Risman, Barbara J., and Kyung Park. 1986. "Parents Without Partners: A Comparison of Single Male and Female Custodial Parents." Paper presented at the American Sociological Association Meeting (September), New York.

Robinson, Bryan E. 1986. "Men Caring for the Young: A Profile." In *Men's Changing Roles in the Family*, pp. 151–61. Edited by Robert A. Lewis and Marvin B. Sussman. New York: Haworth Press.

Robinson, John P. 1988. "Who's Doing the Housework?" *American Demographics* (December): 24–28, 63.

Rodgers, Fran S., and Charles Rodgers. 1989. "Business and the Facts of Family Life." *Harvard Business Review* (6) (November–December): 121–29.

Roel, Ronald E. 1991. "Parental Leaves Cost Little, Bring Few Problems." *Newsday* (May 23): 55.

Ross, Catherine E., John Mirowsky, and Joan Huber. 1983. "Dividing Work, Sharing Work, and In-Between: Marriage Patterns and Depression." *American Sociological Review* 48 (6) (December): 809–23.

Rossi, Alice A. 1960. "Transition to Parenthood." *Journal of Marriage and the Family* 30: 26–39.

———. 1977. "A Biosocial Perspective on Parenting." *Daedalus* 106 (2): 1–31.

———. 1984. "Gender and Parenthood." *American Sociological Review* 49: 1–19.

Rothman, Barbara K. 1989. "Women as Fathers: Motherhood and Child Care Under a Modified Patriarchy." *Gender and Society* 3 (1): 89–104.

Rotundo, E. Anthony. 1985. "American Fatherhood: A Historical Perspective." *American Behavioral Scientist* 29 (1): 7–25.

Rubin, Gayle. 1975. "The Traffic in Women: Notes on the 'Political Economy' of Sex." In *Toward an Anthropology of Women*, pp. 157–210. Edited by Rayna Rapp. New York: Monthly Review Press.

Rubin, Lillian B. 1976. *Worlds of Pain: Life in the Working-Class Family*. New York: Basic Books.

———. 1983. *Intimate Strangers: Men and Women Together*. New York: Harper & Row.

Rubin, Zick. 1973. *Liking and Loving: An Invitation to Social Psychology*. New York: Holt, Rinehart, and Winston.

Ruddick, Sara. 1989. *Maternal Thinking*. Boston: Beacon Press.

———. 1991. "Thinking Mothers/Conceiving Birth." Paper presented to the New York Institute for the Humanities, Seminar on Motherhood (December 13), New York City.

Russell, Graeme. 1986. "Primary Caretaking and Role-Sharing Fathers." In *The Father's Role: Applied Perspectives*, pp. 29–57. Edited by Michael E. Lamb. New York: Wiley.

Ryan, Mary. 1979. *Womanhood in America: From Colonial Times to the Present*, 2nd ed. New York: New Viewpoints.

———. 1981. *Cradle of the Middle Class*. New York: Cambridge University Press.

Santi, Lawrence L. 1987. "Change in the Structure and Size of American Households: 1970 to 1985." *Journal of Marriage and the Family* 49 (4): 833–37.

Santrock, J. W., and R. A. Warshak. 1979. "Father Custody and Social Development in Boys and Girls." *Journal of Social Issues* 32: 112–25.

Santrock, J. W., R. A. Warshak, and G. L. Elliot. 1982. "Social Development and Parent-Child Interaction in Father-Custody and Stepmother Families." In *Nontraditional Families: Parenting and Child Development*, pp. 289–314. Edited by Michael E. Lamb. Hillsdale, N.J.: Lawrence Erlbaum.

Sattel, Jack W. 1976. "The Inexpressive Male: Tragedy or Sexual Politics?" *Social Problems* 23: 469–77.

Schnaiberg, Allan, and Sheldon Goldenberg. 1989. "From Empty Nest to Crowded Nest: The Dynamics of Incompletely Launched Young Adults." *Social Problems* 36 (3): 251–69.

Schooler, Carmi, Joanne Miller, Karen A. Miller, and Carol Richtand. 1984. "Work for the Household: Its Nature and Consequences for Husbands and Wives." *American Journal of Sociology* 90 (1): 97–124.

Schor, Juliet B. 1991. "Americans Work Too Hard." *New York Times* (July 25): A31.

————. 1992. *The Overworked American: The Unexpected Decline of Leisure.* New York: Basic Books.

Schuman, Howard, and Jacqueline Scott. 1989. "Generations and Collective Memories." *American Sociological Review* 54 (3): 381.

Schwartz, Felice N. 1989. "Management Women and the New Facts of Life." *Harvard Business Review* (January–February): 65–76.

Scott, James C. 1985. *Weapons of the Weak: The Everyday Forms of Peasant Resistance.* New Haven, Conn.: Yale University Press.

Scott, Joan W. 1988. *Gender and the Politics of History.* New York: Columbia University Press.

Scott, Marvin B., and Stanford M. Lyman. 1968. "Accounts." *American Sociological Review* 33 (February): 46–62.

Seccombe, Karen. 1986. "The Effects of Occupational Conditions upon the Division of Household Labor: An Application of Kohn's Theory." *Journal of Marriage and the Family* 48 (4): 839–48.

Seccombe, Wally. 1986. "Patriarchy Stabilized: The Construction of the Male Breadwinner Wage Norm in Nineteenth-Century Britain." *Social History* 11 (1): 53–76.

Secunda, Victoria. 1992. *Women and Their Fathers: The Sexual and Romantic Impact of the First Man in Your Life.* New York: Delacorte Press.

Segal, Lynne. 1990. *Slow Motion: Changing Masculinities, Changing Men.* New Brunswick, N.J.: Rutgers University Press.

Seltzer, Judith A. 1991. "Relationships Between Fathers and Children Who Live Apart: The Father's Role After Separation." *Journal of Marriage and the Family* 53 (February): 79–101.

Seltzer, Judith A., and Suzanne M. Bianchi. 1988. "Children's Contact with Absent Parents." *Journal of Marriage and the Family* 50: 663–77.

Sennett, Richard, and Jonathan Cobb. 1973. *The Hidden Injuries of Class.* New York: Knopf.

Shelton, Beth A., and Juanita Firestone. 1989. "Household Labor Time and the Gender Gap in Earnings." *Gender and Society* 3 (1): 105–12.

Sherman, Norman, and Ginny Sherman. 1988. *Hunger Action Forum* 1 (15): 2.

Sidel, Ruth. 1986. *Women and Children Last: The Plight of Poor Women in Affluent America.* New York: Viking Penguin.

————. 1990. *On Her Own: Growing Up in the Shadow of the American Dream.* New York: Viking Penguin.

Silk, Leonard. 1988. "Now, To Figure Why the Poor Get Poorer." *New York Times* (December 18): 1–5.

Skocpol, Theda. 1987. "The Travails of Feminism—and Its Promise—in a Nation Without a Welfare State." *Gender and Society* 1 (3): 332–41.

Skolnick, Arlene. 1991. *Embattled Paradise: The American Family in an Age of Uncertainty.* New York: Basic Books.

Slade, Margot. 1991. "Siblings: Growing Up Closer." *New York Times* (July 25): C1.

Smart, Carol, and Selma Seven-Huijsen. 1989. *Child Custody and the Politics of Gender.* New York: Routledge.

Smelser, Neil J. 1959. *Social Change in the Industrial Revolution.* Chicago: University of Chicago Press.

Smelser, Neil J., and Erik H. Erikson. 1980. *Themes of Love and Work in Adulthood.* Cambridge, Mass.: Harvard University Press.

Smith, Ralph E. 1979. *The Subtle Revolution: Women at Work.* Washington, D.C.: Urban Institute.

Smith, Richard M., and Craig W. Smith. 1981. "Childrearing and Single-Parent Fathers." *Family Relations* 30: 411–17.

Smith, Vicki, Kathleen Gerson, Carmen Sirianni, and Peter Stein. 1990. "Gender and Workplace Participation: A Sociological Perspective on the 'Mommy Track' Debate." Paper based on presentations at the 60th Annual Meeting of the Eastern Sociological Society (March), Boston.

Snarey, John. 1988. "Men Without Children." *Psychology Today* (March): 61–62.

Sorenson, Annemette, and Sara McLanahan. 1987. "Married Women's Economic Dependency, 1940–1980." *American Journal of Sociology* 93 (3): 659–87.

South, Scott J. 1988. "Sex Ratios, Economic Power, and Women's Roles: A Theoretical Extension and Empirical Test." *Journal of Marriage and the Family* 50 (1): 19–31.

Spalter-Roth, Roberta, and Heidi I. Hartmann. 1990. "Unnecessary Losses: Costs to Americans of the Lack of Family and Medical Leave." Washington, D.C.: Institute for Women's Policy Research.

Spitze, Glenna D. 1986. "The Division of Task Responsibility in U.S. Households: Longitudinal Adjustments to Change." *Social Forces* 64: 689–701.

Stacey, Judith. 1990. *Brave New Families: Stories of Domestic Upheaval in Late Twentieth Century America.* New York: Basic Books.

———. 1991. "Backwards Toward the Post-Modern Family." In *America at Century's End*, pp. 17–34. Edited by Alan Wolfe. Berkeley and Los Angeles: University of California Press.

Stack, Carol B. 1974. *All Our Kin: Strategies for Survival in a Black Community.* New York: Harper & Row.

Staines, Graham L. 1986. "Men's Work Schedules and Family Life." In *Men's Changing Roles in the Family*, pp. 43–65. Edited by Robert A. Lewis and Marvin B. Sussman. New York: Haworth Press.

Stein, Peter J. 1984. "Men in Families." *Marriage and Family Review* 7 (3–4): 143–62.

Steinberg, Ronnie. 1988. "The Not-So-Subtle Revolution." Unpublished manuscript, Department of Sociology, Temple University.

Steinmetz, George, and Erik O. Wright. 1989. "The Fall and Rise of the Petty Bourgeoisie: Changing Patterns of Self-Employment in the Postwar United States." *American Journal of Sociology* 94 (5): 973–1018.

Stigler, C. J., and Gary Becker. 1977. "De Gustibus non est Disputandum." *American Economic Review* 67: 76–90.

Stinchcombe, Arthur L. 1968. *Constructing Social Theories.* New York: Harcourt, Brace, and World.

Stoltenberg, John. 1989. *Refusing to Be a Man: Essays on Sex and Justice.* New York: Penguin Books.

Stone, Lawrence. 1989. "The Road to Polygamy." *New York Review of Books* 36 (3) (March 2): 12–15.

———. 1990. *Road to Divorce: England, 1530–1987.* New York: Oxford University Press.

Strauss, Hal. 1989. "Freaks of Nurture." *American Health* (January–February): 70–71.

Sullivan, Mercer L. 1986. "Ethnographic Research on Young Fathers and Parenting: Implications for Public Policy." Conference on Young Unwed Fathers, Catholic University (October 1–3), Washington, D.C.

Suro, Robert. 1991. "The New American Family: Reality Is Wearing the Pants." *New York Times* (December 29): sec. 4, p. E2.

———. 1992. "For Women, Varied Reasons for Single Motherhood." *New York Times* (May 26): A12.

Sweet, James A., and Larry L. Bumpass. 1987. *American Families and Households.* New York: Russell Sage Foundation.

Swidler, Ann. 1980. "Love and Adulthood in American Culture." In *Themes of Work and Love in Adulthood,* pp. 120–47. Edited by Neil J. Smelser and Erik H. Erikson. Cambridge: Harvard University Press.

———. 1986. "Culture in Action: Symbols and Strategies." *American Sociological Review* 51 (2): 273–86.

Tavris, Carol. 1992. *The Mismeasure of Woman.* New York: Simon & Schuster.

Teltsch, Kathleen. 1992. "As More People Need Care, More Men Help." *New York Times* (July 22): B1, B4.

Thompson, Linda, and Alexis J. Walker. 1989. "Gender in Families: Women and Men in Marriage, Work, and Parenthood." *Journal of Marriage and the Family* 51 (November): 845–71.

Thornton, Arland, and Deborah Freedman. 1983. "The Changing American Family." *Population Bulletin* 38 (4): 2–44.

Tilly, Charles. 1987. "Family History, Social History, and Social Change." *Journal of Family History* 12 (1–3): 319–30.

Tilly, Louise A., and Joan W. Scott. 1987. *Women, Work, and Family.* New York: Methuen.

Tresemer, David W. 1975. "Assumptions Made About Gender Roles." In *Another Voice: Feminist Perspectives on Social Life and Social Science,* pp. 308–39. Edited by Marcia Millman and Rosabeth M. Kanter. Garden City, N.Y.: Anchor Books.

Uchitelle, Louis. 1990a. "Surplus of College Graduates Dims Job Outlook for Others." *New York Times* (June 18): A1, B9.

———. 1990b. "Not Getting Ahead? Better Get Used to It." *New York Times* (December 16): sec. 4, pp. 1, 6.

———. 1992a. "Hardships the Job Numbers Miss." *New York Times* (January 8): D1, D4.

———. 1992b. "Pay of College Graduates Is Outpaced by Inflation." *New York Times* (May 14): A1, B12.

U.S. Bureau of the Census. 1981. Current Population Reports, ser. P-20, no. 336.

Household and Family Characteristics: March 1980. Washington, D.C.: U.S. Government Printing Office.

———. 1986. Current Population Reports, ser. P-20, no. 411. *Household and Family Characteristics: March 1985*. Washington, D.C.: U.S. Government Printing Office.

———. 1989a. "The Earnings Race: Are Wives Really Catching Up?" *The Census and You* 24 (10) (October): 1.

———. 1989b. Current Population Reports, Special Studies, ser. P-23, no. 163. Arlene F. Saluter. *Changes in American Family Life*. Washington, DC.: U.S. Government Printing Office.

———. 1990. Current Population Reports, ser. P-20, no. 447, *Household and Family Characteristics: March 1990 and 1989*. Washington, D.C.: U.S. Government Printing Office.

———. 1991. Current Population Reports, Special Studies, ser. P-23, no. 173. *Population Profile of the United States, 1991*. Washington, DC.: U.S. Government Printing Office.

———. 1992a. Current Population Reports, P70-30. Martin O'Connell and Amara Bachu. *Who's Minding the Kids? Childcare Arrangements: Fall, 1988* (Data from the Survey of Income and Program Participation). Washington, D.C.: U.S. Government Printing Office.

———. 1992b. Current Population Reports, ser. P-20, no. 458, *Household and Family Characteristics: 1991*. Washington, D.C.: U.S. Government Printing Office.

U.S. Department of Labor. 1980. *Perspectives on Working Women: A Databook*. Bulletin 2080. Washington, D.C.: U.S. Government Printing Office.

———. 1991. *Working Women: A Chartbook*. Bulletin 2385 (August). Washington, D.C.: U.S. Government Printing Office.

Vanek, Joann. 1974. "Time Spent in Housework." *Scientific American* 231 (November): 116–21.

Vogel, Lise. 1990. "Debating Difference: Feminism, Pregnancy, and the Workplace." *Feminist Studies* 16 (1) (Spring): 9–32.

Waller, Willard. 1937. "The Rating and Dating Complex." *American Sociological Review* 2: 727–34.

Wallerstein, Judith S., and Sandra Blakeslee. 1989. *Second Chances: Men, Women, and Children a Decade After Divorce*. New York: Ticknor and Fields.

Warner, Rebecca L. 1986. "Alternative Strategies for Measuring Household Division of Labor: A Comparison." *Journal of Family Issues* 7: 179–95.

Weisburg, Herbert F. 1987. "The Demographics of a New Voting Gap: Marital Differences in American Voting." *Public Opinion Quarterly* 51: 335–43.

Weiss, Robert S. 1990. *Staying the Course: The Emotional and Social Lives of Men Who Do Well at Work*. New York: Free Press.

Weitzman, Lenore J. 1984. "Sex-Role Socialization." In *Women: A Feminist Perspective* (3rd ed.), pp. 157–237. Edited by Jo Freeman. Palo Alto, Calif.: Mayfield.

———. 1985. *The Divorce Revolution: The Unexpected Social and Economic Consequences for Women and Children in America*. New York: Free Press.

Weitzman, Lenore J., and Ruth B. Dixon. 1980. "The Transformation of Legal Marriage Though No-Fault Divorce." In *Family in Transition* (3rd ed.), pp. 217–30. Edited by Arlene S. Skolnick and Jerome H. Skolnick. New York: HarperCollins.

Welter, Barbara. 1966. "The Cult of True Womanhood: 1820–1860." *American Quarterly* 18 (Summer): 151–74.

Wikler, Norma. 1981. "Does Sex Make a Difference?" New York: NOW Legal Defense and Education Fund.

Wilensky, Harold L. 1960. "Work, Careers, and Social Integration." *International Social Science Journal* 12 (Fall): 543–60.

———. 1963. "The Moonlighter: A Product of Relative Deprivation." *Industrial Relations* 3 (1): 105–24

Williams, Christine L. 1989. *Gender Differences at Work: Women and Men in Nontraditional Occupations.* Berkeley and Los Angeles: University of California Press.

Willis, Paul. 1977. *Learning to Labor: How Working Class Kids Get Working-Class Jobs.* New York: Columbia University Press.

———. 1979. "Shop Floor Culture, Masculinity and the Wage Form." In *Working-Class Culture: Studies in History and Theory*, pp. 185–98. Edited by J. Clarke, C. Critcher, and R. Johnson. New York: St. Martin's Press.

Wilson, William J. 1978. *The Declining Significance of Race: Blacks and Changing American Institutions.* Chicago: University of Chicago Press.

———. 1987. *The Truly Disadvantaged.* Chicago: University of Chicago Press.

Wolfe, Alan. 1989. *Whose Keeper?: Social Science and Moral Obligation.* Berkeley and Los Angeles: University of California Press.

———. 1991. *America at Century's End.* Berkeley and Los Angeles: University of California Press.

Wright, Erik O., Karen Shire, Shu-Ling Hwang, Maureen Dolan, and Janeen Baxter. 1992. "The Non-Effects of Class on the Gender Division of Labor in the Home: A Comparative Study of Sweden and the United States." *Gender and Society* 6 (2) (June): 252–82.

Wrong, Dennis H. 1961. "The Oversocialized Conception of Man in Modern Sociology." *American Sociological Review* 26 (April): 183–93.

Zaretsky, Eli. 1982. "The Place of the Family in the Origins of the Welfare State." In *Rethinking the Family: Some Feminist Questions*, pp. 188–224. Edited by Barrie Thorn and Marilyn Yalom. New York: Longman.

Zavella, Patricia. 1989. "Sun Belt Hispanics on the Line." Paper presented at the History and Theory Conference, University of California (April 1), Irvine.

Zelizer, Viviana A. 1985. *Pricing the Priceless Child.* New York: Basic Books.

———. 1988. "From Baby Farms to Baby M." *Transaction: Social Science and Modern Society* 25 (3): 23–28.

———. 1989a. "Beyond the Polemics on the Market: Establishing a Theoretical and Empirical Agenda." *Sociological Forum* 3 (4): 614–34.

———. 1989b. "The Social Meaning of Money: 'Special Monies.'" *American Journal of Sociology* 95 (2): 342–76.

Zinsser, Caroline. 1990. *Born and Raised in East Urban: A Community Study of Informal and Unregulated Child Care.* New York: Center for Public Advocacy Research.

Zussman, Robert. 1987. "Work and Family in the New Middle Class." In *Families and Work,* pp. 338–46. Edited by Naomi Gerstel and Harriet E. Gross. Philadelphia: Temple University Press.

INDEX